Christ Church Papers No. 2

EDUCATION AT CHRIST CHURCH, OXFORD
1660–1800

A VIEW taken from CHRIST CHURCH MEADOWS
OXFORD.

Cyril Jackson Dean   Webber Censor

Dean Jackson and the Censor, James Webber

EDUCATION AT CHRIST CHURCH OXFORD
1660–1800

E. G. W. BILL

OXFORD
AT THE CLARENDON PRESS
1988

Oxford University Press, Walton Street, Oxford OX2 6DP

Oxford New York Toronto Melbourne Auckland
Delhi Bombay Calcutta Madras Karachi
Petaling Jaya Singapore Hong Kong Tokyo
Nairobi Dar es Salaam Cape Town

Associated companies in Beirut Berlin Ibadan Nicosia

Oxford is a trade mark of Oxford University Press

Published in the United States
by Oxford University Press, New York

British Library Cataloguing in Publication Data
Bill, E. G. W.
Education at Christ Church, Oxford
1660–1800.—(Christ Church papers; no. 2).
1. Christ Church. (University of Oxford)
—History
I. Title   II. Series
378.425'74'09   LF565
ISBN 0-19-920158-7

Library of Congress Cataloging in Publication Data
Bill, Edward Geoffrey Watson.
Education at Christ Church, Oxford, 1660–1800.
(Christ Church papers; no. 2)
Includes index.
1. Christ Church (University of Oxford)—History—
17th century. 2. Christ Church (University of Oxford)—
History—18th century.   I. Title.   II. Series.
LF565.B52   1987   378.425'74   87-7743
ISBN 0-19-920158-7

Printed and bound in Great Britain by
Butler & Tanner Ltd, Frome and London

TO MARGARET

PREFACE

THE purpose of this study is to attempt to discover who went to Christ Church between the Restoration and the end of the eighteenth century, what they were taught, and who taught them. It is therefore concerned with the education of those sections of society which, particularly in the eighteenth century, provided the government of the country nationally and locally, and from which the clergy were recruited. The period has no natural boundaries, though defined by the towering presences of John Fell at the beginning and of Cyril Jackson at the end, but is limited on the one side by the relative poverty of the evidence and on the other by educational reforms which presented a convenient point at which to terminate the inquiry. The book is based mainly on the records at Christ Church, and in particular on the immensely valuable series of Collections Books, which are a source without parallel in the records of any other Oxford college. Nevertheless the evidence is often incomplete. Much remains to be discovered, and many aspects of the subject deserve more extended treatment than has been possible here. Bacon's words at the end of the *Advancement of Learning* are not amiss:

this writing seemeth to me, as far as a man can judge his own work, not much better than that noise or sound which musicians make while they are tuning their instruments; which is nothing pleasant to hear, yet is a cause why the music is sweeter afterwards. So have I been content to tune the instruments of the muses, that they may play that have better hands.

I am grateful to Dr J. F. A. Mason, Librarian of Church Church, for reading the book in manuscript and making many valuable suggestions. Above all I am grateful to my wife for her unwavering encouragement and unselfish support without which the book would never have been completed.

E. G. W. B.

CONTENTS

LIST OF PLATES

LIST OF TABLES

I

Introduction

DURING its long history the meaning of 'liberal education' has been subjected to many changes of emphasis but it is nevertheless a sufficiently constant and coherent concept to allow definition. In England in the seventeenth and eighteenth centuries it was a harmony of ideas on education formulated by the Greeks, and especially by Aristotle, with the aspirations of the governing class in society. Far from being an abstract or artificial system, its moral and intellectual assumptions were deeply rooted in society and in turn had a great influence on the nature and political character of that society. It achieved its most complete expression in the universities. Historically the universities were seminaries for the clergy and so continued throughout the seventeenth and eighteenth centuries, but liberal education aimed to educate gentlemen rather than clergymen. The English gentleman, a term which has no exact equivalent in any European language, and especially the belief that gentility rested on education rather than on birth, was the product of liberal education. For better or for worse it was a potent force in English political history when the governing class was drawn from a comparatively small section of the community. Partly owing to its identification with this class, liberal education lost its comprehensive character in the eighteenth century when the scientific developments of the time, particularly those which benefited trade and commerce, were excluded from it, and it became to a large extent synonymous with a classical education.

Aristotle believed that education had an ethical and political purpose. He taught that the ultimate good was happiness, and that happiness was an activity of the soul. In common with Plato, he held that the soul was divided into two parts, the rational and the irrational or appetitive, and that there were two kinds of virtue, intellectual and moral, corresponding to the two parts of the soul. Intellectual virtue consisted in the exercise of reason. In its highest form it was contemplative and united man with the gods. Moral virtue was the result of habit, and it was the duty of the legislator to make citizens good by forming good habits. Through the acquisition of good habits men eventually derived pleasure from the performance of good actions. Virtue was opposed to excess because extremes were hostile to reason. 'He who greatly excels in beauty, strength, birth or wealth, or on the other hand who is very poor, or very weak, or very much disgraced, finds it difficult to follow reason.'[1] This led Aristotle to the famous doctrine of the golden mean. Every virtue, he maintained, was a mean between two extremes, each of which was a vice. Thus courage was a mean between cowardice and rashness. Aristotle used the idea of virtue in a special sense. Through virtue man developed the essential nature implanted within him. It was thus a means to an end. From this belief it followed that there were different kinds of virtue. The virtue of the ruler, for example, was not the same as that of the ruled, nor the virtue of the master or husband the same as that of the slave or wife. In order to attain virtue, it was necessary to have leisure, and it was therefore necessary that the freeman should not engage in what came to be regarded as illiberal pursuits.

In the state which is best governed the citizens who are absolutely and not merely relatively just men must not lead the life of mechanics or tradesmen, for such a life is ignoble and inimical to virtue. Neither must they be husbandmen, since leisure is necessary both for the development of virtue and the performance of political duties.[2]

Slaves might be taught useful arts, such as cooking, but these were no part of education. 'Any occupation, art, or science, which makes the body or soul or mind of the freeman less fit for the practice of virtue, is vulgar; wherefore we call those arts vulgar

[1] *Politics* 1295^{b}6–9.
[2] Ibid. 1328^{b}37–1329^{a}2.

which tend to deform the body, and likewise all paid employments, for they absorb and degrade the mind.'[1]

Christianity absorbed Aristotle's ideas on education as on much else, but the purpose of liberal education was not to make men religious. 'Liberal Education', Newman wrote in a famous essay, 'makes not the Christian, not the Catholic, but the gentleman.'[2] Liberal education emphasized the importance of ethical instruction, but ethics, despite attempts to give them the sanction of the religious conscience, rested on a foundation of reason rather than revelation. In 1810 Edward Copleston, the Provost of Oriel, stated the orthodox view of the connection between ethics and religion in his reply to the *Edinburgh Review*. He declared that without the authority of religion the purest system of ethics was comparatively lifeless and unfruitful, and without ethical instruction religion itself was vapid and even dangerous. 'Hardly any man but the Enthusiast', he wrote, 'contends that the Gospel was designed to supersede moral reasoning. It adds a sanction to Ethics, which the sublimest philosophy could never give: it corrects some errors, into which the purest philosophy without that guide, had fallen. But it displays no entire and systematic code.'[3] A similar view had been expressed at the end of the eighteenth century by the Headmaster of Westminster, William Vincent. It was the practice at Westminster School, he wrote, 'to explain the sentiment of Sophocles by the text of St Paul, and contrast the eternal unwritten law of the Gentiles with *the law engraven on the heart*', to compare the teaching of Plato, Socrates, and other philosophers with the doctrines of Revelation, and to show 'how far those doctrines approach the truth, and how infinitely they fall short of the Word of God'.[4] In such passages Copleston and Vincent answered critics

---

[1] Ibid. 1337^{b}8–15.

[2] J. H. Newman, *Idea of a University* (1852), discourse v, s. 9.

[3] E. Copleston, *Reply to the Calumnies of the Edinburgh Review*, (1810), 178–80.

[4] W. Vincent, *Defence of Public Education* (1801), 23. Vincent added this comment on Markham's religious instruction at Westminster: 'Upon such opportunities as authors or sentiments like these afford, I remember to this hour the tone, the manner, the elevated warmth of my own preceptor, the venerable Metropolitan of York; and I feel at this moment, that I owe the firmest principles of my mind, and my first reverence of the Scriptures, to his instruction'.

who have questioned why Christian morals were studied in pagan classical authors. Newman, however, perceived that the religious conscience was only too likely to elude a liberal education. The object of such an education, he argued, was 'nothing more or less than intellectual excellence', which by its nature was averse to immorality and created a disposition favourable to virtue. Reason thus combated the moral disorders denounced by Revelation, and thus far he was in agreement with Copleston. But, he continued, there was nothing specially Christian in this, for there was a vast difference between mental refinement and genuine religion. Conscience in such circumstances might be no more than a moral sense, and the command of duty a matter of taste. Sin became not an offence against God but against human nature. 'The world is content with setting right the surface of things; the Church aims at regenerating the very depths of the heart.'[1] The charge that liberal education taught a superficial morality was also taken up by Wilberforce, who complained that morality was deprived of spiritual roots because of the fatal habit of considering Christian morals as distinct from Christian doctrine.[2]

The cause of this moral anaemia in education, if such it was, may be traced to Aristotle's belief that education was concerned with training the faculty of reason and inculcating good moral habits. In the eighteenth century, the virtues most admired were the Aristotelian virtues of prudence, justice, fortitude, and temperance. Asseline Eustachius, whose compendium of ethics based on Aristotle and Aquinas was widely read in the first half of the century, called them the four cardinal virtues, and Cicero described them in his *De Officiis* as the constituent elements of the good action. Prudence, which reinforced the lessons of recent English history, was the most important of the virtues. Daniel Whitby, whose *Ethices Compendium* first published in 1684 was much read at Oxford, placed prudence at the head of the virtues. It was not, he remarked, itself a moral virtue but the instrument through which virtue was attained. A similar view was expressed by Dean

---

[1] Newman, *Idea of a University*, discourse viii, s. 8.
[2] W. Wilberforce, *Practical View of the Prevailing Religious System*, 3rd edn. (1797), 383.

Markham in a sermon preached in 1753. 'By a sound mind', he said, 'I understand Moderation or Prudence ... Prudence is said to preside over and direct the other virtues; Moderation, to contain them: as being the opposite to excess, by which vice is constituted.'[1] In order to achieve the golden mean of moderation it was necessary to train and control the passions by the use of reason. 'The grand design of a liberal education', wrote Edward Bentham, 'is to strengthen the powers of your understanding, to enrich, but at the same time to correct your imagination, to moderate and guide your passions, in short, to form and confirm the habits of piety, wisdom, justice, temperance, and fortitude.'[2]

Because the training of character and intellect was achieved by developing the power of reason, liberal education was concerned with logic, and, in its highest form, with philosophy. Aristotelian logic was an instrument for detecting the differences between objects. It was not primarily a method for discovering new facts but for establishing the relationship between facts already known. Thus liberal education was not concerned with the accumulation of facts but with the relationship between the various branches of knowledge. Through logic liberal education originally embraced the whole of human experience. Undergraduate studies at Christ Church show that logic as a discipline was learnt by the study of grammar, rhetoric, and prosody, but that once perfected it was applied philosophically to the study of metaphysics and the classical philosophers. Thus comprehended, logic was the foundation of the view that education was 'not the complete carrying out of any one branch of knowledge, but the laying a foundation on which the Student may subsequently build up a thorough knowledge of any.'[3] In the middle of the eighteenth century, however, an important change in the traditional character of liberal education occurred when natural science was relegated to a comparatively secondary position and some aspects of science were

---

[1] W. Markham, *Sermon at the Consecration of James, Bishop of Gloucester* (1753), 25.
[2] E. Bentham, *Advices to a Young Man ... upon his Coming to the University* (c. 1760), 7.
[3] *Report of the Oxford University Commission* (1852), evidence, 138.

banished from the university altogether. Logic as a discipline continued to be taught, but it ceased to be the intellectual framework within which all knowledge was reconciled. Liberal education then diminished and tended to become synonymous with classical education.

The exclusion of natural science from the curriculum was not caused by a conflict between religion and science. In the middle of the eighteenth century men still believed that religion and science were in mutual harmony. Scientists such as Boyle and Newton were not troubled that their discoveries were at variance with their religion, and the movement for a rational theology associated with the deists was based on the belief that faith and reason were reconcilable. Nor was the exclusion of science caused, as has sometimes been suggested, by the supposed veneration of the university for the authority of Aristotle. So little was the university mesmerized by the authority of Aristotle that, when in the eighteenth century it became apparent that the findings of natural science were inconsistent with Aristotle's view of the natural order, his scientific writings were promptly expelled from the curriculum.[1] Although the syllogistic method of logic was said to be inconsistent with the inductive method of natural science, both methods of inquiry long existed in the university side by side, and because they served different purposes there was no intrinsic reason for the one to prejudice the other. Natural science was dropped from the curriculum mainly because the collegiate tutorial system was unable to provide tuition, but also because some branches of science were considered to be in conflict not with Aristotle's ideas on logic but with his ideas on education.

Aristotle had taught that certain studies were not fit to be included in a liberal education, and he identified them as those activities which occupied men's minds to such an extent that they denied the opportunity and the leisure necessary to develop the power of reason. Thus liberal education was concerned with training the character and intellect and not with vocational training or the acquisition of specialized skills. In the universities, the

---

[1] Copleston, *Reply to the Calumnies*, 15–16.

existence of faculties of theology, medicine, and law demonstrated the belief that such specialized knowledge should be acquired when liberal education was completed. By the middle of the eighteenth century, however, the momentum of the Industrial Revolution had reached a pitch where there was a rapidly increasing demand for new skills, such as chemistry and engineering. It was not the intellectual discoveries of natural science which clashed with the idea of a liberal education but their practical application in trade and industry. The Industrial Revolution required a more utilitarian education, but liberal education was concerned with the education of a landed governing class and not with the skills needed by merchant and manufacturer.

The defenders of a liberal education equated with a classical education found an able champion in Edward Copleston, the Provost of Oriel, who in 1810 answered an ill-natured attack in the *Edinburgh Review* in which it was claimed that Oxford studies lacked utility. The controversy continues to have interest. Copleston argued that if the object of society were the accumulation of wealth, then the separation of the professions and the division of labour would be the best means of obtaining it. But, he said, 'There must be surely a cultivation of the mind, which is itself good: a good of the highest order; without any immediate reference to bodily appetites, or wants of any kind.'[1] If rightly studied, science enlarged the mind and enabled a man to perform the public and private duties of life more correctly, but it was best studied when the mind had been properly disciplined and trained.

If this liberal instruction be first provided [he wrote] and if the intellect be duly prepared by correct Logic and pure Mathematical science—there is no analysis, which the business of life may afterwards call upon him to investigate, beyond the reach of a moderate understanding. The habit of discrimination, the power of stating a question distinctly, and of arguing with perspicuity, are of much greater importance than the hasty acquisition of miscellaneous knowledge. Not that I would be understood to exclude the study of those matters from an University. They are taught, and esteemed and encouraged here: but we do not deny that they

[1] Ibid., 168.

are subordinate, and not the leading business of education: and (what I think should never be forgotten) they are much more easily attained by a well disciplined mind, after he enters into life, than the other studies upon which we lay the greatest stress.[1]

The premature pursuit of specialized knowledge, he continued, might benefit the individual but was harmful to the community. 'Society requires some other contribution from each individual, besides the particular duties of his profession. And if no such liberal intercourse be established, it is the common failing of human nature to be engrossed with petty views and interests, to under-rate the importance of all in which we are not concerned, to carry out partial notions into cases where they are inapplicable, to act, in short, as so many unconnected units, displacing and repelling one another.'[2]

When, having stated the ends of education, Copleston turned his attention to the means of achieving them it was to defend 'the cultivation of literature' against 'the acquisition of science'. Classical literature inspired and elevated the spirit of man, and provided a unifying culture in opposition to the divisiveness of utilitarian education.

Whatever may be the advancement later ages have made in the knowledge of the properties of bodies, the temper and constitution of the human mind cannot have changed ... Never let us believe that the improvement of chemical arts, however much it may tend to the augmentation of national riches, can supersede the use of that intellectual laboratory, where the sages of Greece explored the hidden elements of which man consists.[3]

[1] Ibid., 176–7.

[2] In the course of developing this argument, Copleston attacked the importance attached to economics, or political economy, by politicians. His words remain worthy of consideration. 'The attainment of this science', he wrote, 'seems almost to have supplanted all the other branches of knowledge requisite for a statesman; to have often narrowed his views, and to have made him regard every public measure simply in the relation it bears to national wealth. But this object, as I have already contended, and ever will contend, against the clamorous sciolists of the day, is not the prime business of true policy. However important and even necessary it may be, it is a subordinate and not a predominant concern in public affairs.' (Ibid., 172.)

[3] Ibid., 111.

Later in the nineteenth century, when industrial wealth rivalled land as the source of political power and when a new middle class emerged based on the differentiation of industrial and commercial function, the exclusion of science from liberal education came under strong attack. Although in the universities utilitarianism made little impact even during the reform movement of the 1850s, an attempt was made by critics such as Mark Pattison and Newman to redefine liberal education by restoring scientific studies. Just as one strand in Aristotle's ideas on education had led to the severance of natural science, so now a different one was invoked to justify its restoration. Pattison said that the classicists rightly held to the fundamental idea of intellectual culture as the end of education, but

> Their error lies in their not understanding that the study of antiquity, of the past, even when much more profound that it usually is, cannot *now* convey that culture. Their opponents . . . have lost sight of the truth, that for the purpose of education, knowledge is only a means . . . to intellectual development. They *will* stake the issue on the comparative utility of the Classics and of Science, whereas they ought to place it on the comparative fitness of the two subjects to expand the powers, to qualify for philosophical and comprehensive view.[1]

He proposed an ideal of education which was derived from the Greeks but was considerably more exacting than the more modest aims of liberal education in the eighteenth century. For Pattison education really began when the training of the faculties had been completed, and *that* training could be pursued by means of many different kinds of studies.

> When [he wrote] disciplined studies have done their best, we come to those whose purpose is to liberalise or expand the mind, here we have no discretion, no latitude of choice. The end here is the cultivation of mind in itself, for its own sake; the nurture and growth of the mind to the full proportions; no mere training of particular faculties to be employed in special services . . . The means are nothing less than all the extant knowledge of the age in which we happen to live . . . If we fix our aim steadily on a perfect culture, a philosophical comprehensiveness

---

[1] *Oxford Essays, by Members of the University* (1855), 264.

of thought, we cannot afford to ignore any important class of ascertained facts; for a liberal culture is not the knowledge of facts, but intellectual grasp—not a collective acquaintance with many sciences, but a harmonious survey of knowledge, in all its parts, as a whole.[1]

In practice liberal education did not always achieve the ideal described by Pattison. Aristotle taught that virtue was the means to an end, and that the end was the exercise of reason and philosophy. But the virtue of the good citizen fell short of the virtue of the philosopher king. Mark Pattison expressed the divergence of theory and practice when he wrote that 'though a useful and practical life may be the end of education, yet the perfection of education consists in the perfection and enlargement of the intellect *per se*',[2] and Newman reluctantly conceded that, 'If a practical end must be assigned to a University course, I say it is the training of good members of society'.[3] But who were the good members of society and what were their characteristics? Educational theory reflects social conditions, and in the seventeenth and eighteenth centuries, when the conception of government by cultured gentlemen, which Aristotle had described in the *Politics*, was at its height, liberal education was the education of the governing classes. The gentry and aristocracy, who did not need to occupy their time in labour and seldom entered a profession, could afford the leisure which Aristotle declared the prerequisite of education. This, as Allestree noted, put liberal education beyond the reach of the poor, 'the indigence of whose condition doth on the contrary determine their pursuits to that only which may bring them in a subsistence, fastens them to the Shop or Plough, and so leaves their minds uncultivated and unapt for those more excellent productions which the happier Institution of Gentlemen enable[s] them for.'[4] For the governing classes a liberal education was a useful education: had it been otherwise they would not have flocked to the university in such large numbers. But it was not useful in terms of commerce and industry.

---

[1] Ibid., 265.
[2] Ibid., 264.
[3] Newman, *Idea of a University*, discourse vii, s. 10.
[4] R. Allestree, *Gentleman's Calling* (1668), 13.

Liberal education prepared them for their political and social responsibilities as governors and magistrates, good citizens and loyal subjects. 'The great object of education', wrote Charles Barker in 1783, 'is to prepare us for the due discharge of those various and extensive obligations which belong to us as men and citizens.'[1] For those entering political life, liberal education was particularly relevant. In an age when parliamentary oratory was at its height, rhetoric or the art of public speaking was, as the Revd Roger Pickering noted in 1749, an important acquisition 'for every Gentleman, especially such as have seat in that House, where the occasion of delivering our sentiments is sudden and requires consequently an inward fund to supply the want of premeditation. Reason and arguments themselves often owe their force to the ornaments with which they are delivered.'[2] Classical literature abounded in precepts and examples for the aspiring parliamentarian, from the speeches of Thucydides, which the Earl of Bristol recommended to his son in 1704 as models suitable for either House, to the great orations of Cicero.[3] No less an authority than Dean Markham told the young Gilbert Elliot, who came up to Christ Church in 1768, that 'only classical and historical knowledge could make able statesmen, though mathematics and other things were very necessary for a gentleman'.[4] Classical history served the moral ends of education by showing that virtue was rewarded and vice punished, and it provided a pantheon of heroes worthy of emulation.

He who in his early age [wrote Vicesimus Knox] has been taught to study and revere the characters of the sages, heroes, statesmen, and philosophers, who adorn the annals of Greece and Rome, will necessarily imbibe the most liberal notions. He will catch a portion of that generous enthusiasm which has warmed the hearts, and directed the conduct, of the benefactors and ornaments of the human race.[5]

[1] C. T. Barker, 'On the Use of History', Chancellor's English Essay, in *Oxford Prize Poems* (1783), 125. Barker became an energetic tutor and Senior Censor of Christ Church.

[2] J. Nichols, *Literary Anecdotes of the Eighteenth Century* (1815), ix, 332.

[3] *Letter-Books of John Hervey, First Earl of Bristol* (1894), i, 203.

[4] Countess of Minto, *Life and Letters of Sir Gilbert Elliot* (1874), i, 38.

[5] V. Knox, *Liberal Education* (1781), 167.

Liberal education not only realized the ideals of those entering politics and government but it embodied the intellectual and moral ideals of the English tradition of gentility. Locke described the essential qualities of the gentleman as virtue, wisdom, breeding, and learning. In English society, where there was no constraint of caste and the social structure was fluid, gentility owed more to education than to birth or wealth. In a letter to his pupil John Alford in 1666 Locke wrote,

Though your ancestors have left you a condition above the ordinary rank, yet tis your self alone that can advance your self to it. For tis not either the goeing upon two legs, or the liveing in a greate house, or possessing many acres that gives one advantage over beasts or other men, but the being wiser and better.[1]

Under the influence of Locke, the eighteenth century believed that civility was a gentlemanly quality. Civility was based on the universal principles of human nature and reflected the view that moral behaviour was based on reason, which was common to mankind. It was therefore distinct from those external accomplishments recommended by Lord Chesterfield, whom Dr Johnson castigated as inculcating 'the morals of the whore and the manners of a dancing-master'.[2] Parents wishing to give their children a liberal education sometimes failed to discriminate between true civility and polite manners. 'The greatest and most general error of parents', wrote Obadiah Walker, 'is that they desire their children to be more plausible then knowing, and to have a good mine rather than a good understanding, or at least to have both together: to employ the same time to acquire serious studies and a-la-modeness.'[3] It was not an error of which Sir Heneage Finch was guilty, when in 1663 he rebuked his son Daniel for spending his time at Christ Church in frivolous pursuits. 'My chief cares and desires for you', he wrote, 'are that you may prove a knowing and a vertuous man, that which the town calls a fine gentleman

---

[1] J. Locke, *Correspondence*, ed. E. S. de Beer (1976), i, no. 200.
[2] J. Boswell, *Life of Johnson* (L. F. Powell's revision of G. B. Hill's edition) (1934–64), i, 266.
[3] O. Walker, *Of Education*, 3rd edn. (1677), 15.

being to my understanding rather a libell than a commendation.'[1]
It was not the purpose of liberal education to impart such social
accomplishments, which might properly be acquired after leaving
the university by attending the Inns of Court or by foreign travel.

Education also laid the foundation of taste, which, like civility,
was a characteristic of gentility, and like gentility was based on
morality. Vicesimus Knox described taste as 'That delicate faculty
which is sensibly delighted with all that is beautiful and sublime,
and immediately disgusted with all that is inelegant in composition, and must be affected with similar appearances in the conduct
of human life'.[2] Henry Kett, a tutor of Trinity College, called it
'a power of distinguishing right from wrong applied to works
of art'.[3] Through its ennobling effects, good taste elevated and
purified, but bad taste debased. Good taste restrained the passions
by regulating that nurse of passion a disordered imagination.[4]
Because taste was founded on moral criteria, it was subject to
rules, and since rational morality was based on human nature, the
moral truths of good and bad taste were universal. Good taste
was good judgement. It was in accordance with the principles of
liberal education that appreciation of the arts did not extend to
the ability to perform, which was a sort of specialization. In 1677,
Obadiah Walker wrote that it was permissible for a young man
to sing for the sake of his health, but 'Musicke I think not worth
a Gentlemans labor, requiring much industry and time to learn,
and little to lose it. It is used chiefly to please others, who may
receive the same *gusto* from a mercenary (to the perfection of many
of whom few Gentlemen arrive) at a very easy rate.'[5]

In training the rational, moral, and aesthetic faculties, the study
of classical literature, as Copleston noted, had no equal. In 1804,
A. D. Hendy, like Copleston a member of Oriel, wrote that

It enlivens the imagination, refines the taste, and strengthens the powers
of the judgment; in a word, it tends more than any other study to

---

[1] HMC, *Finch* (1913), i, 244.
[2] Knox, *Liberal Education*, 194.
[3] H. Kett, *Elements of General Knowledge* (1802), ii, 140.
[4] Knox, *Liberal Education*, 11.
[5] Walker, *Of Education*, 115.

preserve that just equilibrium among the mental powers, which, as it is the most favourable to virtue and to happiness, is also the best preservative against prejudice and error.[1]

A knowledge of classical literature was the necessary accomplishment of a gentleman. 'Every scholar', said Vicesimus Knox, 'ought to be a gentleman; and indeed I can hardly conceive a true gentleman, by which I mean a man of an elegant, a liberal, and an enlightened mind, who is not in some degree a polite scholar.'[2] A polite scholar, however, was not the same thing as a profound scholar. Classical authors were not included in a liberal education for the sake of scholarship nor even to acquire proficiency in Greek and Latin, but for the sake of mental discipline and moral improvement. 'The language of Greek and Latin', wrote that anxious parent Sir Heneage Finch, 'are no part of learning themselves, but only helps to it; they serve as keys to open those treasures of wisdom and knowledge which ly buryed in ancient authors.'[3] It was indicative of this approach to classical literature that until late in the eighteenth century it was common for Greek texts to be read in editions with facing Latin translations. John Fell deliberately restricted the critical apparatus in his editions of classical authors, and Locke advised that texts should be read rather than commentaries. Classical authors were often read attentively but not critically—scholarship was a form of specialization properly pursued by scholars (though in eighteenth-century Oxford it seldom was) but not by young students. In accord with this view Bentley had been brushed aside at Christ Church as an irritating irrelevancy, and Oxford as a whole was slow to recognize that he had had the better of the argument over Phalaris.[4]

Liberal education was thus a powerful influence on the intellectual and moral climate of English society in the seventeenth and eighteenth centuries. Its impact on the aristocracy and gentry, who constituted the core of the ruling classes, was especially strong, but it also permeated the clergy. It provided a common

[1] A. D. Hendy, *Essay on the Utility of Classical Literature* (1804), 7.
[2] Knox, *Liberal Education*, 79.
[3] HMC, *Finch* (1913), i, 244.
[4] See pp. 258–60.

educational background with shared assumptions and a secure foundation for political and cultural beliefs. It taught that the duties and responsibilities of the just man in society were based on reason and morality. It cemented social stability, for it valued those qualities, such as moderation, prudence, temperance, and fortitude, which held society together. It believed that the training of the mind was more important than the accumulation of knowledge. It was not without its defects. It encouraged learning but not scholarship; it respected the established order rather than inspired the breast of the reformer; it inculcated a system of morality which sometimes degenerated into a mask of habit; the belief in moderation could become a defence of mediocrity; it produced statesmen, politicians, clergymen, and men of sense and principle, who did great service to the State, but it distrusted the imagination and did not produce poets and artists. Liberal education produced the English gentleman, whose qualities, for better or for worse, were eloquently described by Newman in these words:

It is the education which gives a man a clear conscious view of his own opinions and judgments, a truth in developing them, an eloquence in expressing them, and a force in urging them. It teaches him to see things as they are, to go right to the point, to disentangle a skein of thought, to detect what is sophistical, and to discard what is irrelevant. It prepares him to fill any post with credit, and to master any subject with facility. It shows him how to accommodate himself to others, how to throw himself into their state of mind, how to bring before them his own, how to influence them, how to come to an understanding with them, how to bear with them.[1]

Christ Church in common with other colleges in Oxford and Cambridge was historically a seminary for the clergy, but training for the ministry, such as it was, began after education had been completed, and all undergraduates, whether intended for the Church or for secular employment, received in essential points the same liberal education. Christ Church presented a microcosm of that education in the seventeenth and eighteenth centuries. In

[1] Newman, *Idea of a University*, discourse vii, s. 10.

the historical structure of the foundation of Christ Church, in its social organization, in the nature of the exercises and studies pursued within it, in the tutorial system, the principles and practices of liberal education are clearly articulated.

II

The Governing Body of Christ Church

(*a*) THE DEANS OF CHRIST CHURCH

By the foundation of Christ Church, Henry VIII established a cathedral and a college within a single institution. It was an act of imaginative parsimony which testified to the connection between religion and education. The dual character of the foundation was united in the Dean and Chapter, who constituted the Governing Body and legal corporation of Christ Church. They administered the large estates belonging to the foundation; they regulated the internal economy; they exercised a large ecclesiastical patronage by electing to Studentships and by presenting to the many livings in the gift of the college. But the Chapter as such exercised remarkably little control over the educational work of the college. It elected the college officers annually, occasionally promulgated decrees requiring the more strict observance of college exercises, and granted graces for degrees. But it did not concern itself with the tutorial arrangements, nor with the plan of study represented by the curriculum. Such practical limits on the authority of the Chapter could hardly have been avoided, for a body composed of men of learning and experience, often advanced in age, regarded within the walls of Christ Church in Lord Hardwicke's telling phrase as 'in the nature of coadjutors of the Dean', and within the university as of equal standing with the Heads of Houses,[1] was unsuitable for the supervision of studies or the laborious duties of instruction. For the Canons of Christ

---

[1] When in 1674 the Heads of Houses disputed the college's right to deliver the university sermons exclusively in the cathedral, the Dean and Chapter asserted that the Canons possessed the 'right of being esteemd as heads of houses, every prebend having alwaies had in the University the respect and honour of that station' (Ch. Ch. Archives, Estates Register, 1659–75, p. 514).

Church, the Chapter was frequently the avenue to even greater preferment. Beyond it lay deaneries, bishoprics, even the Archbishoprics of Canterbury and York, as well as livings equal to the dreams of clerical avarice. The educational work of Christ Church was in the main discharged by the Dean and the Sub-Dean assisted by the Students. Of these the most important was unquestionably the Dean, on whose character and abilities the reputation of the college largely rested.

In July 1660, George Morley became Dean of Christ Church. In 1648 he had been ejected by the parliamentary visitors from his canonry, which was said to have been the only preferment he ever desired,[1] and spent the ensuing twelve years in exile. During this period he laid the foundation of his subsequent career by cultivating the friendship and patronage of Sir Edward Hyde, later Earl of Clarendon, whose 'particular friend' he became.[2] For three years he was a member of Lady Hyde's household at Antwerp while her husband was ambassador in Spain, and he was later chaplain to Anne Hyde, Duchess of York. In Church matters, Morley did not belong to the discredited Laudian party, but had Calvinist sympathies and was 'esteemed one of the main patrons of those of that persuasion'.[3] Shortly before the Restoration, Hyde sent him as an emissary to the Presbyterians in England. His broad religious sympathies, his exemplary piety, and his independence of mind—what Burnet called his obstinacy and Hyde his contrariness—made him a suitable person to settle Christ Church, for he was acceptable both to the old Cavaliers and to the Presbyterians, who held many of the Studentships. It was probably through Hyde's interest that he was designated for the Deanery at least as early as July 1659.[4] At the Restoration Morley and Sheldon were the two men who had 'the greatest credit' in Church

---

[1] A. Wood, *Athenae Oxonienses*, ed. P. Bliss (1820), iv, 150.

[2] G. Burnet, *History of my Own Time*, ed. O. Airy (1897), i, 177.

[3] Wood, *Athenae*, iv, 154.

[4] *Cal. Clar. SP* (1932), iv, 273. The Nicholas Papers in the British Library contain a note of earlier date in which Robert Payne was designated for the Deanery of Christ Church, Morley for the Savoy, and Hammond for the Deanery of Westminster. Payne was expelled from his canonry in 1648 and died in 1653 (BL Egerton MS 2542, fo. 270).

affairs,[1] and although Morley's appointment to Christ Church is evidence of the importance attached to the university by the government, it is likely that from the start he was earmarked for even higher preferment. On 25 April 1660 occurred the death of Hammond, who had been intended for the Bishopric of Worcester. Morley was installed in the Deanery in July and in the following October became Bishop of Worcester. Thus he was Dean of Christ Church for only three months, but during that time the royal commission appointed to visit the university completed most of its work.

Although disappointed royalists might claim that the Restoration meant indemnity for the King's enemies and oblivion for his friends, they had little cause to complain that in the composition of the Chapter of Christ Church loyalty was unrewarded. The surviving Canons expelled by the parliamentary visitors, Morley himself, Richard Gardiner, Edward Pococke, and Robert Sanderson, were immediately restored, and Jasper Mayne, John Fell, Richard Allestree, and John Dolben, who had been deprived of their Studentships in 1648 and had subsequently kept the Anglican liturgy alive in Oxford, were appointed to canonries.[2] Morley's old tutor, John Wall, who had been appointed to a canonry in 1632, expelled in 1648, and restored in the same year, retained his stall undisturbed. He was a patristic scholar, 'a quaint preacher', and in Anthony Wood's remarkable phrase 'spent his life in celibacy and books'.[3] This unworldly eccentric was the only Canon in 1660 who had not suffered for his loyalty. Although the incoming Canons seem to have been ready to forgive his pliant principles, they found it more difficult to accept his refusal to contribute to the cost of rebuilding the north side of Tom Quad, which severely strained the college finances, and were outraged by his gift of a substantial sum to the city of Oxford. On the day of his death, Gardiner visited him and offered to pray for him, but Wall refused. 'Upon which', Wood related, 'old Gardiner

---

[1] Burnet, *History of my Own Time*, i, 313.
[2] Dolben married the niece of Sheldon, who in May 1660 sought a canonry at Christ Church for him (*Cal. Clar. SP* (1970), v, 3).
[3] Wood, *Athenae*, iii, 734.

being inraged said that he was "a mudde wall, a tottered wall, a toren wall, nay! a towne wall"; and broke his windows with his staff'.[1] When Sanderson became Bishop of Lincoln towards the end of 1660, William Creed, a Fellow of St John's College, succeeded him in his canonry and in the Regius Chair of Divinity. The Chapter then contained two Canons who had submitted to Parliament in 1648, though unlike Wall, Creed had subsequently atoned by becoming 'a defender of the church of England in the worst of times'.[2]

According to Wood, 'Dr. Morley, in that short time that he governed the coll. restored the members thereof then living, that had been ejected in 1648, and such that remained factious Dr. Fell either removed or fixed in loyal principles'.[3] During the summer and early autumn of 1660, fourteen of the ejected Students were restored. They were Christopher Bennel, Henry Croone, Walter Dayrell, Richard Hill, Richard Howe, William Holloway, Samuel Jackson, Thomas Severne, Stephen Skinner, George Smith, Samuel Speed, Ralph Tounson, Giles Waring, and David Whitford. Not all the Students deprived in 1648 were restored. Some were dead or were ineligible because of marriage. Others were established in their professions and had no reason to return to Oxford, for a Studentship was not in itself a career, and few chose to remain in the university after taking their degrees except to obtain a college living. Most of the Students who sought reinstatement in 1660 had been prevented by their expulsion or by service in the royalist armies from taking their degrees or pursuing their vocations, and for them restoration to their Studentships meant the resumption of interrupted careers. Samuel Jackson, for example, had been prevented by service in the royalist army from taking his medical degrees, and although he was appointed to a medical Faculty Studentship in 1661 did not take his degree of MD until ten years later. Richard Hill had been 'forced to turn tutor for a subsistence.'[4] David Whitford, who

---

[1] A. Wood, *Life and Times*, ed. A. Clark (1892), ii, 90.
[2] Wood, *Athenae*, iii, 637.
[3] Ibid., iv, 194.
[4] *Cal. SP Dom. 1660–1*, 225.

was wounded and captured at the Battle of Worcester,[1] was a Bachelor of Arts at the time of his expulsion. In December 1660 he petitioned the Crown because, although he had been reinstated in his Studentship, he was unable to keep it 'by a custome of the Colledge', for the effect of dating his seniority from his expulsion had been to place him among those Students who were required to be Masters of Arts. His petition was referred to Morley, then Bishop of Worcester, and in the following January he was made Master of Arts by creation.[2] A similar dispensation was accorded at the same time to Walter Dayrell.

The restoration of some Students could not be achieved without the removal of approximately an equal number, for the foundation limited the number of Students to one hundred. As Visitor of Christ Church, the King had the power to remove Students, and it was a power he later exercised in the case of John Locke, but in 1660 he acted through a commission appointed by letters patent on 13 July to visit the whole university. F. J. Varley has questioned the legal basis of this commission on the ground that the Crown had no title to visit the university as a whole,[3] but Queen Elizabeth I had exercised such a power in 1559. Burnet states that Clarendon 'resolved not to stretch the prerogative beyond what it was before the wars',[4] and it is unlikely that he would have acted on a different principle in dealing with such a vexatious and litigious body as the university. Nevertheless, the appointment of the commission was a political act which reshaped Christ Church at the Restoration.

Wood declared that the commissioners acted with moderation, and that they were concerned to remove those not statutably elected and 'especially such that were factious'.[5] Varley has questioned whether the commission was really so moderate, and Mor-

---

[1] His elder brother was one of the murderers of Isaac Dorislaus.

[2] PRO, SP 29/24/120.

[3] J. Varley (ed.), *The Restoration Visitation of the University of Oxford and its Colleges*, Camden Society, 3rd series (1948), vol. xviii, p. vi.

[4] Burnet, *History of my Own Time*, i, 159.

[5] A. Wood, *History and Antiquities of the University of Oxford*, ed. J. Gutch (1796), ii, pt. 2, 701.

ley's belief that nothing had contributed to the ruin of the Church
so much as nominal conformity, a belief enshrined in his maxim
that 'it is better to have a schism without the church than within
it',[1] seems to give grounds for this view. On the other hand the
instructions to the commission lend support to Wood's verdict.
By an order under the sign manual on 30 July 1660, the commissioners were directed to remove only persons appointed during
the troubles 'where some others duly qualified can lay a legall
clayme, or where the places are forfeited by insufficiency or scan-
dall'.[2] In a further order on 1 August, these instructions were
enlarged to include the good of the Church in general and of the
university in particular.[3] At Christ Church the commissioners
seem to have followed their brief without undue severity.

At the Restoration, five Students remained of those appointed
by the parliamentary commissioners in 1648 or elected with their
sanction. Two of them, Richard Russell and Thomas Vincent,
appear to have resigned without appearing before the commission.
Two were examined by it. One of them was William Segary, who,
when asked by what authority he held his place, replied that it
was by virtue of his admission in 1648 'authorised by Dr. Reynolds
then Deane of Ch. Ch.'. He was deprived. The other was Anthony
Radcliffe, who replied to the same question that he was admitted
'by the then pretended Visitors of this University'. He kept his
Studentship, eventually became a Canon, and on his death bequeathed over £2,000 for the rebuilding of Peckwater. George
Atherton, who was appointed in 1650, was not examined by the
commission and retained his Studentship.[4]

A further six Students were ejected from those appointed after
the Dean and Chapter had recovered their right of election in

---

[1] H. C. Foxcroft (ed.), *Supplement to Burnet's History of my Own Time*, (1902),
69.

[2] BL Egerton MS 2618, fo. 81.

[3] Ibid., fo. 83.

[4] Atherton was appointed to John Busby's Studentship but was appointed to
another vacancy when Busby was restored in 1651. Since Busby kept his Studentship in 1660, it was hardly possible to remove Atherton, since both Students
had identical tenure. Busby was the nephew of Richard Busby, Headmaster of
Westminster.

1650. Robert Lovell was removed because he owed his nomination to Christopher Rogers, who had been intruded into a canonry in 1648 and ousted in 1660. Henry Tilley, Nathaniel Whitehorne, Thomas Johnson, and John Rogers were removed, but for reasons unknown. Whitehorne and Rogers were Canoneer Students,[1] and were presumably nominated by intruded Canons. Henry Stubbe was removed because it was said that he was 'unduly brought in' by Dean Reynolds and because there were 'many complaints of his carryadge'. Stubbe had in fact been deprived of his Studentship several months previously by Dean Reynolds for writing in defence of Sir Harry Vane, through whose interest he had originally obtained his Studentship.[2] Four other Students were interviewed by the commissioners but were allowed to keep their Studentships. They were Esay Ward, Nathaniel Hodges, William Cutler, and George Nurse. Ward said that he had been appointed by Dean Reynolds prior to the sessions of the parliamentary visitors and without application to them. Hodges had succeeded to the Studentship from which Samuel Speed had been expelled in 1648 and to which he was restored in 1660. Three Students, John Singleton, John Thompson, and Richard Dyer, surrendered their Studentships without appearing before the commission. With Segary and Stubbe they are the only deprived Students mentioned by Calamy.[3]

Thus out of a total of 100 Studentships, twelve became vacant by deprivation or resignation in 1660. Seven Students were deprived and five resigned. The majority of them were Canoneers, and the main cause of deprivation seems to have been the illegality of their appointment, whether by the parliamentary commissioners in 1648 or through the illegal exercise of their patronage by intruded Canons whose own tenure was also illegal. It is unlikely that religious convictions played an important part, for many Students remained in 1660 who were removed for religion in 1662. Not all Canoneer Students, however, were deprived, and

---

[1] Canoneer Students, unlike Westminster Students, were appointed on the nomination of individual Canons. See p. 107.
[2] Wood, *Athenae*, iii, 1069.
[3] *Calamy Revised*, ed. A. G. Matthews (1934).

it is tempting to suppose that a distinction was drawn between those appointed by Presbyterian Canons and those appointed by Independent Canons, but in the absence of an electoral roll for the period it is not possible to determine this question. In contrast with the Canoneers, few Westminster Students vacated their places in 1660, doubtless because the legality of their tenure, which depended on letters patent, was not in question. Thus the royal commission in 1660 seems to have been moderate in character in that it strove to base its actions on legal principle and to avoid the indulgence of political or religious revenge.

In order, however, to restore the Students ejected in 1648, it was necessary not only to provide Studentships for them but also to restore them to their rightful seniority on the Student roll. It was a consequence of the illegality of the Interregnum that their seniority was calculated from the date of their deprivation in 1648. Consequently all the restored Students were placed at the top of the roll among the twenty senior Students known as Theologi, except for one Faculty Student who was placed according to custom at the head of the Philosophi. But room for the restored Students could only be found amongst the Theologi by removing some of the existing Theologi to a lower part of the roll occupied by the Philosophi, for not all the Students who resigned or were deprived in 1660 were Theologi, and their departure did not thus create enough vacancies in the appropriate part of the roll. In order, therefore, to make room for the restored Students it was necessary to demote six senior Students, who thus lost their seniority. By what may well have seemed a belated act of justice, the *main* sufferers were those Students who had submitted to Parliament in 1648 and still held their Studentships. Although Richard Heylin, John Busby, and Thomas Lockey kept their seniority at the top of the list of Theologi, Thomas Tyas fell from fourth place to sixth, Lewis Palmer from fifth to eleventh, Edward Bagshaw from seventh to seventeenth, John Vincent from eleventh to twenty-first, and Edward Fettiplace from twenty-first to twenty-third.[1] The restoration of Students to the top of the

---

[1] Fettiplace held one of the Faculty Places tenable by laymen which in order of seniority came after the Theologi, who were in holy orders.

roll, and the deferred expectations of those reduced in standing, caused disruption at the bottom of the roll because the usual turnover of Studentships was interrupted. No Students were admitted until Easter term 1661.

In 1660 many Students turned their coats as their predecessors had done in 1648. Amongst them were Charles Pickering, Henry Bold, and Henry Thurman, who, as Wood scornfully remarked, were 'the most ready men to cring to and serve these times', and, having previously complied with the Presbyterians and Independents, complied again at the Restoration 'like so many Protei'.[1] Until the failure of the Savoy Conference some entertained reasonable hopes that their religious opinions would not prevent them from remaining at Christ Church, but when the Cavalier Parliament inaugurated the second stage in the settlement of the university, whereby its exclusively Anglican character was established, a number of Studentships became vacant between the spring of 1661 and the summer of 1662. Calamy names seven Students who then vacated their places: Samuel Angier (Easter 1661), Obadiah Hughes (Michaelmas 1661), Edward Bagshaw (Hilary 1662), Thomas Stafford (Easter 1662), James Janoway (Easter 1662), John Dod (Michaelmas 1662), and William Maddock (Michaelmas 1662). Of these, all seem to have resigned except Obadiah Hughes, who, having been warned by the Dean and Sub-Dean on several occasions to take orders, was finally expelled on 13 August 1661 as 'rebellious and incorrigible'.[2]

The increasing rigour of the Restoration settlement was also seen in the treatment of the college chaplains. The visitors restored two of those ejected in 1648, Richard Washbourne and John Read, but referred the cases of several other chaplains appointed subsequently to the Dean and Chapter. One of them almost immediately incorporated in a Scottish university, but of the others Benjamin Berry informed the visitors in October 1660 that although he had been ordained in London five or six months previously by the Presbyterians he would not scruple to read the

---

[1] Wood, *Life and Times*, i, 359, 369.
[2] Chapter Act Book, 13 Aug. 1661.

Book of Common Prayer if continued in his chaplaincy; John Hibbot said that he had been made a chaplain by Dean Owen three years before but was not in orders; John Ward said that although he too was not in orders he had endeavoured to obtain ordination from a bishop and intended to continue to do so. All three retained their chaplaincies at the Restoration but were deprived in 1661.

When George Morley left Christ Church for the Bishopric of Worcester, the college was in a pitiful state. During the previous twenty years many of the buildings had fallen into decay and some had been pulled down. The estates had been neglected or ravaged by war and the coffers were empty. The Chapter was crippled by elderly Canons, several of whom had been born in the previous century. The restored Students had little learning and with rare exceptions were unqualified to hold the Censorships or other college offices or to act as tutors.[1] Many of the Students who had survived the king's return were time-servers or disaffected. Parents often viewed the university with suspicion and preferred to have their sons taught at home or sent abroad.[2] The immense task of revival and reconstruction required a man of great practical and administrative ability. Such a man was John Fell.[3]

At the time of his appointment to a canonry Fell was thirty-five. He and John Dolben, who was born in the same year, were the youngest members of the Chapter. Almost immediately he became Sub-Dean, and much of the administration of the college was in his hands during Morley's frequent absences. When the Deanery became vacant, he was a notable candidate for the succession. Although he had no influential relatives and few friends at court, he was well known to the small and influential group of clerics, which included Morley himself, who advised on Crown appointments. He was the friend and biographer of Hammond, whom he knew at Oxford and visited at Westwood Park where Hammond died and where *The Whole Duty of Man*, first published

---

[1] Wood, *Life and Times*, i, 360.
[2] Ibid., 355.
[3] For the life of Fell see S. Morison, *John Fell The University Press and the 'Fell' Types* (1967).

in 1658, and sometimes attributed to Fell, was written. He had served in the King's army in the early part of the Civil War, and had suffered for his loyalty under the Commonwealth. He had been deprived of his Studentship in 1648, and his father, who was Dean of Christ Church, had been expelled. In the years that followed he had with Dolben and Allestree courageously braved the authorities by continuing to celebrate the sacraments of the Church of England in Oxford, first in Christ Church itself in the lodgings of his brother-in-law Thomas Willis and then in a house belonging to Willis opposite Merton. His appointment to the Deanery acknowledged the loyalty of those who had suffered during the Commonwealth.

The Civil War had a decisive influence on the development of Fell's religious and political beliefs. It broke out when he was at the impressionable age of seventeen and ended when he was only twenty-four. During the intervening years he had witnessed the execution of the King, the disintegration of the State, and the destruction of the Church of England, besides the misfortunes which overtook him and his family. Throughout his life he remained haunted by the fear that the second Civil War might be followed by a third, that brother might again be set against brother. In 1681, at the time of the Rye House Plot, he wrote to Sir Richard Newdegate,

We remember very well the time when blood and rapin put on the mask of Godliness and reformation, and we lost our king, our libertie and property, and religion by fighting for them. As it then appeared that we poor Cavalliers were protestants, tho scandald with the names of malignants and papists, so I hope we shall still continue and be as willing to suffer and die for our religion, as others are to talk of it.[1]

Rebellion was not only illegal and treasonable, but, as the *Book of Homilies* taught, it was sinful. Fell was a man of great personal piety. Burnet remarked that he and Allestree were two of the devoutest men in England,[2] and Wood declared that 'He was the

---

[1] Warwick Record Office, Newdegate Papers, B. 413, Fell to Sir R. Newdegate, 11 May [1681].
[2] Foxcroft, *Supplement to Burnet*, 47.

most zealous Man of his time for the Church of England, and none, that I yet know of, did go beyond him, in the performance of the rules belonging thereunto'.[1] He attended public prayers four times a day and had family prayers twice a day, he fasted often, and in Burnet's phrase was 'much mortified to the world'. His piety was deeply rooted in the traditions and sacraments of the Church. During the troubles, when everything seemed lost, it was the sacramental life of the Church of England that sustained him, nourished not only by his own sufferings but by the blood of the royal martyr. The defence of the Church of England against schismatics and papists became the central purpose of Fell's life. Loyalty to the Church of England, and to the Crown as Head of the Church, was the foundation of stability in society and the bulwark against rebellion.

In his quest for stability and continuity, which the war had destroyed, Fell looked back to the example of Archbishop Laud, who bestrode the social order in which he grew to manhood. The makers of the Restoration Church, Sheldon, Morley, Hammond, all of whom had incurred Laud's displeasure, respected his memory but did not seek to emulate him. But Fell, who belonged to a politically less experienced generation, had witnessed at Oxford the glittering peak of Laud's achievements, and endeavoured, as Wood expressed it, 'to reduce the University to that condition as it stood in Laud's time'.[2] Laud's influence was very deep. In 1682, Fell published his great edition of St Cyprian. The choice of the saint was highly significant, for Cyprian, who had opposed schism, confronted the Pope, and endured martyrdom, was regarded as a symbol of the suffering Anglican Church in the seventeenth century. Laud himself was seen as a latter-day Cyprian, and Peter Heylyn, whose biography of the Archbishop was entitled *Cyprianus Anglicus*, described him as 'a martyr of the English Church and State, for it was his Sad Fate to be crusht betwixt Popery and Schism'.[3] Fell shared Laud's ambition to make the Church of England a learned Church which traced its descent

---

[1] Wood, *Athenae*, iv, 196.
[2] Wood, *Life and Times*, i, 348.
[3] P. Heylyn, *Cyprianus Anglicus* (1668), dedicatory epistle.

from the Apostolic Church and maintained the traditions of the Greek Fathers. He also shared Laud's conception of a Christian society with an educated laity brought up in Christian principles and loyal to the Crown and to the Church of England. Learning and education were complementary instruments of social stability. They were the means by which society was prevented from relapsing into anarchy and civil war.

Christ Church soon felt the posthumous influence of Laud. One of Fell's first acts was to restore Anglican worship to the cathedral. The college accounts record the purchase of a damask altar cloth, a pulpit cloth, new staves for the vergers,[1] mats for the Masters and scholars to kneel on, and new bell ropes. The sum of £12. 8s. 3d. was spent on prayer books and a lectern bible. George Dallam repaired the organ, and it is probable that Fell was one of the 'Reverend Persons' in obedience to whose commands Edward Lowe, the cathedral organist, published his *Short Direction for the Performance of Cathedrall Service* in 1661. In November 1660, the Canons and Students attended the services wearing surplices. The surpliced choir was restored, and Wood relates that early in the following year 'some varlets of Christ Church' removed all the surplices they could find from 'the chamber under the common Hall (where the choiresters learne their grammar)' and thrust them deep into the privy in Peckwater. So enraged were the Dean and Canons by this aesthetically arcane but politically imaginative manifesto that they threatened to deprive the offenders, if caught, of their places, to expel them from the university, and to have their ears cut off in the market place.[2] Even more significant of Laud's influence were the changes in the services. In July 1660, Latin prayers were revived. In the same year monthly communion was instituted and later *weekly* communion. Monthly communion was rare enough, and in the early part of the century George Herbert had observed that 'touching the frequency of the Communion, the parson celebrates it, if not duly once a month, yet at

---

[1] The staves survive. They are surmounted by a dove, and bear the inscription 'CIIR In convertendo captivitatem Sion 1660'.

[2] Wood, *Life and Times*, i, 358.

least five or six times in the year'.[1] From a report sent to Henry
Compton, Bishop of London, towards the end of the century it
would seem that Christ Church was unique among cathedrals and
colleges in having weekly communion.[2] When Fell made the
change is not known, but it had doubtless occurred by the time
Dean Granville discussed the introduction of weekly communion
at Durham with him in 1680.[3] New communion plate was purchased in 1661.

In pursuit of social stability, Fell believed that the education of
the ruling classes was of crucial importance, and he strove with
unremitting vigour to attract the aristocracy and gentry to Christ
Church. In this he had a large measure of success, but his success
was less with the older aristocratic families, which were often
intellectually marooned amid their comfortable acres, than with
the families recently ennobled in the reign of Charles I or at the
Restoration, such as Annesley, Finch, Hyde, Perceval, and Savile,
which were amongst the most vigorous and politically active
sections of society. Thus it was fitting that the first Nobleman
to be admitted after the Restoration was Edward Hyde, son of
the future Earl of Clarendon, who matriculated on 7 December
1660.

The influence of the Noblemen and Gentlemen Commoners
at Christ Church was more pervasive during Fell's time and
throughout the eighteenth century than their numbers would
suggest. Frequently they were connected with Students or Commoners by ties of blood, and widespread imitation and adoption
of their mode of life undoubtedly contributed to the rising cost
of university education. In particular, aspects of a liberal education
which was especially suited to their needs were absorbed by other
undergraduates, so that an education which fitted the gentry for
their position in society also suited Students and Commoners, the
majority of whom were destined for the Church. The country
parson was often a pale reflection of the squire.

[1] G. Herbert, *A Priest to the Temple*, ch. xxii, 'The Parson in sacraments'.
[2] Bodl. MS Rawlinson C. 983, fo. 46.
[3] Surtees Society, *Miscellanea* (1861), p. 172; and *Remains of Denis Granville*
(1865), 49.

Those classes which dominated court, Parliament, and magistracy strongly approved of the education Fell gave to their sons. When Lord James Butler came up, his grandfather the Duke of Ormonde, who was Chancellor of the University, expressed the hope that he might be 'confirmed and perfectly instructed in the religion professed, practised and best taught in that University, wherein is comprehended the principles of honour, virtue, and loyalty'.[1] Sir Robert Southwell wrote of Fell, 'I know no man has his thoughts and genius so much turned to the care and education of youth as this good man.'[2] In 1671, Sir George Rawdon wrote to Viscount Conway, 'I intend to send you over my sons when the days lengthen ... Such as I advise with here are generally for Oxford, and Mr. Solicitor is for Christ Church, where he approves highly of Dr. Fell's government.'[3] Fell was specially anxious to win over the sons of papist and puritan families. In 1677, the eldest son of the Roman Catholic Marquess of Worcester was sent to Christ Church because his Presbyterian mother 'will have him bred up a Protestant'.[4] The King himself on several occasions caused the sons of Irish peers to be sent to the college. In 1675 he ordered that Lord Courcy, 'hitherto brought up in the Romish religion', should be sent to be educated by Fell,[5] and in 1680 he desired that Lord Dunkellin's son should be sent to Christ Church so that he might be 'instructed in religious and loyal principles and so be in safety in England and by that means out of reach of Popish designs and dangers'.[6] In 1682, one Bourke was sent by the King 'to be brought up in learning and in the Protestant religion'.[7] The King, apparently believing that in education what was good for his subjects was also good for his bastards, sent the Duke of Southampton to Christ Church, his mother presumably

---

[1] HMC, *Ormonde,* NS (1906), iv, 306.
[2] Ibid., 551.
[3] *Cal. SP Dom. 1671–2,* 27.
[4] Wood, *Life and Times,* ii, 394.
[5] HMC, Le Fleming, *12th Report,* app. vii (1890), 123.
[6] *Cal. SP Dom. 1679–80,* 499.
[7] HMC, *Egmont* (1909), ii, 110. Probably Richard Bourke, subsequently 8th Earl of Clanricarde.

having forgotten or forgiven the libel circulated in the university on the occasion of her visit in 1665.[1]

Fell devoted himself with enthusiasm to the education of the aristocracy and gentry. He was, said Wood, 'admirable in training up youth of noble extraction, had a faculty in it peculiar to him, and was much delighted in it'.[2] Laud had complained of the lack of government of noblemen and gentlemen by their tutors 'as if they had nothing to do but only to read to them',[3] but no such charge could be levelled against Fell, who 'would constantly on several mornings in the week take his rounds in his coll. go to the chambers of noblemen and gent. commoners, and examine and see what progress they made in their studies'.[4] He had, said Humphrey Prideaux, a most exact knowledge of all the young gentlemen under his care and a constant account of their actions so that nothing escaped him.[5] Noblemen and Gentlemen Commoners were required to take part in college exercises, apparently with other members of the college without distinction of rank. Thus in 1674, Sir Philip Perceval, who had matriculated as a Nobleman in the previous year, took part in disputations,[6] and as early as 1663, Sir Heneage Finch wrote to his son Daniel, 'Bee sure to be present at all disputacions in the Hall, whither the fellow commoners seldome came in my time, and study the question beforehand, for one argument of your own choosing, out of those books which write upon the question, will be better managed by you then any argument which your tutor can putt into your head'.[7] Fell's energies were not always crowned with success. On one occasion he wrote that Lord Kingsale was 'addicted to the tennis court, proof against all Latin assaults, and prone to kicking, beating and domineering over his sisters, fortified in the conceit that a title of honour was support enough, without the pedantry and trouble

[1] Coyly quoted in Wood's *Life and Times*, ii, 67.

[2] Wood, *Athenae*, iv, 196.

[3] W. Laud, *Works*, ed. W. Scott and J. Bliss (1847–60), v, pt. 1, 260.

[4] Wood, *Athenae*, iv, 196.

[5] Sir H. Ellis (ed.), *Original Letters of Eminent Literary Men*, Camden Society, 1st Series (1843), 185.

[6] HMC, *Egmont* (1909), ii, 34.

[7] HMC, *Finch* (1913), i, 237.

of book learning'.[1] The Duke of Ormonde stoically observed, 'I take it for granted that he is past profiting in learning what is taught there, and if he be well established in point of religion, I can console myself for his want of proficiency in his other studies.'[2]

At Christ Church, Fell's energies were mainly directed to the education of undergraduates, but he also tried to encourage learning amongst those who remained at Oxford after completing their education and taking a degree. Most of these were Students intent on a career in the Church. Fell's great ambition to produce a learned clergy, familiar with the origin of their beliefs and able to defend them against papists and sectaries, centred on his great work for the university press, and it was this work which furnished opportunities for the encouragement of young scholars from Christ Church. In 1672, for example, he employed Humphrey Prideaux to edit Florus, and in 1676 caused him to undertake an edition of *Marmora Oxoniensia*. William Taswell, who said that Fell 'frequently made me a present of two pounds, at the same time telling me it was designed as a reward of merit', was engaged in collating manuscripts of Cyprian.[3] Thomas Sparke edited the Oxford Herodian in 1678, and William Foster, a Servitor, was 'corrector' of the Oxford Bible in 1675, and of the Oxford Homer the following year. Fell also encouraged the Coptic studies of Thomas Edwards to whom he gave a college living.[4] The publication in 1674 of a translation of Johann Scheffer's *History of Lapland*, the first anthropological book printed at the university press, arose in unusual circumstances. Hearne relates that the translation was made by a Student named Acton Cremer as 'an Imposition set him by Bp. Fell for courting a Mistress at yt Age, which the Bp. dislik'd, yet for all that he married'.[5] Fell's use of his patronage for the benefit of Christ Church caused Wood to complain that 'He had a hand in all public elections and endeav-

[1] GEC VII.

[2] Ibid.

[3] *Camden Miscellany II* (autobiography and anecdotes by William Taswell), Camden Society, 1st Series (1853), 18, 23.

[4] T. Hearne, *Collections* (1885–1921), vii, 351.

[5] Hearne, *Collections*, iii, 318.

oured to promote his own men, tho not so fit as others. He had a fond conceit that none could dispute better than a Ch.Ch. man, none preach better, speech it, or any thing else. He was exceeding partial in his government even to corruption.'[1] These charges come strangely from Wood who, although not a member of Christ Church, was one of the most notable beneficiaries of Fell's patronage. He was not the only one, for amongst other scholars with no Christ Church connection helped by Fell were Narcissus Marsh and Robert Huntington.

The idea of education as a means of preparing young men for their position in society and also of strengthening the moral foundations of society itself was never far from Fell's thoughts. To the end of his life he felt beleaguered by the enemies without.

You cannot be ignorant [he wrote to Dean Granville in 1684] what endeavors are usd by the Papists, fanatics, travaild fops, witts, virtuosi, & Atheists, a list of men that makes a great number in the kingdom, to disparage and decry university education, and afright all persons from sending their children hither; by which means, much of the growing youth of the nation are bred by little pedagogues in ignorance, and either without principles or with such as are worse than none.[2]

When his pupils went out into the world, Fell followed them, proferring advice, and not hesitating to point out their short-comings. To Sir Walter Bagot he once wrote: 'Although you put off your university concernments with your gown ... I not only continue the same care I had for your welfare and improvement, and have the same comforts in the notice of them both, but I am own'd by you to have a right to these pretensions.'[3] He was the perpetual pastor. He also took pains to advance his pupils to positions of influence. Thus in 1663 he is found writing to thank Henry Bennet, a former undergraduate and soon to become Lord Arlington, for his protection of the college and for the appointment of a Student to be his chaplain.[4] In 1666 he drew Sir Joseph Williamson's attention to verses written by members of the college

[1] Wood, *Life and Times*, i, 348.
[2] Bodl. MS Rawlinson D. 850, fo. 267.
[3] W. Bagot (ed.), *Memorials of the Bagot family* (1824), 77.
[4] *Cal. SP Dom. 1663–4*, 233.

on the victories over the Dutch.[1] He obtained for William Wake, a future Archbishop of Canterbury, his first perferment by recommending him as chaplain to Lord Preston. No one, said Wood grudgingly, could 'be a chaplaine or have preferment at court or under such bishops that were Oxford men, but such that had letters testimonial under his hand; and those that expected such letters would be at his devotion'.[2] To any that might be won over from popery or dissent he was especially indulgent. His encouragement of Peter Birch, for example, is well known, and he recommended the converted Irish Jesuit Andrew Sall to the Duke of Ormonde for the Chancellorship of Cashel.[3] Many other examples could be found.

What should be the judgement of posterity on Fell as Dean of Christ Church? His achievements were many and were recognized in his own time and by his successors. During the reign of Charles II the college enjoyed an immense reputation which extended far beyond the university. Its buildings were magnificently restored and embellished; matriculations increased year by year, and the aristocracy and gentry flocked to Christ Church in greater numbers than ever;[4] the educational system flourished and the statutory exercises were performed. The ascendancy of Christ Church was the work of Fell, and his success illustrates the decisive importance of the Dean in shaping the fortunes of the college. Fell possessed great qualities of character and intellect, but the driving force which lay behind his achievements was the ever present fear of the return of anarchy. It inspired in him a fierce determination to make Christ Church a bastion of Anglicanism and loyalty through which, by the education of the governing classes and the training of a learned clergy, the collapse of authority might be averted and the security of the State preserved. Authority was personified by the King as head of the State and head of the Church. In his autobiography, William Wake referred to Fell's political creed when describing his own reaction to the Glorious Revolution.

[1] *Cal. SP Dom. 1666–7*, 17.
[2] Wood, *Life and Times*, i, 348.
[3] Bodl. MS Carte 45, fo. 256.
[4] Bodl. MS Tanner 147, fo. 71; Oxf. Hist. Soc. *Collectanea*, iv, (1905), 183.

'By ye prejudices of my education', he wrote, 'first under my own
father and then under Bp. Fell [I] had been accustomed to think
yt all princes were absolute and yt subjects were not to contradict
but merely to obey.'[1] Even this principle, however, could be
sacrificed in certain circumstances for the sake of stability, for,
according to Hearne, Fell was one of the two bishops to vote for
the exclusion of the Duke of York.[2] His insistence on the need
for stability in society, his reverence for the ideas of Laud, which
belonged to an earlier generation, his dislike for the new philo-
sophies, all marked him out as a man of conservative instincts.
His achievements, great as they were, were bought at a price, for
he did as much as anyone to extinguish the ferment of ideas which
had begun to germinate at Oxford during the Commonwealth.[3]
To those who had not experienced his own painful history, his
quest for stability may have seemed a too ready acceptance of the
status quo.

When Fell died in July 1686 it was rumoured that he was to be
succeeded by Henry Aldrich,[4] but James II appointed Obadiah
Walker's old Servitor the convert John Massey, who was a Fellow
of Merton and a Master of Arts of only eleven years' standing,
and he was installed by Aldrich on 29 December 1686. Matriculations at once fell to their lowest level since 1660. Hardly had the
Prince of Orange set foot in England when Massey fled to France
dressed as a woman,[5] or, if the newsletter seen by Wood is to be
believed, in a red cloak like a trooper.[6] On 8 December 1688, the
King nominated Benjamin Woodroffe to the Deanery, but the
patent had not passed the Great Seal when he too left the kingdom.
Woodroffe owed this sign of the royal favour, as he had previously
owed his appointment to a canonry in 1672, to his long acquaintance with James, on whose flagship he had served as chaplain at
the Battle of Southwold Bay. Aldrich at length became Dean in

---

[1] Quoted in N. Sykes, *William Wake*, (1957), i, 10.
[2] Hearne, *Collections*, iii, 444.
[3] No Christ Church men attended the opening of the Ashmolean in 1683.
[4] HMC, Verney, *7th Report* (1879), app., 503.
[5] Bodl. MS Rawlinson B. 407ᵃ, fo. 85.
[6] Wood, *Life and Times*, iii, 287.

April 1689, having been recommended to the Crown, so it was said, by Gilbert Burnet.[1]

Aldrich spent his whole adult life at Christ Church. For him, as for Fell, Christ Church seems to have been the summit of his ambition.[2] First as a Westminster Student in 1662 and later as Canon in 1682, he witnessed the progress of Fell's reconstruction for almost twenty-five years. His relationship with Fell is not well documented, but appears to have been as close as that stern and forbidding personality would allow. In 1672 he composed the music for Fell's Latin ode written for the Act in that year.[3] He was one of those appointed in Fell's will to guide the fortunes of the university press—a trust which amply demonstrates Fell's confidence in his abilities—and when Fell died he composed the epitaph for his tomb. There is evidence, however, that his relationship with Fell was more significant than these facts suggest, and that Fell may have groomed him for the succession. The Dean appointed the tutors, and the records at Christ Church show convincingly that Fell systematically appointed Aldrich to be tutor to the nobility and gentry. In this way Aldrich became associated with the policy of attracting the governing classes to Christ Church which was one of the corner-stones of Fell's achievements.[4]

The qualities which caused Fell to consider Aldrich suitable as a tutor to the aristocracy were many. He was, like Fell himself, a man of exemplary piety, who received the sacrament every week and throughout the year rose at five o'clock for prayers. He was a sound theologian, well versed in Anglican doctrine, an excellent mathematician as befitted a pupil of William Oughtred, and a classical scholar whose famous compendium of logic, published after he became Dean, was written for one of his noble pupils. He was, in the words of the author of his life in *Biographia Britannica*,

[1] BL Add. MS 36707, fo. 63ᵛ.

[2] He was Rector of Wem, Salop, and was appointed chaplain extraordinary to William III in 1694, but seems to have held no other preferment.

[3] F. Madan, *Oxford Books* (1895–1931), no. 2927.

[4] His acquaintance with the noble families entrusted to him may have stood him in good stead in other ways. Thus it is possible that while accompanying his pupils on the grand tour he was able to acquire his great artistic and musical collections and even his skill in architecture.

'a most universal scholar'.[1] But Aldrich was no mere clerical pedagogue, for he also possessed aesthetic gifts rare amongst university dons at any period and unique amongst the Deans of Christ Church. He was the architect of several notable buildings in Oxford, including Peckwater, which was rebuilt to his designs. He was the discriminating collector of a notable collection of prints and drawings. He was a gifted musician, who composed music and acquired a very remarkable collection of early musical manuscripts.[2] Architect, musician, collector, connoisseur, Aldrich's interest in the arts joined with his many other talents made him an eminently rational choice as tutor to the nobility.

When Aldrich became Dean he pursued the same policies as Fell and governed the college in much the same way as Fell had done. Continuity was unbroken, and many of Aldrich's acts echoed those of his predecessor. For example, he took great interest in the educational work of the college, and is said, following the example set by Fell, to have 'visited the Chambers of young Gentlemen on purpose to see that they imploy'd their time in usefull and commendable Studies'.[3] In 1700 it was reported that all the Noblemen of Christ Church dined at his table once a week.[4] He held the office of Vice-Chancellor, as Fell had done, for three successive years, and with equal zeal endeavoured to enforce the traditional exercises of the university. On his first appointment to the office he declared that he would 'severely look after the discipline of the universitie, disputations in Austins, wall-lectures, examinations, Lent exercises'.[5] He continued Fell's New Year Books and faithfully carried on the same personal super-

---

[1] *Biographia Britannica* (1747–66), i, 96.

[2] A contemporary has left a vivid account of the impact on Christ Church of his interest in music. 'The Musick', he wrote, 'do now since ye Death of Bishop Fell come into Christ Church & play in long winternights, & twelfe Day they are to play at dinner to ye Schollars in ye Hall where each Scholler of concern do give ye musick halfe a crown a piece, & after dinner they Retreat to ye Common Fyre Room where they play to ye Masters of Art till they depart.'(Bodl. MS Rawlinson D. 810, fo. 12).

[3] Hearne, *Collections*, iii, 89.

[4] HMC, *11th Report*, app. vii (1888), (Bridgwater), 155.

[5] Wood, *Life and Times*, iii, 404.

intendence of the university press. Although the political mould was shattered in 1688 and university and Crown were estranged for a decade, during which the aristocracy and gentry neglected Oxford, by 1700 the Earl of Bridgwater was of the opinion that 'Christ Church collidge has a great commendation',[1] and the lavish accommodation in Peckwater undertaken in Aldrich's last years was an indication that Noblemen and Gentlemen Commoners had returned to Christ Church. But, although he continued the traditions of Fell's Christ Church, Aldrich was not forged in the same fiery furnace as Fell. Almost everything Fell did was integrated with the overall purpose of his life. Aldrich lacked this intensity of purpose. He was the capable custodian of his inheritance but it is doubtful whether he could have created it.[2]

When Aldrich died in 1710 he was succeeded, not by George Smalridge, whom the Queen wished to appoint, but by Francis Atterbury. The choice proved disastrous. Atterbury became prominent and achieved considerable popularity in Oxford during the convocation controversy in the reign of William III, but his previous connection with Christ Church lacked the distinction of that of either Aldrich or Smalridge. He came up in 1680 as a Westminster Student, took his MA in the normal course in 1687, and resigned his Studentship in 1694 prior to his marriage. He was never appointed to either of the Censorships, but held the junior office of lecturer in logic in 1684, 1685, and 1686, and

[1] HMC, *11th Report*, app. vii (1888), (Bridgwater), 155.

[2] Aldrich was described by his friend Hearne as 'humble and modest to a Fault' (Hearne, *Collections*, iii, 89), and it was considered an example of his modesty that in his will he expressed the wish to be buried in the cathedral without a memorial, a desire with which his thrifty nephew Charles Aldrich hastened to comply. The present monument was erected at the expense of Dr George Clarke, Fellow of All Souls, in 1737 (Hearne, *Collections*, xi, 136), but the following elegant epitaph had already appeared in the edition of the *Symposium* published as a New Year Book in 1711: 'Qui in omni vitae cursu praeclarum aliquod vel benignum alumnis suis paravit. Qui patronus fuit munificentissimus; amicus amicissimus; mortalium, pene dixerim, optimus: illum denique opum honorum contemtorem animum, omnium scientiarum omnium virtutum capacem, caelo (unde profectus fuit) redditum, juvat, & juvabit usque, plausu & gratulationibus prosequi' (quoted in *Biographia Britannica*, i, 96). A warm tribute was paid to Aldrich by John Wigan in the preface to his edition of the *Opera Omnia Medica* of John Freind in 1733.

became lecturer in rhetoric in 1690. He displayed little desire to establish a reputation as a tutor and took very few pupils, though one of these was Charles Boyle, the illustrious editor of the *Letters of Phalaris*. It is apparent that by 1690 Atterbury had become disillusioned with university life and with Christ Church. 'The only benefit I ever propose to myself by the place', he wrote at this period, 'is studying, and that I am not able to compass.'[1] In the same year his father wrote reproachfully to him, 'You seemed to rejoice at your being moderator, and of your *quantum* and sublecturer; but neither of these pleased you; nor was you willing to take those pupils the House afforded you, when Master; nor doth your lecturer's place or Nobleman satisfy you.'[2] Ambition beckoned Atterbury away, and it was ambition which caused him to return some seventeen years later. He was never a Canon of Christ Church and thus had no opportunity to become familiar with the traditions of the governing body, and when he became Dean showed little inclination to acquaint himself with them.

Atterbury owed his appointment and his political allegiance to the High Tory party of Henry St John and Lord Harcourt. Politicians of all persuasions attached great importance to Oxford, and particularly to Christ Church, during the bitter party conflicts which raged during the reign of Queen Anne. 'This greatest of clerical seminaries', Dr G. V. Bennett has written, 'had an influence which spread far beyond the confines of the city and its colleges. A powerful interest of country parsons and Tory aristocrats took their lead in religion and politics from this place of their education.'[3] The creation of such an interest at Christ Church had been one of the most successful ambitions of Fell and Aldrich, and it was appropriate that at his installation dinner Atterbury should have spoken of them and declared his intention of following their example. 'He spoke at large of both these excellent men,' Hearne remembered, 'told his Auditors how exemplary they had been for their Religion, Virtue and Learning; what publick Benefactors they had been not only to the College but to the

[1] F. Atterbury, *Epistolary Correspondence*, ed. J. Nichols (1783–90), i, 10.
[2] BL Add. MS 5143, fo. 102.
[3] G. V. Bennett, *The Tory Crisis in Church and State* (1975), 144.

whole University ... He concluded with a promise to imitate them.'[1] But whereas Fell had sought to establish a powerful interest for the defence of the Church of England against papists and schismatics, the interest which Atterbury sought to establish was that of a faction.

His political patrons expected him to extend his and their influence not only within the college but in university, city, and county. Atterbury for his part, although armed with no more than the modest mandate of a provincial satrap, saw himself as nothing less than a second Wolsey. Speaker Onslow said of him that, 'His views were not only to be the first churchman, but the first man also in the state, not less than Wolsey, who he admired and thought to imitate',[2] and according to Hearne he intended to write a life of Wolsey, the founder of Cardinal College, and made historical collections for the purpose.[3] His first step, and as it turned out his last, was to seek the aggrandizement of the Dean's powers. This was not in itself an impossible ambition, for the Dean's authority was not defined by statutes but by sometimes uncertain custom and tradition, and always depended on the personality of the Dean himself. A strong and tactful Dean could alter and invent tradition, and Atterbury was not unmindful of the example of Fell, whom he described 'as one who he thought stretched the authority of the Dean to the utmost'.[4] Atterbury, however, was no Fell, and he chose to govern not by influence nor by the gradual resolution of ambiguous rights but by the subversion of matters which were well established and defined. In 1716, after he had left Christ Church, he told Swift that as Dean he had claimed the power 'to make, punish, and unmake all the officers'.[5] He also claimed the exclusive right to present to college livings, and to control the conduct of all Chapter business. These were powers no previous Dean had claimed.

Almost immediately after his arrival in Christ Church he became embroiled in a conflict with the members of the Chapter, many

[1] Hearne, *Collections*, iii, 237.
[2] W. Coxe, *Memoirs of Sir Robert Walpole* (1798), ii, 553.
[3] Hearne, *Collections*, viii, 274.
[4] HMC, *Portland* (1901), vii, 69.
[5] F. E. Ball (ed.), *Correspondence of Swift* (1911), ii, 309.

of whom owed political allegiances which differed from those served by him. In its dramatic intensity the ensuing conflagration rivalled the internecine warfare which had recently erupted at Cambridge between Bentley and the Fellows of Trinity. The frequent skirmishes, ambushes, and occasional pitched battles at Christ Church were gleefully reported by one of the Canons, William Stratford, who like Smalridge had been disappointed in his expectations of the Deanery. In one of his letters he related how the Dean fell into such a passion with Canon Gastrell that he nearly came to blows. 'He pushed him with great violence several times, and cried "Get out of my house, you pitiful fellow". We all expected he would have struck him, it was plain he had much ado to forbear it. I never yet saw any man so much under the power of rage, his face looked black and every joint about him trembled.'[1] The tale has no doubt lost little in the telling, but Atterbury's passionate and volatile temperament was noted by other less partial observers. Speaker Onslow described him with much truth as 'a man of great parts, and of a most restless and turbulent spirit, daring and enterprizing, tho' then very infirm and capable of any artifice; but proud and passionate, and not of judgment enough for the undertakings he engaged in'.[2] To the relief of his Brethren in the Chapter, Atterbury departed in 1713 and later achieved a sort of immortality by becoming the only Dean of Christ Church to be convicted of high treason.

In 1713, peace was restored by George Smalridge, who, on following Atterbury into the Deanery of Carlisle, was heard to 'complain of his hard Fate, in being forc'd to carry Water after him, to extinguish the Flames, which his Litigiousness had every where occasion'd'.[3] In 1714, he was consecrated Bishop of Bristol, having vainly sought to persuade Harley to prevail on the Queen to withdraw the offer.[4] Smalridge was the son of a Lichfield dyer, and his education was due in part at least to the assistance of the antiquary and astrologer Elias Ashmole, who was himself the son

---

[1] HMC, *Portland* (1901), vii, 137.
[2] Coxe, *Memoirs of Sir Robert Walpole,* ii, 553.
[3] T. Stackhouse, *Memoirs of Atterbury* (1733), 63.
[4] HMC, *Portland* (1899), v, 321.

of a Lichfield saddler. Ashmole cast Smalridge's nativity, and Smalridge paid graceful tribute to his patron's supernatural powers by presenting to him a translation of the first book of Cicero's treatise *De Divinatione*.[1] Smalridge was elected to Christ Church on a Westminster Studentship in 1682. He was awarded the Bostock exhibition for three years, and was made lecturer in logic after taking his BA. He was appointed lecturer in Greek in 1692, Junior Censor in 1693, Senior Censor in 1694 and 1695, and for over ten years was a very active tutor. From 1700 to 1707 he was deputy to William Jane, the Regius Professor of Divinity, but when Jane died the chair was given to John Potter. On that occasion Hearne described Smalridge as 'an eloquent, ingenious Gentleman, an Excellent Divine and of a deep, rational Understanding; a true Friend to the Church, resolute and brave, of steddy Principles and not likely to be turn'd as ye Party would have'.[2] Having been disappointed in the professorship Smalridge was again disappointed in the Deanery on the death of Aldrich, but received a canonry of Christ Church in the following year.

Christ Church was not immune from the disaffection which followed the Hanoverian Succession. Although Smalridge did not welcome the new dynasty he accepted it as he had accepted the much more drastic change of 1688. In a letter to Walter Gough in 1696 he wrote of the Glorious Revolution,

I know of no persons in the University that either are, or ever were, disaffected to the Government, but some very few, who have suffered for their non-compliance with it. I know some, indeed, that do not like every thing that has been done these eight years last past, and who would not care to be obliged to approve and justify some turns that have been made by those principles which they formerly espoused, and cannot yet shake off; but I know of none that have pretended to comply, but what have done it sincerely and steadily.[3]

As Dean, Smalridge sought to avoid conflict with the government. On the Pretender's birthday in 1715 he invited all the Noblemen and Gentlemen Commoners to dine in the Deanery in order

[1] Bodl. MS Rawlinson D. 176.
[2] Hearne, *Collections*, ii, 88.
[3] J. Nichols, *Illustrations of the Literary History of the Eighteenth Century* (1817–58), ii, 257.

to avoid any disturbance, and in December he admonished the members of the college to take the oaths. Although he forbade prayers to be said for the Duke of Ormonde in Christ Church, his refusal at the instigation of Atterbury to sign the declaration of the Bishops condemning the Jacobite Rising in 1715 led to the Duke's health being drunk openly in Christ Church Hall. David Wilkins told Bishop Nicolson that at Christ Church, 'They boast at the name of Tories still; that is, of occasionally conforming Jacobites, and as long as they see their Dean refuse to sign the abhorence of the last rebellion, together with so many of his brethren, what can their principle be but to be pleased with the Rebels'.[1] But when the fever of Jacobite feeling in the university threatened to provoke a parliamentary bill of reform, Smalridge was one of those who presented an address to Archibishop Wake designed to avert it,[2] and his earnest attention to the state of education at Christ Church, particularly his reform of Collections, was no doubt designed to restore discipline and to remove some of the arguments for reform. Smalridge was not without friends at court, for he was popular with the royal family as a preacher and was on friendly terms with the Prince of Wales. Indeed hardly was Queen Anne in her grave before he was found administering the sacraments to the Prince of Wales.[3] It was such acts which caused Hearne to revise his earlier favourable opinion of Smalridge, whom on reflection he found 'a Man of little Prudence or Wisdom, very unfit to be a Governour ... He cringes and sneaks to the present Government, on purpose to get Preferm'. He does what he can in opposition to K[ing] J[ames]'.[4] The posthumous edition of his sermons, which Johnson, who, like Smalridge and Ashmole, was a native of Lichfield, described as amongst the best English sermons in point of style,[5] was dedicated to the Princess of Wales. He and Robert Freind, the Headmaster of Westminster, had married sisters, and Robert Freind's brother John, who married the sister of Atterbury's son-in-law

[1] Lambeth Palace Library, MS 2686, fo. 130.
[2] J. Nichols (ed.), *Correspondence of Bishop William Nicolson* (1809), ii, 457.
[3] Lambeth Palace Library, MS 941/42.
[4] Hearne, *Collections*, vi, 59.
[5] Boswell, *Life of Johnson*, iii, 248.

and was implicated in Atterbury's plotting, was physician to Queen Caroline. Robert Freind wrote the epitaph for Smalridge prefixed to the edition of his sermons and printed in Gutch's edition of Wood. A less familiar tribute was that paid by Arthur Charlett, the Master of University College, in a letter to Archbishop Wake on 10 October 1719. In it he wrote,

I ever found him one of the most ready, most faithful and most sincere friends ... ever willing, equally in lesser as well as greater matters, very able and sound in his advice ... He much condemned the heads of all parties ... always ready to forgive, willing to promote any public business, rarely out of humour, seldom complaining, severe sometimes upon himself and friends, generally very candid, not easy to believe the worst of any, too apt to believe better of some than they deserved.[1]

The death of Smalridge paved the way for the strengthening of the Whig interest at Oxford. The Lord Chancellor, the Archbishop of Canterbury, and some members of the Chapter favoured the appointment of John Potter, who was not only Bishop of Oxford but held the canonry at Christ Church to which the Regius Professorship of Divinity was attached. The burden of plurality did not weigh heavily on Potter. Hardly had he been appointed to his professorship when Stratford's malicious tongue was wagging. Allestree and Jane, he said, who had previously held the chair, used occasionally to miss giving a lecture as they grew old, but Potter was 'the only professor who ever made a sinecure of their chair, and that too upon his first entering on it; but the saints always had and will have their peculiar privileges'.[2] Potter, however, who was the author of a large progeny and had other game in view, pleaded poverty and begged to be excused. Henry Egerton, the Earl of Bridgwater's son, who had been given a canonry in 1716, was briefly considered, but King George decided to appoint as Dean his chaplain Hugh Boulter and gave him the Bishopric of Bristol as well. Unlike his three immediate predecessors, Boulter had never been a Westminster Student, nor indeed a Canoneer, and he had never held a canonry. In fact his connection with Christ Church was slight. He came up in 1687 as

[1] Ch. Ch. Library, MS Wake 16 (66).
[2] HMC, *Portland* (1901), vii, 24.

a Commoner and after two years migrated to Magdalen as a Demy and was subsequently Fellow. At Christ Church his tutor was Thomas Burton, who became a Canon in 1702 and retained his stall until his death in 1733. Hearne, always disinclined to detect merit in Whiggish clergy, said that Boulter was 'never reckon'd good for anything as to Learning', and that as an undergraduate he performed his disputations 'meanly'.[1] Oxford did not prove a congenial field for Boulter's considerable abilities and in 1724 he became Archbishop of Armagh, but not before Lord Townshend had abused him in public, 'calling him beast and wretched fellow, who being made Dean in order to strengthen the Whig interest there, did nothing but laze away his time, and suffered the Tories to increase their power and numbers in that university'.[2] He was a man of considerable means and by his will founded several exhibitions for Servitors and poor deserving Commoners. It is impossible not to feel warmly towards a Dean who in 1724 was unable to resist the temptation to appoint Charles Este tutor to Gilbert West.

Boulter was succeeded by William Bradshaw, a convinced Whig 'much of the same Principles with Bradshaw the Regicide'.[3] He had been appointed to a canonry in 1723 when rumours of Boulter's dissatisfaction with Oxford were current, but he had no previous connection with Christ Church, having been a Fellow and successful tutor of New College.[4] He had carefully courted the Whig interest, went on the grand tour as tutor to the second son of the Duke of Devonshire, and was rewarded for his political perspicuity by Archbishop Wake with a Lambeth doctorate. In 1724, Edmund Gibson reported that the ministry was 'much set' upon his appointment, 'and particularly ye D. of Devonshire'.[5] The Tory Canons of Christ Church were not unduly perturbed by the news. 'He will be more *busy* than Hugo was', Stratford

---

[1] Hearne, *Collections*, vii, 64.

[2] HMC, *Egmont, Diary of Viscount Percival* (1920), i, 225.

[3] Hearne, *Collections*, x, 53.

[4] Hearne, *Collections*, xi, 138. Bradshaw had, however, given £100 towards the rebuilding of Peckwater in 1718 (Dean's Benefactions Book).

[5] BL. MS Lansdowne 1017, fo. 6.

wrote, 'but not to any more purpose ... He loves his bottle, and if he will give drink he will meet with those who will help him to drink it. But farther than this I apprehend nothing, either without or within doors.'[1] Alas, it was not long before there was a familiar whiff of gunpowder in the air.

Under Dean Bradshaw the political balance within the Chapter changed, and as it did so tempers frayed. When he became Dean, five of the eight Canons had been appointed in the reign of Queen Anne. Although the majority were Tories, Terry was already a tepid Whig, and Potter, who was later Archbishop of Canterbury, had been accused of having republican principles when appointed to his canonry because his father was a Presbyterian and his wife a relative of the Fifth Monarchist Thomas Jenner. But the balance did not finally shift in favour of the ministerial influence until 1726 when John Gilbert succeeded to the stall made vacant by the death of Francis Gastrell. The Students viewed this development with concern sharpened by the prospect of deprivation. When Bradshaw became Dean, some of the senior Students had been elected in the time of Atterbury, and many more had been nominated by Canons appointed in the reign of Queen Anne or had come from Westminster School, where Jacobite sympathies still lingered. The government looked upon them as a body with not unjustified suspicion, and proceeded to fill the canonries with imported Whigs. For a decade after the Hanoverian succession, no Student was given a canonry until Peter Foulkes, a protégé of Archbishop Wake, received Bradshaw's stall in 1724. The traditional preference enjoyed by the Students in the succession to the non-professorial stalls thus fell into abeyance, and the bond of common interest between the Students and the Governing Body, between the governors and the governed, was weakened. The cohesion of the society was so far relaxed that in 1726 Stratford complained that the college 'cannot be long without being divided into distinct parties of Whig and Tory, a thing hitherto unknown in that place'.[2]

---

[1] HMC, *Portland* (1901), vii, 381.
[2] HMC, *Portland* (1901), vii, 441.

Bradshaw soon found himself at war with his rebellious subjects. The first fusillade was fired over the grave of Francis Gastrell, Bishop of Chester, who was buried in the cathedral on 25 November 1725. Gastrell had been a thorn in the side of the government for many years, and in 1719 a dispute occurred in his own diocese which enabled him to take up arms in defence of the university against the Crown. It was occasioned by the King's appointment of Samuel Peploe to the Wardenship of Manchester College. The foundation charter of the college stipulated that the Warden should be Bachelor of Divinity, but Peploe, although a Master of Arts of Jesus College and qualified for the degree from his own university, obtained a Lambeth degree from the Whiggishly inclined Archbishop of Canterbury. Gastrell refused to institute him, and maintained that only degrees obtained in the university were legal qualifications for ecclesiastical preferment. The issue was eventually decided in the courts in Peploe's favour, but Gastrell's able statement of the case, which was published in 1721, alarmed those, of whom Bradshaw was one, who had obtained Lambeth degrees. Bradshaw indeed hastened to regularize his position on his appointment to a canonry by obtaining a Doctorate of Divinity by diploma from the university. It was not only as a defender of the university that Gastrell claimed the respect of the Students of Christ Church. He had been elected from Westminster in Fell's time; he was consecrated to Chester on the same day that Smalridge was consecrated to Bristol; he was a strenuous defender of Atterbury in 1723. Moreover, his death paved the way for John Gilbert's appointment. Against this background George Wigan, the lecturer in rhetoric, preached Gastrell's funeral sermon against the wishes of the Dean. Hearne reported that the assembled Canons were much displeased

at his speaking and taking notice of the Bp's being educated amongst them in their own College, at a time when all Virtue, Honesty, Arts, Sciences, and good Learning were promoted & encourag'd, and not discountenanc'd there. And, withall, it vex'd them that he should be prais'd for the great Service he hath done to Religion and the Universities by his publick Writings.[1]

---

[1] Hearne, *Collections*, ix, 60.

The Chapter shrank from its first intention, which was to deprive Wigan of his lectureship, and contented itself with replacing him at the Christmas election of officers. The 'mutineers', as Stratford called them, retaliated by circulating a couplet which ran

> Would you have all as dull as he that does preside,
> Keep Sherman in, and Wigan lay aside.[1]

As the quarrel grew more heated Bradshaw petulantly omitted to invite the Noblemen and Gentlemen Commoners to the Deanery on Christmas Day or the Masters on New Year's Day. 'He seems', commented Stratford, 'to signify to all his subjects that he has no regard for them.'[2] In the following year the Students successfully opposed David Gregory's candidature for the Proctorship despite the assurances of support he had received from the Dean and Chapter. The Dean's choleric temper was quickly roused by real or fancied affronts, and his subjects lost no opportunity to provoke him. They affected to forget his name and addressed him as *John* Bradshaw after the regicide, or failed to remove their caps as they passed, claiming not to have seen him.[3] The accumulation of slights and insults was enough to drive the Dean to drink, and seems to have done so, for Hearne believed that it was 'excessive drinking that shortened his Life'.[4]

The composition of the Chapter was the source of disappointed expectations not only amongst the Students but for the Sub-Dean also. Thomas Terry, who had been tutor to Edward Harley, was for many years intimate with Atterbury at Christ Church and at Westminster, but when he realized that the political tide had turned irrevocably he trimmed his sails, and in 1724 sought to follow Boulter into the Deanery with, it was said, the support of Boulter himself. Of the five previous Deans all but one had been Students, and three of them Westminster Students. As the representative of a tradition welcome to Chapter and Students

---

[1] HMC, *Portland* (1901), vii, 413.
[2] Ibid., 413.
[3] Ibid., 414.
[4] Hearne, *Collections*, xi, 138.

alike, Terry's aspirations were not unreasonable. His mortification on Bradshaw's appointment was thereby all the greater, and he was heard muttering to himself, 'I have been nine years Sub-dean, and am as loyal as he for the heart of him. I say I shall not care to serve long under him.'[1] His injured feelings were briefly mollified by the convivial Bradshaw, and he was seen leaving the Deanery at one o'clock in the morning. 'A bottle of port has worked wonders and brought on a good understanding between them,' Stratford commented tartly.[2] But at the Christmas election in 1725 the wound opened when Terry ceased to be Sub-Dean. 'The breach betwixt Thomas Terry and the Governor is now pretty notorious,' wrote Stratford. 'Thomas jokes on him before all companies.'[3] In 1728 mutual resentment flared out in public when Bradshaw declined to allow the college to provide a new coach-house for Terry, who 'gave the Dean very foul language. The Dean was wise enough to make his return in the same dialect. The quarrel lasted long, to the great diversion of all present. It was wholly personal, in calling one another names ...'[4] For Stratford, the chronicler of Atterbury's feuds, it must have seemed quite like old times.

Bradshaw died on 16 December 1732 after a long illness. Amongst those who observed his passing with some impatience was Robert Freind, the Headmaster of Westminster, a learned man whose success as a composer of epitaphs was perhaps stimulated by the professional failures of his brother John, the physician. On 25 September he informed the Duke of Newcastle that the Dean was unlikely to recover, adding 'I am press'd to apply for being his successor at Ch.Ch. by severall who thinke I am more capable of doing services to the Colledge than I thinke myself. 'Tis no idle Post to any one yt thinkes of doing the Duty of it, tho so much less laborious than the worke I am now ingaged that it may seem a relief to me.'[5] Yielding, however reluctantly, to the wishes

---

[1] HMC, *Portland* (1901), vii, 382.
[2] Ibid., 383.
[3] Ibid., 414.
[4] Ibid., 466.
[5] BL Add. MS 32687, fo. 488.

of his friends, he was not prevented from pressing his suit with vigour and from contributing a fulsome and opportune panegyric on Queen Caroline to the edition of his brother's works, but during the King's absence abroad it fell to the Queen to tell him that at sixty-five he was too old. He then suggested the name of his old pupil George Wigan, only to discover that the Deanery had been promised to John Conybeare. No Student had interest enough.

Conybeare, like Bradshaw, had no previous connection with Christ Church. At the time of his appointment he was Rector of Exeter, and he was the only Dean then or subsequently to have been Head of another Oxford college. His combination of Whig and Anglican orthodoxy brought him to the attention of Edmund Gibson, Bishop of London, who in 1732 accepted the dedication of his attack on Tindal's *Christianity as Old as the Creation*, and it was to Gibson that he now owed his advancement.[1] At Exeter he had introduced useful reforms, and he set about the task of restoring discipline at Christ Church with great energy. Hearne wrote that he

makes a great Stir in the College at present, pretending to great matters, such as locking up the gates at nine Clock at night, having the keys brought up to him, turning out young women from being bedmakers, having the kitchen (which he visits) cleansed, and I know not what, aiming at a wonderful character, even to exceed that truly great man Bishop Fell.[2]

Peace was restored to the Chapter when at Christmas 1733 Dr Terry became Sub-Dean again, and in the following year the college built for him the coach-house which he had vainly sought from Bradshaw.[3] In 1738 Conybeare reformed the regulations concerning disputations and themes, and in the next year the procedure for taking degrees.[4] In 1734 he encouraged a young Bachelor Student named George Crochley to undertake an edition

[1] Hearne, *Collections*, xi, 152.
[2] Ibid., 169.
[3] Chapter Act Book, 9 Dec. 1734.
[4] Ibid., 16 May 1738, 3 May 1739.

of Cicero's *De Oratore*, an ill-advised venture, according to Hearne, abruptly terminated when Crochley was drowned in Sandford lock. Signs of public approval were not lacking. In 1733 the Prince of Orange, who had come to England to marry George II's eldest daughter Princess Anne, stayed at Christ Church. It was a further mark of approval that a large majority of the Canons appointed in Conybeare's time had formerly been Students. Perhaps even more remarkably, in 1737 Archbishop Wake bequeathed not only his great library of books but also his official papers to his old college in preference to his own excellent library at Lambeth.

Despite these outward signs of prosperity, Conybeare's tenure of the Deanery was not an auspicious period. The nobility and gentry lost confidence in the education provided in the university. Tory squires were not reassured by reports that the education of their sons was in the hands of a Chapter composed of Whigs, and the Whigs were constantly alarmed by rumours of Jacobitism in Oxford and preferred to send their sons on the grand tour. Matriculations in the 1740s and 1750s fell to their lowest level since the reign of James II, and the Earl of Shelburne, who came up in 1755, complained that apart from Hamilton Boyle, later Earl of Cork, 'the college was very low: a proof of it is, that no one who was there in my time has made much figure either as a publick man or man of letters'.[1]

Although matriculations declined and the influence of the Noblemen and Gentlemen Commoners on undergraduate society thereby diminished, the number of Students remained constant at 101, and the proportion of Students to other members of the college increased substantially. This imbalance contributed to an outbreak of indiscipline in the 1740s which culminated in the famous disorders in the wake of the Jacobite Rebellion. Most of the Students involved in these disorders were Westminster Students or had been educated at Westminster. Conybeare had no close connection with Westminster and neglected the Westminster

[1] E. Fitzmaurice, *Life of William, Earl of Shelburne*, 2nd edn. (1912), i, 15. Although he was not strictly contemporary with the Earl of Shelburne, the name of Henry Flood, who came up in 1750, may be added to the list of distinguished Christ Church men of the period.

interest for many years. The Senior Censorship, for example, was held by a Westminster Student for only three years between 1732 and 1745. It is only under Conybeare that evidence is found of ill feeling between the Westminsters and the Canoneers. The Earl of Shelburne remarked that his tutor William Holwell, a Canoneer Student, 'was fool enough to set himself up in a pointed opposition to the Westminsters',[1] and in 1744 two Bachelor Students from Westminster were summoned before the Chapter because they had abused the Senior Censor Richard Hind, who was also a Canoneer Student, and 'treated him with great insolence of words and action proceeding so far as to curse and hisse at him'.[2] It was perhaps with Conybeare's unruly Students in mind that Robert Freind complained to the Duke of Newcastle in 1742 that the college was 'at a very low ebb for want of a proper Head'.[3] After ruminating further he wrote to the Duke again in September, and this time to the Archbishop of Canterbury also, suggesting that the malaise at Christ Church would be ameliorated if the Dean were elevated to the vacant Primacy of Ireland.[4]

Freind's solicitude went unheeded, and Conybeare's hope of lawn sleeves was deferred by the political eclipse of his patron Bishop Gibson. As the years rolled by and the promised land continually receded, a note of urgency, even of reproach, entered the Dean's correspondence. 'I am possess'd', he wrote to the Duke of Newcastle in 1747, 'of no Living or Preferment of any Kind beside my Deanery of Christ Church, which hath scarce prov'd the Case of any Dean here since the first Foundation.'[5] In the following year he entreated the Duke to recommend him to the King for the Deanery of St Paul's.

My attachment to the Interests of the present Royal family ever since its Accession to the Throne of Great Britain is well known [he wrote] and my Endeavours to serve them thro' every Stage of my Life have not been without good Effects. Yet I am so thoroughly sensible of His

---

[1] Fitzmaurice, *Life of Shelburne*, i, 13.
[2] Chapter Act Book, 12 June 1744.
[3] BL Add. MS 32699, fo. 313.
[4] Ibid., 427.
[5] BL Add. MS 32710, fo. 358.

Majestie's Goodness in placing me where I am that I have never prov'd troublesome to Your Grace for any farther Favour excepting once only, when I sued for a Presentation to the living of Marsh Gibbon about the Beginning of the last year. Had my Great and Good Friend the Late Lord Bishop of London been stil alive I should not have wanted an Intercessor with Your Grace on such an Occasion as this.[1]

Newcastle, concerned that the Chapter was composed of unenthusiastic Whigs, was disposed to recommend Conybeare, whom he wished to replace by John Fanshawe, the Regius Professor of Divinity and a firm Whig, but he met without success.[2] Finally, in 1750 Conybeare was rewarded with the Bishopric of Bristol, which for most of the eighteenth century was almost a pocket borough of Christ Church. His appointment was made by the King 'very readily and with pleasure'.[3] It would, said the Duke, make Conybeare 'rather a better Dean of Christ Church with it than without it'.[4]

Conybeare died in July 1755, but almost ten months elapsed before a new Dean was appointed. The Duke of Newcastle, the Duke of Marlborough, Archbishop Herring, and Lord Chancellor Hardwicke discussed the succession, but could not agree on a suitable name to recommend to the King.[5] Newcastle thought that he should be one 'who shall support the King's Interest, which is I hope, now establish'd in the County, and endeavour to promote it to the utmost in the University',[6] and Hardwicke that he should be a man of learning and spirit as well as a staunch Whig.[7] The question which exercised them was whether to appoint a sound Whig or a member of Christ Church, if a sound Whig who was also a member of Christ Church could not be found. In August, the Bishop of Oxford, Secker, who was consulted about the appointment, set out the dilemma in the following words:

---

[1] BL Add. MS 32716, fo. 297.
[2] Ibid., fo. 282.
[3] BL Add. MS 32722, fo. 232^v.
[4] Ibid.
[5] BL Add. MS 32857, fo. 231^v.
[6] Ibid.
[7] BL Add. MS 32721, fo. 419^v.

I am no Judge at all, whether the propriety of placing a Christ-Church man at the Head of Christ-Church, or the apprehension of uneasiness amongst the Whigs ought to prevail. If your Grace prefers the former consideration, I need say nothing of Dr. Fanshaw and Dr. Gregory. Their qualifications are very well known: and the senior of them was reckoned the best Subdean that had been of many years. Of Dr. [William] Freind I can say with truth that he hath approved himself a most careful parish-minister in my diocese: that I never heard the least objection against his political principles, for which I think his late sermon before the House of Commons a sufficient voucher, and that I believe him to be a serious and prudent as well as ingenious and well-bred man, and one who will be capable and desirous of filling the place with reputation. If on the other hand your Grace conceives the second point to be of more consequence, my brother Hume,[1] I am fully persuaded, will make an excellent Bishop, and if, along with the superintendancy of a diocese he can be brought to undertake another troublesome office, as undoubtedly the Deanery of Christ-Church is, will set himself conscientiously to perform the duties of it, and will certainly go through them, not only with the sweetest good temper, but with a due degree of spirit and confessed ability.[2]

The King's choice fell on David Gregory, who was installed on 18 May 1756. He was the first Dean to have held a Studentship since the death of Smalridge, and his appointment finally restored the equilibrium between the Governing Body and the Students. Gregory had been elected from Westminster in the closing months of the reign of Queen Anne, and in 1724, a mere three years after taking his MA, became the first incumbent of the chair of modern history at Oxford founded by George I. The secular character of the professorship may explain his apparent reluctance to take holy orders, which he delayed until 1727 when further delay would have led to the forfeiture of his Studentship. In 1735 he was instituted to the college living of Semley, and, having completed his year of grace, resigned his Studentship on 18 May 1736. A fortnight later letters patent confirmed his appointment to a canonry at Christ Church, whereupon he also resigned his pro-

---

[1] John Hume, Bishop of Bristol (1756).
[2] BL Add. MS 32858, fo. 108, the Bishop of Oxford to the Duke of Newcastle, 11 Aug. 1755.

fessorship. By the time he became Dean, he had held his canonry
for twenty years, a longer period than any of his predecessors. As
Sub-Dean for part of this period he had proved a valuable coadju-
tor to Conybeare and had acquired some experience of college
affairs. Gregory's career was remarkably deficient in the conventional symbols of success of the aspiring clergyman. As a
Student, he made no great mark at Christ Church. He held none
of the college offices, nor was he a tutor. No sermons or fulsome
dedications flowed from his pen. He was not a royal chaplain nor
a chaplain to any of the nobility, and he seems to have received
no ecclesiastical preferment apart from his canonry until he was
given a college living. If he had political friends, they did not
conspicuously include the Duke of Newcastle, for the Duke had
no hand in his appointment. But Gregory had one advantage
which more than compensated for his lack of the usual scaffolding
of preferment, for he was known in court circles and had at an
early age attracted the attention of the King. At every stage his
advancement was due to the royal favour, a debt which he grace-
fully acknowledged by placing busts of George I and George II
by Rysbrack in Christ Church Hall.

   Gregory was not a mere courtier, however, but a man of ability
and accomplishment whose appointment as Dean of Christ Church
heralded a period of notable educational and intellectual advance.
Under his energetic and enlightened rule, Christ Church resumed
its role as the nursery of the governing classes, and the great
landed families, who for a generation had ignored the university,
began once more to send their sons to the college. At his installation, an ancient custom of Christ Church enabled him to make
symbolic affirmation of his determination to restore this connection when William Harley, a Canoneer Student and son of the
third Earl of Oxford, received his grace for the degree of MA 'by
the appointment of Dr. Gregory the new Dean according to
custom upon his Promotion to the Deanery'.[1] In 1756, the Duke
of Marlborough sent his second son, Lord Charles Spencer, to
Christ Church, and in 1762 his third son, Robert. The Duke of

---

[1] Chapter Act Book, 24 May 1756.

Manchester in 1759, the Duke of Portland in 1761, and the Earl of Ilchester in 1765 followed suit. Gregory, who had married a daughter of the Duke of Kent, mixed easily with the aristocracy and was far removed from the caricature of the uncouth wine-bibbing Oxford don. He was, said Lord Shelburne, 'very kind to me, conversed familiarly and frequently with me, had kept good company, was a gentleman, though not a scholar, and gave me notions of people and things which were afterwards useful to me'.[1] By the middle of the eighteenth century, Oxford's reputation for Jacobitism and disaffection had receded, if it had not yet disappeared, and political and social changes had restored much of the esteem in which the university was held. Gregory did not create these conditions but he understood them and endeavoured to enable Christ Church to recapture its traditions and reflect the spirit of the age.

When the landed classes returned to the university in the middle of the eighteenth century, there was renewed emphasis at Christ Church on education as a preparation for public life. Gregory was well suited to guide such a development, for it had been the intention of the Professorship of Modern History, which he had held for twelve years, to achieve a similar object. The foundation, which was the brain-child of Bishop Gibson, was meant to win over the universities to the new dynasty, and to provide opportunities for what Gregory himself called 'the generality of young gentlemen of distinction' to serve the State.[2] In 1728, Gregory wrote to Lord Townshend, 'The methods of Education in our Universities have been in some measure defective, since we are obliged to adhere so much to the rules laid down by our forefathers ... the old scholastic learning has been for some time despised, but not altogether exploded, because nothing else has been substituted in its place.'[3] Under his aegis the professorial curriculum embraced the study of history, law, and modern languages. These were useful for the diplomatic service, which was their primary

---

[1] Fitzmaurice, *Life of Shelburne*, i, 15.
[2] Gregory to Lord Townshend, 24 May 1728, quoted by C. H. Firth, *Modern Languages at Oxford 1724–1929* (1929), 14.
[3] PRO, SP 36/6, fo. 227.

intention, and also for other areas of public life. Gregory brought to his professorship a remarkable knowledge of modern languages gained, according to his anonymous biographer, in foreign travel.[1] He also brought an enthusiasm for the study of history, though his own historical scholarship was such that Hearne, a not unprejudiced observer, described his inaugural lecture as 'a strange Medley of Stuff, without any Method or Connexion, and in a most wretched, barbarous Latin stile'.[2] His interest in historical studies was, however, important, for the study of history was a significant development in the intellectual history of the university during the second half of the eighteenth century.[3]

Thus Gregory was well prepared for the task which lay before him when he became Dean, and he lost no time in reforming the curriculum. His biographer described his achievement in these words:

The Plan of Study, however excellent it might have been, as no doubt it was, when centuries back it was first established, he now found to have become infinitely too superficial and contracted; for Literary Knowledge being in these times so generally diffused through mankind, as that it is less an honour to have it, than scandal to be without it, so he found the Youth of his College more animated than heretofore with a desire of breaking through, and exploring into all the mysteries of Learning ... Dr. Gregory therefore, upon these considerations, but principally from his own zeal for the advancement of literary knowledge, broke up the old plan, and selecting out from it whatever things he therein found good and usefull, wrought them in together with his own admirable materials, and framed at length a System of Study, the most regular, the most beautiful, and the most extensive, that was ever proposed to the youth of the university. It comprehends all the Classics, Poets and Historians, Logic, Mathematics, Philosophy, Divinity, and the several branches which spring from them; in this, all the parts are so curiously and so beautifully arranged, that the various gradations and transitions from one to the other are smooth and natural, and seem, like

[1] *Essay on the Life of David Gregory* (1769), 11.

[2] Hearne, *Collections*, viii, 364.

[3] It is perhaps an example of Gregory's enthusiasm for history that he installed a bed said to have belonged to Queen Elizabeth I in the deanery, where it remained until the accession of Cyril Jackson. (Bodl. MS Top. Oxon. c. 33, fo. 23).

the colours of the rainbow, imperceptibly to rise out of each other; so that the progress through the whole scheme, formidable as it may appear, is in truth found to be both easy and entertaining.[1]

Gregory's reform of the plan of study, that is, of the study required by the college for a degree, was far reaching. He increased the study of Roman history, revitalized the study of Greek, introduced algebra, and extended the quantity and variety of reading. Undergraduates, said his biographer, 'in the course of four years go through the whole circle of Early Learning, and lay a broad and lasting foundation to build their future studies upon'.[2] By improving Collections, by insisting that Noblemen and Gentlemen Commoners took part in declamations and other exercises, and by rewarding industry and providing opportunities for excellence, he stimulated enthusiasm and emulation. 'Our Dean', wrote Lord Beauchamp to Horace Walpole, 'is a very vigilant active governour and does every thing in his power to raise emulation among the undergraduates. I dare say in time his endeavours will succeed, but you are sensible yt much time is required to bring about a total reformation.'[3]

The total reformation of Christ Church was brought a step nearer by the appointment of William Markham to the Deanery in 1767. Markham had been elected from Westminster in 1738, and was an active and successful tutor for ten years. He held the college lectureship in rhetoric from 1747 to 1750, and became Junior Censor in the following year. Any hopes he may have had of the Senior Censorship were quashed by his appointment as Headmaster of Westminster on the resignation of John Nicol in 1753. Two years previously, in 1751, Nicol had been given the canonry at Christ Church which had become vacant by the death of Robert Freind, and he seems to have taken advantage of his appointment to discover a suitable successor among the Students. In May 1752 he is found warmly recommending Markham to the Duke of Newcastle, who took an almost proprietary interest

---

[1] *Essay on the Life of David Gregory*, 17–20.
[2] Ibid., 20.
[3] BL Add. MS 23218, fo. 17ᵛ.

in Westminster School.[1] As Headmaster, Markham was a great success, and even to such a captious critic as the youthful Jeremy Bentham he was 'an object of adoration'.[2] His son-in-law H. F. Mills, who went to Westminster after Markham had departed, has left a description of him of which the accuracy is amply confirmed by others.

It is [he wrote] difficult to say whether he most excelled in the manner of conveying knowledge, or in exciting youth to laudable pursuits. His knowledge of Grecian and Roman literature was universal; his taste pure. His geography was of such extensive range that it descended to all the minuteness of topographical accuracy; so that he never failed to secure the attention of his scholars by enlivening his lectures with the most pleasing descriptions and the most interesting anecdotes. He was at the same time so perfectly master of different incentives for different dispositions, that the studious were ever ambitious of his praise, and the idle feared his rebuke.[3]

When Gregory died, the Duke of Newcastle, unbeknown to Markham, sought to obtain the Deanery for him and recommended him to Archbishop Secker as 'the fittest man in England for it'.[4] The Archbishop agreed with the Duke while still maintaining the political argument he had advanced when Gregory was appointed. 'I think very well, & very highly of Dr. Markham', he replied, 'and know but one man likely to make so good a Dean of Christ Church. I mean the Bishop of Oxford, who perhaps would not accept it, and the Society would have one prejudice at least against him.'[5]

Westminster was the key to Markham's success at Christ Church. As Headmaster he taught youths of almost the same age as those he had tutored at Christ Church, and it was thus possible to design an integrated scheme of education from school to

---

[1] BL Add. MS 32727, fo. 149.

[2] J. Bentham, *Works*, ed. J. Bowring (1843), x, 30.

[3] Quoted in C. R. Markham, *Memoir of Archbishop Markham* (1906), 22, and Nichols, *Literary Anecdotes*, ii, 368.

[4] BL Add. MSS 32985, fo. 176ᵛ; 32986, fo. 273.

[5] BL Add. MS 32985, fo. 196. The Bishop of Oxford was Robert Lowth, of St John's College, who had been translated to the see of Oxford as recently as the previous October.

college. As Headmaster he was closely involved in the reforms of the plan of study introduced by Gregory, whose biographer observed that without Markham's participation they would not have been possible.[1] The twenty-three years during which he was in succession Headmaster and Dean provided the continuity needed to build firm educational foundations. The historic connection between Westminster School and Christ Church was strengthened at a time when the school was at the peak of its renown, and Markham ensured that many of his best pupils came up to Christ Church as Students or Commoners.

The pace of reform at Christ Church quickened. Markham was helped by circumstances not always of his creation: the renaissance in Greek studies, for example, had already germinated; undergraduates came to the university more mature; the wide disparities in age between them diminished owing to the growing popularity of the public schools and the decline of private education. But Markham harnessed these developments and added important contributions of his own. One of his first acts was to reform Collections, and this was followed by the institution of public lectures in ethics, mathematics, logic, history, and divinity.[2] Year by year the curriculum was enriched by the addition of new authors, particularly the Greek dramatists and the Latin historians (both imports from Westminster). The curriculum became more varied and coherent, and was commended by no less a critic than Gibbon. If some undergraduates continued to elude the benefits of education with almost hereditary dexterity, there was a perceptible improvement in the general level of attainment. In 1774, Markham achieved an ambition of long standing when he required the Noblemen and Gentlemen Commoners to take up their Collections with the rest of the college rather than separately as before. This was a significant reform which improved the educational standard not only of the Noblemen and Gentlemen Commoners but of the whole college. The reputation of Christ Church grew rapidly, and in 1771 the college received the accolade of royal

---

[1] *Essay on the Life of David Gregory*, 18.
[2] Ibid., 29.

approval when Markham was appointed preceptor to the Prince of Wales and his brother.

In 1771, Markham became Bishop of Chester, and in 1776 he was rewarded with the Archbishopric of York. Even before he had accepted, George III recommended Lewis Bagot to Lord North as his successor.[1] Bagot was the younger son of a Staffordshire baronet who represented the university in Parliament from 1762 until his death six years later. He was at Westminster under Markham, and entered Christ Church in 1757 as a Canoneer Student on the nomination of John Fanshawe. He took his degree in the normal course, but his career at Christ Church was only marginally more distinguished than Gregory's had been. He was never a tutor, and held none of the college offices except one of the junior lectureships in logic. On becoming Rector of Jevington in 1767 he resigned his Studentship after the customary year of grace, but returned to Christ Church as a Canon in 1771. When Markham departed, he was Sub-Dean and Censor Theologiae.[2]

Bagot had less experience of college or university affairs than any of his predecessors since the Restoration except Boulter. But he was not unlearned, and it is said that as a boy he used to steal away to the parsonage at Blithfield, where he spent many hours reading with the scholarly rector Thomas Townson.[3] His courteous manners and extensive family connections fitted him to deal with the nobility and gentry at Christ Church. Those who knew him best were agreed that his most conspicuous qualities were his piety and moral earnestness. In 1820, an anonymous writer in the *Gentleman's Magazine*, who had been an undergraduate at Christ

---

[1] Sir J. Fortescue (ed.), *Correspondence of George III* (1928), iii, no. 1923.

[2] On his arrival in the Deanery, Bagot found, as Boulter had done before him, that his old tutor was a member of the Chapter. This was Edward Smallwell, who, unlike his pupil, had had a distinguished career at Christ Church. He had been elected from Westminster in 1739, was lecturer in Greek from 1747 to 1750, lecturer in rhetoric in 1751, Junior Censor in 1752, Senior Censor from 1753 to 1759, Librarian in 1757, and a busy tutor for some thirteen years. Despite his great experience and undoubted ability, Smallwell was not a candidate for the succession, having been appointed to his canonry only in 1775. Preferment came to him later, for in 1783 he became Bishop of St David's, and in 1788 Bishop of Oxford.

[3] *Gentleman's Magazine* (1802), 1005.

Church under Bagot, remarked that 'An anxious persevering earnestness was, to a very remarkable degree, the predominant feature of his natural character; influenced, wherever duty was concerned, by the most scrupulous sense of religious obligation'.[1] A similar view was expressed with more subtlety by Cyril Jackson in a letter to the Duke of Portland in 1794 in which he recommended Bagot, who was then Bishop of St Asaph, for the Primacy of Ireland. He spoke in it of

a general earnestness to do good, which gives a tinge to his whole character. The affections of his heart seem always engag'd in what he is doing so that if he acts contrary even to your wishes and opinions, you cannot help loving and esteeming him. He would be as Primate, the liberal patron of learned men, the liberal promoter of public works, his hospitality and beneficence would be splendid and exemplary, and always decent. To be sure he does not like a Dissenter, and the very earnestness of his desire to do good, the very sincerity of his own conviction that he is always acting under that desire and acting too with the firm persuasion that he is right, betrays him sometimes into warmth and sometimes into imprudences.[2]

His moral rectitude sometimes made him intolerant, and Richard Polwhele, who had also observed him as an undergraduate, quoted in his *Reminiscences* a remark of Hannah More that he had 'a great deal of that charity which giveth her goods to the poor, but not quite so much of that which consists of *tenderness to the opinions* of others'.[3] The religious and moral aspects of Bagot's character were not unknown to George III, who in the education of his own sons had had occasion to consider the qualities needed by the successful tutor and guardian, and they were doubtless significant factors in his appointment. In 1782 Bagot obtained the Bishopric of Bristol and in the following year left Christ Church on being translated to Norwich.

Bagot's departure opportunely set the stage for Cyril Jackson, who as Dean of Christ Church dominated the college in the

[1] *Gentleman's Magazine* (Jan. 1820), 1.
[2] Nottingham University Library, Portland Papers P.W.F. 5765, Jackson to the Duke of Portland, 23 Oct. 1794.
[3] R. Polwhele, *Reminiscences* (1836), ii, 167.

eighteenth century as completely as John Fell had dominated it in the seventeenth. He was born[1] in 1746, the son of a country doctor who practised at York,[2] and was educated at Manchester Grammar School until 1760 when he entered Westminster as a King's Scholar under Markham. On two occasions in Jackson's life, events occurred which in retrospect threatened the prospect of him ever becoming Dean. On the first occasion it was possible for a time that he would not become a member of Christ Church at all, for in 1764 he was elected head to Trinity College, Cambridge. He decided not to take up his election but to go to Oxford instead, and he was duly elected to a Canoneer Studentship on 22 December in the same year. The second occasion was in 1778. On 19 August Jackson was granted a year of grace on being instituted to the living of Carlton in Lindrick in Nottinghamshire, and, had that year run its course, would infallibly have surrendered his Studentship. But it so happened that two days later, on 21 August, William Conybeare, who was not only a Student but Librarian, notified the Dean and Chapter of his marriage, and his Studentship was accordingly declared void. On 28 October, when the college reassembled after the summer vacation, Jackson was appointed to the vacant office of Librarian, which carried with it the valuable privilege of holding with a Studentship a living not in the gift of the college, and his year of grace was simultaneously revoked. It is difficult not to suspect collusion in these events. In 1776 Jackson had completed his task as sub-preceptor to the two eldest sons of George III, an office secured for him through the interest of Markham in 1771. The Dean was subsequently elevated to the Archbishopric of York, but Jackson received no tangible reward. Can it be supposed that, having enjoyed the royal favour, he was content to creep away, unrecognized and unknown, to a remote country rectory, even though Markham was, as Arch-

---

[1] Entered in the baptismal register of St. Crux, York, as 'Sorril son of Sorril Jackson'. Archbishop Drummond's order in 1763 allowing the entry to be amended was quoted into the following century as a precedent for altering parish registers (Lambeth Palace Library MS 3416, f. 28).

[2] With the exception of Atterbury and Conybeare, all the Deans of Christ Church in the eighteenth century where the sons of laymen.

bishop of York, its patron? May it not rather be that the threat to do so was a bold indication of his discontent, but one which, given his knowledge of Conybeare's impending marriage, offered a safe means of withdrawal? Whatever the truth, Jackson was given a canonry at Christ Church in the following year.

Jackson was an impressive example of the benefits a tutor might expect from a judicious choice of pupils, for there is little doubt that he owed his elevation to the Deanery to the royal favour he had earned as tutor to the sons of George III. The Prince of Wales even went so far as to claim the credit for his appointment, and on 27 May 1783 wrote to his brother, 'I have been fortunate enough to have it in my power to do a piece of service to a very old friend of our's, I mean Dr. Jackson, by getting him thro' my interest ye Deanery of Christ Church'.[1] Throughout his life Jackson continued to be held in the highest esteem by the royal family. When he retired in 1809, Lord Liverpool wrote to him at the King's command

to express in the strongest terms the deep sense which he entertains of your services during the twenty-six years which you have presided over Christ Church and of the important advantages which have resulted from them to the country. His Majesty added that he regretted most sincerely the determination which he knew you had long formed to retire from all public employment.[2]

These were not empty words and Jackson well understood the practical value of royal approbation. In his reply he wrote to Liverpool,

My success has at all times been principally owing to the generous mention which his Majesty was so often pleased to make of my conduct and the favourable terms in which he always condescended to speak of Christ Church. That was in fact the protection and support which enabled me to overcome opposition and even to set it at nought.[3]

He was held in no less regard by the Prince Regent, whom he often visited at Brighton after his retirement to nearby Felpham.

[1] A. Aspinall (ed.), *Correspondence of George Prince of Wales* (1963), i, no. 76.
[2] BL Add. MS 38243, fo. 221.
[3] Ibid., 242ᵛ.

George IV's esteem for him continued even after his death, for when Lord Liverpool offered the Deanery to Samuel Smith in 1824, Liverpool remarked that the King had expressed 'in the strongest terms' his interest in the college on public and personal grounds from his early connection. 'The King', he added, 'has felt that he owes it to the memory of the late Archbishop of York and the late Dr. Cyril Jackson.'[1]

The marks of royal approval conferred upon him and the opportunities he had had of observing the manners of the court enabled Jackson to move with ease and confidence in society, and particularly in political society. Few things in his career are more remarkable than the extent of his acquaintance, and in some cases friendship, with many of the leading politicians of the time, amongst them Lansdowne, Liverpool, Perceval, Malmesbury, Canning, and particularly the third Duke of Portland. When the Duke died in 1809, Jackson wrote to William Howley, who was then Regius Professor of Divinity, that he had lost a friend to whom 'next to my duties at Christ Church, my whole mind and its affections were chiefly directed—so that for many years the end of Term and the finishing of Collections have been delightful to me, only or at least principally as it enabled me to say to myself, on such a day I shall see the Duke of Portland'.[2] When Portland was Prime Minister, Jackson was a frequent visitor to Downing Street, where he was apparently welcomed without formality. In 1807 he wrote to his pupil Hugh Chambres Jones, for whom he had obtained the appointment of secretary and chaplain to the Duke, advising him to

go down to Downing Street *not before* twelve and ask to see the Duke. Any difficulty of admission will be removed by telling the porter that you come on particular business from the Dean of Ch.Ch. You will then be told fairly whether he is at home or not, and if at home you will soon receive a word from the D. when he can see you. Make your bow and say simply that as I did not seem to be certain in my letter when he would be at Bulstrode you thought it your *duty* to come up and receive

[1] BL Add. MS 38576, fo. 35.
[2] Lambeth Palace Library, MS 2186, fo. 10ᵛ.

his Grace's final *commands*. Mind my two words. I know this will please on many accounts.[1]

But although he moved freely in the highest political circles and followed the course of events with keen interest, Jackson had little political influence, nor did he seriously seek to acquire any. Even in ecclesiastical appointments his advice was seldom asked and often ignored.[2] It is said that he had some share in the retirement of Addington in 1804, but otherwise the only political event in which he seems to have taken an important part was the resignation of the Duke of Portland. In August 1809 he described the deterioration in the Duke's health in these words,

I almost offended him when I was last in town by going too far and speaking too plainly on the other side [i.e. in favour of retirement] ... I know from two different quarters on wch I can thoroughly depend that the—[the recipient has added here the word 'king'] is impracticable on the subject and will hear no reason. And I very much suspect also that there is something which lurks in the D's mind, which perhaps he has never fairly avow'd even to himself, and most certainly to no one else, which forms the greatest obstacle of all. But I cannot mention even to you, to whom I wd confide every thing, what my suspicion is. Let me however add what I conceive to be a third difficulty, or at least to have some influence on this business. Do not you think yourself that if matters had been so managed as that a £10,000 had been left him to amuse himself with at Bulstrode, it might have made a little difference. As things are, Bulstrode can furnish no resource to him. And no man, Heaven knows, has fewer resources or wants them more for the latter end of life.[3]

When a few months later the Duke actually resigned, Thomas Grenville wrote that 'The Duke of Portland was forced into his

---

[1] Jackson to H. C. Jones, 27 Aug. 1807, letter in the possession of the late Lt.-Col. H. M. C. Jones-Mortimer; photocopy at Christ Church.

[2] An example was the Duke of Portland's disregard of Jackson's advice when William Newcome was made Primate of Ireland in 1795 (Nottingham University Library, Portland Papers P.W.F. 5765, Jackson to the Duke of Portland, 23 Oct. 1794.)

[3] Jackson to H. C. Jones, 14 Aug. 1809, letter in the possession of the late Lt.-Col. H. M. C. Jones-Mortimer; photocopy at Christ Church.

letter of resignation by Lord Titchfield, aided and seconded by that great man the Dean of Christ Church'.[1]

If, then, Jackson did not aspire to political influence, why, it may be asked, was he so assiduous in cultivating the acquaintance and friendship of politicians? His reason was not personal ambition, for many offers of preferment were refused by him. In 1794, he was offered the Bishopric of Bristol, and in 1807 he might have followed Markham at York. His reply to the Prince Regent's offer of the see of Oxford has passed into legend. The Deanery of Christ Church was in fact the summit of his ambition because it enabled him to devote himself to the real business of his life, which was the education and advancement of young men. Jackson sought the friendship of politicians and enjoyed the reflection of power because politics were central to his conception of education. He was an energetic exponent of the tradition that the purpose of liberal education was to produce good citizens, and that the highest form of citizenship was to be found in public life and especially in government. Nowhere was this conception more clearly demonstrated than in the education of those under-graduates, particularly the Noblemen and Gentlemen Commoners, who came from sections of society likely to pursue a career in Parliament or public life. Jackson understood their aspirations. 'No one', wrote his anonymous biographer, 'better knew the essential qualifications of an English gentleman, and no one, therefore, could better inspire the breasts of young men in the middle stage between adolescence and manhood, whose destination was to the higher walks of life, with generous sentiments, and a lively sense of the nature and importance of their future duties.'[2] He achieved the remarkable feat of encouraging a considerable proportion of them to study, and the best of them to study as industriously as the best of the Students and Commoners. They were, wrote W. D. Conybeare, 'from a previous state of licentious disorder reduced by him to the most strictly disciplined body among us, and urged to an honourable competition in our

---

[1] HMC, *Fortescue* (1915), ix, 332.
[2] *Gentleman's Magazine* (Nov. 1819), 462.

literary race'.[1] He succeeded in a task which had defeated so many of his predecessors by making the Noblemen and Gentlemen Commoners his willing accomplices. By means of living example he demonstrated the connection between the education they received at Christ Church and the arena of public life which followed. He showed them that the contemporary equivalent of Plutarch's noble Greeks and Romans might be sought in the Palace of Westminster, and that the study of the Greek city-state and the Roman republic, of the masterpieces of classical oratory, rhetoric, and drama, was the foundation necessary for a political life. Through his most brilliant pupils, Jackson pursued vicariously the political career for which his holy orders disqualified him, and the Deanery of Christ Church uniquely allowed him to savour at a distance the political life otherwise denied to him. Occasionally in his correspondence he sought to discuss matters of policy, but more often he is found exhorting his pupils to apply the methods and principles which their education at Christ Church had taught. When, for example, he wrote to Canning in 1807 to congratulate him on the skill with which he had drawn up the so-called Russian Declaration, he seized the opportunity to draw a parallel with classical antiquity. The arguments, he wrote, were

as fine specimens of real and commanding eloquence, founded as all true eloquence must be on strict logick, as I have ever read *even in Greek*, and they are also perfect examples of that which I have learnt from Homer and Demosthenes and from the Scriptures, that the strongest things may be most strongly said by the most simple words.[2]

Jackson's cultivation of politicians had its practical side. Often he used it to help young men at the start of their careers. When, for example, a crop of legal offices was created by Pitt, he urged Canning to 'think sometimes of Ch.Ch.', and pressed on him the claims of Henry Dickens, whom he described as 'not a bad or unindustrious lawyer, but gets no business, just going to be cut

---

[1] W. D. Conybeare (ed.), *Letters and Exercises of the Elizabethan Schoolmaster John Conybeare ... with Notes and a Fragment of Autobiography by the Rev. W. D. Conybeare* (1905), 115.

[2] Leeds Public Libraries, Canning Papers, Jackson to G. Canning, Dec. 1807.

out of his Studentship'.[1] On other occasions he used his influence to help his friends. On the Regius Professorship of Divinity falling vacant in 1809, he persuaded a reluctant William Howley to accept it when Spencer Perceval assured him that to do so would oblige the ministry and perhaps lead to a Bishopric for Howley. When Perceval expressed his pleasure at Howley's acceptance, and, perhaps referring to the common belief that the professorship was more easily accepted than got rid of, remarked that *he* had not done Howley a favour, Jackson reminded him of his promise. 'I told him laughingly', he recorded, 'that I would not trust any Minister without witnesses, and as Lord Liverpool was in the next room, I desired he might be called in, in which he consented to with equal good humour.'[2] In most cases the patronage Jackson sought was minor, but because it was small and was sought from so many different patrons he never incurred heavy obligations in return, and the patronage which might have imposed such obligations he neither sought nor was given. Through such small acts of benevolence he created a freemasonry of Christ Church men in public life. Above all he sought the good of Christ Church. In 1813 he explained his refusal to use his influence on behalf of his only paternal relative, the granddaughter of his father's eldest brother. She married George Hutchinson, Vicar of St Mary's, Nottingham, and her son Cyril George Hutchinson was maintained at Westminster School by Cyril Jackson and his brother William. When this marriage took place, Jackson told George Hutchinson and his wife that they could count on him for money, but that

they must not in any degree build upon my Interest for Promotion, that whatever interest I had was in my own mind most religiously dedicated to Ch.Ch. and to Ch.Ch. only. I will not trouble you with a detail of the principles which led me to this determination, but I always adhered to it, and experience has convinced me that it was wise and that I could not have done half so much for Ch.Ch. ... if I had ever asked for any one else or in any other capacity than as Dean of Ch.Ch.[3]

[1] Ibid., Jackson to G. Canning, [1800].
[2] Lambeth Palace Library, MS 2186, fo. 6.
[3] Ibid., fo. 51.

The emphasis placed by Jackson on the connection between education and public life, with its implication that those in government ought to be adequately educated for their position in society, enhanced the public reputation of Christ Church. Within the walls of the college it was potently symbolized by the Dean who was himself on terms of respectful friendship with the King and the royal family, and was *persona grata* at Westminster with ministers of the Crown, many of whom had been educated at Christ Church.

In the eighteenth century it was still possible for the Dean of Christ Church to be familiar with all aspects of the curriculum which he had studied as an undergraduate and perhaps taught as a tutor. Education evolved slowly within a stable tradition. Jackson was not an innovator by temperament or conviction, and accepted the traditional idea of liberal education as the distillation of wisdom. His success was due to the vigour and vitality he brought to that tradition, and to the strength of intellect and character which enabled him to inspire a higher level of attainment at Christ Church than at any time since the death of Aldrich. His own accomplishments, interests, and opinions thus become worthy of further investigation. In many ways they were typical of the eighteenth century.

Between Fell and Gaisford, no Dean of Christ Church published any serious work of classical scholarship. Jackson indeed made a half-hearted attempt to edit Herodotus, and, although the first book was completed under the superintendence of the Revd John Stokes and printed at the Clarendon Press, it was suppressed before publication and almost every copy destroyed. Jackson's scholarship was the traditional classical scholarship found in the university during the eighteenth century. The anonymous author of the memoir which appeared in the *Gentleman's Magazine* at Jackson's death wrote, not without lapidary licence, that

His strength undoubtedly lay in an intimate knowledge of the Greek language. In this he yielded to none of his contemporaries, neither to Porson, Parr, Burney, Wakefield, or Huntingford, of whom, whenever he spoke, he expressed himself, although not intimately acquainted with any of them, in terms of the most profound respect and admiration. In points in which he never practised himself, or essayed his own powers, he might be excelled by some of them, such as conjectural criticism, and verbal emendation; but in feeling and understanding the force and intensity of each particular word of that most expressive and copious language, and in an historical acquaintance with its terms and idioms, with the time, namely, when each came into use, varied its meaning, or became obsolete, no scholar, however eminent, surpassed him.[1]

Of all the writers of antiquity, Jackson's favourite was unquestionably Homer. He read the *Iliad* and the *Odyssey* repeatedly throughout his life, and unceasingly recommended them to his pupils.[2] To Peel he wrote in 1810,

Give the last high finish to all that you now possess by the continual reading of Homer. Let no day pass without your having him in your hands. Elevate your own mind by continued meditation on the vastness of his comprehension and the unerring accuracy of all his conceptions ... He alone of all mere men thoroughly understood the human mind.[3]

Homer was to be read, not for the sake of scholarship nor even for an understanding of the ancient world, but for his knowledge of the human mind and heart. Homer, he said on one occasion, 'serves me on all occasions of hope, fear, grief, or joy',[4] and to a pupil he remarked that 'a real taste is to be acquired only from him'.[5] Discussing Homer's descriptions of the sea, he once wrote to Lord Granville:

The fact is that the sea is one of his favourite subjects. He seems to have observed it very much and his descriptions of it are throughout perfect examples of truth and accuracy. If you should by chance have him with you and should find an hour now and then to turn to his descriptions of it you will find not only that you understand him better by having the object so before you, but you will find also that he will assist your mind in viewing and examining the object truly. In general the foundation of a real taste for Homer must be your own perfect knowledge of the subjects which he describes. You will then know how to estimate his merit and on the other hand he will conduct you to the habit of

---

[1] *Gentleman's Magazine* (Nov. 1820), 462.
[2] C. Wordsworth, *Annals of my Early Life* (1891), 68.
[3] BL Add. MS 40605, fo. 12ᵛ.
[4] Wordsworth, *Annals of my Early Life*, 68.
[5] PRO 30/29/8.

viewing and understanding things accurately. Thus for instance he is of all others the best instructor in the nature of the human mind and will teach you to observe mankind with accuracy. And when you have done this for twenty years and read Homer twenty times over you will then know how to value the delineations of character which you meet with in him.[1]

He referred to the theme of accurate observation by 'having the object before you' in a letter to Isaac Hawkins Browne in 1772, in which the almost tangible pleasure he himself derived from the classics and was able to communicate to others is apparent.

The mechanical operation of remembering is indeed a little reliev'd when a passage of a favourite poet or historian helps to fix them in the mind [he wrote] but they are much more agreeably as well as much more indelibly fix'd when the real object can be seen. It is impossible for instance for me to describe to you the increase of rapture with which I read the Georgics since I had the opportunity to seeing with my own eyes the culture of the vine and olive . . . with what pleasure do I recollect the Provencales paysannes when for the first time I saw them as Nausicaa and her attendants are described in the Odyssey.[2]

Classical literature was able to illuminate and explain experience because human nature was unchanging, and if the noble Greeks and Romans sometimes seemed to be disguised as eighteenth-century English gentlemen, it was because Jackson related literature to life rather than to the scholar's study. When the Bishop of London consulted him about the appointment of a chaplain, he dismissed the claims of the learned Gaisford because he doubted whether he 'would ever learn the manners of the world . . . I have long wished and laboured to coax him into becoming a Divine, and have often tried to shew him that with his abilities Greek was only a means to an end'.[3]

When he retired, Jackson borrowed from the college library a small case of silver mathematical instruments, which he retained until his death.[4] It was the characteristic act of one whose love of

---

[1] PRO 30/29/8.
[2] Trinity College Library, Cambridge, R. 4.57[29].
[3] Lambeth Palace Library, MS 2186, fo. 48.
[4] Lambeth Palace Library, MS 2186, fo. 11[v].

mathematics and natural science was surpassed only by his passion for Homer. Mathematics and science on the one hand and classical literature on the other expressed the unity of creation, the one representing the reality of the physical world and the other the moral and intellectual. Jackson's practical turn of mind may have been acquired from his father. In 1758 John Smeaton sent an account of the erection of the third Eddystone lighthouse to Jackson's father,[1] and it was perhaps from his father that Jackson learnt the anatomical nomenclature which enabled him to describe correctly the specimens recorded at the annual visitations of the Anatomy School at Christ Church. At Collections Jackson would test his more able pupils by inventing mathematical problems for them. 'Instead of examining me in trigonometry according to the book', George Chinnery once wrote, 'he made corollaries and deductions of his own in which he questioned me.'[2] Chinnery relates how on another occasion Jackson set a problem of such abstruseness for Charles LLoyd that neither the Dean nor LLoyd was able to solve it. LLoyd received his Studentship for his prowess in mathematics, which, Jackson informed Howley, 'have given him a hardness of head and a solidity of thinking which few possess',[3] and in 1808 LLoyd told Chinnery that the previous four or five Studentships given by the Dean were all rewards for taking up great Collections in mathematics.[4] When Jackson tried to define his conception of a good lecture, it was the mathematical image which came to his mind. 'My idea', he wrote, 'has always been that certain great points should be taken lying in the same right line which should be made the centres of circles greater or less as the occasion required, but every one of them touching the two on either side of it.' The most perfect model of this construction was Machiavelli's *History of Florence*, where 'the centres are all well chosen and the intervals are filled up with a master hand so that, as I have said, his circles touch one another'.[5] For

---

[1] Nichols, *Illustrations*, iii, 353.
[2] Ch. Ch. Archives, xlviii.a.44, fo. 104.
[3] Lambeth Palace Library, MS 2186, fo. 50.
[4] Ch. Ch. Archives, xlviii.a.45, fo. 96^v.
[5] Lambeth Palace Library, MS 2186, fo. 35.

many years he amused himself by applying his mathematical skills to problems of economics, and particularly to the public distrust of paper currency, or, as he usually referred to it, 'the bullion question'. He corresponded with Liverpool and Canning on the subject, and in 1810 sent Peel a report on the Mint which had been presented to Lord Shelburne when Prime Minister.[1]

Although it was as a classical scholar and mathematician that Jackson was pre-eminent, his lively and inquisitive mind embraced most of the cultural attainments of the educated man of his day. It is true that music was not among his accomplishments, and posterity has not been allowed to forget his pronouncement that a boy 'with no more ear nor a stone nor no more voice nor an ass' would make an excellent chorister in Oxford Cathedral.[2] He was widely travelled, and on one occasion in 1804 was arrested as a spy, an experience much relished by the wits of Christ Church, which prompted him to advise a friend that 'There is one exceedingly useful letter with which I always travelled, except once and then I was stopped as a spy. This is a general letter from the Customs to the Water Guard.'[3] His journeys to Italy and Provence, which proved so beneficial to his intellectual development, have already been mentioned, and he was sufficiently familiar with the sights of Paris to advise Charles Abbot, who made a tour of the Continent in 1775, that he should 'almost every day pay your veneration to Rafaelle and Annibale Carracci at the Palais Royal'.[4] He was well read in French literature, but not an uncritical admirer of it, and warned Abbot of its dangers.

The want of simplicity [he wrote to him] is such a blemish in the greatest part of it that it is not possible to pardon it. I believe there are few Englishmen that have read more French authors than myself and no Frenchman is more ready to allow them their proper merit. But I have strove always to be above prejudice and while I can acknowledge an Euripides in Racine, whose Athalie in particular might rank even with

---

[1] BL Add. MS 40381, fo. 390.

[2] W. Tuckwell, *Reminiscences of Oxford* (1900), 69.

[3] Lambeth Palace Library, MS 2186, fo. 46; A. Allardyce (ed.), *Letters from and to Charles Kirkpatrick Sharpe* (1888), i, 215.

[4] PRO 30/9/12/2/pt. 1.

the Grecian Drama, I must own that the French tragedy is not answerable to my idea of tragedy. I must confess likewise that the Henriade is to me a tiresome book. But I would wish you to be much on your guard against what they call Criticism—they are not possess'd either of good Logick or Metaphysics which are the foundation of true criticism.[1]

Jackson's interest in travel, whether at home or abroad, enabled him to get to know the young men in the college. He adopted a practice not unlike the vacation reading parties popular later in the nineteenth century. The Deans of Christ Church were intimidating figures in the eyes of their subjects, but travellers' tales were sometimes conducive to an easy social conviviality. So important were the benefits of travel that Jackson's biographer felt obliged to discuss them at length. It was, he wrote, the Dean's almost daily habit to entertain six or eight members of the college to dinner.

On these occasions he set foot and encouraged conversation, he started topics, provoked inquiries, and thus excited the prevailing bent and genius of each of his guests. It was the habit of the Dean during each long vacation, to travel through different parts of England, Wales, Scotland, or Ireland, taking some young friend with him, whose expenses he bore, as a companion. In these journies knowledge was his end;—he explored every nook and promontory on the coast, by walking and by sailing; he ascended every mountain; he visited every manufacture, and he avoided no place but a friend's house, which, if but once entered, he foresaw that his whole leisure would be expended in a series of visiting. He sought for information, and obtained it from every one that came his way, from sailors, fishermen, workmen, and artisans. In this mode he accumulated on every subject connected with the internal economy of the country, a store of knowledge probably not in its great variety equalled by that of any other individual. Topics of this nature formed the subjects of discourse with the young men of his College, while enjoying his hospitality. If any one had travelled during a vacation, it was always a matter of inquiry what he had seen; if any one was about to undertake a tour with the acquisition of knowledge in view, the Dean not only commended his purpose but assisted his researches by pointing out to him objects of curiosity, and explaining their nature and value.

[1] Ibid.

By means of this friendly intercourse, the Dean both received and gave information: he furthered his own plan of becoming personally acquainted with every individual who was placed under his government; and he at the same time communicated, wherever he saw it would become useful, the result of his own labours or inquiries, without effort, parade, or ostentation.[1]

By such methods Jackson acquired an intimate knowledge of the characters and capacities of his young men. No detail was beneath his notice. B. C. Roberts, for example, in one of his letters described with obvious gratification how the Dean jokingly imitated his manner of taking snuff, and in another how, having learnt of his interest in numismatics, Jackson employed him to catalogue the Wake coins in the library.[2] Charles Kirkpatrick Sharpe was invited to dine at the deanery and exhibit his drawings,[3] and it is related that 'evening after evening ... those who showed any talents for composition were taken into his private study, encouraged, and guided by his own taste which was very perfect'.[4] Those who received such marks of favour were stimulated thereby to even greater exertions, and their loyalty became the foundation of discipline.

'Under Dean Jackson', wrote his biographer, 'the government of Christ Church was an absolute one.'[5] No Dean since John Fell had ruled with such authority, though Atterbury had tried. To W. D. Conybeare it seemed reasonable to compare Jackson with Bonaparte.[6] His subjects affectionately accorded him regal honours. In a letter to C. K. Sharpe, William Fitz-Gerald described him as 'our Great King',[7] and in another letter Webb Seymour began an account of an interview with him with the words, 'His Majesty granted me two very long closet audiences'.[8] When Jackson progressed through the college, hats were removed while

---

[1] *Gentleman's Magazine* (Nov. 1819), 460–1.
[2] *Letters and Miscellaneous Papers by Barrè Charles Roberts* (1814), 28, 34, 73, 81.
[3] *Letters from and to Charles Kirkpatrick Sharpe*, i, 105.
[4] Conybeare, *Elizabethan Schoolmaster*, 130.
[5] *Gentleman's Magazine* (Nov. 1819), 460.
[6] Conybeare, *Elizabethan Schoolmaster*, 129.
[7] *Letters from and to Charles Kirkpatrick Sharpe*, i, 140.
[8] Ch. Ch. Library, Hallam MS 7, fo. 9ᵛ, 15 Feb. 1798.

he was in sight by all members of the college, including the
Noblemen and tutors, except the Scouts, who remained covered
because on one embarrassing occasion the Dean had mistaken one
of their number for an undergraduate.

He was a benevolent despot who by the force of his personality
held together the disparate elements which formed the college.
'He had the art, more than any one I have ever seen,' wrote
Conybeare, 'of establishing at once the ascendancy of his own
mind over every other with which it came in contact.'[1] Like other
despots he believed that power was indivisible, and particularly
where the Brethren in the Chapter were concerned. Of his brother
William he was jealous and suspicious. Conybeare, expressing
an opinion which does scant justice to the requirements of the
episcopate, remarked that although Cyril obtained a bishopric for
his brother he despised his judgement too much ever to entrust
any part of the discipline of the college to him.[2] This is borne out
by the fact that William Jackson had been Lee mathematical
lecturer for fourteen years, had held the college lectureships in
Greek and rhetoric, had occupied the office of Junior Censor for
four years, and had been a distinguished tutor, but from the
moment his brother became Dean he never held any college office
and shortly afterwards ceased to be a tutor. In 1783 he was shuffled
into the Regius Professorship of Greek, which unlike Hebrew
and divinity was not annexed to a canonry, and sixteen years
elapsed before he became a Canon of Christ Church in 1799.
Unlike John Fell, Jackson had no favoured son in the Chapter
destined to succeed him, and pretenders were severely discouraged. As a Student the future Dean Hall had basked in Jackson's
favour, and when he gave up his Studentship in 1795 on taking
the living of Broughton in Yorkshire, the Dean recommended
him to the Duke of Portland for preferment in Ireland. 'He would
be the very man to be brought forward hereafter. He has *real
learning* and real good qualities.'[3] However, when Hall became a

[1] Conybeare, *Elizabethan Schoolmaster*, 129.
[2] Ibid.
[3] Nottingham University, Portland Papers P.W.F. 5765, Jackson to the Duke
of Portland, 23 Oct. 1794.

Canon of Christ Church in 1799 through the influence of his patron the Earl of Liverpool, Jackson took a different view of him. In 1807 he became Regius Professor of Divinity, but Jackson thought he added little lustre to the chair and dismissed his lectures as 'sadly sterile and jejune'.[1] Gradually in the absence of a better candidate Hall emerged as the great Dean's successor, though this was not a prospect which Jackson relished. Within a few months of his appointment to the regius professorship, Hall wrote to Liverpool begging for a bishopric and complaining of Jackson's antagonism to him. 'Remain he will I doubt not', he wrote, ' 'till I am gone or till he has intrigued, if I do not go, to place some other person over my head. I know he wishes me gone.'[2]

Authoritarian at Christ Church, Jackson was also a staunch upholder of authority in society at large. When called on to advise the Duke of Portland about the vacant Headship of Hertford College, the most damning thing he could find to say about one of the candidates was that he was 'suspected of being democratically inclined'.[3] Lord Holland was one of those who believed that his respect for authority was excessive and harmful.

He taught, and I believe, felt, so indiscriminate a veneration for all received opinions because they were received [Holland wrote] that he became, without meanness, a worshipper of rank, and although not destitute of sagacity and utterly exempt from the mean passions of envy or jealousy, a favourer of mediocrity. The effect, though not the intention, of his system, could it have prevailed, would have been to leave all prejudices unmolested, and thereby to slacken and discourage improvement, to inculcate caution on his pupils till he had damped their genius, and to reduce all political and literary merit to deference for authority and prudent admiration of acknowledged excellence.[4]

---

[1] Lambeth Palace Library, MS 2186, fo. 34. Jackson tempered his criticism by casting an impartially baleful eye on the lectures of Hall's predecessors. 'Bentham's', he wrote, 'were an unformed heterogeneous mass—Wheeler never possessed one clear idea on any subject whatever. Even the B[ishop] of L[ondon] had read much more than he had thought.'

[2] BL Add. MS 38242, fo. 63.

[3] Nottingham University Library, Portland Papers P.W.F. 5780, Jackson to the Duke of Portland, 12 Aug. 1808.

[4] H. R. V. Fox, Lord Holland, *Further Memoirs of the Whig Party* (1905), 323.

Such criticisms, coming from a political opponent, perhaps do Jackson less than justice, but applied to the traditional idea of liberal education they are not without force. Liberal education supported rather than subverted the existing order. It was not abrasively critical in spirit and tended to acknowledge rather than to challenge received opinion. Yet such defects were often political virtues. Jackson sought to ensure that through the education received at Christ Church the country was governed and administered by men of character and ability. In the eighteenth century such men came in the main from the landed gentry who, having grown rich on the profits of the agrarian revolution, sent their sons to the college as Noblemen or Gentlemen Commoners. What Lord Holland condemned as deference for authority and admiration of acknowledged excellence was from another point of view a realistic recognition of the relationship between education and the nature of social and political power in society.

The recognition of this connection was the ultimate source of the success of both Jackson and Fell, between whom many parallels may be drawn. Both of them shared the same tradition of liberal education and both conceived its highest form to be the training of the aristocracy and gentry for public life. In their methods too they were not unalike. Both of them had an aptitude for teaching young men. Fell informed himself about them by visiting their rooms. In Jackson's time they were usually older and often wealthier than in previous generations and less easily ruled. He managed them by giving them their head wherever possible, but even more he depended on an unrivalled knowledge of the undergraduate members reinforced by a discreet but efficient system of espionage. 'With a view to a certain detection of offences, and a fear of such detection', wrote his biographer, 'he instituted, through the intermediate gradations of tutors, porters, and other servants, such a system of police, that it was impossible any irregularity could take place without the knowledge of the Dean.'[1] Under both Deans the external forms of discipline were enforced with vigour, and the ancient rules and customs of the college were

---

[1] *Gentleman's Magazine* (Nov. 1819), 459.

meticulously observed. Under Jackson punctual attendance at Hall and Chapel was enforced; undergraduates were not allowed to lodge out of college on any pretext, or to attend public entertainments, or to sleep out of their own rooms, and those who returned to college after Great Tom had struck were received with instant retribution. Only after repeated offence without the prospect of amendment were delinquents expelled, and then, in order not to blast their prospects, they were privately required to leave the college, though the cause of their departure was made sufficiently well known to act as a deterrent to others. Both Fell and Jackson were assiduous in encouraging merit.

There never existed any one [wrote Jackson's biographer] more sagacious than himself in discerning or more strenuous in rewarding merit. His was a system of rewards as well as of punishments; and in this course he was most materially assisted by an extraordinary degree of perspicacity in detecting and appreciating the latent talent and disposition of those around him. To this end he spared no pains, and omitted no opportunity.[1]

Merit was founded on industry. 'Work very hard and unremittingly', Jackson wrote to Peel in 1810. 'Work, as I used to say sometimes, like a Tyger or like a Dragon, if Dragons work more or harder than Tygers.'[2] He 'inspired with new vigour' competition for the prizes for Latin prose and hexameters; he insisted on the ancient practice of reading weekly themes and verses in Hall; he reformed the public lectures in logic and mathematics, and he appointed young and energetic tutors 'dependent on his favour and protection, in the habit of reporting to him daily all matters within their several departments, and receiving from him instruction upon all subjects'.[3] Fell attended the public exercises; Jackson ruled over Collections, which in his time were the principal forum of excellence. Fell, as Wood had complained, exalted Christ Church above all other colleges. Jackson followed his example. He restored the vigour of the Censors' annual

---

[1] Ibid., 460.
[2] BL Add. MS 40605, fo. 16.
[3] *Gentleman's Magazine* (Nov. 1819), 460.

speeches in which 'honourable mention was made of all those young men who in the course of the year had distinguished themselves either by superior diligence in the mathematics or the classics at Collections, or by having gained any of the University or College prizes', and according to Cox even discouraged members of Christ Church from forming acquaintances with members of other colleges. Like Fell, Jackson could claim that the good of Christ Church 'has bin . . . and must be ever the business of my life'.

Between Fell and Jackson, however, there were wide differences in character and belief. Fell's unyielding temperament inspired admiration but not affection. Beneath his dignified and awesome exterior, Jackson was a humane, benevolent, and warm-hearted man capable of inspiring loyalty and affection. In a letter to the youthful Canning in 1791 he revealed unsuspected depth of feeling.

Try [he wrote] to make me, to permit me, to be the friend I wish to be to you ... the earnest wish I have to be on the terms of real affection with you. The misfortune is that in the school in which unhappily you live too much, affection is not looked upon as a thing respectable in itself, but rather by one of those false uses of words of which Thucydides complains it is called a weakness which a man should be ashamed to shew. My dear C., I have seen moments when the heart has belied all such maxims—believe me you are infinitely more amiable when you do act from the heart than at another time.[4]

Fell was a man of profound piety and deep religious conviction. Jackson was a more secular figure. Undergraduates were agreeably surprised by his courtly and unclerical manner. When Charles Kirkpatrick Sharpe met him for the first time in 1798 he noted that 'instead of an old, cold, wrinkled creature ... I beheld a very handsome oldish man, with a well-powdered wig and a black gown'.[5] A similar impression was formed by Cox, who visited

---

[1] Ibid.
[2] G. V. Cox, *Recollections of Oxford* (2nd edn. 1870), 174.
[3] Bodl. MS Rawlinson D. 317, fo. 50.
[4] Leeds Public Libraries, Canning Papers, Jackson to G. Canning [1791].
[5] Allardyce, *Letters from and to Charles Kirkpatrick Sharpe* i, 78.

Jackson in his retirement at Felpham and found him simply dressed as a fine, venerable old man, without anything decidedly clerical in his appearance.[1] When Chantrey perpetuated this aspect of Jackson in the statue of him placed in the north transept of the cathedral in 1824, it provoked the angry comment that 'the sitting figure with its back to the altar, the academical instead of the priestly garb, are indeed symbolical of a place where learning has triumphed over religion and the Bishop is overshadowed by the scholars'.[2] Jackson's religious faith judiciously combined prudent expectation with the teachings of Bishop Butler. In a letter to Howley he recommended 'the necessity that the mind should feel strongly that there is a direct moral obligation to adhere and be governed by the strongest evidence which the case will admit, even tho' it should stop short of demonstration'.[3] He drew spiritual consolation as much from the classical authors he loved as from the Scriptures, and in counselling his young friends seldom quoted from the New Testament when suitable advice was to be found in Homer. From classical antiquity he also learnt a stoical optimism, and once confided to a friend[4] that the two lines in the *Oedipus Tyrannus* which had been his guide through life were:

> ... even our woes,
> When brought to their right issue, shall be well.[5]

Jackson retired in 1809 at the age of sixty-four to the small Sussex village of Felpham. He had occupied the Deanery for the same length of time as John Fell. His physical health was excellent and on the day that he executed his deed of resignation he walked the ten miles from Chichester to Felpham,[6] but in other ways he was exhausted by a life which his biographer described as characterized by unceasing activity.[7] The possibility of retirement seems first to

---

[1] Cox, *Recollections of Oxford*, 176.
[2] Quoted in S. A. Warner, *Oxford Cathedral* (1924), 142.
[3] Lambeth Palace Library, MS 2186, fo. 53.
[4] Jackson to H. C. Jones, 20 Feb. [1809], letter in the possession of the late Lt.-Col. H. M. C. Jones-Mortimer; photocopy at Christ Church.
[5] ll. 86–7, translated by Campbell Dodgson.
[6] PRO 30/58/10/144.
[7] *Gentleman's Magazine* (Nov. 1819), 461.

have been raised in 1806, and E. B. Impey then noted signs of flagging energy when he observed that the Dean 'is no longer that sturdy and inexorable magistrate that we remember him'.[1] At Felpham he lived very quietly. He took no part in public affairs and even ceased to read the newspapers. For a while he received occasional and welcome visits from Canning and other old pupils, or made forays to Brighton to see his first pupil, the Prince Regent. He spent his time reading Homer yet again, contemplating the wine-dark sea, tending his garden (in 1809 he requested Howley to send him a Pococke fig[2] from Oxford), and distributing generous charity to the poor of Felpham. He died in 1820 after a short illness and lies buried in Felpham churchyard.[3]

(*b*) THE CANONS

The Students of Christ Church were disenfranchised by their exclusion from the Governing Body, which was composed of the Dean and Chapter. In such important matters as their emoluments, leave of absence, and leave to proceed to degrees, the appointment of college officers, presentations to college livings, and the very tenure of their Studentships they were subject to the Dean and Chapter. In other colleges, the Fellows constituted the governing body, and such matters were regulated by statute, but at Christ Church not only were the Students unrepresented on the Governing Body but the college had no statutes and was governed by traditions and customs established by the Dean and Chapter. How delicate the balance was between Chapter and Students became apparent in 1628 when a violent dispute occurred between them. Its ostensible cause was the claim by the Students that they had not received the benefit due to them under the Statute of Provisions of

---

[1] Allardyce, *Letters from and to Charles Kirkpatrick Sharpe*, i, 289, 294.

[2] 'Arbor Pocockiana', as it used to be called, was according to tradition planted in the garden of the Regius Professor of Hebrew at Christ Church by Edward Pococke, probably at the Restoration.

[3] Unlike John Fell, Jackson did not endow Christ Church in his will. He was, however, as Dean a man of great generosity, and is said to have maintained a fund of £2,000, an immense sum at the time, for providing clandestine assistance for those in need (Conybeare, *Elizabethan Schoolmaster*, 130).

18 Eliz. I, c. 6, but it rapidly degenerated into a struggle for power. The Chapter told the Bishop of London that the Students were 'meere accidentalls and collateralls' in the college, and the Students retorted by denying that the Chapter had authority over them. Eventually the Chapter felt obliged to ask the Visitor to grant a body of statutes, but although the King took a sufficiently serious view of the disturbance to submit it to the Privy Council, none was granted.[1] In such circumstances the composition of the Chapter was an important issue, and the custom developed for a proportion of the canonries to be held by former Students, and for the Dean himself to be selected wherever possible from former Students of Christ Church. By the prospect of succession and the recollection of a common origin, a bond was established between the governors and the governed, and those who had themselves been Students might be depended upon to guarantee and maintain the traditions and customs by which they had been governed.

The importance of the composition of the Chapter was well understood not only by the Students but by the Dean and Canons, to whom it gave the best assurance of tranquillity. Thus when in 1679 William Nichols, a Master of Arts of Christ Church, reported the rumour that Henry Godolphin, a Fellow of Eton and formerly of All Souls, might be appointed to succeed to the canonry held by Samuel Speed, he noted that the appointment would 'grieve the Students very much. The bishop will certainly hinder it if he can, not for the person's sake, but to prevent so ill a precedent.'[2] A precedent no less harmful was averted when the appropriation of a canonical stall to the public oratorship was discontinued at the Restoration. Charles I annexed a canonry to the office of public orator by letters patent in 1636, but the grant was never confirmed by Parliament. When John Fell succeeded to this canonry in 1660 he was not appointed public orator, and the office was shortly afterwards bestowed on Robert South, then a Student, who complained publicly when the Chancellor visited the university in the following year that 'he was deprived of his right of cannonship

---

[1] Ch. Ch. Archives, Estates 145, fos. 245, 251; *Acts of the Privy Council of England May 1629 to May 1630* (1960), 816.
[2] HMC, *Egmont* (1909), ii, 86.

of Xt.Ch.'.[1] The appropriation of the canonry was strongly resented at Christ Church because the university statutes, which regulated the appointment of the orator, forbade the office to be held by members of the same college in succession. This ensured that on every alternate appointment a Canon from another college was imposed on Christ Church. Charles Allestree, who was a Student himself, condemned the practice as prejudicial to the interests of the Students in general, 'who think they have most right to be promoted to this dignity in the church upon any voidance of it'.[2] So anxious was Fell to resist the appointment of these 'aliens', as Allestree called them, that in 1683 he was accused by Thomas Hyde of having obtained through Bishop Compton 'some kind of promise to bestow canonships only on Christ Church men'.[3] Fell did not deny the charge and admitted having written to the Bishop, but added, 'I presume to think it is not unsuitable to my obligation to be so concerned in so important an interest of this society'.[4] Wood accused him of promoting members of the college regardless of merit, but his actions were not prompted by chauvinistic patronage, nor to any marked extent by a desire for complaisant colleagues, but by a determination to preserve a beneficial tradition.

It was a tradition which went back to a period before Fell was born. When Dean Smalridge was obliged in 1715 to urge the appointment of Students to the canonries of Christ Church, he noted that, except for Thomas White in 1591, John Perin in 1604, Henry Hammond, who was public orator, Henry Compton, who had incorporated as a Nobleman, and some of the regius professors, all the Canons appointed since 1571 had previously been Students. He excluded from these calculations those appointed during the Interregnum, and shared Bishop Fell's opinion that they were no more than 'Holy Robbers'.[5] Smalridge's

---

[1] Wood, *Life and Times*, i, 414. South was appointed to a canonry in 1670. He resigned the public oratorship (but not the canonry) in 1677. Thereafter the office was never held with a canonry.

[2] BL Add. MS 27440, fo. 15ᵛ.

[3] *Cal. SP Dom. 1683*, pt. 1, 188.

[4] Bodl. MS Rawlinson D. 317, fo. 50.

[5] Ch. Ch. Library, MS Wake 15, Smalridge to Wake, 20 Dec. 1715.

hope that the practice would continue was dashed when Oxford became a centre of disaffection after the Hanoverian succession. The ministerial exercise of Crown patronage was then used to promote the Whig interest in the university. Among the Students of Christ Church bred by Fell and Aldrich there were few impeccable Whigs, and between 1714 and 1736, when David Gregory was appointed, only two former Students received canonries. Christ Church became a shining example of the policy which Archbishop Herring commended to a receptive Duke of Newcastle in 1750. 'Tho it will be a work of time', he wrote, 'no way seems so likely to bring that University into a wise way of thinking and acting as to pick out and distinguish those valuable men in it who are Friends to his Majesty and the Protestant succession.'[1] By this date there was no shortage of such valuable men among the Students, and the government was able to revive the tradition of giving them preference in the appointment of Canons. Between 1736 and 1760, all but three of the Canons appointed had been educated in the college, and Robert Freind could inform the Duke of Newcastle with truth that 'it seldome happens that a canon's place is supply'd by any but a Ch.Ch. man'.[2]

For a century after the Restoration, except during the troubled years after the death of Queen Anne, most of the Canons were not only former Students but former Westminster Students. From 1660 to the end of the eighteenth century, only ten Canoneer Students were appointed, and five of these (Jasper Mayne and William Jane in the seventeenth century, and Edward Vernon and Deans Bagot and Jackson in the eighteenth) had been educated at Westminster though not elected to Westminster Studentships.[3]

Neither the Duke of Newcastle's management of clerical patronage nor the preference given to former Students long survived the accession of George III. In 1761, the Duke noted that ecclesiastical

---

[1] BL Add. MS 32721, fo. 425.
[2] BL Add. MS 32701, fo. 11ᵛ.
[3] During the same period, three canonries were held by members of Christ Church who had never held Studentships: Henry Compton, Thomas Hunt, and Jonathan Shipley.

preferment had to be settled with the Earl of Bute,[1] and by 1765 his influence had so far declined that, as he complained to Lord Rockingham, William Digby's warrant was signed 'without my having said one word to the king'.[2] The number of Canons with no previous connection with Christ Church increased, and between 1760 and 1800 less than half of those appointed to the non-professorial canonries were former Students. All those who were native members of Christ Church were, however, Westminster Students or had been educated at Westminster, and the Westminster presence in the Chapter thus remained dominant even though not so pervasive as before. Many of the appointees were Etonians and may reflect George III's predilection for Windsor rather than Westminster. But whatever the cause, by the end of the century the tradition that the Students of Christ Church had an almost prescriptive right to the canonries was seriously weakened.

The professorial stalls of Hebrew and divinity were held even less often than the remaining stalls by former Students. Between 1660 and 1800 less than half were occupied by members of Christ Church. Although intermittently held by scholars of distinction, the professorial canonries were no less immune to political considerations than the unappropriated canonries. When, for example, the Regius Professorship of Hebrew fell vacant in 1747, the Duke of Newcastle, besieged by candidates for preferment who little expected their political loyalty to be rewarded by the obligation to teach Hebrew, considered separating the professorship from the canonry. This was not difficult to achieve because, although the canonry was annexed to the chair by Charles I in 1630, the grant, as in the case of the public oratorship, was not subsequently confirmed by Parliament. It was Lord Hardwicke who seems to have persuaded the Duke not to proceed with a judgement so uncharacteristically reminiscent of Solomon. In a letter asserting the claims of Thomas Hunt he wrote,

---

[1] BL Add. MS 32929, fo. 7ᵛ.
[2] BL Add. MS 32968, fo. 265.

I beg leave to recommend him most heartily for this reason, because I am fully persuaded that he is the most worthy to succeed. I am sensible that as a Canonry of Christ-Church has gone along with it, your engagements as to these preferments may create difficulty. But if the Canonry is de jure annexed to the professorship, it certainly was done to meliorate the professorship and to encourage the ablest persons in that kind of learning to accept it. For this reason the professorship ought to draw the canonry after it, and not the canonry the professorship, which latter seems to be destroying the intent of the annexation. And indeed it must strike every body as being extremely wrong to appoint a Hebrew professor who knows nothing of the language, which I remember was said to have happened in the last instance. If these two preferments are not so strictly annexed but that they may be severed, and Mr. Hunt cannot succeed for the canonry, I believe he will be content with the professorship *sole*, to which I should hope there would be little or no objection.[1]

The Regius Professorship of Divinity, to which James I had annexed a canonry in 1605, was less vulnerable than Hebrew to political interference because the annexation was confirmed by Parliament in 1711.[2] Even so, a similar tendency to consider the professorship and the canonry separately appeared when John Fanshawe, a determined Whig, was appointed in 1741. On that occasion Robert Freind wrote to Newcastle, 'I dare say after a

---

[1] BL Add. MS 32712, fo. 195. Lord Macclesfield also supported Hunt's appointment, and in a letter to Newcastle on 20 July 1747 noted that he gave instruction in Hebrew to two persons from every college in Oxford twice a week (Ibid., fo. 171ᵛ). Hardwicke's charge that Clavering knew no Hebrew seems exaggerated. A Latin translation of two tracts by Maimonides and a compendium of Hebrew grammar, both published in 1705, are attributed to him. Hearne records that 'Some few years ago this Dr. Clavering used always to preach upon Rabbinical affairs (he having studied Hebrew), wch when People used to laugh at, he at length turned himself to another way of preaching, and undertook to confute Aristotle's Definitions. The Bp. of Chester, Dr. Gastrel, having heard one of these sermons, was surprized at its badness; said he, "he did well to intermix formerly Rabbinical Stuff in his Sermons, because few could then find him out; but now all are able to judge of him & he sufficiently discovers himself" ' (Hearne, *Collections*, x, 65).
[2] 10 Anne, c. 45.

little practice he will make a good figure in the chair ... As to the canonry, he is the very man to be wisht for.'[1]

By the end of the eighteenth century the seeds were sown of the constitutional struggle which racked the college in the middle of the next century. The friction between the governors and the governed which had split the college in Dean Bradshaw's time was replaced by a more serious threat to stability. Under Bradshaw the dispute was about patronage, under Liddell it was about power. By the end of the eighteenth century the proportion of Students who entered a secular career and were thus necessarily excluded from the Chapter had increased, but the Students that remained enjoyed a more important role in education at Christ Church as the tutorial system developed, and as they did so they looked more and more to a career in the university. Although the seeds of discontent did not germinate under Cyril Jackson, exclusion from the Governing Body was to become a humiliating grievance.

[1] BL Add. MS 32697, fo. 152. The question has been raised whether the occupiers of the professorial stalls at Christ Church were professors first or Canons first. The Act of 10 Anne, c. 45, and the Act establishing the chairs of ecclesiastical history and pastoral theology in 1840, refer to the annexation of the canonries to the professorships, and Lord Hardwicke's argument on behalf of Thomas Hunt also suggests that the canonries were subordinate to the professorships. On the other hand it was established in the time of John Fell that the Canons of Christ Church had the standing of Heads of Houses, and in 1736 Lord Hardwicke himself had described them as 'in the nature of coadjutors of the Dean'. Dr Claude Jenkins, who was appointed Regius Professor of Ecclesiastical History in 1934, always maintained that the correct form of address for the professorial Canons, as for all other Canons of Christ Church, was 'Doctor', and that to apply the term 'Professor' was incorrect. It is worth noting that although the Canons had the standing of Heads, there was an unwritten law that no Head of a college could hold a canonry at Christ Church. There were two exceptions to this rule. In 1615, John Prideaux, then Rector of Exeter, was appointed to a canonry, but his patent included a dispensation from residence and from all other duties of the stall. In 1820, Lord Liverpool inadvertently appointed the Principal of Brasenose, Frodsham Hodson, to the Regius Professorship of Divinity, but, as Canning informed Phineas Pett, 'the difficulty was not foreseen by Lord L.' (BL Add. MS 38193, fo. 131).

III

Students and Others

(*a*) THE WESTMINSTER STUDENTSHIPS

At the foundation of Christ Church, 100 Studentships were established. In 1665, the number was increased to 101 by the addition of the Studentship founded by William Thurston. The Studentships represented the college as a place of education and learning. Within its walls they always constituted a numerically substantial part of the undergraduate population and an even larger part of the resident graduates. There were two[1] categories of Students, namely those elected from Westminster School by the Dean acting on behalf of the college, and the Canoneer Students elected by the Dean and Chapter on the nomination of individual members of the Chapter.

The Westminster Students were elected annually by an examination held in public. The election occurred on the second Monday in Easter term until 1726 when the date was altered by royal decree to the sixth Monday after Easter Day. The principal electors were the Dean of Christ Church, and the Master of Trinity College, Cambridge, and the examination consisted principally of the recitation of Latin verse compositions, declamations, and epigrams in Latin and Greek on themes given to the candidates by the examiners. In 1661, John Evelyn was present at an election and wrote, 'I heard & saw such Exercises at the Election of Scholars at Westminster Schoole, to be sent to the Universitie, both in Lat: Gr: & Heb: Arabic & in Theames & extemporary Verses, as wonderfully astonish'd me'.[2] A more critical opinion

---

[1] The Faculty Students were appointed from the Westminster and the Canoneer Students.

[2] Evelyn, *Diary,* ed. E. S. de Beer (1955), iii, 287.

of the examination was given by George Smalridge, who was elected in 1682, in a letter to Walter Gough in 1697. 'You will be pleased, if I mistake not', he wrote, 'with the Westminster Election: but the questions to be asked of school-boys are only grammatical, and not of that puzzling nature that we should prepare them, or critical, so as to please a more critical ear. *Extempore* verses will be a diversion.'[1] Charles Abbot, who was elected in 1775, possessed copies of epigrams and verse declamations by Freind and Markham probably similar to those produced at the elections, and it is likely that examples of such exercises circulated in the school as a model for the able and a crutch for the incompetent.[2]

The Westminster elections were designed to demonstrate the candidates' self-confidence and quick-wittedness, but were not intended to be a searching examination. Students were often chosen, moreover, because of financial need, and the electors were not indifferent to the claims of kindred, the blandishments of preferment, and the interference of politicians. Thus in 1669, Sir Joseph Williamson wrote to Fell at the King's desire asking him to elect a grandson of Richard March to a Westminster Studentship,[3] and in 1675 Charles Bertie approached Williamson to use his influence, successfully as it happened, to obtain the election of Henry Stead.[4] According to William Taswell, the election of Samuel Wilson in 1670 was due to 'the recommendation of the Earl of Montgomery, his godfather.'[5] The diversity of the factors which determined an election are illustrated in a letter which Smalridge wrote in 1698 to his friend Walter Gough, who had tried to enlist his support in favour of one Henry Arnold. Dean Aldrich, he wrote,

is already determined to three of those who stand, if he finds them qualified, and if they lie in his way, so that he can have them if he pleases. These are, Frewin, the captain of them; one that the Dean has had his

---

[1] Nichols, *Illustrations,* iii, 266.
[2] PRO 30/9/3/31.
[3] *Cal. SP Dom. 1668–9,* 314.
[4] *Cal. SP Dom. 1675–6,* 67.
[5] *Camden Miscellany II* (Autobiography of William Taswell), 15.

eye upon for some years, as an ingenious deserving young man, whom he cannot pass by without doing him an injury. Another is Mr Mostyn, who stands, as I am told, the third, that is the second in the Dean's way, and who must appear very ill not to be chose to Oxford for his Brother's sake, and whom you may be sure I am bound to serve to the utmost, being as much obliged to Sir Roger, as it is almost possible for one man to be obliged to another. There is one Cremer, godson to the Dean, and son to a school-fellow, fellow-student, and intimate acquaintance of the Dean's, who, when he died, recommended this young child to the Dean's care and favour; so that, if there be any room for favour, that young man has a very good title to it.[1]

Since this letter was written on 22 March and the election did not take place until 21 April, it is evident that on this occasion, and doubtless on many others, the public examination was not necessarily decisive in the selection of the successful candidates, and that many elections were settled beforehand. The Deans of Christ Church were familiar figures in Westminster, both in the Chapter and in the School, and were able to keep themselves well informed about the candidates. In 1800 it was still very desirable to obtain the Dean's interest prior to an election. In that year Elijah Impey wrote to Hugh Chambres Jones, 'I would by no means advise you to offer yourself as candidate to Vincent the Headmaster before you have received a *favourable* answer from the Dean.' Cyril Jackson was reported to be 'particularly solicitous' to secure the election of Jones, but he was defeated by the Master of Trinity, who on his turn elected him to Trinity despite Vincent's assurance that even if elected he would not go to Cambridge, as proved to be the case.[2]

By an order of Queen Elizabeth I, Christ Church and Trinity College, Cambridge, were required to elect not less than three candidates each year. The colleges chose in rotation in alternate years, and also selected candidates alternately during the election

---

[1] Nichols, *Illustrations*, iii, 269. At the election in 1698 Richard Frewin, John Mostyn, and Henry Cremer were elected to Christ Church. Henry Arnold was elected to Trinity.

[2] E. B. Impey to H. C. Jones, 23 Feb. 1800, and W. Vincent to E. B. Impey, 14 May 1801, letters in the possession of the late Lt.-Col. H. M. C. Jones-Mortimer; photocopy at Christ Church.

itself.[1] The candidates were allowed to express a preference for either university by means of a Latin address to the Dean of Christ Church or the Master of Trinity. The elegant petition composed by John Locke when seeking admission to Christ Church in 1652 survives in his papers.[2] If the Dean and Master were unable to agree about an election it might be referred to the whole body of electors, who included the Headmaster, the Dean of Westminster, and in the case of the election attended by Evelyn the Regius Professor of Divinity at Oxford, and, it is said, 'by any that would'.[3] But although the electors might elect, they were unable to impose their will on a reluctant candidate. Edmund Smith, for example, 'so signally distinguish'd himself by his conspicuous Performances' at the election in 1688 that both colleges wished to elect him.[4] Although Trinity prevailed, having the option on that occasion, Smith preferred to go to Christ Church, where he was given a Canoneer Studentship.

The refusal of election to Trinity was rare in the seventeenth century, and occurred only twice between the Restoration and the end of the century, once in the case of George Man in 1681 and again in that of Edmund Smith. It became very common in the eighteenth century, when a tenth of the candidates elected to Trinity failed to take up their election and matriculated instead at Christ Church, where, often after waiting as much as one or two years for a vacancy to occur, many of them received Canoneer Studentships. During the same period, election to Christ Church seems never to have been declined in favour of Trinity. Amongst those who declined their election was Cyril Jackson, who was elected head to Trinity in 1764 but went up to Christ Church as a Canoneer Student. Alexander Akehurst, who followed him to Christ Church a year later, recalled the circumstances in a letter to Philip Bliss in 1826. 'When the election was over', he wrote, 'Dean Gregory of Ch.Ch., one of the electors, being himself

---

[1] *Camden Miscellany II*, (Autobiography of William Taswell), 15.

[2] Locke, *Correspondence*, i, no. 5.

[3] *Report from Select Committee of the House of Commons to Inquire into the Education of the Lower Orders in the Metropolis* (1816), 445.

[4] E. Smith, *Works* (1714), [ii].

disappointed and knowing the same of Cyril, said to him, "Do'nt mind them. Come and enter yourself a Commoner of Ch.Ch. and I will give you a Studentship", which he did.'[1] Election to Trinity was most frequently refused during the Mastership of Bentley and was an unforeseen consequence of his famous dispute with the wits of Christ Church concerning the letters of Phalaris.

Thomas Newton relates in his autobiography that, although it might have been better for his subsequent career if he had followed 'the most considerable' of his schoolfellows to Oxford, he preferred to go to Cambridge,

thinking the studies there more manly, and knowing the fellowships of Trinity College to be much more valuable than the studentships of Christ's Church; [and he] accordingly made interest to Dr. Bentley to be by him elected first to Cambridge. The Doctor was not displeased, but wondered at the strangeness of this application, the Westminster Scholars, if ever they applied to him, applying more usually that he would not, than that he would elect them to Cambridge. For they supposed him to have no friendly disposition towards them ever since his famous dispute with the Christ Church men concerning the Epistles of Phalaris; and he had sometimes been heard to say that the School had produced only one good scholar, old Prideaux; but after his son married a niece of Dr. Freind, and he had lived and conversed more among them, he conceived a better opinion of them, and declared that Freind had more good learning in him than he had ever imagined.[2]

Newton added that Bentley was also reluctant to elect Westminsters because they were apt to side against him in the college. After Bentley's death the number of those opting for Christ Church after election to Trinity declined, but in the last decade of the eighteenth century some nine elections to Trinity were refused in favour of Christ Church. The practice of refusing election at one university and attending the other was finally prohibited in 1830.[3]

The number of Students elected to Christ Church far exceeded the number of Scholars elected to Cambridge. In the course of

---

[1] BL Add. MS 34569, fo. 304ᵛ.
[2] T. Newton, *Works* (1782), i, 18.
[3] Ch. Ch. Archives, Estates 142, fo. 80.

the eighteenth century Christ Church elected 429 Westminster Students, but Trinity elected only 368 Scholars, including those who refused their election in preference for Oxford. This had not always been the case. Between the Restoration and the end of the seventeenth century, both Christ Church and Trinity exceeded the minimum number of three elections a year required by Queen Elizabeth, but Trinity did so more frequently than Christ Church, and averaged some five elections a year compared with four by the House. There is evidence that Christ Church would often have been content to have elected no more than the minimum, and in some years even less. In 1668, the King himself found it necessary to command the college to elect three Students from Westminster instead of two as intended,[1] and George Smalridge reported in 1698 that whenever Dean Aldrich attended an election he 'resolved to take but three, but has always hitherto been overruled by the earnest persuasions of Dr Knipe and the Bishop of Rochester'.[2] In the eighteenth century, on the other hand, Christ Church elected five Westminster Students on thirty-five occasions whereas Trinity elected the same number of Scholars on only four.

The disproportion between the numbers elected to Oxford and to Cambridge was caused not only by Bentley's feuds but by the closer relationship between Westminster and the Dean of Christ Church compared with that between Westminster and the Master of Trinity. When the Dean had himself been educated at Westminster the number of elections was generally higher than when he had not, but the situation at Trinity, where Bentley believed that the Westminster Scholars opposed him, was not repeated at Christ Church, because the Westminster Students were permanently excluded from the Governing Body, and it was not possible for the Dean to recruit a body of supporters amongst them however many were elected. Atterbury, however, seems in the course of his quarrel with the Canons to have pursued a deliberate policy of increasing the number of Westminster elections. In 1712, five Students were elected, but in 1713 the number

---

[1] *Cal. SP Dom. 1667–8*, 35.
[2] Nichols, *Illustrations*, iii, 270.

rose to seven, which was without precedent and was never equalled. Between the two elections, having demanded that the college muniments be brought to him, he transcribed the regulations governing Westminster elections into a small volume which was kept in the deanery, noting that they were 'collat. cum originali in Archivis Ecc. Xti. asservato Oct. 14 1712'.[1] It is possible that Atterbury intended to set up in opposition to the Chapter a body of Students who owed allegiance to him, but he was also able to injure his opponents in the Chapter by curtailing their opportunities to nominate Canoneer Students, for the larger the number of Westminsters appointed the fewer vacancies existed for Canoneers. Martin Benson spoke no less than the truth when he informed Richard Rawlinson that he was the only Canoneer Student elected during the whole of Atterbury's time.[2] Before the potentially inflammable consequences of Atterbury's actions could be felt he had been removed from Christ Church. Other Deans were more tender of the patronage of their Brethren in the Chapter in the appointment of Canoneer Students. Thus when the Duke of Newcastle tried to obtain the election of five Students from Westminster in 1734, Dean Conybeare wrote to him,

I am in no small concern because I know not how to comply with your Grace's request of taking five Students from Westminster this election. It is not only inconsistent with the rule I set myself upon a thorough consideration of matters when I came here first, but will lead me into difficulties from which I can never hope to free myself whilst I live. I am aware of the ill consequences which have attended some of my predecessors as often as they have gone out of the way in taking an extraordinary number from Westminster, and I hop'd I should never be press'd to do the like, especially since I have determin'd with myself never to take less than four.[3]

---

[1] Liber Ecclesiae Christi Oxon, 47.

[2] Bodl. MS Rawlinson J. fol. 2, fo. 181. His age may explain why an exception was made in his favour, for he was 23 and soon to take his degree, which would have made him ineligible for a Studentship.

[3] BL Add. MS 32689, fo. 202. Conybeare adhered to his resolution to take a minimum of four except in 1737, 1742, 1748, 1751, and 1754, in each of which years he took five, and in 1752 when he took only three.

The preference at Westminster for Christ Church rather than Trinity was even greater than the disproportion in elections and the frequency of refusal of election to Cambridge suggest, for between 1660 and 1800 more than a hundred Canoneer Studentships were filled from Westminster in addition to the Westminster Studentships. Although some of them were awarded to those who had refused election to Trinity, the majority were given to nominees for Canoneer Studentships *ab initio*. This practice too became increasingly common in the eighteenth century. When in 1717, no less than three Canoneer Studentships were filled from Westminster, Hearne described the event as 'a thing never known before, the Canons usually on such occasions making choice from other Places, especially if they had relations, or could oblige some leading Men'.[1] The colonization of the Canoneers by Westminster contributed to the harmonious relationship which existed between them and the Westminster Students. Domestic concord was also nurtured by the not uncommon practice of electing one brother to a Westminster Studentship and another to a Canoneer. For example, in 1674 one of Archbishop Dolben's sons was elected to a Westminster Studentship and four years later another son was elected to a Canoneer. In 1764 a son of William Freind was elected to a Canoneer Studentship while in 1772 another son was elected to a Westminster, and of Archbishop Moore's three sons at Christ Church two were elected to Canoneer Studentships and the third to a Westminster. The fathers of the Students in all these cases had been Canons of Christ Church and were thus familiar with the traditions and prejudices of the college, and would not have subjected their sons to a disadvantage had one existed. Nevertheless on financial grounds there was a preference for Westminster compared with Canoneer Studentships because by the early eighteenth century several valuable trusts had been established for the benefit of the former. This may explain why Dean Smalridge nominated his son to a Canoneer Studentship, 'having little else to leave him', but the boy came

[1] Hearne, *Collections,* vi, 75.

up on a Westminster,[1] and why Henry Forester, having been nominated to the roll by his father, Dr Paul Forester, in 1756 and again in 1758 was not elected to a Canoneer Studentship but came up instead on a Westminster.

The connection between Westminster and Christ Church was cemented by the closest ties and constantly renewed by family and professional relationships. At Christ Church in the eighteenth century there was usually a Harley or a Mostyn, a Dolben or a Freind, who had been educated at Westminster. The majority of the Deans and Canons had been educated at Westminster, and all the Headmasters from Camden to Markham had been to Christ Church.[2] Two of the Headmasters, Robert Freind and John Nicoll, returned to Christ Church as Canons, and a third, Markham, came back as Dean. Busby founded the Senior Common Room at Christ Church and endowed lectureships in mathematical and oriental studies. Former Westminster Students, such as Matthew Lee, who became a fashionable physician, and Robert South, who was a Canon of Christ Church, founded exhibitions and scholarships at Christ Church for the benefit of Westminster. It was small wonder that Robert Freind had no doubt that it was better for his scholars to go to Oxford than to Cambridge.

We remember [he wrote to the Duke of Newcastle in 1742] many Men of Character from Ch.Ch. both in Church and State, but upon rummaging my Memory I cannot recollect any of our breed from Trinity since Ld Hallifax and Mr. Stepney who left the Colledge 50 years ago. Those who have gone to either Colledge from West^r. went away, generally speaking, equally qualify'd. Whence then could ye Difference arise but from the care that was taken of them afterwards?.[3]

---

[1] Nichols, *Illustrations*, iii, 274.

[2] Wood suggests that Camden's predecessor Edward Grant may also have been educated at Christ Church (*Athenae*, i, 711). In the whole of its history only four Masters of Trinity have been to Westminster.

[3] BL Add. MS 32699, fo. 323. Freind was a scholar of distinction despite Hearne's disparaging reference to him as 'eminent at making Epitaphs and Epigrams in Latin' (Hearne, *Collections*, ix 340), and was admired by no less a judge than Bentley. Samuel Wesley wrote of him,

What Scholar found and great as Freind,
His Worth to future ages shall commend

So effective was the preference for Christ Church that when Lord Shelburne came up in 1755 he found that 'Christ Church is composed, nineteen out of twenty, of those who have been bred at Westminster'.[1]

The influence of Westminster was not confined to the Studentships. The aristocracy and gentry whom Fell had tried to bring to Christ Church were usually privately educated, but by the eighteenth century they came to a remarkable degree from Westminster, which by common consent was the foremost school in the country, the cradle of the wealthy, the famous, and the aspiring. In prestige and social acclaim it surpassed Eton and Winchester, its only rivals. In 1772, James Wadham Whitchurch acknowledged its precedence when he noted that in 'the Three great Schools of Westminster, Eton, and Winchester ... the greater part of our Nobility and many Persons of the first Distinction have been, and are still educated'.[2] It owed much of its reputation to the energy and abilities of a succession of outstanding Headmasters, but it owed even more to the rapid growth of London and the proliferation within it of the organs of government and the sinews of trade, to the prosperity of the aristocracy and gentry which enabled them to leave their country estates for the salubrious western suburbs of the metropolis, and to the emergence of a vigorous professional class. Its prosperity was not without political consequences. Within a decade of the accession of George I, after a period of estrangement when, under the malign influence of Atterbury (who retained the Deanery of Westminster *in commendam* with the see of Rochester), Westminster was tainted with Jacobitism, it was the deliberate policy of the

> Not Busby's self in equal height maintain'd
> The School, where half a Century he reign'd.
> Daily through Freind her swelling numbers rose,
> The hate, but more the envy of her Foes.

(Epilogue spoken at the Westminster meeting in the year 1732–3, printed in *Some Account of the Life and Character of Samuel Wesley* (1743), 3). In view of this effusion, it was perhaps poetic justice that Wesley was refused the post of Second Master in 1733.

[1] Fitzmaurice, *Life of Shelburne*, i, 13.
[2] J. W. Whitchurch, *Essay upon Education* (1772), 113.

government, and particularly of the ever busy Duke of Newcastle, to promote the connection between school and college. In 1731, the Prince of Wales informed Viscount Perceval that the youth of Westminster could be expected to support the government, and that he 'looked on gaining one school to be worth gaining fifty families'.[1] Towards the end of the eighteenth century, as London became more and more unhealthy, Westminster yielded the primacy to Eton, which basked in the favour of royal Windsor, and the historic connection which had been on balance beneficial to Christ Church became an increasingly intolerable burden.

Although the Westminster Students were elected only from the King's Scholars, their social origins were diverse and reflected the broad spectrum of society represented at the school. The majority of Westminster Students, particularly in the seventeenth century, were the sons of clergymen, or, more frequently, of gentlemen, a vague term which embraced the small landed gentry, the professions, and sometimes those engaged in the more respectable and lucrative branches of trade. Since those who described themselves as the sons of gentlemen did not require the approval of the College of Arms, they included a number of social optimists. One of these was probably Edward Hannes, who described himself in the university matriculation register in 1682 as the son of a gentleman, though according to Le Neve his father 'kept an herb shop in bloomsbury mercate'.[2] During the eighteenth century, this amorphous group became more exactly defined by wealth and social position, and, particularly during the first half of the century, there was a large increase in the number of Students whose fathers

---

[1] HMC, *Egmont,* Diary of Viscount Perceval (1920), i, 160. Amongst those implicated in Atterbury's plot was the physician John Freind, brother of the Headmaster of Westminster. John Freind, who like Atterbury had been a Westminster Student, married Anne Morice, the sister of the Bishop's son-in-law William Morice. Fortune, however, smiled on the Freinds from an unlikely quarter. In 1728, Lord Townshend became gravely ill and was cured by John Freind, who, becoming thereby a man of consequence at court, was himself cured of his Jacobite tendencies. William Morice told Atterbury that it was through John Freind's connections at court that the Prince of Wales visited Westminster School and saw a play performed by the King's Scholars (Coxe, *Memoirs of Sir Robert Walpole,* ii, 240).

[2] G. W. Marshall (ed.), *Pedigrees of Knights,* (Harleian Society, 1873), 491.

were either armigerous or were members of one of the professions, or indeed were both of these.

Prominent among the professions was the law. If the *Record of Old Westminsters* is to be believed, few sons of lawyers were elected in the seventeenth century, but the number rose substantially in the following century. After the sons of lawyers came the sons of medical practitioners, led by the offspring of such luminaries as John Arbuthnot, physician to Queen Anne, John Freind, physician to Queen Caroline, and James Ford, physician to Queen Charlotte. The sons of government officials, such as the storekeeper of Chatham Dockyard, the Auditor of the Duchy of Lancaster, and the Master of the Mint, were not infrequently elected, and in a century given to endemic foreign wars the sons of soldiers, amongst them William Markham. The University contributed its quota—Dean Gregory was the son of the Savilian Professor of Astronomy, and John Randolph, one of the reformers of the tutorial system at Christ Church, was the son of the President of Corpus Christi College, Oxford. Few Westminster Students were the sons of merchants or prosperous tradesmen, though Andrew Stone, the crony of Walpole, and his brother George, the grasping Archbishop of Armagh, were the sons of a wealthy London goldsmith.

Many of the Westminster Students came from more humble backgrounds. Throughout the eighteenth century about a third were the sons of the inferior clergy, many of whom were very poor. Dean Smalridge was the son of a Lichfield dyer, and Fifield Allen, according to Hearne, was the son of an Oxford mercer 'said to have been hang'd at London'.[1] Of similarly modest origins were Bonnell Thornton, the son of an apothecary, Edward Vardy, the son of an architect, Robert Nares, the son of a musician, Philip and Samuel Dwight, the sons of the Fulham potter, and George and Richard Crochley, the sons of a schoolmaster in Bloomsbury. But, as the eighteenth century advanced, the number of Students from wealthy or socially eminent families rose steadily. This was particularly evident in the proportion of those whose fathers were

[1] Hearne, *Collections*, ix, 117.

among the higher clergy (archbishops, bishops, deans, and the like), or were peers or baronets. Indeed the number of Students who were the sons of peers or baronets almost doubled between 1750 and 1800. The great majority of them were younger sons or brothers of peers and had to make their way in the world. Many did so with signal success, amongst them Lord Mansfield, who was the fourth son of the fifth Viscount Stormont, and Arthur Paget, the younger son of the Earl of Uxbridge. The election of the sons of peers was a phenomenon of the eighteenth rather than of the seventeenth century. Fell sought to attract the sons of the aristocracy and gentry in order to train the governing class in sound religion and a just appreciation of their position in society. Studentships he regarded as fit for men of learning, and especially for those intending to enter the Church. In his time only the brothers of Viscount Preston in 1674 and the Earl of Peterborough in 1680 were elected to Westminster Studentships. Such elections continued to be infrequent under Dean Aldrich, but from 1719, when the brother of Lord Hervey was elected, until the end of the century about a score of sons of peers were elected from Westminster, and from 1750 over a dozen sons of baronets. The influence of such socially distinguished Students was out of proportion to their number. They helped to make academic life more respectable in the eyes of Noblemen and Gentlemen Commoners, but they also weakened the historic conception of Studentships as primarily intended for the supply of a learned clergy, and so contributed to the gradual secularization of studies.

The election of wealthy and socially privileged Students also made the traditional claim that Studentships were awarded in case of financial need more difficult to sustain. This applied equally to the many exhibitions established in the eighteenth century for the exclusive benefit of the Westminster Students. Apart from the Fell and Hill foundation,[1] the earliest of these exhibitions was founded by Robert South, who died in 1716. He bequeathed the reversion of his property at Kentish Town and Caversham to

[1] The Fell and Hill trust was established in 1685 for the benefit of two Westminster Students. The first appointments were not made until 1714 and the exhibitions were only worth £2–£3 a year.

Christ Church on the death of his housekeeper Margaret Hammond, the widow of Edward Hammond, 'a Sot, commonly called Crony Hammond',[1] who had been his curate at Islip. The will provided for the improvement of certain small livings belonging to Christ Church by means of annual grants, and directed that any surplus income should be applied to the maintenance of six poor Westminster Students to be nominated by the Dean and Chapter at the rate of 20 nobles each, a sum interpreted as £6. 13s. 4d. throughout the eighteenth century. The foundation had a shaky start, and the first appointment of an exhibitioner was not made until 1738. Between 1741 and 1751 none at all was made, though the payments to poor livings continued, because the income was severely strained to meet the cost of repairs on the Kentish Town estate, then a field on the edge of the metropolis, the dilapidated state of which was probably not unconnected with the injunction in South's will that Margaret Hammond should remain a widow 'for that otherwise neither she nor I can tell what havock an husband will make upon the premises'. At first the exhibitions were given mainly to Bachelors, but from 1755 more often to Students who were undergraduates at the time of their first appointment. Because there was no fixed tenure, awards were made at irregular intervals, and no vacancies occurred in 1758, 1762–3, 1770, 1773, 1776, 1786, 1792–5, and 1798. In the 1790s they seem to have been used in order to encourage promising Students to remain in residence until taking their MA, so securing the supply of tutors. The value of the exhibitions by themselves was too small to have much effect, but South was often held with one or more of the Lee exhibitions.

Matthew Lee was a fashionable physician with lucrative practices in London and Bath. When he died on 26 September 1755 he bequeathed the major part of his estate amounting to approximately £30,000[2] to Christ Church mainly for the benefit of the Westminster Students. By the terms of the bequest, which took effect ten years later in 1765, he founded an anatomy lectureship,[3]

---

[1] Hearne, *Collections*, v, 271.
[2] Benefactors' Register, 65.
[3] See p. 314.

four mathematical exhibitions for Westminster Students, and an annual prize, or Certamen, open to Students and Commoners of Christ Church. For the better support of the Westminster Students during the first year after their election a fund of £50 was set up. Lee also founded an unspecified number of other exhibitions for Westminster Students nominated by the Dean and Chapter. They were worth £10 a year and were tenable for a maximum of eight years. Nearly every Westminster Student held one of them, and it was clearly Lee's intention that all should do so. From about 1786 the exhibitions were usually given some two years after matriculation. Unlike the Fell and Holford exhibitions,[1] which were held by Commoners, neither Lee nor South was awarded as the result of examination, presumably because the Westminster election was itself considered to be a qualifying examination. The Lee foundation was very wealthy. South was incapable of improvement until the Dean and Chapter were empowered to grant building leases of the Kentish Town estate in 1851, but Lee increased rapidly in value. Whereas South remained fixed, Lee exhibitions were increased to £30 a year in 1807, and in 1818 Cyril Jackson, then in retirement at Felpham, advocated a further increase to £50.[2]

The Westminster Students were also eligible for two exhibitions founded in the seventeenth century for Students, but not exclusively for Westminster Students. These were the Morris exhibitions, which are discussed elsewhere (Chapter V, section *e*), and the Bostock. In 1633, Joan Bostock gave to Christ Church three houses in Peascod Street, New Windsor, and directed the Dean and Chapter to distribute the income annually to four Students in need and 'of the towardliest hope for learning and conversation'.[3] The estate yielded a small income and the exhibitions were only

---

[1] See pp. 184–9.

[2] Ch. Ch. Archives, Estates 90, fo. 301ᵛ. In 1761, Richard Frewin, another Westminster Student who made a successful career in medicine, bequeathed an estate near Ramsbury, Wilts, for the benefit of the Westminster Students during the period between election and admission. It proved an uncertain source of income and was sold in 1775 for the sum of £2,000, which was invested in South Sea Annuities.

[3] Ch. Ch. Archives, lv. b. 1.

worth on average £4 a year until 1727 when they were increased to £5. In the seventeenth century the Bostock was awarded much more often to Westminster Students than to Canoneer, and although the gap narrowed in the following century it continued to be given more frequently to the Westminster Students, who often held it with Lee and South. Until about 1770, most of the Bostock exhibitioners were Bachelors at the time of their election, but thereafter, as in the case of other trusts, they tended to be undergraduate Students.

In the December after their election, the Westminster Students-elect were formally admitted to their Studentships in the north chapel of the cathedral. The Canoneer Students-elect were admitted at the same time. Both groups of Students took the oaths prescribed by law, swore to observe all existing and future statutes, ordinances, and decrees of the House, to obey the Dean, Sub-Dean, and all officers with lawful authority over them, and to advance the usefulness, dignity, and splendour of Christ Church. They then knelt in turn before the Dean who pronounced the formula, 'Ego authoritate mea admitto te [speaking the Christian name] in perpetuum Alumnum Cathedralis hujus Ecclesiae in nomine patris et filii et spiritus sancti Amen'. After the completion of these formalities, which continued unchanged except for alterations in the oaths until the nineteenth century, the new Students attended morning service wearing their Students' gowns for the first time. The residential qualification for a degree for the Westminster Students was calculated from the time of admission,[1] but they were required to come into residence in the Trinity term after their election, and from 1763, and perhaps earlier, were taught as a single class separate from other undergraduates until their admission. By an ancient tradition the Westminster Students of the previous election rode out to Nuneham and escorted the Students-elect to Christ Church, where they were entertained with sometimes excessive hospitality. By an equally ancient tradition the Dean and Chapter sought to suppress this practice, and in 1788, when the Students defied the Junior Censor by riding out

---

[1] Chapter Act Book, 7 Dec. 1714.

to Nuneham, resolved 'in the most public and peremptory manner
that the practice above mentioned of going to meet the election
must absolutely be abolished'.[1] According to H. L. Thompson[2] it
was the advent of the railway rather than the fulminations of the
Dean and Chapter which eventually caused the ride to Nuneham
to be discontinued.

(*b*) THE CANONEER STUDENTSHIPS

Every year a number of Studentships fell vacant for one reason
or another, and any that remained after the Westminster election
were in the gift of the Dean and the individual Canons of Christ
Church. Candidates nominated by them for election became
Canoneer Students. Dean Fell wrote of them to Lord Hatton that
'Westminster Schole is our Nursery, and that unless upon casualty
none who are not chosen from thence can be Students here, and
that those few who come in here upon contingency of super-
numerary and unexpected voidances are the nominations of privat
men who are under preingagements'.[3] The Westminster Students
had precedence over the Canoneers in point of election, but no
other distinction was observed between the two categories of
Student after their admission.[4] Both were entered on the roll in
the Chapter Book, both received the same meagre emoluments,
both were subject to the same rules and regulations.

Although the number of Canoneer Studentships to be filled
each year was unpredictable, there were never enough vacancies
to enable the Dean and Canons to make an annual nomination.
The opportunity for them to exercise their patronage occurred
irregularly and usually at intervals of several years. In order
therefore to record their rights of precedence an electoral roll was
drawn up.[5] On it were stated the names of the members of the

[1] Chapter Act Book, 30 May 1788.

[2] H. L. Thompson, *Christ Church* (1900), 180.

[3] BL Add. M S 29583, fo. 25.

[4] The terms Senior and Junior Student are anachronistic prior to the ordinance
of 1858 though occasionally met in casual usage.

[5] The electoral roll is to be distinguished from the Student roll, which was
the list of Students entered annually in the Chapter Book.

Chapter in order of seniority, always headed by the Dean, followed immediately by the Sub-Dean who subsequently, when he vacated office, took his place on the list according to seniority. The names of candidates nominated for election when a vacancy should occur were entered against the appropriate patron. Whenever the electoral roll was filled, the Dean had two turns and each of the Canons a single turn. The nominees were elected to Canoneer Studentships in the order in which they appeared on the roll, and, since those at the top were thus the first to be elected, nomination by the Dean, Sub-Dean, or senior Canon was often especially valuable because it led to speedier election than did nomination by other members of the Chapter. Once completed, the electoral roll was not made up again until all the nominees on it had been elected to Studentships or had withdrawn their candidature.[1]

Originally the electoral rolls consisted of sheets of paper or parchment on which were inscribed the names of the Dean and Chapter and their nominees. A few examples survive for the period immediately preceding the Civil War,[2] but most have perished. When, after a careful examination of the college records, Bishop Tanner sent a list of the Canoneer Students to Richard Rawlinson, he remarked, 'I shall not, I fear, be able to recover their several patrons, the rolls on which they were nominated not being preserved nor entered in the Chapter book as of late'.[3] The practice, to which Tanner alludes, of entering the electoral rolls in the Chapter Book began in 1671, and is there described as

[1] There is some evidence to suggest that in the sevententh and early eighteenth centuries, nominations were not entered systematically on the rolls. Thus the roll opened on 19 July 1682 contains the names of John Fisher, Matthew Loveday, and one Holloway. Fisher was elected in 1684 and Loveday in the following year. Holloway was never elected. But if all the members of the Chapter exercised their rights of patronage there were presumably eight other nominees for whom there is no record of nomination between 1682 and the opening of the next roll on 28 June 1686. In fact the eight missing nominees were probably the eight Canoneer Students elected during this period in addition to Fisher and Loveday. Their names were: Armstead, Chapman, Greaves, and Urry (17 July 1682); Lloyd and Willoughby (21 July 1684); Okeover (5 January 1685); and Wotton (13 July 1685).

[2] Ch. Ch. Archives, Estates 141, fos. 19, 21, 25, 29, 33.

[3] J. Aubrey, *Letters by Eminent Persons* (1813), ii, 111.

representing 'the auntient custome of the house'. They continued to be entered until 1750, but after that date appear only in the Draft Act Books. New rolls were filled up on the following occasions:

1671 (23 September)	1747 (24 December)
1675 (30 June)	1749 (22 December)
1679 (7 October)	1750 (22 December)
1682 (19 July)	1756 (9 July)
1686 (28 June)	1758 (7 July)
1690 (12 July)	1760 (5 January)
1694 (6 July)	1761 (24 December)
1700 (4 July)	1763 (23 December)
1703 (8 July)	1765 (24 December)
1706 (23 July)	1770 (24 December)
1709 (11 November)	1772 (23 December)
1713 (19 December)	1774 (4 July)
1716 (14 December)	1775 (23 December)
1719 (23 December)	1778 (20 June)
1721 (29 July)	1779 (24 December)
1723 (23 July)	1781 (22 December)
1726 (8 July)	1783 (23 December)
1728 (19 December)	1785 (23 December)
1732 (15 August)	1788 (23 December)
1735 (10 July)	1790 (23 December)
1738 (26 June)	1792 (22 December)
1740 (26 June)	1795 (23 December)
1742 (28 June)	1799 (18 December)
1744 (26 June)	1800 (12 December)

This list shows that a new roll was made on average every two or three years, except during the seventeenth century when the average was nearer four years. Six years elapsed between the roll made in 1694 and the next roll, and in 1750 and 1765 five years passed before a new roll was needed. Only in 1749–50, 1760–1, 1774–5, 1778–9, and 1799–1800 were new rolls made in consecutive years. The incidence of canonical patronage was thus very unpredictable. A Canon resident for ten years might reasonably expect to nominate no more than four or at the most six Students. Dr Stratford, for example, who held his canonry for twenty-six years from 1703 to 1729, nominated only nine Canoneer Students during the whole of this period. Dean Jackson, who enjoyed the extra patronage allowed to the Dean, made nineteen nominations between 1783 and 1800.

Nomination to the electoral roll could take place at any time either before or after matriculation, but not after graduation. In the eighteenth century almost half the nominees matriculated within a year of nomination, and about a third within two years. Because vacancies in the Studentships could not be predicted with any exactness, and because the electoral roll operated in such a way that some nominees might expect early election while others might have to wait many years, there was often a wide difference in the ages of nominees at the time of enrolment. The most usual age was between sixteen and eighteen, and tended to rise towards the latter part of the eighteenth century as the age at matriculation generally in the university increased, but youths of nineteen were frequently nominated, and on a few occasions the nominees were twenty-one years old. At the other end of the scale it was common for youths of fourteen or fifteen to be nominated, and as late as 1799 a thirteen-year-old boy was placed on the roll. The youngest person ever to have been nominated appears to have been John Potter, who was nine years old when placed on the roll by his father in 1723. Because members of the Chapter might die before the next roll was drawn up or might receive preferment elsewhere, they often felt obliged to nominate their sons or close relatives whenever the opportunity arose, and many of the youngest nominees arose from this cause.

Once nominated to the roll, a candidate for a Studentship normally presented himself for election according to his seniority on the roll. If he was considered too young to matriculate, or if the election of an older candidate was jeopardized by the possibility that he would have graduated before another vacancy occurred, an exchange might be effected in order to place the nominee higher up or lower down on the roll. This was probably the reason that Edward Pococke, a relative of the famous Hebraist, appeared on no less than four rolls between 1686 and 1700. In 1686 he was nominated by Dr Hammond, in 1690 and 1694 by Dr Wake, and in 1700 by Dr Radcliffe: after so much effort it is disappointing to discover that he failed in the end to obtain election. The exchange of patronage created obligations and counter-obligations which were more than debts of honour, as the Duke of Newcastle discovered when he recommended James Morrice to Dean Gregory on 4 June 1758. At first the Dean expected no difficulty and thanked the Duke for 'putting it in my power to shew my gratitude to your Grace in obeying your commands'.[1] But he soon found his optimism misplaced and on 13 June was obliged to write to the Duke again.

I am sorry, [he wrote] to inform your Grace that all my endeavours to obey your commands have at present proved ineffectual, as all the Canons who have a right to the nomination to the present vacant Studentships are absolutely engaged. If Mr. Morrice is inclined to take his chance here, I will do my best to procure him a Studentship as soon as possible from one of my brethren, for I am afraid my own turn of nominating is at too great a distance to be of such service to him as I could wish; the truth is I am in debt for two Studentships which of late I was glad to borrow, and till I have repaid them I can get no more credit.[2]

Hardly had he written when events again proved him wrong. Some six Studentships fell vacant in July, and five of them were at once filled from the old roll which had been made in 1756. At the head of the new roll on 7 July 1758 was James Morrice, the first of the Dean's two nominees. He was elected the same day.

The uncertainty of the date of election to a Studentship and the long interval which might precede it caused a considerable proportion of nominations to fall by the wayside. Some entered other colleges or went to Cambridge, and others abandoned the idea of a university education. Of the forty-four separate names to appear on the rolls between the first roll recorded in the Chapter Book in 1671 and the year 1700, no less than twelve failed

[1] BL Add. MS 32880, fo. 325.
[2] Ibid., fo. 429.

subsequently to be elected to Studentships. From the middle of the eighteenth century the number of unsuccessful nominees declined, because as the age at nomination rose the interval before matriculation diminished, and the prestige of Studentships was increasing.

After nomination followed election and admission. Before the election of Canoneer Students the Act of 31 Eliz. I, c. 6 for the prevention of corrupt elections was read. Until 1713 it was usual for the Canoneers to be elected in June or July soon after the Westminster election had taken place, but thereafter they were usually elected at Christmas, though summer elections continued occasionally until 1786 when they were abandoned by Cyril Jackson. At admission the proceedings with regard to Canoneers were the same as for Westminsters, and emphasized that henceforth no distinction of status existed between the two categories of Student. Election and admission were corporate acts of the Chapter without which nomination, which was the exercise of individual canonical patronage, was ineffective. Although the number of Canoneer Students elected annually varied considerably, over the whole period the average was about four a year and in total was only slightly less than that of the Westminsters.

Candidates for Canoneer Studentships were not examined at the time of nomination, and the tender years of many of them would have made an examination difficult at that time, but the Dean and Chapter required them to submit to examination when they were elected. On 24 December 1633, the Chapter resolved that 'no scholler shall be admitted to be Student of Christ Church who is not first examind and found sufficient in learning by such examination as ye Deane and Chapter shall think fitting',[1] and in the same year a candidate named Gregory was rejected as 'not found sufficient'. In 1739, Dean Conybeare complained to Lord Kinderton that on examination Gilbert Repington, who had been nominated to the Studentship in the patronage of the Vernon family by an award made in 1599, 'appeard so miserably deficient in point of necessary learning that I am desired by the Chapter to

---

[1] Ch. Ch. Archives, Estates 141, fo. 7.

acquaint you we think him to be unqualifyd and do request it of you to nominate some other qualifyd person'.[1] Lord Kinderton however, stood by his candidate, who was duly elected at the following Christmas and thereby acquired the dual distinction of being the only candidate for a Studentship in the eighteenth century known to have been rejected for illiteracy, and also the oldest candidate to be elected, having attained the ripe age of twenty-six. Other elections were less controversial. In 1740, for example, Robert Gibson, the son of the Bishop of London, was elected 'having been previously examin'd',[2] and in 1772 Edmund Burke wrote, when his son Richard was elected on the nomination of the latter's godfather Dean Markham, 'The Dean was very much pleased with him upon his examination'.[3]

In the absence from the Chapter Books of any regulations or decrees concerning the examinations, their nature remains a matter for conjecture. It would appear that they were informal and that they were conducted in private, perhaps by the Dean as in the case of Richard Burke but never by the Censors or other college officers, since Canoneer Studentships were in the gift of members of the Chapter. A public examination of the sort observed at Westminster, where the candidates were chosen from the King's Scholars, was not possible, since the candidates for Canoneer Studentships were limited to those nominees on the electoral roll eligible for Studentships which were actually vacant, and the number of such vacancies at any one time was seldom more than two or three at the most. It is unlikely that the examination was intended to do more than ascertain whether a candidate possessed a sufficient minimum level of competence. To have done more, and particularly to have made the examination a test of excellence, would have invaded the rights of patronage possessed by the Chapter.

Although nomination to a Canoneer Studentship could be obtained at a very early age, election did not follow until the nominee was old enough to pursue his studies with profit. The

---

[1] Ibid. 120, fo. 74.
[2] Chapter Minute Book, 26 June 1740.
[3] E. Burke, *Correspondence* ed. T. W. Copeland (1958–78), ii, 401.

Dean and Chapter never made a formal ruling concerning the age of Canoneer Students at election, but the existence of such a rule is implied by a minute dated 23 December 1747 in the Chapter Book that 'Mr John Rye was entered upon a former Roll in the late Dr Rye's turn who soon after died, when the said John Rye being too young to be admitted that turn was charged down this Roll'.[1] Its existence is further confirmed by many instances of nominees entered on the rolls being passed over for election in favour of older candidates. In some cases this probably occurred because of the need of the older candidates to obtain election while they were still undergraduates, but in many instances election was clearly delayed because of the youthfulness of the candidates. Thus the roll in 1760 emptied so quickly that another roll was drawn up in the following year. Within the space of little more than a year ten Students were elected, but all except three had been substituted for nominees on the roll drawn up on 5 January 1760. The ages of the successful candidates varied from sixteen to nineteen. Of the seven displaced candidates, three were not heard of again, but of the remaining four, three were the sons of Canons of Christ Church and were aged eleven, fifteen, and sixteen, and the fourth was aged fourteen. The sixteen-year-old was elected to a Westminster Studentship in June 1760, and the rest to Canoneer Studentships in 1763 and 1764, when they were aged between sixteen and eighteen. Of the seven nominees displaced in 1760, three had already been nominated to the roll made four years previously in 1756, and one to the roll made in 1758. Between the Restoration and the middle of the eighteenth century most Canoneer Students were elected when they were between sixteen and nineteen years old, the majority being seventeen. In the latter part of the eighteenth century the average age rose slightly in step with the general increase in the age of undergraduates at matriculation. The rigid enforcement of an age limit for election would have been as much an infringement of canonical rights of patronage as an effective examination, and very young Students were occasionally elected during the eighteenth century.

[1] Chapter Act Book, 26 June 1744, annotation.

The last occasion when a Student was elected at the age of twelve—always an extremely rare event—was in 1717, when Daniel Burton was elected on the nomination of his father, and the last election of a thirteen-year-old was in 1741. Richard Burke was fourteen when elected on the nomination of his decanal godfather in 1772. From about 1740 it was rare for youths of fifteen to be elected.

In addition to ensuring that candidates for Canoneer Studentships had a modicum of learning and were of a suitable age, the Chapter considered a third qualification. This was 'fitness' to become a Student, and it embraced such considerations as social and financial circumstances and also moral character. In 1782 the Chapter refused to allow Andrews Windsor, who had been nominated by Canon Conway, to seek election because of their 'disapprobation of his behaviour'.[1] Servitors were deemed unfit to be Students. This had not always been so. Wood records that Jasper Mayne, who became a Student in 1627 and a Canon at the Restoration, entered Christ Church as a Servitor. Under John Fell several Servitors were elected to Studentships: James Hulet in 1663, Francis Davis in 1665, Thomas Price in 1672, and Charles Nelme in 1681. When Thomas Price was nominated by Dr Compton on 23 September 1671, Gilbert Knight, also a Servitor, was nominated by South. It is related that Knight deferred his BA seven times in the hope of a Studentship 'which afterwards fell not'.[2] The eligibility of Servitors was not in dispute until the latter part of the seventeenth century provided that they could find a patron to nominate them to the roll. They ceased to be eligible when the numbers of Servitors at Christ Church fell dramatically as many who in former times might have come up as Servitors came up instead as Commoners. The menial character of the remaining Servitorships was thereby emphasized. This

---

[1] Chapter Minute Book (cover), 16 Dec. 1782. At the same time the Chapter resolved that his brother Henry Windsor should be a candidate as soon as he was qualified. The effect of this decision was to disqualify an unsatisfactory candidate but at the same time to safeguard by an act of substitution the right of the Canon who made the original nomination.

[2] HMC, *Ormonde*, NS, (1906), iv, 607.

change in the status of Servitors may be seen taking place in the appointment of Charles Nelme, who matriculated as a Batteler Servitor in 1676 and re-entered as a Commoner in June 1681 three weeks prior to his election to a Studentship. No Servitor was elected to a Studentship after the appointment of Dean Aldrich in 1689. The ineligibility of the Servitors was an indication of the rising status of Students, who by the eighteenth century were considered comparable to the Gentlemen Commoners. In 1721 Edward Trelawny entered as a Gentleman Commoner after vacating his Studentship, and Enoch Markham, who obtained a Studentship in 1750, surrendered it three years later, soon after taking his degree, and re-entered as a Gentleman Commoner. Isaac Price Maddox entered Christ Church as a Gentleman Commoner in 1757 two days before his election to a Studentship, and in 1778 Richard Colley Wellesley, the son of the Earl of Mornington, entered as a Nobleman prior to his election to a Studentship. By the eighteenth century the idea of fitness for a Studentship had, for Canoneers as for Westminsters, largely lost its ancient association with financial need.

When nominees were of an age to enter the university, many preferred to come into residence and commence their studies rather than to wait for a Studentship to become vacant. The college thus usually contained resident undergraduate Commoners who were not yet Students but held nominations to Studentships and looked forward to eventual election. Most nominees were elected to a Studentship within six months or a year of matriculation, but some remained in residence for two years prior to election. The tendency during the eighteenth century as a whole was for the period between matriculation and election to shorten, but until about 1760 there are rare instances of residence for more than two years and of Students-designate on the point of taking their degree before being elected. Thus Brooke Hector was elected to a Studentship on 22 December 1721, but in the Battel Book for the week ending 26 January 1722 he is described as a Bachelor of Arts. Similarly, Guy Fairfax was elected on 8 July 1757 and on 15 July appears in the Battel Book as a Bachelor of Arts. The fact that Students-designate were prepared to reside for lengthy periods, without knowing when a vacant Studentship would occur, suggests that the emoluments of Studentships were not of crucial importance. The acceptance of a Studentship within a few weeks of taking a degree is an indication that Studentships were held in considerable esteem, not least perhaps because they opened the way to tutorships and to college offices such as the Censorships. Once elected, a Student was placed on the roll according to his seniority calculated from the date of matriculation, and Students whose election had been delayed for any considerable time appeared to make a meteoric ascent of the roll. This was not an indication of merit but a consequence of seniority.

A period of residence after nomination was not a prerequisite of election and should not be regarded as the equivalent of a period of probation. Nor was election to a Studentship after a period of residence an indication of the award of a Studentship for merit or good behaviour, unless *nomination* had occurred after residence had commenced. Nomination was the essential stage in obtaining a Canoneer Studentship and once it had been secured election was almost inevitable. Because residence was not a necessary qualification for election, a small but steady stream of nominees to Studentships matriculated at other colleges in Oxford or at university halls before coming into residence at Christ Church shortly before election. The reasons for this practice were partly economic and partly a consequence of the unpredictability of vacancies in the Studentships. Those who adopted it were usually low on the electoral roll, and at the time of their admission to Christ Church tended to be older than the majority of Students. They chose to pursue their education at a less expensive college than Christ Church rather than to wait for a vacant Studentship, by which time they might otherwise have been older than was desirable for beginning their studies. Strictly speaking these candidates for Studentships were elected from other colleges, but it would be misleading to suppose that Studentships were open to the university at large as they were in the following century, for undergraduates could only seek election if they had a nomination. In most instances nomination had been obtained prior to matriculation, but in very rare cases nomination was obtained *after* matriculation at another college. Jeremy Bentham was the most celebrated example of such a nomination.[1] Cyril Jackson put an end to residence in another college after nomination whether before or after matriculation. In 1825 Dr Phineas Pett, who had been Canning's tutor before receiving a canonry, invited his old pupil to nominate a Student on his turn when the roll was made up in the following year. Canning proposed to nominate a son of Sir Robert Chester, saying that it would indemnify the boy for his disappointment at not being elected from Westminster to Christ Church and inquiring whether it would be necessary for him to remove himself from Cambridge where he was a Commoner at Trinity. Pett replied without delay, 'I grieve that the thing is utterly impossible. It has been for many years an invariable Regulation to admit none to Studentships from any other college or university. The having belonged ab initio to Christ Church is indispensable.'[2] Sir Robert Chester, who had himself come up to Christ Church in 1786, retorted by quoting the case of Henry Cay Adams, who had migrated from Pembroke College to a Studentship in 1782. In a private memorandum Pett stated the custom at Christ Church. 'Dr. Cyr. Jackson made Dean June 1783', he noted, 'and from that time no Student (nor, I believe, Commoner) has ever since been admitted from any other College.'[3]

Jackson's prohibition of residence in another college prior to election was not only an example of Christ Church exclusiveness but a consequence of his desire to improve the quality of Canoneer Students. One way in which he sought to achieve this was by awarding some of the Studentships in his gift for merit, par-

---

[1] See p. 128.

[2] Leeds Public Libraries, Canning Papers, Pett to G. Canning, 7 June 1825.

[3] Ibid. Adams matriculated at Pembroke on 15 Dec. 1781 and a week later, on 22 Dec., was nominated to a Studentship by Dr Kennicott. He was admitted to Christ Church, according to the Dean's Register, on 22 Oct. 1782, and was elected to a Studentship on the following 24 Dec. Those who were elected to Canoneer Studentships after refusing election from Westminster to Trinity are not an exception to Pett's statement because they did not matriculate at Cambridge.

ticularly in mathematics. In the absence of a satisfactory examination at election, merit was best ascertained at Collections. This
implied residence not only prior to election, which was a common
phenomenon, but prior to nomination, which was very unusual
until Jackson's time. If undergraduates were to give proof of
merit prior to nomination it was clearly necessary for them to do
so by residing at Christ Church rather than in another college.
Under Jackson there was a significant increase in the number of
undergraduates nominated to Studentships after they had been in
residence for a year or more. In these cases residence became
what it had not been previously, namely a period of probation.
Undergraduates nominated a year or more after coming into
residence should be distinguished from those nominated soon
after coming into residence, for the latter increased as the interval
between nomination and election contracted for the majority of
Canoneer Students towards the end of the eighteenth century.
They should also be distinguished from Students, such as Hector
and Fairfax, who were elected after a lengthy residence but had
been nominated before matriculation. Jackson's attempt to treat
at least some of the Studentships as prizes is in marked contrast
with the way in which even such notable Deans as Fell and Aldrich
had regarded the Canoneers. Fell attached little importance to
them. He made no nomination to the roll in 1682 and only one
in 1679, and about half the nominations attributable to him failed
to obtain election. Aldrich was equally indifferent, and nominated
only once to the rolls made in 1690, 1694, and 1700. Jackson's
effort to improve the quality of the Canoneers occurred at a time
when Westminster School was in decline, and, had his successors
pursued his policy with equal determination, would have partly
compensated for the procession of undistinguished Westminster
Students who came to Christ Church in the nineteenth century.

There were two important exceptions to the method of appointing Canoneer Students so far described. These were by suspension
of the electoral roll and by the intervention of the Crown. Both
methods disregarded the ordinary course of Chapter patronage,
but whereas suspension of the roll was the voluntary act of the
Dean and Canons, the intervention of the Crown did not require

their agreement. During the first half of the seventeenth century the appointment of Students by common consent was not uncommon, but from the Restoration to the end of the eighteenth century only about a score of Students were appointed in this way. In a few cases the roll was suspended to allow the election of Students of special ability, amongst whom were two future Deans of Christ Church. In 1764 the roll was suspended for the election of Cyril Jackson, and in 1800 for Gaisford. In November 1751 two Students were expelled and others punished for drinking the Pretender's health, and the Chapter ordered the suspension of the roll, 'to which the Dean and all the Canons as well absent as present have consented', because it was conducive to the good discipline of the House 'to distinguish some exemplary young man by electing him into one of these places'. The exemplary young man was William Pemberton. In 1763, Francis Burton was elected 'for his good behaviour'. In other cases the roll was suspended in order to enable the Dean and Chapter to pay a graceful compliment to a benefactor. Thus in 1671 Francis Morley was nominated at the request of his uncle the Bishop of Winchester and former Dean of Christ Church, and at the filling up of the roll in 1675 it was again suspended at the Bishop's request, this time in favour of Richard Windebancke. In 1721 it was suspended for another Bishop of Winchester, when, as a gesture of thanks for a benefaction, a Studentship was given to Hele Trelawny, the son of the old age of Jonathan Trelawny.[1] A similar gesture was made in 1799 when the Chapter decided that William Freind should be placed on the roll immediately after the Dean's nomination, 'intending by this mark of their favour to shew their respect and gratitude to their munificent benefactor Dr Richard Robinson, late Primate of Ireland in the person of his relation'. The Primate's sister Grace was William Freind's grandmother. Occasionally the roll was suspended in favour of the son of a college official. Thus in 1671 it was suspended for the election of William Bedford, the son of Samuel Bedford, formerly the college

---

[1] Trelawny gave £200 to Christ Church in 1712 and a further £100 in 1717 (Benefactors' Register, 50, 55).

auditor, and in 1675 for John Willis, the son of another John Willis who was Chapter Clerk and died in that year. In 1792 it was suspended for Deacon Morrell in consideration of his father James Morrell, the Chapter Clerk. For the roll to be suspended it was necessary for the Dean and all the Canons, including any who might be absent, to be in agreement. They had to agree not only on the identity of a candidate but also on the surrender of their individual patronage.

The Crown claimed an absolute right to appoint Students. The legal foundation of the claim was never tested nor defined, but probably relied on the alleged rights of the Founder and a generous interpretation of the prerogative. From the foundation until the outbreak of the Civil War, the Crown intervened frequently in order to appoint Students. The most dramatic instance occurred when by royal mandate Queen Elizabeth I gave to Westminster School the right to Studentships at Christ Church and to Scholarships at the sister foundation at Trinity College, Cambridge. After the Restoration the Crown exercised its power of appointment less frequently. Thus no attempt seems to have been made to influence the royal visitors of the university in 1660 to replace deprived Students with royal nominees, though in 1662 the King ordered the Dean and Chapter to admit John Gaches 'into such Student's place of that our Colledge as is now void or which shall become next vacant after ye arriuall of these our letters'.[1] The King did not abandon his powers but used them more discreetly. In 1669, for example, Sir Joseph Williamson wrote to Fell that Richard March, an old servant of the King, had sought a letter of recommendation for his grandson who was 'of years and proficiency sufficient to render him deserving', to be elected from Westminster at the next election. The King, said Williamson, was anxious to gratify March 'in so small a matter', and had asked him to write privately to Fell, 'being desirous that *mandamuses* should not issue too lightly, in cases of this kind, as being of ill consequence to the foundation of all learning ... believing it will have

---

[1] Ch. Ch. Archives, Royal Letters; *Cal. SP Dom. 1661–2*, 254.

the same effect as if a *mandamus* had been issued'.[1] In this instance a Westminster Studentship was involved, but there is no reason to suppose that similar persuasion was not applied to the appointment of Canoneers.

During the eighteenth century, and especially under the first two Georges, the powers of the Crown were sometimes exercised by ministers. In the disposal of such patronage the ecumenical sympathies of the Duke of Newcastle knew no bounds. When even the appointment of the Chapter Clerk was not beneath his notice, the Studentships, whether Westminster, Canoneer, or Faculty, could not be ignored. The Duke's usual practice was to communicate his wishes to the Dean. In 1758, for example, he recommended to Dean Gregory the appointment of William Russell to a vacant Faculty Studentship in law, suggesting that he might speak 'to such of the Canons as you shall have reason to believe may be dispos'd to shew regard to my recommendation'.[2] The Dean conveyed the message to William Freind, who, owing to the interest of his father Robert Freind with the Duke, had succeeded to his father's canonry at Christ Church. William, although anxious to please, had promised his vote to Lord Harcourt's protégé Thomas Carter, who was duly elected, but on the same day Russell was appointed to a Faculty Studentship in medicine, despite the absence of any medical qualifications. A year later Gregory informed the Duke that 'Dr. Forester has promised to nominate young [John] Davis to a Studentship, who was recommended to you by Lord Halifax and for whose success your Grace seem'd so solicitous, when I had the honour of waiting upon you in the Spring'.[3] The Dean went on to describe Davis as 'a very good scholar to our Society, who from his own merit deserves all encouragement', but the more thoughtful members of the Chapter may have considered the Dean a trifle sanguine when in 1763 Davis, by then a BA, was ordered to be confined to the college 'for his frequent & scandalous practice of gameing

---

[1] *Cal. SP Dom. 1668–9*, 314–15.
[2] BL Add. MS 32886, fo. 549.
[3] BL Add. MS 32898, fo. 315.

& for other irregularities' and to prepare a speech in English about gaming which he was to repeat to the assembled college.[1]

In the reign of George III ministers ceased to concern themselves with such appointments but the Crown resumed the practice of recommending to Studentships. Its recommendations had the force of commands, and the Dean and Chapter usually felt obliged to accept them, albeit with reluctance. The esteem in which Cyril Jackson was held by the royal family, however, allowed him on at least one occasion successfully to oppose the wishes of his old pupil the Prince of Wales when he felt the interests of Christ Church to be threatened. In 1800 William Percy was elected from Westminster to Trinity College, Cambridge, but refused his election and applied for admission to Christ Church as a Commoner with a view to obtaining a Canoneer Studentship. The Dean 'peremptorily refus'd' to admit him on any footing whatever, whereupon his father sought the assistance of the Prince. An enraged Jackson complained that the Prince had been tricked because the circumstances of the case had been concealed from him. There were, he conceded, a number of unfilled Studentships that year, though none of them was in his own gift, but it was 'of serious consequence to Westmr. School, to Christ Church & myself that my original refusal shd. be persisted in'.[2] The Prince decided not to press the matter and Percy entered Lincoln College. However, after Jackson's resignation the Prince continued to assert his right of recommendation and in 1817 did so with success on behalf of W. F. Hook.[3] Seven years later in 1824 he recommended that Studentships should be awarded to Frederick Calvert, the son of Sir Henry Calvert, and Richard Seymour, the son of a naval hero. Dean Smith was not cast in the same mould as Jackson and his attempt to dispute the royal wishes met with ignominious defeat. On 12 February 1824 Lord Liverpool informed him that the King insisted on both appointments, and added, 'I am under the necessity of adding that as the individuals recommended are in no respect *improper* you have no alternative

---

[1] Chapter Act Book, 6 Dec. 1763.
[2] Aspinall, *Correspondence of George Prince of Wales,* iv, no. 1545.
[3] BL Add. MS 38576, fo. 44ᵛ.

but to obey the King's commands'. He then suggested that the nominees should stand in the name of the whole Chapter so that the royal command would not fall solely on the Dean but equally on the Canons, who did not have the same public obligations imposed upon them. Calvert and Seymour were duly elected the same year.[1]

In the exercise of their patronage, most of the Deans of Christ Church acted with independence of mind and consideration of the good of the college. On more than one occasion Dean Fell disregarded nominations by so great a person as the Chancellor, the Duke of Ormonde, and Aldrich was described by Richard Steele, then vainly seeking nomination, as one who 'would rather prefer one that was a Scholar before another'.[2] To Jackson, as has already been shown, the use of patronage was a method of rewarding Commoners of merit. When Lord Belham requested his nomination in 1802, Jackson wrote to him, 'The fact is that I laid it down as a rule from the time of my appointment to my present situation, that I would always give my nominations to a Studentship as rewards to those Commoners whom I consider'd as the most deserving, and I have therefore invariably excus'd myself from listening to any application'. He indicated that he had returned a similar answer to the Archbishop of York, the Duke of Portland, and the Earl of Malmesbury, and, presumably referring to the case of William Percy, added

I have been graciously permitted to oppose the very same reason even to those applications which otherwise it would have been my duty to have considered as commands ... I will say also honestly that the rule itself is so necessary and so very essential to my system of government here that I could not even on that ground depart from it, were all other considerations out of the question.[3]

Although not blind to merit, the Deans were often defeated by the clamour of their kindred for preferment, and it was not uncommon for them to award Studentships to their sons,

---

[1] Ibid., 41.
[2] R. Blanchard (ed.), *Correspondence of Richard Steele* (1941), no. 5.
[3] BL Add. MS 33109, fo. 189.

nephews, and more distant connections, who, it may be assumed, were no less well qualified for them than other candidates. Few Deans were men of wealth, and many had risen from modest origins. It was not unreasonable for them to dispose of their patronage in order to provide for their families, though the recipients of such family piety may sometimes have been in the uncomfortable position of prefects in a school where their father was headmaster. Conybeare, Gregory, and Markham all had sons in Studentships, and the more sons the Deans of Christ Church had the more Studentships they distributed to them. Four of Markham's sons held Westminster Studentships, and three of Gregory's Canoneer. Atterbury's son Osborn was elected to a Westminster Studentship long after his father had vacated the Deanery. Fell and Aldrich, neither of whom married, had nephews elected from Westminster, and Fell himself was nominated to a Canoneer by his father when the latter was Dean. The claims of kin were almost hereditary. Thus in 1749, Robert Freind gave his nomination to George Smalridge, who was not only Dean Smalridge's grandson but was tortuously related to his patron, for Freind and Dean Smalridge had married daughters of the Revd Samuel de l'Angle. Dean Bagot occupies a special place of honour. If he exercised his patronage as resolutely as circumstances suggest he may be deemed to have added a new meaning to the phrase 'patron saint'. To him may be attributed in large measure the increase in the number of Studentships awarded to the sons of peers in the later eighteenth century. Nepotism became a significant factor in raising the status of Students. Bagot's social aspirations were well known in Christ Church. Richard Polwhele, who came up in 1778, remarked to a friend, 'It is said that Bagot betrays a partiality for men of rank'.[1] He was connected with the Earls of Dartmouth by his mother, who was a daughter of the

---

[1] Polwhele, *Reminiscences,* i, 41. Bagot's partiality was not uncritical, and Polwhele qualified his remark by noting that Bagot had rusticated Robert Lowth, the Bishop of London's son, and the two sons of a judge. Robert Lowth's main claim to fame, however, was as the purchaser while an undergradute of a pony which lived to the age of 37 (R. Lowth, *Billesdon Coplow, a poem ... to which is Prefixed a Brief Memoir of the Author* (1831), 5).

first Earl, and by his brother, who married a granddaughter of the first Earl. In addition, a nephew and a niece married offspring of the second and third Earls. Three of the second Earl's sons, Heneage, Henry, and Edward Legge, were elected to Canoneer Studentships in 1777, 1781, and 1785 respectively. Bagot himself married a niece of the eighth Earl of Kinnoull, and through this alliance a host of Hays and Drummonds flocked into Studentships. Edward Auriol Drummond was elected in 1774, Thomas Hay and George Auriol Drummond in 1776, and William Robert Hay in 1778. Only the Dean's elevation to the episcopate saved the college from further colonization by his ubiquitous relatives. In contrast, Cyril Jackson, who never married, repudiated family claims on his patronage even before they were made.

The Canons, less directly involved than the Deans in the educational work of the college and in many instances having no previous connection with it, had, as Lord Liverpool observed, fewer public obligations in the use of their patronage. For some patronage was the currency of private obligations to be preferred unsolicited, but in the course of time not unrequited, to their political mentors. George Jubb offered the first nomination to fall to him after his appointment as Canon in 1780 to Charles Jenkinson, the future Earl of Liverpool, who coldly declined and advised him not to enter into long-term commitments.[1] In 1799, C. H. Hall, who later owed his appointment to the Deanery mainly to Liverpool, followed in Jubb's footsteps with almost indecent ardour. 'I gladly embrace the opportunity', he wrote, 'of offering to your Lordship what I have only delayed till I could do it pleno jure the nomination to my first Studentship.'[2] He asked to be allowed to nominate Cecil Jenkinson, adding that a new roll was to be made at Christmas so that should anything happen to him in the meanwhile (presumably translation to a bishopric rather than to paradise) the nomination would stand. In the event he nominated John Banks Jenkinson, who was elected forthwith. Although such Abrahamic sacrifices were not infrequent, they

---

[1] BL Add. MS 38307, fo. 159.
[2] BL Add. MS 38233, fo. 298.

were balanced by instances when the Canons proved less complaisant. In 1713, for example, the Lord Treasurer, the Earl of
Oxford, wished to obtain a Canoneer Studentship for one Lewis.
Dr Stratford, who had no vacancy on the electoral roll at his
disposal, approached Canon Terry, who had yet to nominate.

> I told him your Lordship would not press him to do anything he thought
> improper, that he was to be the judge who was fit to be nominated by
> himself, but that I did not know that your Lordship had any thoughts
> of recommending any other, if Lewis should be unfit ... The Sub-dean
> said what I allowed, that after so much negligence it would be necessary
> to have a proof, as well as a promise, of his future behaviour.[1]

On further inquiry Lewis was found to have absented himself
from chapel, to have missed his tutor's lectures, and to have slept
out of college, and at length had to be literally hauled out of bed
so that Stratford could speak to him. The Lord Treasurer did not
press his election.

So far as their kith and kin were concerned, the Canons obedi-
ently followed where the Deans so often led with enthusiasm.
Edward Pococke and Peter Foulkes each obtained the election of
four sons to Canoneer Studentships. Hammond, Allestree, and
Wake in the seventeenth century, and Burton, Fanshawe, Forester,
William Freind, Potter, and Tanner in the eighteenth, all ensured
the election of more than one son or nephew. Occasionally family
piety obscured objective judgement as when Bishop Tanner discovered that the namesake and nephew he had nominated in 1726
was in fact 'a vile, rakish, sad young man',[2] and even Archbishop
Potter may have entertained doubts when one of his sons was
expelled for marrying his bedmaker and another was reputed to
be the author of the notorious *Essay on Woman*. Sometimes the
influence of genealogy is not at once apparent. When Dr Peter
Foulkes nominated William Holwell on 26 June 1740, he was in
fact giving a Studentship to his stepson, for he had married
Holwell's widowed mother, who was a daughter of Offspring

---

[1] H M C, *Portland* (1901), vii, 187.
[2] Hearne, *Collections,* x, 425. Tanner nominated his nephew in 1726, but the
nomination was later exchanged with Dr Terry.

Blackall, Bishop of Exeter. When Robert Price was nominated by
Shute Barrington in 1765, his merits were no doubt undiminished
because his mother was the daughter of the first Viscount Barrington. In 1788 Charles Anson was nominated by Edward Vernon.
His father, whose name was George Adams until he changed it
to Anson in 1773, married a daughter of the first Baron Vernon,
which made Charles Anson a nephew of Edward Vernon.

Unbridled nepotism was restrained by the rules and regulations
of the college, and it was because of them that Jeremy Bentham
failed to obtain a Studentship. Before Bentham matriculated at
Oxford, his father applied to Dr Edward Bentham, a distant
relative who was Regius Professor of Divinity and also Sub-Dean,
'but got for an answer that his patronage was engaged. Afterwards,
he spontaneously offered one to Bentham; who was so humbled
by neglect and annoyance, and so desponding, that, after con-
sulting his morose tutor, Mr Jefferson, he declined the favour
which the doctor proffered.'[1] The facts show Dr Bentham in a
better light than this sour version of them. His patronage was
indeed engaged. A new roll had been drawn up on 5 January
1760, and Dr Bentham nominated one George Rous, who was
elected to a Studentship on 24 December the same year. On
26 June 1760, Jeremy Bentham matriculated and entered Queen's
College. He was then twelve years and four months old. When
the next roll was made on 24 December 1761, Dr Bentham
nominated Jeremy Bentham to it, and his name is inscribed on
the roll. Dr Bentham, however, ceased at this time to be Sub-
Dean and his nomination dropped from third in seniority on the
roll to eighth, and Thomas Bagot, who was eventually nominated
in place of Jeremy Bentham, had to wait for two years, until
December 1763, for his election. Dr Bentham's goodwill to the
youthful Jeremy did not stop at his nomination to the roll, for,
perhaps realizing that an interval of as much as two years between
nomination and election would mean that Jeremy Bentham would
be on the point of taking his degree before he obtained a Studentship, he arranged to exchange the nomination with Dr Barton,

[1] J. Bentham, *Works*, x, 38.

who stood fourth on the roll immediately after the Sub-Dean. The effect of this exchange was to place Jeremy Bentham on the roll in a position of seniority similar to that which he would have enjoyed in 1760 if a vacancy had existed. Thus Dr Bentham seems to have taken considerable pains to obtain a Studentship for his ungrateful kinsman despite the fact that in 1760 Jeremy Bentham was too young to be elected.

Patronage as a method of dispensing preferment by means other than sale had respectable historical origins. In the universities Fellowships were originally clerical, and most of those who held them entered the Church, where patronage was the usual method of appointment for archbishop and curate alike. Because they were eleemosynary they were awarded for need rather than for merit, though no college which depended on the selection of Fellows for its government and tuition could afford to neglect merit as an appropriate qualification. At Christ Church, the Dean and Chapter, although subjected to the pressures of politics and the undeniable exigencies of family obligations, on the whole exercised their patronage with discrimination. At the election of Students the recital of the Act of 31 Elizabeth I, c. 6, against corrupt elections constantly reminded them that they had inherited from a celibate clergy a condemnation of simony, though not of its sister nepotism, which until the nineteenth century was widely regarded less as a social evil than as a social duty and at All Souls was for centuries elevated to the level of principle. It is related that Canon Barnes once remarked, 'I don't know what we're coming to. I've given Studentships to my sons, and to my nephews, and to my nephews' children, and there are no more of my family left. I shall have to give them by merit one of these days.'[1] In capacity and attainments the Canoneer Students were not inferior to the Westminster Students, who unlike them were appointed by public examination, and amongst the many distinguished men elected were Archbishop Wake (1675), Gilbert West (1723), William Eden, first Baron Auckland (1762), Viscount Wellesley (1778), Frederick North, fifth Earl of Guilford (1782), George Canning

---

[1] Tuckwell, *Reminiscences of Oxford,* 134.

(1789), and 'Monk' Lewis (1790). In the latter part of the eighteenth century Studentships were increasingly awarded to well-to-do young men, and their eleemosynary nature declined at a time when society increasingly demanded an educated middle class. Studentships then came more and more to be given for merit, though they were not yet prizes to be awarded in open competition. The use of patronage in making university appointments eventually fell into disfavour in the nineteenth century, except in the case of the regius professorships, and was replaced by competitive examination.

Canoneer and Westminster Students alike were recruited from broadly similar sections of society. Had this not been so it is probable that the college would have been beset by jealousies and disputes. Some differences, however, arose from the fact that the Westminsters came from a particular school whereas the Canoneers did not. Fewer Canoneers than Westminsters came from the professional classes, and in particular fewer seem to have been the sons of lawyers or government officials, occupations which flourished in London. More Westminsters than Canoneers were sons of the inferior clergy. The general tendency throughout the period, however, was for Students in both groups to come from wealthy or socially prominent backgrounds. It was a tendency more pronounced in the case of the Canoneers than the Westminsters. In the seventeenth century, a sizeable proportion of Canoneer Students came from poor backgrounds. Under Dean Fell, as has been shown, Studentships were sometimes given to Servitors, and in the university matriculation registers an average of about one Student each year described himself as 'filius plebis'. In the eighteenth century, by contrast, and especially during the second half, the number of Students who were able to describe their fathers as armigerous or who were sons of the higher clergy increased rapidly. Furthermore, while it was very rare in the seventeenth century for a member of the aristocracy to be elected to a Studentship, between 1750 and 1800 eighteen sons of peers and fourteen sons of baronets were elected. Among them were Frederick North, son of the celebrated Lord North, and Richard Colley Wellesley, who was son of the Earl of Mornington.

Canoneer Studentships became increasingly coveted objects of ambition as their status improved. A Studentship, wrote Cyril Jackson in 1802, 'is of such value besides many other circumstances to recommend it over and above the mere emolument, that I know very few things which are more the objects of solicitation'.[1]

(c) THE FACULTY STUDENTSHIPS

Included among the 101 Studentships were the Faculty Studentships, which were tenable only by laymen. Although relieved of the obligation to enter holy orders, in other respects the conditions of tenure were the same as for other Studentships. In order to obtain a Faculty Studentship it was necessary to be a graduate Student. From this two consequences followed. Firstly, the Faculty Studentships were never filled from outside Christ Church. Secondly, since candidates were already Students, appointments were not made by the exercise of individual canonical patronage, and indeed had it been otherwise the Westminster Students would not have been eligible. Appointments were made by the Dean and Chapter collectively. The Dean's support was important, and indeed decisive in the case of a strong Dean such as John Fell, who, according to Humphrey Prideaux, actually appointed the Faculty Students,[2] but the votes of the Chapter were not a formality. When Noel Broxholme sought a Faculty place in 1713, Dr Stratford remarked that by siding with Atterbury he 'had put it out of our power to serve him',[3] and when in 1758 Dean Gregory sought the vote of Dr William Freind for the Duke of Newcastle's protégé William Russell he found it already engaged to another candidate.[4]

To the four Faculty Studentships established at the foundation, a fifth was added in 1665 when the Studentship founded as a consequence of a bequest by William Thurston became a Faculty

---

[1] BL Add. MS 33109, fo. 190.
[2] BL Add. MS 28929, fos. 28, 30, 67.
[3] HMC, *Portland* (1901), vii, 157.
[4] See p. 122.

place almost by chance. Under the terms of his will, Thurston, who so far as is known had no direct connection with Christ Church, left the residue of his estate after certain bequests to 'King's College' in the university of Oxford for the maintenance of a Fellow and the support of learning. The question arose which college was meant by a description which did not exactly fit any of them. Brasenose and Oriel, both of which claimed to be royal foundations, disputed the title with Christ Church, and in 1662 the suit was taken to the Court of Arches.[1] Christ Church submitted in evidence a lease made in 1545 in which the college was described as 'King Henry the Eighth's College', but the case, as did many others, foundered in the Court of Arches without coming to a conclusion, and the executors sued out a commission of delegacy under the Great Seal. The matter was eventually submitted to the Archbishop of Canterbury, and on 22 March 1665 the legacy, which litigation had reduced from £1,020 to £920, was awarded to Christ Church by an order of Charles II, which stated that 'one Student more bee added to the number of one hundred already founded'.[2] Although Thurston was instrumental in the creation of a new Studentship, his bequest was not applied to this purpose. Even before the King's award had been made, the full amount had been paid into the building account on the previous 19 December.[3] In his award the King referred to the 'good management of the general revenue of our said colledge', and the stipend of the extra Studentship was defrayed from the ordinary revenues of the Dean and Chapter. That this was possible illustrates the rapid recovery in the finances of Christ Church after the Restoration.

When Thurston's executors received their discharge at the hands of Leoline Jenkins and George Croyden, a former Westminster Student who became Canon of Christ Church in the following year, they were given the first nomination of the new Student, 'as it was ever our desire', and on 22 June they notified

---

[1] J. Houston, *Index of Cases in the Records of the Court of Arches* (1972), no. 6381.
[2] Ch. Ch. Archives, Estates 121, fo. 183, and Royal Letters; *Cal. SP Dom. 1664–5*, 266.
[3] Ch. Ch. Archives, Disbursement Book 1642–3, fo. 77.

the Dean that their choice had fallen on James Vernon, an under-graduate of Christ Church, who was promptly elected early in July.[1] The election of an undergraduate to the Thurston Studentship is a clear indication that the original intention was not to make it a Faculty Studentship. It became so because of the intervention of the King, to whom it offered a convenient solution to an immediate problem. On 24 March, two days after he had settled the bequest on Christ Church, the King ordered that Thomas Ireland should be restored to his Studentship. When Ireland had resigned his Studentship in 1664 in order to become a candidate for the Readership of Moral Philosophy, he stood fifth on the Student roll at the top of the list of Philosophi immediately after the four Faculty Students. In 1665 this place was occupied by another Student, and in order to restore Ireland to his seniority without injustice to his successor the King ordered that he should have 'the Student's place which we have commanded by our letters of the two & twentieth instant to bee added to the number already founded ... and that for this turne hee be admitted Junior Master in his former seniority & so continue without the obligation upon him of being farther advanced to any higher Table, ranke, or order in that colledge'.[2] Ireland owed this remark-able example of royal favour to the visit which Charles II had made to Christ Church in 1663. On that occasion the King was received in the Hall, accompanied by the Queen and her retinue, and 'Mr. Thomas Ireland, one of the Students, spake to them 116 English verses on his knees, which soe much pleased the king that he thanked him for them, gave him his hand to kiss, and commanded a coppy of them'.[3] Although the King's command exempted Ireland from the necessity of taking orders, its wording does not suggest that a similar dispensation was intended to apply to future occupants of the Studentship, but the precedent was quickly created that the Thurston Studentship was tenable by

---

[1] James Vernon was the son of Francis Vernon, of London, by Anne, widow of William Welby, of Gedney, Lincs., and daughter of George Smithes, a London goldsmith.

[2] Ch. Ch. Archives, Royal Letters.

[3] Wood, *Life and Times,* i, 497.

laymen. In 1675 Ireland was succeeded by William Allestree. In the previous autumn, Allestree, who was then employed on an embassy to Sweden, wrote to John Locke expressing the hope that he might retain that employment. 'If', he wrote, 'I should be out of the Kings service here, or out of all businesse at home, I may be press'd to the bad choise of either taking orders, or loosing what I possesse in Ch:Ch:.'[1] The fifth Faculty Studentship seems to have been established more by chance than from any desire to encourage secular studies.

Of the four Faculty Studentships created at the foundation, it was intended that two should be held only by civil lawyers and two only by physicians, but this division was often disregarded. Between the Restoration and the death of Queen Anne, for example, neither of the legal Studentships was held by a civil lawyer, and only one of the medical Studentships was held continuously by physicians. For this state of affairs there were several reasons. The civil law, despite a flurry of activity in the ecclesiastical courts in the late seventeenth century, was in decline. For some, impartially innocent of attachment to the law, to medicine, or to the Church, the retention of their Studentships unencumbered by the duty to take holy orders provided a pension which could be enjoyed for life provided they remained celibate. The situation was aggravated by the government's reliance on the universities for well-educated laymen capable of serving as diplomats or civil servants. The Crown was able to relieve Students of the need to take holy orders by means of the dispensing power, but the same object could be achieved by means of the Faculty Studentships without the disruption caused by the royal prerogative. Locke's career is not untypical. On 14 November 1666 Charles II granted him a dispensation from holy orders, which Locke, who was already a Theologus, would otherwise have been compelled to take, probably by the following Christmas, on pain of forfeiting his Studentship. The dispensation not only assured him an income while he was on a diplomatic mission to Brandenburg but enabled him to keep his Studentship until one

[1] Locke, *Correspondence*, i, no. 292.

of the Faculty Studentships tenable by laymen fell vacant. Such a vacancy occurred in 1675, and the Dean and Chapter duly appointed him to it. Amongst other Faculty Students employed on government service in the second half of the seventeenth century was John Ellis, who was secretary to Sir Leoline Jenkins and subsequently Under-Secretary of State and Comptroller of the Mint. After the accession of George I, recruitment for the government service diminished, and when it was revived a decade later the government looked to the Regius Professorship of Modern History to supply the need rather than to the Faculty Studentships. Until the middle of the eighteenth century the Faculty Studentships in medicine were filled by physicians more often than the legal Studentships were filled by civil lawyers, partly because the government service had a greater need of lawyers than of physicians, but also because of a tradition, which stemmed from the time when Oxford was visited by plague, that one of the Faculty Students in medicine should attend the health of the members of the college, for which purpose he had to be resident in Oxford.[1]

In 1715 the Dean and Chapter passed a decree repeating the 'antient Rule of the Church' that the four Faculty Studentships should be divided equally between civil law and medicine.[2] No reference was made in the decree to the fifth Faculty Studentship, which was subsequently known as the Studentship in Humanity,[3]

---

[1] Dean Aldrich was attended on his deathbed by one of the Faculty Students in medicine, Richard Frewin (Hearne, *Collections*, iii, 90), and in 1774 the Chapter ruled that 'it is the opinion of the Dean and Chapter that physicians who are likely to be resident and useful to the college ought to have a preference in the disposal of two of the Faculty places' (Chapter Minute Book, 16 Dec. 1774). George Chinnery wrote on 15 March 1808 that Cyril Jackson required all undergraduates of Christ Church to receive medical attention from Sir Christopher Pegge, the Regius Professor of Medicine (though not a Faculty Student). 'He wished the men of his College to be attended by a Ch. Ch. physician because no other medical man thinks it worth his while to attend the men regularly or to give him a faithful and daily account of the manner in which they are going on' (Ch. Ch. Archives, xlviii a. 43, fo. 55).

[2] Chapter Act Book, 12 Nov. 1715.

[3] It was first referred to in the college records as the Studentship in Humanity in 1776 (Draft Minute Book), and first used in the Chapter Act Book when William Garthshore was appointed in 1794.

and was devoted to classical or literary studies. The decree met only intermittent success and it became increasingly difficult to find Students qualified in medicine or civil law as the eighteenth century advanced.

In the case of civil law the difficulty was partially obscured by the longevity of William Wall, who held one of the Studentships from 1738 until 1791, when he died at the age of eighty-six, but the companion Studentship was not held by a civil lawyer after 1767. The shortage of suitably qualified Students reflected not only the suddenly accelerated decline of the Church courts during the first half of the eighteenth century but also the absence of legal education at Christ Church. Most undergraduates who wished to take a degree in civil law migrated to All Souls, where the Regius Professorship of Civil Law was held by a Fellow of the college almost without interruption from 1672 until the end of the following century. Students who migrated to All Souls, having automatically surrendered their Studentships, were ineligible for the Faculty places at Christ Church. The BCL was the least exacting degree open to undergraduates, but the attempt by the Chapter in 1740 to raise the standard by requiring the prior completion of the curriculum for the BA had little effect, though those who subsequently took the degree of BCL were often better qualified to do so than had been the case previously.[1] Faced with a lack of candidates, the Chapter resorted to filling the two legal Faculty Studentships with common lawyers.

In the case of the medical Studentships matters were no better. One of them fell vacant in 1756 and remained so for eight years. It was not occupied by a physician after 1772 but by a succession of lawyers. The second medical Studentship was vacant from 1751 to 1758, when it too was filled by a lawyer, and with one notable exception all subsequent occupants for the rest of the century were lawyers. The Dean and Chapter became so resigned to their inability to appropriate particular Studentships to particular studies that they appointed Charles Abbot to one of the Faculty Studentships reserved for physicians although he was one of the

---

[1] See p. 146.

few Students in the latter part of the eighteenth century qualified to hold a legal Studentship by virtue of the possession of a BCL. The difficulty of filling the medical Studentships with physicians arose in part from the decline in medical studies at Oxford and the emergence of thriving medical schools in London and Edinburgh but perhaps even more from the fact that the emoluments and privileges of a Studentship did not compare with the professional opportunities open to the ambitious medical practitioner in or near London. The difficulty was further compounded by the practice of filling the Studentships from those who were already Students of Christ Church. The unsatisfactory consequence of the system was illustrated by the experience of Sir Christopher Pegge, a physician of dubious distinction who ultimately became Regius Professor of Medicine. Pegge had been an undergraduate at Christ Church but not a Student. In 1790 he was appointed Lee Reader in Anatomy in succession to William Thomson, but since he was not a Student he was not appointed to the Faculty Studentship vacated by Thomson. This was given to Thomas Carter, 'no Student in the Faculty of Physick being qualified'.[1]

By the end of the eighteenth century the Faculty Studentships, legal and medical alike, were held almost invariably by common lawyers. Many of them achieved considerable eminence in the law. Sir Archibald Macdonald, for example, became Solicitor-General, and Sir John Skynner Chief Baron of the Exchequer. Others, such as William Eden and Nicholas Vansittart, were distinguished in other walks of life. Few merited Lord Macclesfield's description, written without Christ Church in mind, that 'those who have the Faculty places get them purely to avoid going into Orders, and that they may live a more gay life without designing to follow any profession'.[2] The Dean and Chapter, acquiescing in the fact that few wished to study civil law and that the medical profession flourished elsewhere, accepted that the Studentships provided opportunities for laymen to pursue secular studies and thereby fulfilled their original intention albeit not in the manner intended.

---

[1] Chapter Act Book, 10 Nov. 1790.
[2] J. Gutch (ed.), *Collectanea Curiosa* (1781), ii, 61.

No attempt was made to reform the Faculty Studentships. The Chapter, for example, never considered removing the disabling restriction on the choice of candidates to those who were already Students of Christ Church. Theoretically this was possible in the absence of restraining statutes, but in practice it would have encountered strong vested interests, for the Faculty Studentships could not be opened to members of other colleges unless the undergraduate Studentships were also opened, and that would have undermined the foundation of canonical patronage on which seniority and emoluments were calculated. Nor, for different reasons, was it possible to appoint the Faculty Students to tutorships. Historically they acted as tutors on rare occasions, but they were usually non-resident, and neither medicine nor law was a study suitable for undergraduates. The conventional wisdom in the eighteenth century was that tutors ought to teach every subject in the curriculum: the Faculty Students were laymen and specialized in particular disciplines.

(d) THE TENURE OF STUDENTSHIPS

The original intention of Studentships at Christ Church, apart from the Faculty Studentships, was to provide for the training of the parochial clergy. Thus, although Students were appointed for life, the rules and regulations of the college were designed to reduce the tenure in practice to a shorter period, thereby ensuring that Students were discharged into livings more rapidly. 'Our colleges', Fell wrote to Sunderland in 1684, 'are nurseries and become useful as they make quick removes and frequent successions, and this will be stopped if men can find means to continue here.'[1] The Victorians delighted to depict the Senior Common Rooms of the university in the eighteenth century as congested with ancient Life-Fellows, useless drones whose umbilical cords were anchored in the college cellars, but so far as

---

[1] *Cal. S P Dom. 1684–5,* 211.

Christ Church is concerned the picture does less than justice. It is true that many Students, then as now, held their Studentships for twenty years or more, and in a few instances for very much more. The sterile record for the longest tenure of all is held by John Ellis, who was appointed in 1664 and retained his Studentship for seventy-four years until his death in 1738, and he was closely rivalled by James Howell, who was Student from 1767 to 1838. The Faculty Students, not being required to vacate their places for omitting to take orders or on accepting institution to a living, often held their Studentships for long periods. Lawyers in particular seem to have aspired to immortality. But for the majority of Students such instances were rare and unrepresentative. Between 1660 and 1800 the average length of tenure of both Westminster and Canoneer Studentships was a little over twelve years, and throughout the period the tendency was for the length of tenure to become shorter.[1] Thus although the average tenure between the Restoration and the end of the seventeenth century was more than fourteen and a half years, it had fallen by the end of the eighteenth to a little more than ten and a half years. At no time was the college filled with superannuated sinecurists, for the average age of the resident Students was about thirty.

From the time of his appointment a Student was confronted by a series of obstacles, the failure to overcome any one of which led inexorably to the loss of his Studentship. When he had accumulated sufficient residence he was required to take the degrees of BA and MA at the times prescribed by statute. On entering the ranks of the Theologi, or twenty senior Students, he was obliged to take priest's orders, unless by that time he had been appointed to one of the Faculty Studentships. Having taken holy orders, he forfeited his Studentship if he accepted a living with cure of souls more than a short distance from Oxford. Finally, a Student could retain his Studentship for so long as he did not marry or commit a grave breach of college discipline or public morality. In the long

---

[1] These averages are based on *all* Studentships. If Students who failed to take a degree are excluded, the average is 13·4 years. Similarly the averages given for the late seventeenth and eighteenth centuries are increased to 15·1 and 11·3 respectively.

run the advantages of surrendering a Studentship outweighed the benefits of retaining it, and such was the intention of the 'quick removes and frequent successions' advocated by Fell. The diminution in the length of tenure of Studentships between the Restoration and the end of the eighteenth century was due to variations in the incidence of the various causes of forfeiture and to the changing expectations of Students as they came increasingly to be recruited from wealthy and socially prominent backgrounds during the second half of the eighteenth century.

Since a Student lost his Studentship if, having accumulated the statutory residence, he failed to take the degrees of BA and MA, the majority of Students were successfully propelled through the Schools by self-interest if other motives failed. Even more Students took degrees than would appear from the university registers, for until the first quarter of the eighteenth century, and occasionally thereafter, degrees are sometimes ascribed to Students in the college records that are not entered in the university records. Amongst the records at Christ Church in which evidence of this paradox may be found are the Act Books of the Dean and Chapter. From 1665 they contain annual lists of Students in order of seniority, and from 1667 these lists are authenticated by the Registrar or Chapter Clerk, one of the legal officers of the college. Bachelors and Masters are distinguished respectively on the lists by the prefixes 'Dominus' and 'Magister', and in the majority of instances the possession of a degree implied by this usage is confirmed by the university records. But in a number of cases the terms Dominus and Magister appear in the lists without such confirmation. In addition to the special category of Students who entered the law line under the terms of a Chapter order in 1740,[1] about thirty other Students appear from the Act Books to have possessed the degree of BA or MA, and in some cases both degrees, but to have received neither of them from the university. Of this number, a dozen were Bachelors; a further dozen were Masters according to the college records but had only received a BA from the university; and five received the degrees of BA and

[1] See p. 146.

MA according to the college records but are not recorded in the university records. All but one in the last category occurred when John Fell was Dean.

It is unlikely that the discrepancies between college and university records were caused by irregularities in keeping the university registers. It was important for the university to keep a proper record of its degrees, and any hypothesis which assumed frequent acts of self-denial in the collection of fees would be insecurely based on the observation of human nature. If the university registers do not record the grant of a degree it is because none was granted by the university. The explanation must, therefore, be sought within Christ Church. It then becomes apparent that degrees were recognized in the college for which the university gave no authority. To understand how this arose it is necessary to examine the practice of granting graces.

After presenting himself for examination by the university it was necessary for a Student to obtain the consent of the Dean and Chapter. This he did by petitioning them for a grace. The petition took the form of an oration which was recited in the presence of the Dean and Chapter. In 1713 a Student was admonished to prepare a better speech and to take care to deliver it *memoriter*, and in 1772 the Chapter noted that one Barton should have his grace, but, because he had been prevented from speaking his oration at the stated time, he was to do so on the next occasion allotted by custom for the exercise, even though he had delivered the text to the Dean.[1] The oration was an opportunity for the orator to demonstrate his accomplishments. In 1763 William Weller Pepys not only received his grace for the degree of BA but was rewarded with a book 'for his much approved Critical Dissertation on the third book of Apollonius Rhodius in his speech by him this day pronounced in the Hall with great propriety of Elocution'.[2] In 1779 Charles Abbot delivered a speech on the orations of Demosthenes. The manuscript is entitled 'Oratio habita Aed. Xti Oxon. ante grad. Baccalaur. adept. Oct. XIX

[1] Chapter Act Book, 16 Dec. 1772.
[2] Chapter Act Book, 17 Mar. 1763.

MDCCLXXIX'.[1] Under Cyril Jackson graces were sometimes given to undergraduates of exceptional ability, and conferred upon the recipients the privileges of a Bachelor of Arts within Christ Church even though the degree had not yet been received from the university. In 1786 Henry Harrison, who had been prevented by illness from completing the necessary residence, received his grace 'with all the privileges of a Bachelor in the House', but he did not receive his degree from the university for a further two years.[2] In 1783 the future Dean Hall was given his grace though not of full standing 'as a reward for his having from the time of his entrance distinguished himself by his diligent attendance upon the public lectures, by his exemplary performance of the college exercises, and his good conduct in every respect',[3] and in December 1786 George Bisset, who was not of standing for BA until the following Easter, received his grace for his 'extraordinary proficiency and good behaviour, particularly his diligence in his Collections, both the Censors having publicly borne testimony to the same'.[4]

The grant of a grace was a solemn event which signified the formal certification that a candidate was qualified for his degree, and on rare occasions was actually withheld until the necessary state of preparedness had been reached. In 1782, for example, a Student named Brodrick was summoned before the Chapter for various offences, and it was resolved that his degree should be put back a year and that he should perform satisfactorily a scheme of exercises which were to be given to him as a condition of his becoming a candidate for a degree in the following year.[5] The grace was not intended to dispense with the need to submit to examination by the university. Thus in 1780 the Chapter ordered that two Students who had 'had their Grace for the degree of MA in the House, but not having proceeded to the said degree in the

---

[1] PRO 30/9/3/31. Abbot took his BCL in 1783, but Foster records no grant of a BA.

[2] Chapter Act Book, 7 Nov. 1786.

[3] Ibid., 10 Mar. 1783.

[4] Ibid., 22 Dec. 1786. See pp. 328–9.

[5] Chapter Minute Book, 25 June 1782.

University, be moneoed to take the degree of MA before the expiration of next term'.[1] Nevertheless in a college such as Christ Church, where the standard of education was relatively high, the grant of a grace was such evidence of merit as to make the university examination almost a formality, and indeed the university examinations in the eighteenth century have been criticized on these very grounds. At Christ Church the grant of a grace became almost indistinguishable from the grant of a degree by the university, and in their private correspondence the Canons referred to the granting of degrees when they meant the granting of graces. In 1713 Dr Stratford wrote that 'honest' Periam and Thomas Terry were ready to take the degree of Doctor, 'but neither of them can proceed unless our Dean comes down, and we hear nothing of him. We cannot hold a Chapter to give them their degrees in the House',[2] and in 1728 he complained that owing to the absence of several Canons there was 'no proxy in the College, nor consequently any power to give degrees, or do any other business of any kind'.[3]

It would seem, therefore, that those who are recorded in the college records, but not in the university records, as possessing a degree had received their grace from the Dean and Chapter but had not subsequently been admitted to their degree by the university. For some of them, as has been suggested, the possession of a degree was a superfluous formality. Having satisfied the Dean of Christ Church, undergraduates for whom a degree had little practical value had no sufficient inducement to obtain the accolade of the university. Richard Cox, the Archbishop of Cashel's son, perhaps fell into this category. He received his grace on 19 April 1763 but, according to Foster, never received his degree. Yet

---

[1] Ibid., 22 Dec. 1780.

[2] H M C, *Portland* (1901), viii, 139. On 16 Nov. 1657 George Percivall informed his brother John that his degree would be conferred on him in the House in the following week, 'although not until Lent in the University' (H M C, *Egmont* (1905), i, 589). Bachelors were required to determine in Lent before receiving their degree.

[3] H M C, *Portland* (1901), vii, 460. The tradition of granting degrees of the House is retained by the Dean of Christ Church to the present time. A similar power has been exercised by the Heads of other Oxford colleges.

when he resigned his Studentship on the following 2 July he was referred to in the Chapter Act Book by the prefix 'Dominus' reserved for Bachelors. But there was a further reason for the omission. During the latter part of the seventeenth century and the early years of the eighteenth it enabled some Students to avoid taking the oath of allegiance. After the accession of William III, this oath, together with the oath of supremacy and subscription to the Thirty-nine Articles, was taken at matriculation and again at the time of presentation for a degree. At matriculation the oaths may well have seemed mere cabalistic incantations to many undergraduates, and were often treated by the university as formalities. Nicholas Amhurst remarked that the oath of allegiance was often neglected in the early years of George I, and quoted the case of an undergraduate who did not know he had taken it until informed by the Vice-Chancellor when signing his certificate of matriculation, 'not one word of it, or his majesty king George' having been mentioned.[1] But the oaths taken on presentation for a degree were a more serious matter. To the Nonjurors the oath of allegiance was particularly obnoxious, and the acceptance in Christ Church of degrees unhallowed by the university perhaps represented an ingenious device which permitted them to retain their Studentships and also the benefits of seniority. In 1691 the Earl of Nottingham ordered the Vice-Chancellor to remove all Nonjurors from Fellowships,[2] and was informed by Aldrich that 'by the best inquiry he can make he does not find any man in Christ Church has refused or neglected to take the oaths'.[3] But John Urry, the editor of Chaucer, was described in the college records in 1689 as a Master of Arts, yet when he died in 1714, Hearne referred to him as a Bachelor of Arts, which was the only degree attributed to him in the university records, and added that, 'He refused the Oaths, & died a Non-Juror. For this reason tho' he had the degree of A. M. yet he was not presented, the time of

---

[1] N. Amhurst, *Terrae Filius*, 3rd edn. (1754), 88, 90.

[2] N. Luttrell, *Brief Historical Relation* (1857), ii, 291.

[3] HMC, *Finch* (1957), iii, 282. Only 8 dons in the whole university resisted the oath to William and Mary in 1689 (*History of the University of Oxford*, v, ed. L. S. Sutherland and L. G. Mitchell (1986), 23).

tendering the Oath of Allegiance to Wm & Mary being then come'.[1] A similar case may be that of Robert Morgan, who also received his MA in 1689, according to the college records, but, according to Hearne, 'scrupled taking the Oaths'.[2] He subsequently complied and was made a Master of Arts by creation in 1702—an honour which neither confirmed nor denied the MA he had assumed at Christ Church since the Revolution. Hardly any Students were removed at the Revolution or at the Hanoverian Succession, but nine Students between 1689 and 1696, and five between 1714 and 1719, appear on this interpretation to have held degrees without taking the oaths.[3]

Although the recognition in Christ Church of degrees which had not received the imprimatur of the university almost ceased after 1720, the practice continued for a particular category of Student, namely those who took the degree of BCL. By the university statutes it was not necessary for a candidate for the degree of BCL to have obtained a BA or MA previously, but the possession of an MA curtailed the period of legal study. If a

---

[1] Hearne, *Collections,* v, 34.

[2] Ibid., xi, 157.

[3] Despite the outbreak of Jacobite sentiment at Christ Church on the accession of George I, it is unlikely that any Student was deprived for refusing the oaths of allegiance, supremacy, and abjuration required of all members of the foundation by 1 Geo. I, c. xiii. There survives at Christ Church the register in which were certified to the Court of Common Pleas the names of all those who subscribed. In 1715 all but eight Students did so. Of the eight, four entered the Church and presumably therefore took the oaths; one, Noel Broxholme, became physician to Frederick, Prince of Wales; one was younger brother to John Wainwright, who became the Prince's secretary; one entered the legal profession; another, John Aubin, retained his Studentship until 1740 and presumably subscribed at a later date. It thus seems unlikely that any of these Students was omitted from the register because of conscience. The position is almost unchanged if Students who surrendered their Studentships in 1714 before the Act came into force are considered. Of these, four entered the Church, two were deprived for failing to take holy orders, one died, one became Junior Lord of the Admiralty in 1717, one became Camden Professor of History in 1727, and one, 'much given to Horse-racing' (Hearne, vii, 123), resigned aged 58 and died a few years later. Only Thomas Bromley resigned because of conscience. The fact that there was no renewal of the Nonjuror Schism following the Hanoverian Succession caused some to allege a degree of cynicism in Oxford over the oaths.

candidate had obtained an MA, he was required to attend the
lectures of the Regius Professor of Civil Law for three years, but
if he was not a Master of Arts he was obliged to attend the
professor's lectures for five years, having first applied himself for
two years to the study of logic, moral philosophy, politics, and
other humane studies, unless bound by the statutes of his college
to commence his legal studies at an earlier date. Thus, if he
proceeded MA before commencing the study of civil law it was
necessary to spend a total of ten years in the university, but if the
study of civil law began after two years in general preparatory
studies it was possible to complete the course of studies in seven
years, which was also the period normally required for an MA.
Once the BCL had lost whatever practical use it possessed in the
courts, the attraction of the degree to undergraduates lay in the
fact that the exercises were minimal and that equivalent status to
the MA could be obtained after two years' study instead of the
usual four.

In 1740 the Chapter created an important precedent, which
continued to be quoted throughout the century, in the case of John
Bettesworth, who was the son of a distinguished civil lawyer. On
27 March it was resolved that he should have permission 'to enter
himself on the law line upon the particularity of his case, he
performing all his exercises in Arts within this House and likewise
proceeding to the several degrees of Bachelor and Master of Arts
within this House'. The important part of this decree lay in the
requirement that candidates for the BCL should complete the
usual exercises for BA and MA. It is clear from the Collections
Books that they were not permitted to enter the law line until
they had completed the normal course of studies for the BA,
lasting sixteen terms, and, although records do not exist at Christ
Church, it is probable that a similar practice prevailed with regard
to the MA in so far as there were exercises for that degree. The
study of civil law ceased to be a refuge for the indolent, and,
although details of legal studies in the period are sparse, it is
probable that the BCL afforded an opportunity for students who
did not intend to enter the law as a profession to study the
principles of natural law enshrined in the works of Grotius,

Pufendorf, and Burlamaqui so much admired by the eighteenth century. The provision that candidates for the BCL should also complete the exercises for the MA ensured that they were competent for both degrees after a period of seven years. Bettesworth, for example, was entered on the roll of Students as a Bachelor of Arts at Christmas 1741, a little over four years after his matriculation, and on 5 March 1744 the Chapter gave him his grace for the degree of MA. In the university records the only degrees attributed to him are BCL in 1744 and DCL in 1749.

In Christ Church candidates for the BCL were considered as graduates from the time they entered the law line, even though the university did not confer the degree upon them. In 1772 John English Dolben was given leave to enter the law line, and it was ordered that he should be considered 'as a Bachelor in the House', and when he was given his grace for the degree of BCL in 1775 he was also accorded 'the privilege of ranking as MA in the House'. In 1778 Sackville Stephens Bale was also given the privileges of a Master of Arts in the House when he received his grace for BCL, and Edward Vernon was given those of a Bachelor of Arts in the House when he was given leave to take up law. In all these cases the award of a BCL is entered in the university registers, but none of the degrees which were recognized within Christ Church is entered in them.

After the death of Smalridge, the Dean and Chapter exercised their right to award degrees within the House more sparingly, and few were given except to those who entered the law line. In 1720 it was decreed that all Bachelors and undergraduates should take their degrees at the times appointed in the university statutes under pain of expulsion, and from 1723 graces for BA and MA as well as for higher degrees were entered regularly in the Act Books. These changes occurred at a time when the political fever of the previous generation had abated, and the Nonjuror Schism had been largely healed by death and reconciliation. They also coincided with the publication of a celebrated pamphlet by Francis Gastrell, a Canon of Christ Church, entitled *The Bishop of Chester's case, with relation to the Wardenship of Manchester, in which it is shewn that no other degrees but such as are taken in the University can be deemed legal qualifications for any ecclesiastical preferment in England* (1721). If he was right to suggest that ecclesiastical preferment might be threatened by a defect of title, it was indeed time to consider whether the claims of conscience of those such as John Urry were too strident.

When the statistics of degrees taken by Students according to the university registers are adjusted to include those entered in the Chapter Act Books, and after the exclusion of Students who died or were expelled for disciplinary reasons before they had graduated, it is found that approximately 90 per cent of Students appointed between 1660 and 1800 took the degree of BA, and that most of them also took their MA. There were occasional fluctuations. Between 1740 and 1760, and again in the 1780s, there was a fall in the number who took their BA, and between 1730 and 1750 there was a decline in the number to take their MA.

Where a Student did not take his degree the cause was most unlikely to have been his failure of the university examinations. Failure in the examination Schools was always a rare phenomenon, and Thomas Salmon writing in 1744 noted that the disgrace of plucking happened 'scarce once in a year'.[1] The most common cause of a Student leaving the university without a degree was lack of the necessary statutory residence. Until quite late in the eighteenth century, residence was often very erratic, and it was not uncommon for undergraduates to absent themselves from the university for a term or two or even longer before returning to their studies, a practice which seems to indicate a lack of continuity and coherence in the curriculum. At Christ Church the Dean and Chapter did their best to insist on residence, but without a great deal of success. In theory the rules were strict. On 18 June 1713 Mathew Skinner was asked by the Chapter why he had been absent for several terms without leave. In his reply he said that he was unaware that he ought to apply for leave, and he was informed that by 'the ancient rules and customs of this House' no Student could be absent without leave for more than ten weeks in the

---

[1] T. Salmon, *Present State of the Universities* (1744), 442.

year. In 1716 the Chapter repeated its ruling, and throughout the 1720s Students were summoned to explain their extended absence. On 9 November 1748 no less than nine Bachelor Students were called before the Chapter to give an account of their absence. In January 1760 the Chapter thought it necessary to re-enact the rule yet again, and on that occasion took the unusual step of recording subsequent grants of leave in the Act Book. By the time the Chapter abandoned this practice in the following April, no doubt exhausted by such unfamiliar application to the details of administration, nine Students had been given leave—John Cleaver to become a tutor at Westminster, Francis Atterbury to attend to his duties as an officer in the militia, and many of the remainder to attend the law courts in London.

One of the principal causes of absence was the cost of almost constant residence throughout the year. Studentships were not especially lucrative, and in the eighteenth century, when Students tended to equate their social standing with that of the wealthy Gentlemen Commoners, were inadequate for the provision of a comparable standard of living. Students' incomes are not easily calculated and varied greatly according to seniority. In common with other colleges, Christ Church did not derive its income from the rack-renting of its estates but from fines at the renewal of leases and from antient rents. These were the benefits which accrued from the system of 'beneficial' leases: the major part of the economic value of the estate was retained by the lessee or his tenant. In the eighteenth century, renewal fines were normally based on a recent valuation and reflected the actual value of a property, but the income from this source the Dean and Chapter understandably chose to divide amongst themselves. During the sixteenth century, the antient rents, which were paid by the beneficial lessee, lost much of their value owing to inflation. They were fixed rents because the outgoings charged on college revenues, amongst which were Students' stipends, were also fixed, and because colleges did not have the machinery to renegotiate them. So impoverished had colleges become in the reign of Queen Elizabeth that Parliament required a third of the customary rents to be converted into corn rents and the proceeds paid to Fellows and Scholars.[1] These rents were known as the improved rents. The Act operated so that a third of the money rent in 1576 was assessed as quantities of wheat and malt which were subsequently valued yearly according to the price of grain certified by the clerk of the market. In 1756, for which year exact figures of the distribution of the improved rents survive, a Senior Master received £53. 2s. 8d. from improved rents, and £5. 6s. 8d. from his fixed stipend and livery. From the Senior Masters' estate at Chatteris in Cambridgeshire he derived a further £6. 10s. 0d. His total income from these sources was thus £64. 19s. 4d. If he was Censor he received a further £7. 10s. 0d. a year plus other minor emoluments; if lecturer in rhetoric £5; if lecturer in Greek £2. 13s. 4d. To these sums he might add the meagre income of a curacy in or near Oxford. He also had his commons and, unless he chose to live in certain rented rooms in the new Peckwater quadrangle, free chambers. If on top of this he was a tutor his income might be augmented considerably.[2] Students of less seniority had to be satisfied with a smaller share of the improved rents and a smaller stipend and livery. Christ Church was wealthier than other colleges and, owing to the impact of the Agricultural Revolution in the eighteenth century, the improved rents appreciated, but on the other hand the size of the foundation, with 101 Students, was larger than that of any other college. Nevertheless, the income of the senior Students seems to have been greater than that, for example, of the Fellows of All Souls, and, although information on this point is scanty, not greatly different from that common in most colleges,[3] where the cost of residence also created problems.

Although not always successful in enforcing residence, the Chapter insisted that degrees should be taken once the statutory residential qualifications had been obtained. Should a Student then fail to seek a grace, a monition was published in Hall, and if

[1] 18 Eliz. I, c. 6.
[2] See p. 231.
[3] Sutherland and Mitchell, *History of the University of Oxford*, v, 238.

that was ignored expulsion followed.[1] Monitions in these circumstances were not uncommon between 1725 and 1760, but ceased when Cyril Jackson expelled two Students for not taking their BA and two more for not taking their MA. The Chapter's insistence on graduation once statutory residence had accumulated, without equal insistence on *continuity* of residence, meant that although a Student might be deprived for omitting to take his degree when qualified to do so he was seldom deprived because of his non-residence, and there are some remarkable instances of Studentships being retained for long periods, and their emoluments received, without their occupants proceeding to a degree. Philip Twysden, who matriculated in 1696, had not acquired sufficient residence for his BA by 1701, but in that year he ceased residence altogether yet kept his Studentship until 1711. An even more arresting example was provided by the case of Sidney Evelyn, an otherwise unremarkable member of the diarist's family, who resided for two years after matriculating in 1736, and then absented himself from the college for twelve years, during which period he did not take a degree being unqualified to do so. Arthur Trevor, who took his BA in 1698, had not taken his MA when he was deprived in 1708, and Richard Stewart, to whom the Chapter Book attributed a BA in 1699, had no MA when he was deprived ten years later. Despite their non-residence, however, Evelyn, Trevor, and Stewart moved inexorably up the list of Students by virtue of seniority, and eventually all three were deprived because, having become Theologi, they declined to take holy orders. But for the necessity of taking orders on becoming a Theologus, and provided that he did not marry, it would seem that a Student could in theory retain his Studentship for life without taking a degree, if he avoided accumulating sufficient residence and satisfied the Chapter that his absence did not predicate his mortality.

Of the Students who left the university without having accumulated the statutory residence necessary for a degree up to the last decade of the eighteenth century, a not inconsiderable proportion

[1] A specimen monition, dated 26 Sept. 1747, is contained in Ch. Ch. Archives, Estates 146, fo. 4.

did so when they were within a term or so of acquiring it. The reasons for this practice can only be surmised. For some Students it perhaps meant the avoidance of university dues paid at examination and of the increasingly irrelevant exercises expected from Determining Bachelors. For others, as has been suggested, the possession of a degree, if not a matter of indifference, was of small practical value. A degree, for example, was not the essential prerequisite of ordination for those entering the Church. Some clergymen had no degree at all, and many more had a BA but no MA. To Students from wealthy or socially prominent backgrounds, a liberal education was one thing, and was obtained by attending the course of studies at Christ Church, but a degree was an unnecessary qualification and perhaps even a badge of servitude.

Only a handful of Students failed to take their degrees for reasons other than absence, resignation, or deprivation. A few migrated. Of these a tiny minority went to Cambridge, where the degree of MA was more easily obtained than in Oxford, but this was always a very rare event at Christ Church, particularly after the expulsion of William Ellis in 1670 for accepting a degree at Cambridge while in attendance on the Prince of Orange, despite the personal intercession of the Prince on his behalf. Of the remainder who migrated, the majority went to All Souls in order to study law, but migration to any other college was practically unknown.[1]

Although, in the matter of residence, there were long periods

[1] Apart from those who went to All Souls, the only Student to migrate to another Oxford college during this period was Robert Leyborn, who was elected a Fellow of Brasenose in 1715. In his case special circumstances existed, for his uncle by marriage was Robert Shippen, Principal of Brasenose, and the advantages of such a relationship outweighed those of a Westminster Studentship. Migration entailed the loss of a Studentship, though not in all cases in which a Headship was concerned. In 1726 John Wigan was made Principal of New Inn Hall but kept his Studentship until he married in 1739, even though he had been granted a year of grace on his appointment. In 1753 William Sharp was appointed Principal of Hertford College, which was almost a pocket borough of Christ Church, but he retained his Studentship until 1760, when he was instituted to the college living of Easthampstead. Bernard Hodgson was also appointed in Hertford but gave up his Studentship a year later, having received a year of grace on becoming vicar of Tolpuddle.

when the Dean and Chapter were remarkably tolerant of a long and comparatively unfruitful association with the university, they unhesitatingly expelled those Students, whether or not blessed with degrees, who did not take priest's orders on entering the ranks of the Theologi, the twenty most senior Students. In them was manifest the ultimate intention of Studentships as ecclesiastical offices. One of Dean Fell's early acts was to insist, after the laxity of the Commonwealth, that the Theologi took priest's orders,[1] and in 1678 George Walls complained to Locke that the Dean 'doth soe drive us into orders, that theres noe livinge without them, and lesse when wee have them'.[2] It was not enough to be in deacon's orders, and Charles Este, the editor of *Carmina Quadragesimalia* and later Bishop of Waterford, was one of many threatened with deprivation for not being in priest's orders. During the eighteenth century, almost 10 per cent of the Students were deprived because they were not ordained, and others no doubt resigned rather than face the inevitability of expulsion. Amongst those who were deprived was James Bruce, who was removed from his Studentship on 12 July 1798 and became thereby the only Student to be deprived posthumously, having been drowned two days before. The restriction of the twenty senior Studentships to those who were in priest's orders was beneficial to Christ Church because it accelerated the turnover of Students. In the ordinary course of events, every Student eventually became a Theologus and was then obliged to take orders. If he wished to remain a layman or to pursue a secular career, he was unable to retain his Studentship.[3]

It was not necessary for a Student to wait until he was a Theologus before taking holy orders—the status of Theologus merely defined the time beyond which a decision could not be deferred. Having taken orders, a Student was forbidden, under pain of deprivation, by a Chapter resolution on 6 February 1639 to take a benefice outside the university worth more than £6. 13s. 4d. in the King's Book, or more than 30 miles from

---

[1] Chapter Act Book, 24 Dec. 1664.
[2] Locke, *Correspondence*, i, no. 409.
[3] This did not of course apply to the Faculty Students.

Oxford without the permission of the Chapter granted 'ab anno in annum'. The original intention of this regulation, which no doubt repeated earlier regulations, was to promote a learned clergy by encouraging Students to reside in Oxford in order to study for the higher degrees in divinity. Because it encouraged residence, the Librarian was excluded from the regulation, since the nature of his duties required almost continual residence, and in 1758 the Wake Librarian was allowed a similar dispensation. The strict rules of residence were relaxed, however, in favour of those Students who held from the Dean and Chapter benefices which had formerly been served by Osney Abbey or St Frideswide's Priory. A small number of these monastic livings had been given to Christ Church at the foundation, and because their spiritual needs had been met without prolonged absence from the mother house they were very poor and almost destitute of endowments. The livings in this category most frequently held by Students were St Mary Magdalen and St Thomas in the city of Oxford, and Binsey, Cowley, and Drayton in the county of Oxford. Permanent employment with cure of souls in parishes which were not under the eye of the Dean and Chapter was not allowed with a Studentship, and since *institution* conferred such permanent employment, institution became the test of what was allowed and what not. Preferment which did not require institution, such as archdeaconries, certain prebends, or sinecures, was tenable with a Studentship. When in the nineteenth century donatives and perpetual curacies, which had been held at the pleasure of the nominator, became benefices, and the power of removal except through the ecclesiastical courts was taken away, the bishop's licence was regarded as the equivalent of institution, thus giving the donee or perpetual curate a permanent cure of souls and thereby removing the grounds on which the loss of Studentships had previously been avoided.

On taking a living, a Student forfeited his Studentship from the date of institution, unless a year of grace had been granted, in which case forfeiture dated from the expiry of the period of grace.[1]

---

[1] The year of grace should not be confused with the grace for a degree.

Fell explained the system of graces to Sunderland in 1684. 'It is our constant method', he wrote, 'that when any of our society has a living with cure of souls, though the acceptance thereof forfeits all right among us, yet to allow the benefit of twelve months' stay in consideration of the charge of first fruits and other incidental expenses, commonly called a year of grace.'[1] Students who entered a secular profession were not entitled to a year of grace, though on one occasion in 1761 when the Dean was absent the Chapter so far forgot why graces were given that it voted one to Dr William Spry, a lawyer and Faculty Student and thus a layman.[2] A month later, reinforced this time by the presence of the Dean, the Chapter ordered that Spry's case should not be taken as a precedent and reaffirmed the traditional view that graces were awarded only on the obtainment of a curacy for life or on institution to a benefice.

At one time it was possible for a Student to receive several graces in succession. In his letter to Sunderland on the subject of graces, Fell noted that John Gaches had been given three separate years of grace and added that further indulgence might follow. In 1694 David Jones was instituted to the college living of Budworth, in Cheshire. He did not surrender his Studentship, but in 1696 gave up the living and returned to Christ Church. Three years later he was instituted to the college living at Marcham, and on 20 October 1699 the grant of a year of grace was recorded in the Sub-Dean's Book. It was no doubt with this case in mind that on the following day the Chapter passed a decree

that whosoever shall accept of a preferment or benefice from this House under the common seal, or from any other patron whereby his place may be avoyded by the rules and customs of the House his place is immediately voydable. And that no man have a year of grace unless requested from the Dean and Chapter. And that to such as request it a year of grace may be granted, but not above one year of grace to any person upon any account whatsoever.[3]

---

[1] *Cal. SP Dom. 1684–5*, 211.
[2] Chapter Act Book, 20 Nov. 1761.
[3] Chapter Act Book, 21 Oct. 1699.

The Chapter's bold words were not accompanied by much resolution. Thus in 1701 Robert Bourne obtained the college living of Chalgrove, but, having entered his year of grace, asked permission to quit it and return to Christ Church. The Chapter agreed to his return on condition that he gave up any future claim to a college living which might be sought by another Student and that no further year of grace was allowed to him. Nevertheless, when he took another living in 1706, the Chapter allowed him a year of grace 'as has bin usual for other Students of this House to have, any act or order of the Chapter to ye contrary notwithstanding'. In 1709 the Chapter repealed the clause in its decree of 1699 which forbade the grant of more than one grace in any circumstances, but by then the practice of granting more than one was almost if not quite obsolete. There were good reasons for disallowing more than one grace. If a Student who had received a grace returned to the college it would be necessary to restore him to his position of seniority on the Student roll, an act of legerdemain which might cause resentment amongst those dispossessed. There was a further reason for discouraging the grant of additional graces, for according to Nicholas Amhurst it was a practice which clogged the succession.

When a college-living falls, [he wrote] the person chosen to succeed (who is usually the senior-fellow of the college, or if he refuses it, the next senior) is allow'd a year of grace (as it is call'd) at the end of which he must resign either his living or his fellowship, as he thinks best; but, at present several persons make use of this indulgence to pocket up a little money: they accept of livings, which they do not intend to keep any longer than one year; when, having received the revenues of that year, they throw it up to the next, who perhaps does the same.[1]

He added that he had heard of one college where it was common for a living to descend in this way until all the Fellows had had a year's income and the last to receive it was obliged to serve it. The college which adopted this ingenious expedient was not Christ Church.

Throughout the period, the Church remained the principal

---

[1] Amhurst, *Terrae Filius*, 212.

vocation of Students. During the eighteenth century at least 60 per cent of them took holy orders, and of these two-thirds resigned their Studentships on taking a living. Many of the remainder lost their Studentships when they married, which often coincided with taking a living. Christ Church was an ample patron and possessed almost ninety livings scattered widely throughout the country. Whenever one of them fell vacant, a notice stating its value was put up in Hall, and the Students were permitted to apply for it in order of seniority. Many of the livings were very poor. In 1778 the Dean and Chapter made a survey of their patronage in response to the Act to Promote the Residence of the Parochial Clergy (17 Geo. III, c. 53). It revealed that fourteen livings were worth less than £50 a year, and a large number of the rest less than £100. Many were neglected and squalid. Ardington, it was reported, was so impoverished that the vicar had not resided for fifty years, 'the necessary consequence of its being an appendage to some better preferment'.[1] At Slapton, the rector had not resided for more than two months during the summer for the previous thirty years, and William Holwell, a former Junior Censor, wrote that what Dean Gregory used to say of Semley was true, namely, that Semley was in the sink of Wiltshire and the parsonage house in the sink of Semley.[2] At Drayton it was reported that the vicarage was habitually used as a poor house by the parish officers.[3] Not unnaturally many Students preferred to take livings more affluent than those in the patronage of the Dean and Chapter.

Since the patronage at the disposal of the Dean and Chapter was offered to the Students in order of seniority, there was a tendency for the richer livings to be claimed by the more senior members of the college. None of the livings, however, was sufficiently well endowed to tempt a Student to remain in the university for the sake of succeeding to it unless he also had some other reason to reside. Students who took the poorer college livings worth up to £100 a year usually did so soon after taking the degree of MA, and thus generally held their Studentships for

---

[1] Ch. Ch. Archives, Estates 2, fo. 26ᵛ.
[2] Ch. Ch. Archives, Estates 30, fo. 145.
[3] Ch. Ch. Archives, Estates 71, fo. 329.

seven or eight years. About half the Students who obtained livings from patrons other than the Dean and Chapter did likewise. Students appointed to the slightly better livings worth up to about £150 a year held their Studentships in the eighteenth century for an average of thirteen years, and those who bided their time for the small number of livings which exceeded this amount might expect to hold them for about twenty years. Of the most valuable of the Christ Church livings, about half were acquired by gift or purchase in the seventeenth and eighteenth centuries. By a curious historical accident, Staverton in Northamptonshire, which was the most valuable of all the livings, was one of these. It had formed part of the endowment of St Frideswide's Priory, but had not been given to Christ Church after the Dissolution and was not acquired until the eighteenth cetury. In 1778 it was worth £400 a year, derived mainly from 344 acres of recently enclosed land. It was confined to Westminster Students. The Censors and lecturers in rhetoric and Greek, whose tenure of their Studentships tended to be lengthy, did not show a marked preference for college livings, and half of them took livings from other patrons than Christ Church. Thus, although the majority of Students still entered the Church in the eighteenth century, the intention of the founders that the college should serve as a seminary for the livings in its patronage was abandoned owing to the poverty of most of them.

The Librarian of Christ Church was not the only Student allowed to retain his Studentship with a living. On two occasions in the eighteenth century, this privilege was extended to successful tutors whom the college did not wish to lose. In the first case Edward Smallwell was allowed to retain his Studentship with the living of Batsford in 1767 'by special favour ... in consideration of his uncommon trouble and great diligence in placing and making catalogues of the books in Peckwater library'.[1] Smallwell had also been Senior Censor for six years and an active tutor for much longer. The second case was that of James Chelsum, who was allowed to keep his Studentship with the vicarage of Lathbury

[1] Chapter Act Book, 23 Dec. 1767.

in 1773 as a reward for executing 'a very useful plan of lectures in divinity', and as an encouragement to him as tutor, catechist, and praelector.[1]

A Student was obliged to resign his Studentship on marriage, but marriage was seldom noted in the college records as the cause of forfeiture, owing to the system of graces. Students often married when they left the university for a parish, but it was to their advantage to vacate their Studentships on institution rather than on marriage because if they did so they were entitled to a year of grace. The eighteenth century saw an increase, albeit a small one, in the number of Studentships vacated specifically by marriage. It was a consequence of the increased age at which undergraduates entered the university, but it occurred most frequently at about the time of taking the degree of MA, and was often an indication that a Student had entered one of the lay professions, which carried no entitlement to a year of grace. The Dean and Chapter sometimes experienced difficulty in discovering whether a Student was married or not. The responsibility for informing them lay with the Student himself. When Canning married, his old tutor Phineas Pett sent him a gentle reminder. 'It is customary', he wrote, 'for a Student upon marriage to acquaint them with the day upon which it has taken place, in order that the Studentship may be declared vacant. The regular wa[y] of proceeding is to write to the Subdean.'[2] Most Students were prompt in informing the Chapter, but constant vigilance was necessary. On one unfortunate occasion the Chapter acted precipitately on information received, and on 14 July 1737 summoned three Students before it charged with concealing their marriages. It transpired that one of them was indeed married, but another solemnly denied that he was or ever had been married, and the third, John Bertie, boldly 'refus'd to answer to the question whether he was marry'd or not but desir'd to know who inform'd against him'.

Finally among the causes for the fortfeiture of Studentships

---

[1] Ibid., 6 Jan. 1773.
[2] Leeds Public Libraries, Canning Papers, Pett to G. Canning, 27 July n.y.

were disciplinary offences. Most often these were repeated violence
or serious disobedience to the college authorities. Despite his
reputation as a stern disciplinarian, Dean Fell is known to have
expelled only three Students. Among them was Nicholas Brady,
the author with Nahum Tate of a famous metrical version of the
Psalms, who was expelled in 1682 for some unknown offence. At
the same time Thomas Cooper lost his Studentship when he was
'caught with a wench at Alsop's house ye bedmaker who has used
the trade of a procurer a greate while and is now turned out of
his employ in ye colledge'.[1] In 1674 a Student was expelled for
wounding with a sword several persons at St Alban Hall when
disordered with drink. On the other hand, in 1664 two Students
were ordered to be expelled, but had their sentences suspended,
for fighting when drunk, climbing out of college, abusing visitors,
killing a sow belonging to a poor woman and for other 'intolerable
misdemeanours'. One of them, William Levett, sufficiently over-
came his youthful indiscretions to become Principal of New Inn
Hall.

In an outbreak of lawlessness in the 1690s several graduate
Students were deprived. A Student named Augustine Spalding,
who had taken his MA in 1686, accused Smalridge, the future
Dean, who was then a tutor and lecturer in Greek, of opening his
letters, fought with him in the quadrangle, called him rascal in
the presence of his pupils, emptied chamber-pots over a bedmaker
named Mary Gristie on two occasions, swore felonies against
three Students of unblemished character, and was, not surprisingly
in view of his other activities, unable to perform his exercises. He
was twice admonished by the Dean and then confined to his room,
where, with more wit than wisdom, 'hee in contempt of his
punishment had hung a bag out of his chamber as the prisoners
do at Bocardo'. He met with expulsion in 1693. In the following
year, Edmund Smith, the author of *Phaedra and Hippolitus* and
many fugitive pieces famous in their day, was admonished 'in
order to his expulsion', having earlier been 'degraded for his
scandalous and profligate behaviour'. He survived the threat of

[1] Bodl. MS Tanner 305, fo. 141, Th. Burton to H. Prideaux, 10 Dec. [1682].

expulsion again in 1700, when he was summoned before the Chapter for riotous behaviour, but was finally removed from his Studentship in 1705 for lampooning the Dean. In 1695 a Student Master was suspended from the benefits of his Studentship for six months, confined to the Library, and required to read the metaphysics of Suarez, as a punishment for beating the college porter.

During the whole of the eighteenth century only two graduate Students were expelled. One of these was turned out in 1742, having previously been suspended from taking his degree for a year and later admonished for threats and violence to the college porter and for forcing his way out of college. He was gated until he had translated the first volume of Stanyan's *Greek History*, but he continued to defy the Chapter by missing prayers, going out of college, sleeping at public houses twice, and not delivering 'so much as one line of the imposition' until patience was exhausted. The other expulsion of a graduate Student was of the Lee lecturer in Anatomy, William Thomson, who was deprived in 1790 for gross immorality committed in the interests of science.[1] Offences against sexual morality were seldom regarded as a hanging matter. A few months after Thomson was expelled from his Studentship, Charles Sandby, also a graduate Student, was summoned before the Chapter because 'an illicit connection had for some time past subsisted between Mr Sandby ... and a woman now resident in the parish of Fritwell'. When Sandby admitted the truth of the charges, the Chapter decided to suspend sentence of expulsion on condition that he surrendered his curacy, did not officiate as a clergyman for three years, and resided outside the dioceses of Oxford and Worcester in a place appointed by the Dean and Chapter and under the eye of a suitable guardian. In 1795 Sandby was presented to the college living of Netherswell in Gloucestershire.

Undergraduate Students were expelled on a number of occasions during the eighteenth century, usually after repeated offence which included acts of violence. Even for Richard James,

[1] See p. 316.

an undergraduate Westminster Student, who on 10 June 1750, 'in violation of his Duty to his Majesty and to the Great Scandal of this House', gave a dinner to celebrate the Pretender's birthday and proposed his health, expulsion was the climax to other mis-demeanours. The Chapter order depriving him states that he had 'for a long time behaved very irregularly, and not been reformed either by the admonitions of his tutor or the censures of the college officers'. After the famous dinner, he had forced his way out of college at a very late hour by threatening to kill the porter, and had ignored a *moneo* of the Dean and Chapter summoning him to appear before them. His accomplices, who were two other Westminster undergraduate Students named Ralph Barnes and William Sealy, were dealt with more leniently. Both were ordered to deliver a penitential speech in Hall and were confined to college for six months, except on Sundays and holy days, when they were accorded the privilege of attending the university sermons, and Barnes was in addition required to spend the first three months of his sentence 'in the college library during all the studying hours' in a course of study directed by the Dean. This outbreak of juvenile treason did not pass unnoticed by the government, and the alacrity with which Dean Conybeare suppressed it may have contributed to his appointment to the Bishopric of Bristol later in the year. 'It is reckon'd the Dean and Chapter of Xt Church have done well', Henry Pelham wrote. 'They expell'd James, who is said to be the ring-leader, and did not appear upon summons. They have inflicted punishment on the rest in an academical way.'[1]

Despite the government's nervousness, this expression of Jaco-bitism was not of political importance but an indication that discipline at Christ Church was at a low ebb. On 23 December 1749 the Dean and Chapter issued a dire warning in the following resolution:

Whereas there have been of late several Disturbances in Christ Church at unseasonable hours to the Great Prejudice of Discipline and of the

---

[1] BL Add. MS 32721, fo. 196, H. Pelham to the Duke of Newcastle, 28 June 1750.

Reputation of this Place, These are to caution young men against any such Excesses for the future and to assure them that whoever shall be found Guilty of such Practices hereafter shall be punished with Great Severity and be obliged to discover his accomplices under pain of immediate Expulsion.

In 1748 a Student Bachelor had been punished for 'great Irreverence & Disobedience to the Subdean & to the Dean and Canons', and the order for the expulsion of James was in fact preceded by the punishment of another Bachelor Student for the intriguing offence of 'great Negligence & Irregularity & of notorious Prevarication before the Chapter'. Neither the fulminations of the Dean and Chapter nor the fate of Richard James immediately restored order to Christ Church. Barnes and Sealy had shared with James the offence of celebrating the Pretender's birthday, but unlike him they had not previously lapsed from grace. Nemesis, however, was waiting in the wings, and in the following year both of them were involved with another Student named William Oliver, son of the inventor of the Bath Oliver biscuit, in a notorious riot at the New Inn. Barnes was expelled having been accused of 'entering forcibly into a gentlewoman's bedchamber there ... and assaulting the said gentlewoman in a very indecent and scandalous manner as she was lying in her bed'. Sealy escaped more lightly with another penitential speech and suspension from his degree for a year, but after nursing his wounds for a month he resigned his Studentship. William Oliver was expelled. For him it was a second offence, for in 1750 he had been summoned before the Chapter for neglecting his duties notwithstanding the censures of his tutor and of the college officers, and for violence to another Student, and was sentenced to be rusticated for a year 'during which time he is to prepare carefully the usual Collections and to employ himself in studies at the Dean's direction'.[1] Thus within the space of two years three

---

[1] In his letter to Newcastle quoted above, Pelham states that Oliver was present at the Pretender's dinner. There is no mention of his complicity in the college records or in the punishment meted out to him on 19 June 1750.

undergraduate Students were expelled from Christ Church. It was enough to restore a semblance of discipline.[1]

The disciplining of Students, the imposition of punishments, and the decision whether or not to expel rested with the Dean and Chapter. From time to time the Censors were involved, but as accusers rather than as judges. In 1718, for example, the Dean and Chapter expelled Edward Taswell, who had been accused by Henry Gregory, the Junior Censor, of excessive and bitter swearing. Both Censors appeared before the Chapter to testify that Taswell's continuance in the college would endanger the morals of the youths committed to their charge.[2] Sometimes the Censors were involved as the victims of undergraduate outrage. In 1760 Thomas Penrose was rusticated for climbing out of college with ropes, abusing the porter, breaking the Censor's windows, and showing rudeness to the Dean. Two years later he was deprived of this Studentship for 'a long course of irregularities', and for

[1] The state of the Young Pretender's health was not a matter of great concern at Christ Church, and, except where it served as a means for the Students to taunt their severely Whiggish masters, Jacobite sentiment was seldom more than an expression of youthful bravado. It was most voluble in the years after the Hanoverian Succession, and in 1716 David Wilkins reported that the health of the Duke of Ormonde, who had sought to raise the west country for the Old Pretender, was openly drunk in Christ Church Hall (Lambeth Palace Library, MS 2686, fo. 129ᵛ). Jacobite sentiment was kept alive by the Westminster connection even after the impeachment of Atterbury. In 1751 an attempt was made to discredit William Murray, the future Lord Mansfield, by reviving the story that as a schoolboy at Westminster he had toasted the Pretender in the house of a Jacobite draper in Cheapside, accompanied by Andrew Stone and James Johnson, both of whom with Murray himself became Westminster Students soon afterwards. The charge was even the subject of a debate in the House of Lords in 1753. On that occasion George Stone, the brother of Andrew, wrote to Lord George Sackville that 'the Pretender's health was frequently drank at Oxford ... It was gone from Christchurch and under discouragement there before our time. Murray's case is particularly hard, for I well remember that the Jacobites of Oxford used to speak of him with resentment and abhorence' (HMC, *Stopford-Sackville* (1904), I, 192). James Johnson became Under Master at Westminster in 1733, and in 1752 was described as a High Tory 'devilishly belied if he has not a deal of the old leaven in him yet' (*Memoirs of a Royal Chaplain, 1729–1763: the Correspondence of Edmund Pyle*, ed. A. Hartshorne (1905), 181). Perhaps James, Barnes, and Sealy celebrated a tradition they had learnt at the feet of their old preceptor.
[2] Ch. Ch. Archives, Sub-Dean's Book, liii.b. 4, fo. 54ᵛ.

absence contrary to an express order 'when he had two crosses upon his name'. The last occasion on record[1] in the eighteenth century when undergraduate Students were actually expelled was in 1778 and arose from threats of physical violence to the college officers. John Soley and John Scriven were put out, 'having in a most daring manner in defiance of the authority of this House attacked the Masters' Common Room, broke into it and committed several outrages there, having attempted to break into the Rhetorick Reader's room with declared purpose of violence against his person and thereby put him in fear of his life'. The unfortunate Rhetoric Reader was Cyril Jackson's brother William. But the most celebrated disciplinary case in which the college officers were involved occurred in 1767, when William Shipley was expelled for casting doubt in print on their impartiality and competence in awarding the Certamen. Shipley appealed to the Visitor, and the Lord Chancellor ruled that the punishment was too severe. He was restored and kept his Studentship until 1771. The Lord Chancellor's judgement is of considerable interest for its definition of the rights of Students to their Studentships, and of the limits to the Dean and Chapter's power as the Governing Body of Christ Church. The Students, it declared, 'had always been considered as possessed of the same general rights with the Fellows of other foundations, holding their Studentships as their freeholds and not liable to be deprived of them without just and legal cause'. What was just and legal was not defined, but in practice it included the deprivation of Students for failing to take their degrees, for receiving institution to a living, for omitting to take holy orders, for marriage, and for miscalculating the tolerance of the Dean and Chapter in matters of discipline. The Student's right to his freehold, it may be noted, had not saved Locke in 1684 when it was in conflict with the superior right of the royal prerogative.

---

[1] Cyril Jackson ensured that offenders departed without the stigma of expulsion. See p. 81.

(*e*) MATRICULATION

There is no single record from which a complete list of the members of Christ Church may be compiled. The magnitude of Joseph Foster's achievement in the *Alumni Oxonienses*, which is based on the university registers, is not diminished by the need to augment the information in the university records by the college records, and particularly by the Battel and Caution Books and the Deans' Registers of matriculations. None of these records at Christ Church is complete in itself. Members of the college may, for example, be discovered in the Battel or Caution Books who eluded the Deans' Registers or the university registers, and others may be found in the Deans' Registers but not in the university registers and vice versa. Such discrepancies occur throughout the period but most frequently during the seventeenth century. The Laudian statutes required colleges to keep registers of admissions, but at Christ Church there is no evidence that such a register was kept until the Restoration, and for some years afterwards it was compiled with considerable irregularity. Between 1660 and 1663 almost fifty undergraduates are entered in the university register but not in the Dean's Register.

When undergraduates were admitted to Christ Church they were entered in the Dean's Register of admissions and in the Battel Books according to their status as Noblemen, Gentlemen Commoners, Commoners, or Servitors, but in the university registers status was indicated only indirectly by the amount of fees paid. The college records are more reliable than the university registers as a record of status because the circumstances of admission to the college made deception impossible, whereas on matriculation in the university an undergraduate might pay the lower fees due from a Commoner but enter Christ Church as a Gentleman Commoner, or he might pay the university dues of a Servitor and seek admission to Christ Church as a Commoner. Although such malpractices were not widely imitated they occur sufficiently often for the university registers to be treated with caution as a source for the status of undergraduates unless confirmed by the college records. The Battel Books are a trustworthy source for determining status because the entries were usually made by the Dean in person and undergraduates were listed according to the manner in which the various orders were seated in Hall, but they are inconvenient to use and for most practical purposes the Deans' Registers are to be preferred.

In Table III. 1 statistics of undergraduates admitted to Christ Church between 1660 and 1800 are arranged by calendar year.[1]

TABLE III.1. Annual Statistics of Matriculation

Year of admission	Westminster Students	Noblemen	Gentlemen Commoners	Commoners[a]	Servitors[a]	Total
1660	0	2	10	20 (7)	6	38
1661	9	2	4	25 (6)	3	43
1662	6	1	10	23 (6)	10 (1)	50
1663	5	2	4	22 (4)	8	41
1664	5	6	8	26 (5)	15	60
1665	4	2	8	18 (1)	15	47
1666	5	2	14	29 (4)	21	71
1667	5	1	12	19 (3)	16	53
1668	4	4	13	11 (1)	10	42
1669	3	2	8	22 (2)	13	48
1670	5	1	10	18 (2)	8 (1)	42
1671	3	1	7	18 (4)	14	43
1672	3	3	11	13 (2)	9	39
1673	5	4	9	28 (4)	12	58
1674	5	3	7	19 (2)	8	42
1675	4	6	8	13 (3)	7	38
1676	4	1	8	19 (5)	5	37
1677	3	3	9	15 (3)	6	36
1678	4	5	6	24 (6)	7	46
1679	3	6	9	19 (3)	13	50
1680	4	8	7	20 (6)	8	47
1681	4	2	5	12 (1)	9	32
1682	5	2	6	17 (1)	5	35
1683	4	1	6	16 (1)	8	35
1684	3	1	7	9 (4)	6	26
1685	3	2	10	19 (4)	6	40
1686	4	1	9	22 (5)	9	45
1687	4	0	2	8 (1)	3	17
1688	4	2	2	11 (5)	8	27
1689	5	1	3	15 (1)	4	28
1690	4	4	2	13 (4)	6	29
1691	4	1	9	19 (4)	1	34

[1] There is often a wide discrepancy between the date of entry at Christ Church in the Dean's Register and the date of matriculation in the university register. In the following statistics the former has been preferred.

Year of admission	Westminster Students	Noblemen	Gentlemen Commoners	Commoners[a]	Servitors[a]	Total
1692	4	1	2	9	6	22
1693	4	1	10	7 (2)	10	32
1694	5	1	6	18 (3)	5	35
1695	4	1	5	14 (1)	5	29
1696	4	0	5	18 (2)	5	32
1697	4	1	6	20 (4)	9	40
1698	3	1	7	12 (2)	6	29
1699	4	2	5	11	5	27
1700	3	1	11	8 (4)	3	26
1701	4	1	3	12 (2)	9	29
1702	5	1	10	18 (3)	4	38
1703	4	5	12	11 (6)	3	35
1704	4	3	12	14 (6)	9	42
1705	4	4	13	7	7	35
1706	4	2	8	8 (4)	4	26
1707	5	2	7	16 (4)	6	36
1708	4	3	7	11 (2)	8	33
1709	4	2	5	18 (4)	5	34
1710	5	2	3	13 (2)	6	29
1711	3	1	3	18 (1)	7	32
1712	5	2	9	21 (3)	8	45
1713	7	3	8	16 (2)	7	41
1714	5	5	7	22 (4)	7	46
1715	4	2	3	18 (4)	5	32
1716	5	2	11	13 (4)	6	37
1717	5	2	10	14 (4)	6	37
1718	4	2	3	13 (3)	9	31
1719	4	3	6	22 (8)	8	43
1720	4	1	9	19 (7)	5	38
1721	4	0	7	17 (4)	7	35
1722	4	2	9	20 (5)	4	39
1723	4	1	5	13	7	30
1724	4	0	7	13 (4)	6	30
1725	4	3	8	17 (7)	7	39
1726	5	3	6	15 (1)	9	38
1727	4	1	5	8 (2)	6	24
1728	4	1	8	20 (5)	6	39
1729	4	1	8	17 (4)	4	34
1730	4	2	5	17 (4)	9	37
1731	5	2	3	13 (4)	5	28
1732	4	1	6	13 (2)	9	33
1733	4	1	3	9 (1)	4	21
1734	4	1	3	18 (7)	11	37
1735	4	2	5	14 (4)	3	28
1736	4	1	5	8 (1)	9	27
1737	5	0	8	17 (5)	7	37
1738	4	0	1	10 (1)	8	23
1739	4	1	2	12 (6)	7	26
1740	4	3	1	11 (4)	7	26
1741	4	0	3	13 (5)	3	23

Year of admission	Westminster Students	Noblemen	Gentlemen Commoners	Commoners[a]	Servitors[a]	Total
1742	5	1	2	8 (6)	4	20
1743	4	0	6	10 (6)	12	32
1744	4	1	6	8 (4)	8	27
1745	4	4	6	9 (3)	7	30
1746	4	0	4	16 (3)	5	29
1747	4	1	5	5 (4)	4	19
1748	5	0	5	(5)	8	23
1749	4	0	4	7 (6)	5	20
1750	4	0	4	13 (7)	4	25
1751	5	0	5	9 (4)	4	23
1752	3	0	5	6 (3)	4	18
1753	4	0	5	8 (3)	7	24
1754	5	0	6	8 (1)	4	23
1755	4	3	7	12 (2)	5	31
1756	4	2	4	8 (3)	8	26
1757	4	1	4	5 (3)	2	16
1758	4	1	6	6 (4)	3	20
1759	4	1	7	11 (6)	4	27
1760	5	1	10	15 (9)	5	36
1761	4	3	7	8 (6)	3	25
1762	4	2	7	8 (4)	4	25
1763	5	3	15	9 (6)	8	40
1764	4	2	10	17 (6)	2	35
1765	4	1	5	9 (5)	6	25
1766	4	0	6	10 (1)	3	23
1767	4	5	7	11 (4)	10	37
1768	4	3	17	16 (4)	2	42
1769	5	4	10	11 (1)	1	31
1770	3	1	6	14 (2)	6	30
1771	4	3	3	8 (4)	5	23
1772	5	0	6	18 (6)	4	33
1773	3	2	5	11 (7)	5	26
1774	4	1	8	14 (6)	4	31
1775	4	1	14	15 (6)	7	41
1776	5	3	4	17 (6)	3	32
1777	4	1	10	20 (7)	7	42
1778	4	2 (1)	10	28 (11)	4	48
1779	3	2	9	21 (5)	4	39
1780	5	1	3	16 (2)	2	27
1781	5	2	6	27 (3)	4	44
1782	5	0	5	27 (8)	2	39
1783	5	2	6	28 (8)	5	46
1784	4	5	8	26 (4)	4	47
1785	5	1	14	14 (2)	6	40
1786	4	0	11	24 (3)	5	44
1787	5	2	8	19 (3)	4	38
1788	5	0	14	24 (7)	4	47
1789	5	3	6	23 (5)	5	42
1790	5	5	10	28 (5)	8	56
1791	5	2	6	26 (7)	2	41

Year of admission	Westminster Students	Noblemen	Gentlemen Commoners	Commoners[a]	Servitors[a]	Total
1792	3	1	11	27 (6)	8	50
1793	3	2	9	18 (2)	2	34
1794	5	4	12	26 (1)	3	50
1795	4	5	10	26 (4)	2	47
1796	5	3	7	17 (1)	3	35
1797	3	3	12	29 (6)	0	47
1798	3	3	12	26 (4)	2	46
1799	4	1	13	31 (8)	2	51
1800	4	0	8	29 (4)	2	43

[a]Figures in brackets indicate totals of Commoners and Servitors subsequently elected to Studentships.

The Westminster Students are entered in the year of their matriculation, which was also that of their election. The Canoneer Students always entered as Commoners, apart from a small number entered as Servitors in the seventeenth century, and are noted in brackets under that head according to the date of their matriculation, which was not necessarily the year of nomination or election. Undergraduates who re-entered are included only in the year and category of their original admission. Thus a Gentleman Commoner who inherited a peerage and was thereby required to re-enter as a Nobleman, or a Commoner who re-entered as a Gentleman Commoner (a not uncommon practice in the 1740s and 1750s when the number of Commoners admitted was extremely small), are only included once. Commoner Bachelors and Masters, who incorporated, are excluded, but the dozen or so Gentlemen Commoners who were admitted with degrees between 1727 and 1769, usually from Trinity College, Dublin, are included in the totals of Gentlemen Commoners.

The rate of admission to Christ Church during the ten years after the Restoration was not equalled until the last decade of the eighteenth century, by which time the population of the country had greatly increased. The totals for admission for the years 1664, 1666, and 1673 indeed were not surpassed during the entire period. After the Revolution of 1688 the trend of admissions was downwards for the rest of the century as the university found

TABLE III.2. Decennial Averages for Matriculation

	Westminster Students	Noblemen	Gentlemen Commoners	Commoners	Servitors
1660–1669	4·6	2·4	9·1	21·5	11·7
1670–1679	3·9	3·3	8·4	18·6	8·9
1680–1689	4·0	2·0	5·7	14·9	6·6
1690–1699	4·0	1·3	5·7	14·1	5·8
1700–1709	4·1	2·4	8·8	12·3	5·8
1710–1719	4·7	2·4	6·3	17·0	6·9
1720–1729	4·1	1·3	7·2	15·9	6·1
1730–1739	4·2	1·1	4·1	13·1	7·2
1740–1749	4·2	1·0	4·2	8·7	6·3
1750–1759	4·1	0·8	5·3	8·6	4·5
1760–1769	4·3	2·4	9·4	11·4	4·4
1770–1779	3·9	1·6	7·5	16·6	4·9
1780–1789	4·8	1·6	8·1	22·8	4·1
1790–1799	4·0	2·9	10·2	25·4	3·2

itself in political opposition to court and government, but it recovered in the reign of Queen Anne, when there was a considerable increase in the matriculation of Noblemen and Gentlemen Commoners, and, after an interval, of Commoners. The Hanoverian Succession did not affect the rate of admission adversely at first, but early in the 1720s a decline set in which lasted until about 1760. This was a period when Christ Church tended to be avoided by the aristocracy and gentry. So great was the decline that the average number of admissions in the middle of the eighteenth century was little more than half of that at the Restoration. The first signs of revival appeared under Dean Gregory and began in earnest with the appointment of Markham, and it was a symbol of his influence that all five Noblemen admitted in 1767, the year in which he became Dean, were from Westminster. For the rest of the century the rate of admission for Gentlemen Commoners continued to rise, but was eventually overtaken by a large increase in the number of Commoners, which almost doubled between the accession of George III and the end of the century.

The average age of undergraduates at matriculation increased steadily between 1660 and 1800. Conspicuous amongst the causes of this trend was the rise in the number of those who received a public as opposed to a private education prior to entering the university. This seems to be confirmed by the fact that the only undergraduates whose average age remained almost unchanged were the Westminster Students, who enjoyed a public education throughout the period. They were usually eighteen or nineteen years old at the time of election. Between the Restoration and the accession of Queen Anne about half the Commoners were aged sixteen or seventeen, about a quarter eighteen, and the rest between thirteen and fifteen. By about 1730 the average age had risen to between seventeen and eighteen. Almost until the end of the century, however, very young Commoners continued to be admitted. When, for example, John Spry came up in 1778 he was a stripling of fourteen, and in Markham's time several undergraduate Commoners matriculated at fifteen. The average age of the Canoneer Students, who were always Commoners at matriculation, was the same as that of other Commoners, which meant that until quite late in the eighteenth century they were often younger than the Westminster Students. In the case of the Gentlemen Commoners there were wider variations in age compared with the Commoners. In the seventeenth century nearly twice as many Gentlemen Commoners as Commoners came up at fifteen, and in the following century they lagged behind the upward trend of the Commoners and tended to range between sixteen and nineteen. By the end of the eighteenth century, however, the average age of the Gentlemen Commoners levelled out and became indistinguishable from that of other undergraduates. A similar trend may be observed in the case of Noblemen. Servitors on the other hand were often older than other undergraduates, until late in the eighteenth century when the higher average age in Christ Church generally reduced the gap. Thus by the end of the eighteenth century differences in age between one group of undergraduates and another had almost disappeared, and the average age had reached the level of modern times.

While wide differences existed between the ages of undergraduates at matriculation, it was difficult to develop the plan of study. The improvement of the curriculum depended on undergraduates coming up to the university at roughly the same age and with a similar level of attainment. The traditional division of undergraduates into four *Classes*, which corresponded to the four years needed for a Bachelor's degree, was adapted for under- graduates of differing ages, and it continued to exist while these differences remained. The small tutorial class consisting of under- graduates of similar abilities, on which the improvement in the curriculum depended, could not develop while the system of *Classes* remained.

The impact of fluctuations in the rate of matriculation is less easy to assess. The numbers of undergraduates admitted often varied greatly in consecutive years. In 1727, for example, 24 undergraduates were admitted, but in the following year the number was 39. In 1762, there were 25 admissions, but in 1763 they rose to 40, while in 1793 and 1794 the numbers were 34 and 50 respectively. The *Classes*, which were intended mainly for oral exercises and disputations, absorbed such fluctuations without difficulty. Thus it was not necessary in the seventeenth and eight- eenth centuries to adopt the later practice of limiting the annual intake of undergraduates, except in so far as the available accom- modation imposed a natural limit, but, when the tutorial system was reformed in the latter part of the eighteenth century, wide variations in the annual intake would almost certainly have created difficulties but for the emergence of the private tutor and the increase in the average age at matriculation, which, because it was accompanied by a higher level of attainment, required less tutorial supervision. The development of the tutorial system was perhaps the main cause of a tendency for undergraduates to matriculate at the same time, or times, in the year. Until about 1786 it was common to matriculate throughout the year, but from that date, as the plan of studies and lectures became complex, there was a marked increase in the number to matriculate at the start of the academic year in October, or in January.[1]

---

[1] The development of the curriculum and tutorial system are discussed in more detail in later chapters.

(*f*) NOBLEMEN AND GENTLEMEN COMMONERS

In addition to Students, there were four categories of undergraduates at Christ Church, namely Noblemen, Gentlemen Commoners, Commoners, and Servitors. They enjoyed a similar
education but were distinguished socially one from another by
differences in academic dress, by separate tables in Hall, and to
some extent by the appropriation of particular sets of rooms.[1] In
the case of the sons of peers and other privileged undergraduates
the period of residence required for a degree was reduced by
statute. This hierarchical structure of undergraduate society
reflected that of society at large, and like it was based to a
considerable extent, but by no means solely, on economics. As in
the case of this wider society, the boundaries between the various
groups were not rigid, and often fused imperceptibly.

　　The term Nobleman was more loosely defined in the seventeenth than in the eighteenth century. Many of the Noblemen
who came to Christ Church in the time of Fell were baronets or
the sons of baronets. In 1744 Thomas Salmon wrote that 'Baronets
are esteem'd Noblemen here, and wear black Gowns trim'd with
Gold'.[2] They continued to be admitted as Noblemen until the
time of Dean Markham. In the latter part of the eighteenth
century, however, when Noblemen shared the general tendency
of undergraduates to come from richer and more elevated levels
of society, the franchise contracted and Noblemen became nobler.
Between Jackson's appointment in 1783 and 1800, sons of the
Dukes of Argyll, Leeds, Marlborough, Portland, and Somerset
were admitted to Christ Church as Noblemen, whereas in the time
of Fell the nearest approach to ducal rank, with the exception of
Charles II's bastard by the Countess of Castlemaine, was Ormonde's grandson. But however the order of Noblemen was defined,
there were often close ties of blood with the Gentlemen Commoners, some of whom were the younger brothers of those who
entered Christ Church as Noblemen. In 1664, for example, Sir
Richard Graham matriculated as a Nobleman, but when his

---

[1] See p. 241n.
[2] Salmon, *Present State of the Universities*, 422.

brother James came up two years later in 1666 he entered as a Gentleman Commoner. Charles Mordaunt, son of the first Viscount Mordaunt, came up as a Nobleman in 1674, but his brother Osmond followed as a Gentleman Commoner in 1686. Occasionally a Gentleman Commoner was obliged to re-enter as a Nobleman on inheriting a peerage or baronetcy. Thus in February 1675 Thomas Isham entered as a Gentleman Commoner, but when his father died in the following month he succeeded to the baronetcy and re-entered as a Nobleman in May. In the eighteenth century, Andrew Leslie, a younger son of the Earl of Rothes, who matriculated as a Gentleman Commoner in 1732, re-entered as a Nobleman in 1735, apparently for social rather than dynastic reasons. Such family relationships softened the social boundaries between Noblemen and Gentlemen Commoners.

Similarly the boundaries between Gentlemen Commoners and Commoners were far from inflexible. Unlike the Nobleman, whose rank identified him in society at all times, the Gentleman Commoner was not readily recognized. He existed in the university, but no one called himself a Gentleman Commoner outside its walls. Even within the university the term was loosely defined. Gentlemen Commoners were the sons of gentlemen and described themselves as such in the university registers, but the term gentleman was too imprecise to distinguish them from the Commoners. In the time of John Fell, over half the Commoners described themselves as the sons of gentlemen. Gentlemen Commoners were often the sons not only of gentlemen but of gentlemen who had consolidated their position in society by the assumption of arms. But this also applied to the Commoners, particularly in the latter part of the eighteenth century. Between 1783 and 1800, over 60 per cent of Commoners described their fathers as armigerous. Moreover, the distinction was not always observed within families between gentlemen who were armigerous and those who were not. In 1691 George Weld described his father as armigerous when admitted to Christ Church, but in 1695 his brothers Charles and Thomas described him simply as a gentleman. In Jackson's time a substantial number of Gentlemen Commoners were baronets or the younger sons of peers, but about a tenth of the

Commoners were also baronets or the sons of peers. The ties of blood which bound the Gentlemen Commoners to the Noblemen also bound them to the Commoners. Thus Arthur Kaye, the eldest son of Sir John Kaye, Bt., entered as a Gentleman Commoner in 1686, but his brothers George and Thomas came up as Commoners in 1690, and whereas Anthony Chester was admitted a Gentleman Commoner in 1679 his brother was a Commoner in 1686. In such cases, primogeniture no doubt decided whether to enter as a Gentleman Commoner or Commoner, but in very many instances the decision probably depended on economic circumstances. On the whole Gentlemen Commoners were distinguished from Commoners by superior wealth rather than by superior social status.

In all essentials the Noblemen and Gentlemen Commoners received the same education as other undergraduates, though many of them, oblivious of the feast prepared for their benefit, departed from the university inoculated against education and anaesthetized by the proximity of scholarship. They did not, however, always receive it *with* the rest of the college, and until the last quarter of the eighteenth century were taught separately from other undergraduates. This was not the effect of social exclusiveness, but reflected the fact that they tended to come up to the university younger and less well prepared than other undergraduates, and were permitted to take a degree, should they wish to do so, after a shorter and presumably less exacting period of study than was required of others. They did not take up Collections with the rest of the college but gave them to the Sub-Dean, and they were not placed in *Classes* with other undergraduates, though in 1652 the Chapter sought, with indifferent success, to require Gentlemen Commoners to perform the usual exercises of themes, declamations, and disputations with the Students.[1] When, in the eighteenth century, Noblemen and Gentlemen Commoners came increasingly from schools such as Westminster and Eton, where they had received the same education as other undergraduates from these schools, and when they

[1] Chapter Act Book, 24 Feb. 1652.

matriculated at the same age as other undergraduates, it was possible to integrate their education with that of the remainder of the college. This process began under Dean Gregory. His biographer relates that he was much concerned that Noblemen and Gentlemen Commoners pursued their studies privately in their chambers 'without ever coming forth and appearing in any public sort of exercise'.[1] He resolved to introduce some manly, useful, and agreeable exercise 'in which they should now and then make their public appearance. It was determined, therefore, that two, one on each side of the question, should, every week in Term time, declaim upon some Historical subject; that the Declamations should be written in the English language, and publicly recited in the Hall of Christ-Church'.[2] Integration of the studies of Noblemen and Gentlemen Commoners with the rest of the college was completed by Markham. These measures paved the way for Cyril Jackson's remarkable success in educating the Gentlemen Commoners, and contributed greatly to improving the character of education at Christ Church.

There were few inducements for Noblemen to take a degree by examination, but between the Restoration and the end of the eighteenth century the following did so.

Charles Finch, m. 29 Aug. 1676	BA 1678
Robert Booth, m. 19 Oct. 1678	BA 1681 MA 1684
Leopold Finch, m. 8 April 1679	BA 1681
Charles Boyle, m. 5 June 1690	BA 1694
Nicholas Herbert, m. 21 Nov. 1726	BA 1730
Andrew Leslie, m. 11 Mar. 1732[3]	BA 1735
Henry Trelawny, m. 2 July 1773	BA 1776 MA 1781
John George Beresford, m. 19 May 1790	BA 1793 MA 1796
Lloyd Kenyon, m. 10 Oct. 1794	BA 1797
Charles Marsham, m. 15 Oct. 1795	BA 1800 MA 1801
Dupré Alexander, m. 11 Apr. 1796	BA 1799
Luke Dillon, m. 28 Apr. 1797	BA 1800

[1] *Essay on the Life of David Gregory*, 24.
[2] Ibid., 24–5.
[3] Matriculated as a Gentleman Commoner.

Thomas Hamilton, m. 13 Oct. 1798   BA 1801 MA 1815

Almost as many Noblemen took a degree by examination between Cyril Jackson's appointment as Dean in 1783 and the end of the century as did so in the whole of the previous period.

Although it was no part of Fell's policy in attracting the nobility to Christ Church that they should take degrees by examination, he was for many years resolved that on their departure the university should as often as possible confer an honorary degree. Many Noblemen thus received an honorary MA on leaving Oxford. In the seventeenth century the Act was a great public occasion, and the conferment of honorary degrees brought honour on the university as well as on those who received its degrees. John Perceval, although a Gentleman Commoner, might equally well have spoken for the Noblemen when he wrote in 1676 that the Act was a ceremony 'where many doe designe to shew theyr parts as well to gett ye honour of giving theyr aid towards the solemnising soe great and publick an assembly as to weare a Master of Arts cap, which is permitted to those (of our gown) who speake in ye Theatre'.[1]

The lavish award of honorary degrees aroused opposition in some quarters. 'Poor folks' sons study hard', wrote Wood, 'and with much adoe obtaine their degrees in Arts and a fellowship. But now (1671) noblemen's sons are *created* Artium Magistri for nothing.'[2] The complaint was well founded. Of the Noblemen who matriculated at Christ Church between the Restoration and 1670, the majority received honorary MAs. Fell himself eventually came to believe that honorary degrees too freely given were harmful, though his conversion did not come until he had ceased to be Vice-Chancellor, an office which he held from 1666 to

---

[1] BL Add. MS 46953, fo. 120. Great though Fell's desire was to award honorary degrees to Noblemen, it was not quite so great as implied by the *Complete Peerage* (1910–40), which attributes the award of an honorary MA to the Earl of Clanbrassill before he had even matriculated. The degree was awarded on 28 Sept. 1663, though according to the university register the Earl did not matriculate until the following 7 Oct. In fact the Dean's Register at Christ Church shows that he actually matriculated on 4 Aug.

[2] Wood, *Life and Times*, ii, 276.

1669. He then wrote to the Duke of Ormonde, the Chancellor, condemning the practice in severe terms which echo Wood.

This, [he observed] as it is greivous to the University at all times, will be peculiarly so in the presence of an Act, when men after long attendance, and performance of troublesome exercises, and the paiment of expensiue fees, are admitted to those honours which others in a moment, without any previous qualification, by creation obtain. I therefore humbly conceive that nothing can be don more to the encouragement of the studies, or more obliging to the thoughts of all in this place, then if your Excellence be pleased to shut the dore against all such, howeuer importunate they may be.[1]

From 1670 until the middle of the following century the number of honorary MAs awarded to Noblemen was small. It increased greatly under Gregory and Markham. Bagot, despite his partiality for the aristocracy, made little effort to encourage Noblemen to seek academic distinction, whether earned or honorary, but with the appointment of Cyril Jackson the full effect was felt of the reform of Collections in 1774 and the integration of the studies of Noblemen with those of other members of the college. There was an almost immediate increase in the award of honorary MAs, and between 1783 and 1800 almost half the Noblemen received them. It is evident that Jackson sought to obtain honorary degrees for Noblemen who had given proof of merit but who for one reason or another were unwilling to take a degree by examination. Sometimes he achieved the same object by means of degrees of the House. In 1795 J. W. Grimston wrote, 'I have been talking very seriously with the Dean, and am happy to tell you that he is highly satisfied with my conduct; insomuch that he said the other day, if having a degree in the House would make my stay here more agreeable, he should be very happy to give it to me'.[2] The award of honorary degrees stimulated competition, and perhaps contributed indirectly to the increase in the number of Noblemen to take degrees by examination in Jackson's time.

Gentlemen Commoners were often younger sons and had their

---

[1] Bodl. M S Carte 38, fo. 375.
[2] H M C, *Verulam* (1906), 156.

way to make in the world. Perhaps for this reason a higher proportion of Gentlemen Commoners than of Noblemen took degrees by examination. Although between the Restoration and the end of the seventeenth century few did so, there was a gradual increase during the first half of the eighteenth century, and between 1756 and 1783 the proportion trebled. It is a remarkable testimony to Jackson's success in educating the Gentlemen Commoners that between the date of his appointment and the close of the century almost a quarter of them took a degree by examination. The average length of residence of the Gentlemen Commoners was a little over two years, but at all periods a considerable proportion of those who took their BA by examination did not avail themselves of the reduced residential qualification for a degree provided in the university statutes but extended their residence to the full sixteen terms. In this matter as in others the distinction between the Gentlemen Commoners and the Commoners tended to be blurred. An education of equal duration and content for all was a necessary preliminary to the effective reform of the public examinations of the university at the beginning of the nineteenth century.

The Gentlemen Commoners, unlike the Noblemen, were seldom given the degree of honorary MA until well into the eighteenth century. James Rushout in 1661 and Robert Shirley in 1669 received honorary degrees, the former certainly and the latter probably through the influence of the Duke of Ormonde, but the only other Gentleman Commoner to do so in Fell's time was James Lane, who was created MA in 1670 after taking his BA by examination in the same year. The award of honorary MAs to Gentlemen Commoners appears at first glance to have been revived by Atterbury, who, for what would appear to be carefully calculated political reasons, gave them to Edward Harley and Simon Harcourt in 1712. Harley came up as a Gentleman Commoner in 1707 and ceased to reside in 1710, and Harcourt came up in 1702, also as a Gentleman Commoner, and went down two years later. Although both of them were thus Gentlemen Commoners during their time at Christ Church, by the time they received their honorary degrees both were the eldest sons of peers,

John Locke when a Tutor

Henry Hallam

William Wyndham Grenville

William Markham

and it appears likely that the award was made to them in that capacity. 'It will be expected, I find,' Canon Stratford wrote to Harley, 'that you should accept of your Master's degree at parting. It will cost indeed twelve or fifteen guineas, but it has been usual for those of your Lordship's quality, who have lived with credit here, to receive that compliment at parting.'[1] It was not usual for Gentlemen Commoners but for Noblemen to be thus honoured. By a curious coincidence the first unequivocal Gentleman Commoner to whom an honorary degree was awarded in the eighteenth century was another Edward Harley. According to Foster the date of the degree is unknown, but Hearne records that it was conferred by Convocation in 1721, adding that 'There was an Opposition in the House about the conferring this Degree'.[2]

Honorary degrees were occasionally awarded to Gentlemen Commoners in the time of Dean Conybeare, and the Irish statesman Henry Flood was distinguished in this manner, but, as in the case of degrees by examination, the award of honorary degrees became more frequent under Dean Gregory. Between 1756 and 1783 about 8 per cent of Gentlemen Commoners received honorary degrees, and under Cyril Jackson the proportion rose to some 13 per cent—significantly below the proportion to take a BA by examination. Most Gentlemen Commoners who received honorary degrees had sufficient residence to qualify for a degree by examination. In such cases an honorary degree was, in Stratford's words, a 'compliment at parting', but it was a compliment which many coveted.

(g) COMMONERS

The Commoners of Christ Church came from a wide cross-section of society, but during the eighteenth century the social basis contracted as more of them came from wealthy or socially prominent backgrounds. In this respect they reflected a general trend at Christ Church. In the time of John Fell, five sons of baronets and

[1] HMC, *Portland* (1901), vii, 46.
[2] Hearne, *Collections*, vii, 238.

thirteen sons of knights entered as Commoners. At the other end of the social scale were undergraduates who described their fathers in the matriculation registers as 'plebeian', a term of rather vague connotation used to designate a poor man who was not a clergyman. Almost two-thirds of the Commoners were the sons of gentlemen, and most of the remainder of clergymen. By the end of the eighteenth century, however, about a tenth of the Commoners were the sons of peers or baronets. None then described his father as 'plebeian', and those who in earlier times had called their fathers gentlemen now increasingly referred to them as armigerous. Only the proportion of parsons' sons remained fairly constant. Thus, as society grew richer, it became more difficult for a poor boy to obtain a university education, and, as will be shown, the difficulty was not removed by the foundation of charitable trusts at Christ Church.

For Commoners, as for many other undergraduates, the acquisition of a degree was not universally regarded as the inevitable culmination of residence in the university. Over the whole period from 1660 to 1800 approximately 48 per cent took a BA or BCL at Christ Church and approximately 24 per cent an MA. Most of those who stayed on to obtain the MA did so to pass the time until they reached the canonical age for ordination of twenty-three. Of those who did not graduate at Christ Church about 8 per cent migrated to other colleges in Oxford and frequently did so there. The statistics of graduation, despite their low level, improved considerably during the eighteenth century. During the period 1660 to 1700 only 36 per cent of undergraduates took a BA or BCL at Christ Church, and in the decade after the Restoration, when Commoners flocked to the college in numbers unequalled until the 1780s, the proportion fell to less than a third. In contrast, 52 per cent of Commoners graduated at Christ Church in the first half of the eighteenth century, and 56 per cent in the second half. Taking the century as a whole, it appears that the proportion of Commoners to take a degree remained fairly constant, and bore little relation to the size of the college. The increase in the number of Commoners in the second half of the eighteenth century thus did not lead to an increase in the proportion of graduates.

Although the standard of education at the end of the century was probably higher than it had been at the beginning, the underlying reasons which caused undergraduates to seek or not to seek degrees changed very little.

As in the case of Students, degrees were occasionally attributed to Commoners in the college records that were not entered in the university registers. The number of such cases was never large, and although they were most frequent during the seventeenth century instances may also be found in the late eighteenth. Philip Astle in 1790, for example, and John Hudson and William Taunton in 1797 and 1799 respectively were described as BAs in the Collections Books, but none in known to have received the degree from the university. It is unclear in such cases whether the degree was recognized only within Christ Church, or whether the silence of the university registers is an indication that the ceremony of conferring a degree, or the ceremony and the public examinations too, had been omitted. Whatever the explanation, it would appear to imply a disregard for the degrees of the university, a disregard perhaps increased by the occasional practice of awarding degrees long after the recipient had ceased to reside. The most notable example of the grant of a degree in such circumstances was to R. H. Leigh, who matriculated in 1781 but did not take his BA until 1837. His was not an isolated case. Walter Hollier matriculated in 1777 but did not take his BA until 1792, and George Jackson received his degree in 1803, eighteen years after he had matriculated.

Most of the Commoners who left Christ Church without a degree did not possess the necessary statutory residence. Many went down after one or two years, and a substantial number after almost three. Hardly any Commoners failed the public examinations of the university. Except in the case of those undergraduates who wished to study law at All Souls, migration to another Oxford college prior to graduation was usually caused by economic circumstances, though occasionally, especially in the time of Cyril Jackson, migration was involuntary. Because Christ Church was amongst the most expensive colleges, emigration was always more frequent than immigration.

The decline in the eighteenth century in the educational opportunities for poor youths of ability was not caused primarily by the
rising cost of a university education. This occurred mainly in areas
of conspicuous consumption, and the cost of such basic items as
commons, chambers, and tuition did not increase to the same
extent. It was, however, a consequence of the increased prosperity
of society. Those who had come up in the seventeenth century as
the sons of 'poor men' came up in the eighteenth, as we have
seen, as the sons of gentlemen. Poor students thus belonged
to a relatively poorer section of society than before. At Christ
Church, such students did not benefit from the educational foundations, such as the Fell, Boulter, and Holford exhibitions, established for Commoners. Although these were charitable in intent,
they were not awarded at the time of admission to the college but
after a period of residence, and by definition poor youths lacked
the means to take up residence of uncertain duration with no
assurance of eventual election to an exhibition. The charities thus
did not help poor students to come to the university: they helped
poor students who were already at the university. Eventually
even comparative indigence yielded to ability as the principal
qualification for election.

The most important of the exhibitions for Commoners were
those created by the will of John Fell and settled by Chancery in
1699. Provision was made for an unspecified number of exhibitions of £10 a year for 'indigent and ingenious Commoners of
Christ Church' who had been resident for not less than a year.
The exhibitions were tenable for up to ten years but were voided
in case of marriage or of failure to reside forty weeks in the year.
At the end of October or early in November, having obtained
leave from the Dean, candidates sat an examination in Hall by the
Dean and Canons, the Censors, the lecturers in rhetoric and Greek,
or any four or more Student Masters. They were examined in the
usual Latin and Greek authors, and in such parts of philosophy
as by their standing they were presumed to have read, and were
required to compose and read publicly a theme on a subject
appointed by the Dean or by the lecturer in rhetoric.

Until the middle of the eighteenth century the emoluments of the Fell exhibitions were often diverted to the payment of room rents, commons, and battels—unmistakable signs of the poverty rather than of the extravagance of the exhibitioners. For many poor Commoners, residence for forty weeks in the year was an insuperable obstacle to election. It was probably for this reason that no exhibitioners were appointed in 1710, and only one in each of the years 1705, 1706, and 1708. The shortage of candidates led the Dean and Chapter to obtain an order in Chancery in 1716 reducing the required residence to thirty weeks, because, it was claimed, many had been forced to give up their exhibitions owing to the cost of prolonged residence and others had been discouraged from seeking them. For several years the change had a salutary effect, but there was no election in 1743, 1758, 1759, 1763, 1764, and 1769, and on eight occasions, the last of which was in 1773, only one appointment was made. In these circumstances the capital of the trust accumulated, even though the rents of the endowment were falling, and in 1765 the investment of surplus income enabled the college to double the value of the exhibitions. This large increase made them much sought after, and was followed by a marked rise in the number of Fell exhibitioners elected to Canoneer Studentships. During the century forty-five exhibitioners received Studentships, among them Canning, Vansittart, and Gaisford. Seventeen of them were nominated by the Dean or Sub-Dean, and of these thirteen received their nomination *after* they had been awarded an exhibition. The practice of awarding Canoneer Studentships to Fell exhibitioners increased in frequency under Jackson and seems to reflect a deliberate policy. It was a development which accelerated the turnover of exhibitions, for Students were not allowed to hold them, and a Commoner elected to a Fell was usually obliged to relinquish it on obtaining a Studentship.

The decline in the poverty qualification and the award of exhibitions to future Canoneer Students were indications that the ancient idea of eleemosynary foundations designed to assist the needy was in course of being replaced by the idea that they were intellectual prizes. This had been far from Fell's mind when he endowed them. His intention had been to support a body of resident Commoner Bachelors and Masters at Christ Church by facilitating a period of residence equal to the average duration of a Studentship. In fact, none of the exhibitions was held for the permitted period of ten years, and the longest tenure was that of Jonathan Stubbs, who was appointed in 1747 and held his exhibition for seven and three-quarter years until 1755. Until Bagot's time, the Fell was often held by Bachelors and Masters. John Dudley, who was appointed in 1770, was the last to retain his exhibition until becoming Master, with the isolated exception of Henry Stillingfleet, who was appointed in 1789. In 1779 the residential qualification for election was raised from one to two years. Even before this date the period of residence often extended in practice to almost two years, because matriculation occurred throughout the year. A Commoner who matriculated in December, for example, was not eligible in the following autumn, when the examination took place, but in the autumn after that. The effect of the alteration in the residential qualification in 1779 was to move the date of election forward even further, for matriculation continued to take place throughout the year. Elections then often occurred nearer the third than the second year, and in 1782 and 1794 exhibitions were actually awarded to men who had already taken their BA. It is reasonable to assume that an examination held after two years was more exacting than an examination held after one, and the main effect of the change in the residential qualification was to raise the standard of the Fell exhibitions. This was reflected in the increased number of exhibitioners after 1779 to take a degree. The alteration in the date of the examination coupled with the decline in the residence of Bachelors and the election of exhibitioners to Canoneer Studentships caused a reduction in the length of tenure of the Fell exhibitions, which in turn increased the number available from about three to about seven or more a year.

In 1757 the first election to the Boulter foundation took place. By his will, Archbishop Boulter, who died in 1742, bequeathed the sum of £1,000 to endow exhibitions for five of 'the poorest and most deserving Commoners', preference being given to the sons of the clergy, other things being equal. The exhibitioners were to be appointed after examination from undergraduates not above three years' standing, and had a maximum tenure of four years. The exhibitions were thus intended to assist undergraduates from matriculation to the time of taking the degree of BA, but the income proved inadequate to provide more than two or three exhibitions a year on this basis. Moreover, the emoluments, which were increased in 1763 from £7. 11s. 4d. a year to £8 a year, were often insufficient to persuade the poor Commoners for whom they were intended to reside. In 1762 only one candidate appeared for election, and in the following year none at all. The majority of the Boulter exhibitioners, however, at some time also held one of the Fell exhibitions, and the examinations for both exhibitions occurred on the same day. Up to 1784 both might be held simultaneously, and the Fell was awarded before, after, or at the same time as the Boulter. Under Cyril Jackson, however, it became the practice for the Boulter to be vacated on election to the Fell, which then took place later. The effect of shortening the tenure of the Boulter by this measure was to increase the number of exhibitions to an average of about five a year. Most of the Boulter exhibitioners subsequently elected to a Fell exhibition enjoyed a tenure of not more than a year. The minority who did not obtain election to Fell seldom held Boulter for more than two years and never for the four permitted by the founder.

If the terms of the Boulter exhibitions had some affinity with those of the Fell, the influence of the Fell was even more apparent in the foundation of the Holford exhibitions established in 1717 by the will of Lady Holford, of All Hallows Steyning. She was the daughter of a coachman of Stanton St John, near Oxford, and, according to Hearne, 'being a handsome, plump, jolly Wench, one Mr. Harbin, who belong'd to the Custom House, & was a Merchant, and very rich, married her, and dying, all he had came to her'.[1] Having taken a rich merchant for her first husband, she took an impoverished baronet for her second. By her first marriage she had an only child, Henry Harbin, who matriculated a

---

[1] Hearne, *Collections*, vii, 189.

Gentleman Commoner at Christ Church in 1696 and died young. In his memory she founded five exhibitions for scholars from Charterhouse at Christ Church, or in their absence for undergraduates from Charterhouse at any college or hall in the university, who were to become resident at Christ Church on election. Although a small number of undergraduates from other colleges received Holford exhibitions, the foundation had little effect in causing migrations to Christ Church. The exhibitions were to be awarded after public examination in the Hall to persons deserving 'in respect of their learning, good lives, and prudent demeanour'. Perhaps because the foundation was commemorative rather than charitable, no mention was made of indigence as a qualification. In defining the nature of the examination, the Holford foundation followed closely the model of the Fell. Candidates were to be examined in the usual Greek and Latin classical authors, and in such parts of philosophy as by their standing they were presumed to have read. They were also to compose a theme on a subject given to them by the Dean or the lecturer in rhetoric. The exhibitions were tenable for eight years, that is up to the MA degree, but, because the length of tenure varied in practice, elections did not take place at regular intervals, and in many years no election at all was made.

When Lady Holford died on 3 November 1720, her estate was found sufficient for only three-quarters of the legacies she intended. In 1728, other demands having been satisfied, the Dean and Chapter accepted the sum of £1,500, and, when this had accumulated to £2,200, an estate of 71 acres at Cutteslowe, then on the outskirts of Oxford, was purchased in 1737. The first exhibitioners were promptly appointed, and the award was generally made within a year of matriculation. Until 1750 the exhibitioners were either Canoneer Students or very often Commoners subsequently awarded the Fell. On two occasions in these early years the Holford was awarded to Servitors.[1] In the middle of the century, however, the foundation encountered grave financial difficulties. The tenant of the estate at Cutteslowe, Isaac Silverside,

---

[1] Servitors were also elected in 1756 and 1762.

'being distressed by frequent losses in his cattle during the late distemper', was unable to pay his rent of £90 a year from 1749 to 1755 and eventually became insolvent. The college ultimately lost £340, and one of the exhibitions was as a result vacant from 1755 to 1762. The fall in income led inevitably to a reduction in the value of the exhibitions. Even before the crisis it had not been possible to award the full amount of £13. 6s. 8d. per annum, and between 1752 and 1758 the emoluments fell to £6 per annum. The foundation never fully recovered from this period of financial difficulty during the eighteenth century.

From 1750 until the appointment of Dean Bagot, about two-thirds of the exhibitions were held either by Canoneer Students or by Fell exhibitioners, but increasingly the Holford was given to Commoners who neither became Canoneers nor held the Fell, and at the same time the number of Holford exhibitioners to take a degree declined sharply. Thus at a time when the Fell exhibitions were more frequently given as rewards for merit, no similar tendency was discernible in the Holfords. Although Holford was closely modelled on Fell, it was a much less successful foundation. The cause of this difference was that, unlike the Fell, the Holford exhibitions were attached to a particular school. It is true that the Westminster Studentships were also attached to a particular school, but Charterhouse in the eighteenth century was not comparable with Westminster School.

(h) SERVITORS

Servitors were appointed by the Dean, and according to a Chapter order in 1636 were required to 'waite upon ye Students, Chaplaines & under Commoners'.[1] No mention was made of Noblemen or Gentlemen Commoners, some of whom probably had their own servants, but Servitors were certainly in attendance on Noblemen early in the eighteenth century. In 1714 Canon Stratford wrote to Harley, 'I told Mr. Benson that Mr. Jenks was one for whom your Lordship was concerned. Mr. Benson upon this promised

[1] Chapter Act Book, 2 Aug. 1636.

to recommend the lad to be servitor and to live with my Lord Lemster, who will be here in a few weeks and is to be under Mr. Benson's care.'[1] Servitors were not on the foundation, but in return for performing menial or domestic duties of a not very onerous nature received a free education. They were not required to pay caution money,[2] and they paid no fees for tuition to the Censors and senior college officers who were their public tutors. They were placed in *Classes* for disputations, and took up their Collections with other undergraduates. Although thus assured of an education, the Servitors were socially isolated, and their subordinate position was constantly emphasized. They dined, for example, at a different time from the rest of the college because their duties included waiting at table, and even in the nineteenth century they continued to wear a distinctive dress to distinguish them from college servants.[3] Aubrey noted that Thomas Willis (1622–75), when a Servitor to Dr Iles, wore a blue livery cloak 'and studied at the lower end of the hall, by the hall-dore'.[4] Until 1770 they alone of all undergraduates wore the seventeenth-century round cap or 'bonnet' instead of the square, and were not permitted tassels on their squares as late as 1855.

In 1636 the number of Servitors was limited to thirty, but at the Restoration the Chapter sought to reduce it to twenty, and ordered that 'none be admitted but upon security given by some Master of Arts and Student … for his education in learninge and payment of Battles'.[5] It may be that the order, which was made a fortnight after the appointment of the royal commission to visit the university, was intended to purge the Servitors of religious extremism, of which an example had been provided in the previous month, when the intruded Canons still resided at Christ Church. The Treasurer had then paid the sum of £1 to three Servitors

[1] HMC, *Portland* (1901), vii, 191.

[2] In 1772 they were required to pay the sum of £4, described as 'caution' to the butler (Draft Act Book, 9 Apr. 1772). There appears to be no earlier record of this or a similar payment.

[3] BL Add. MS 44380, fo. 88, T. E. Brown to W. E. Gladstone, 25 Apr. 1854.

[4] J. Aubrey, *Brief lives*, ed. A. Clark (1898), ii, 303; L. S. Sutherland, 'The Last of the Servitors', in *Christ Church Annual Report* (1975), 36.

[5] Chapter Act Book, 31 July 1660.

'who were troubled in conscience for hanging a dog on ye Sabbath day'.[1] It is, however, more likely that it was a consequence of the financial crisis which faced the college at the Restoration, and was an attempt to curtail the embezzlement of provisions by persons claiming to be servants, or that it was a consequence of the large increase in matriculations which limited the accommodation available for Servitors. The limitation ceased to be observed when the finances of Christ Church rapidly improved and the rate of matriculation settled down. Servitors then continued for many years to constitute a sizeable proportion of the college.

Towards the end of the seventeenth century, the number of Servitors fell considerably. Matriculations throughout the university declined at the same time, but, whereas they recovered early in the following century for other undergraduates, the admission of Servitors remained at a low level because many who in earlier times would have come up as Servitors now entered as Commoners. At the end of the eighteenth century not more than two or three Servitors a year were admitted, and in 1854 there were only about a dozen in the college.[2] The decline in the number of Servitors reduced considerably the places for poor students at Christ Church. Servitors were usually either the sons of poor clergy and impoverished schoolmasters or the sons of Oxford tradesmen, college servants, and the like. As society became more affluent and liberal education more closely identified with the education of gentlemen, it became more difficult especially for the second of these categories to be admitted to the university. In a letter to Arthur Charlett in 1719, White Kennett noted the growing opinion that 'the sons of the poorer sort of farmers and tradesmen had much better be bred up to a like occupation than be supported in schools and universities that would be more creditably fill'd by the sons of those only who are sufficient to maintain them'.[3] The sons of Oxford tradesmen and college servants continued to be admitted occasionally as Servitors, but in

---

[1] Ch. Ch. Archives, Disbursement Book, June 1660.
[2] BL Add. MS 44380, fo. 88.
[3] Bodl. MS Ballard 7, fo. 146ᵛ.

the eighteenth century most Servitors were the sons of clergymen or schoolmasters.

During the seventeenth and eighteenth centuries a number of charitable foundations were established at Christ Church for the benefit of Servitors, but they had little effect in enabling poor scholars to come to the university because they were awarded after matriculation had occurred and not at the time of matriculation. In this respect they resembled the exhibitions founded for Commoners. The earliest of the foundations was the creation of Richard Gardiner, a Canon of Christ Church, who in 1664 gave the college a small estate at Bourton on the Water, in Gloucestershire, to provide exhibitions for two Servitors 'of good merit for learning and honest conversation', who were to be appointed by the Dean and Chapter. The exhibitions were first awarded two years later in 1666. They were tenable until the MA, and were worth £6 a year until 1772 when they were increased to £7. The income of the trust was frequently sufficient to allow the appointment of a third exhibitioner. The Cotton exhibitions were often held with the Gardiner, and were founded by Edward Cotton, a Canon of Exeter, who at his death in 1675 bequeathed to Christ Church his lease from the Dean and Chapter of Windsor of the tithes of Thornmow in the parish of Ottery St Mary, in Devonshire. The profits of the estate were to be used to maintain two Bachelor Servitors, preference being given to persons of indigence and learning from Exeter or from the counties of Devon, Cornwall, or Oxford. The exhibitions were first awarded in 1678. They were tenable for four years and were worth £12 each. The Paul exhibitions, which were also intended for Bachelor Servitors, were founded in 1676 by Rachel Paul, the widow of William Paul, Bishop of Oxford. She gave the college thirty-eight acres at Eynsham in Oxfordshire to provide exhibitions of £5 a year for three poor resident Bachelors of good life and conversation, preference being given to the sons of clergymen.

The following century saw the Pauncefort and Boulter exhibitions founded for undergraduate Servitors. When Edward Pauncefort died in 1726 he directed his executors to purchase and convey to the Corporation of the Sons of the Clergy an estate worth £100 a year. Part of the income was for the payment of £5 a year to each of eight widows of clergymen, and the rest was to be divided equally between ten Servitors to be nominated to the Corporation by the Dean, two Canons, and six Students for their 'sobriety, diligence at their studies, and of parts for a minister of the gospel and designed for Holy Orders'. Although the exhibitions were awarded from 1727, the executors did not immediately purchase an estate, but paid the sum of £100 a year to the Corporation until 1757, when in accordance with a decree of Chancery an estate in Radnorshire was purchased. It turned out an unsatisfactory purchase, not least because the vendor also happened to be the standing counsel and registrar to the Corporation, and the value of the exhibitions dropped from £6 a year to between £4 and £5. The Pauncefort exhibitions were so numerous that it was possible to award one to almost every Servitor. As the numbers of Servitors diminished, the exhibitions came to be held for longer periods, and by the end of the century were commonly held for two or three years. A further five exhibitions were founded by Archbishop Boulter, who gave the sum of £500 for the purpose. The Boulter exhibitions were tenable for three years by Servitors of two years' standing nominated by the Dean and Chapter. When first awarded in 1757 they were worth £3. 15s. 10d. a year, and in 1763 increased to £4 a year. In 1773 the trust had 'a considerable surplus in hand of monies defaulted for nonresidence', and two additional exhibitions were created for a time, but as residence became stricter the funds again sufficed only to maintain the original foundation. Finally, there was a small estate at Eynsham in Oxfordshire given by Bishop Frampton which from 1726 sustained two more exhibitions for undergraduate Servitors.

The exhibitions were individually of small value, but when the number of Servitors declined it became possible for those who remained to hold more than one exhibition simultaneously. The effect of the charities was thus to lengthen the residence of those who were already Servitors at Christ Church, and, because the inability to afford to reside was the main impediment to graduation, to increase the number taking a degree. For Servitors, more than for any other group of undergraduates, a degree was the passport to a career, but many failed to graduate or left the university as Bachelors. Between the Restoration and the end of the seventeenth century, about 60 per cent took a BA, but only half an MA. Under Jackson, over 70 per cent took a BA, and the majority of these an MA. When at the end of the century educational standards improved at Christ Church, and even more after the reform of the public examinations, this advance was not maintained, and the Servitors found themselves at a disadvantage because they lacked the means to engage private tutors. In 1821 T. V. Short, the Junior Censor, told W. F. Hook that although there was no difficulty in obtaining a Servitorship for the son or grandson of a clergyman ('for such the place is intended'), it was unfair to appoint one who was not well prepared, 'for there have been more men plucked among the Servitors the last three years than in the whole college besides'.[1]

[1] Ch. Ch. Archives, W. F. Hook to his mother, Mar. 1821.

IV

The Structure of Education

(*a*) THE ORGANIZATION OF STUDIES AND THE COLLEGE OFFICERS

The Laudian statutes prescribed in detail the course of studies necessary in the university for the degrees of BA and MA. An undergraduate was required to attend lectures by the university lecturer in grammar twice a week during his first year. He was also required to attend lectures twice a week by the lecturer in rhetoric on Aristotle, Cicero, Quintilian, or Hermogenes. From the end of his first year until he took his BA, he went to lectures in logic and moral philosophy, and attended as an observer the disputations *in parvisis,* that is, the disputations of the sophists, every Monday, Wednesday, and Friday. After two years' residence in the university, he heard lectures by the Regius Professor of Greek on Homer, Demosthenes, Isocrates, Euripides, and other classical authors, and he disputed twice in the Schools, once as an opponent and once as a respondent. On the completion of the disputation, the Regent Master, who moderated at the exercise, gave him a book of Aristotle's logic, placed a plain hood over his head, and created him general sophister. He then continued to attend the disputations *in parvisis* until he took his degree, himself disputing once a term and acting as a disputant in the exercises of other scholars. When he had spent four terms studying logic, he responded twice at the Lenten disputations of Determining Bachelors before petitioning for his degree. For the degree of Master, the Bachelor of Arts was required to respond and oppose once a year at the Augustine disputations, to respond in three questions at the Quodlibet disputations, and to deliver six formal lectures. He was also required to attend the lectures of the Savilian

Professors of Geometry and Astronomy, and lectures by the lecturers in natural philosophy and metaphysics, the Camden Professor, and the Regius Professors of Hebrew and Greek. The statutes were amended in 1662 to require two declamations to be delivered by candidates for the MA.

The Laudian statutes were not innovatory but were an attempt to codify and rationalize earlier statutes. How far they were successful is open to dispute, but there is considerable evidence that the traditional exercises were kept up during the eighteenth century, though frequently they were little more than formalities. The gradual decay of university education, that is, of education given by means of university institutions, was caused by the vigorous development of the collegiate system. The colleges developed an organization similar and parallel to that provided by the university, but more efficient. Whereas the university had little control of its professors and found the complex statutes on disputations difficult to administer, the college officers were appointed by the governing body and had authority for the effective regulation of studies. Students had little motive to attend university lectures and to perform university exercises which repeated what they had already learnt from their college lecturers and tutors.

Studies at Christ Church were based on a system of disputations, declamations, lectures, and other exercises which thus duplicated that provided by the university statutes. In Fell's time it had undergone little change since the foundation of the college in the mid-sixteenth century. The fundamental unit for teaching purposes was the *Classis*. There were four of these, corresponding to the four years required to complete the curriculum for the degree of BA. Each *Classis* had a moderator, whose duty was to lecture on Aristotle and to conduct disputations four times a week alternately in Greek and Latin. The moderator of the first or junior *Classis* lectured on the *Prior Analytics* and on Porphyry; the moderator of the second on the *Categories, Posterior Analytics,* and *Topics*; the moderator of the third on the *Ethics* and *Physics*; and the moderator of the fourth on Aristotle's scientific books. On Mondays, Tuesdays, Wednesdays, and Fridays, at 9 a.m., undergraduates attended the college lecturer in rhetoric, who examined them on his lectures of the previous week and set themes, and at 1 p.m. on the same days in each week they attended the college lecturer in Greek. They were also required to declaim in Latin or Greek on alternate Saturdays. The Bachelors declaimed in Hall twice a week in the presence of the Sub-Dean, and disputed on Wednesdays and Saturdays. The Senior Censor moderated at the Wednesday disputations and the Saturday disputations when they took place in Lent, but the Junior Censor moderated at other times. The Senior Censor lectured to the Bachelors on Tuesdays and Saturdays, and the Junior Censor on Mondays, Wednesdays, and Fridays immediately after morning prayers. Before taking the degree of Master, Bachelors were obliged to give six lectures on Aristotle to the satisfaction of the Dean or the Sub-Dean. The Masters then engaged in theological disputations in the Latin chapel every Friday evening, when the Censor Theologiae was moderator, and gave lectures on Wednesdays and Fridays. In essential points this system, which in some respects was more exacting than that prescribed by the university statutes, continued until late in the eighteenth century.

The administration of this system of public exercises depended principally on the college officers, of which there were ten. It did not depend on the tutors, who were not college officers. Until the eighteenth century the tutors played an important but subordinate role in preparing their pupils for the public exercises at Christ Church. The college officers were established when Christ Church was founded, and some of them continue to exist at the present day. In ascending order of seniority they consisted of the four lecturers (praelectors) in dialectic or logic, who were also moderators of the four *Classes,* the lecturers in rhetoric and Greek, the Junior Censor (Censor Naturalis Philosophiae), the Senior Censor (Censor Moralis Philosophiae), the Catechist, and the Sub-Dean, who was also Censor Theologiae.[1] At the apex, though not a college officer, was the Dean. The officers represented the

[1] Referred to as Moderator Theologiae in the Chapter Act Book, 23 Dec. 1663.

traditional framework of education as a progression from logic and grammar to natural philosophy, thence to moral philosophy, and finally to metaphysics and theology. They were elected annually in December by the Dean and Chapter, and a list of them was put up in Hall.[1] With the exception of the Sub-Dean, all of them were Students. In addition to the public offices, there were several endowed lectureships created by benefaction. In 1667 lectureships in mathematics and oriental languages were founded by Richard Busby. In 1750 a lectureship in theology was established with a bequest by Robert Challoner, and in 1766 the mathematical and anatomical lectureships created by the will of Dr Matthew Lee.

The *Classis* continued to be the channel through which the public tuition at Christ Church represented by the college officers was given until the late eighteenth century. Its collapse, which is discussed in Chapter IV, section (*b*), was caused by the reform of the curriculum and by its inability to absorb the large number of Noblemen and Gentlemen Commoners who until 1774 had been educated separately from other undergraduates. Originally all other undergraduates, including Students, were intended to enter the first *Classis* at matriculation, and subsequently to progress through the second, third, and fourth, though practice in this respect did not always conform with theory.[2] The lecturer or moderator for each *Classis* was always a Student Bachelor. He was invariably only a few years older than the undergraduates in his *Classis,* and where he was a Westminster Student, as were the majority of the lecturers, he had often been a pupil at Westminster School with them. More than half the lecturers in logic were appointed for one year only, but where a lecturer was appointed for two or three years he might teach the same undergraduates as they moved into the second and third *Classis,* or he might continue to teach the same *Classis* as before but now composed of a different intake of undergraduates, or he might be reappointed after teaching the first *Classis* to teach the third or perhaps even the fourth. Because of his youthfulness, the lecturer in logic was not always

[1] Hearne, *Collections,* iv, 42.
[2] In 1763 the number of *Classes* was reduced to three. See also p. 216.

in holy orders.[1] Appointment to a lectureship was no guarantee that further preferment would follow, but it was often accompanied by appointment as a tutor.

Next in seniority to the lecturers in logic was the lecturer in Greek. The lectureship changed hands more often than any other college office with the exception of the lectureships in logic. The average tenure was one or two years, though on three occasions it was held for four or five years, and Henry Cremer held it for six years from 1706 to 1711. The lecturer often went on to become Regius Professor of Greek,[2] which, although an entirely separate foundation, was charged on the revenues of Christ Church. From 1712 until the appointment of Benjamin Jowett in 1855, the regius professorship was an academic pocket borough of Christ Church, and, except for a short interval from 1747 to 1751, was filled exclusively by Students, all but one of whom had previously held the Greek lectureship at Christ Church.

Tenure of the lectureship in rhetoric tended to be for longer periods than that in Greek. It was held on average for about two years, but in the eighteenth century it was twice held for six years,

[1] Although most tutors were in orders, this was not an inviolable rule. Before the middle of the 18th cent. even the Censors and lecturers in rhetoric and Greek were not always ordained. John Locke, for example, who was Senior Censor in 1663, and William Breach, who was Senior Censor in 1682 and 1683, were both laymen, and William Taswell relates in his autobiography that he was made lecturer in Greek at Christmas 1681 but did not take deacon's orders until the following Mar. and priest's orders until June (*Camden Miscellany II* (Autobiography of William Taswell), 32). Thomas Fenton, Junior Censor in 1714, Charles Kimberley, lecturer in rhetoric in the same year, James Harcourt, lecturer in Greek in 1736, and James Gilpin, lecturer in rhetoric in 1739, all seem to have been deprived of their Studentships for failing to take orders. Other college officers, such as Henry Watkins, who was lecturer in Greek in 1693–5, and John Wheeler, who held the same lectureship in 1713, were elected to Faculty Studentships (which were tenable only by laymen), after their appointment, and Richard Frewin continued to hold a Faculty Studentship while lecturer in rhetoric.

[2] During the first half of the 18th cent. the academic qualifications for the professorship seem not to have been high. Lord Chesterfield, temporarily at a loss to suggest a career for his son, wrote to him in 1748, 'What do you think of being Greek Professor at one of our Universities? It is a very pretty sinecure, and requires very little knowledge (much less than, I hope, you have already) of that language' (B. Dobrée (ed.), *Letters of Lord Chesterfield* (1932), no. 1518).

and between 1684 and 1771 it was held for four or five years on eight occasions. Although rhetoric was historically a more important study than Greek, the lectureship was in gradual decline. Thus it provided fewer Censors than the lectureship in Greek, and although the traditional progression between the two offices was from Greek to rhetoric it was perhaps an indication of the changing relationship between them that William Freind in 1777 and William Inge in 1785 were both appointed to the Greek lectureship *after* they had held the lectureship in rhetoric. By this date Greek studies were very flourishing, but rhetoric had diminished in importance as disputations fell into disuse and composition was taken over by the tutors.

The most important of the college officers were the two Censors, the Censor Naturalis Philosophiae and the Censor Moralis Philosophiae. The Censorships bear the imprint of their origin in the sixteenth century, and allude to the magistrates in ancient Rome responsible for the census of the citizens and the supervision of public morals. Their essential character has changed little over the centuries, and the present occupants are recognizable in Walter Pope's description of the Censor in 1697 as 'in other Colleges call'd the Dean',[1] and in Lord Grenville's description of him in 1829 as 'the person immediately superintending the conduct of . . . junior members'.[2] Both Censors received equal emoluments from the college. The terms Senior and Junior are not found in the college records until the first half of the eighteenth century, and the distinction between them probably derived from the fact that moral philosophy followed the study of natural philosophy and was thus 'senior' to it.

At the Restoration, the educational duties of the Censors remained much as they had been for the previous century. They lectured to the Bachelors, and presided at their disputations, when, in Walter Pope's words they 'moderate at Disputations and give the scholars questions'.[3] They ensured that undergraduates disputed regularly, and, together with the Dean and the lecturer in

[1] W. Pope, *Life of Seth Ward* (1697), 38.
[2] Lord Grenville, *Oxford and Locke* (1829), 51.
[3] Pope, *Life of Seth Ward*, 38.

rhetoric, they heard themes in Hall. Their importance increased during the eighteenth century with the reform of Collections, and they took the initiative in reforming the public lectures in 1776. In matters of discipline they gradually encroached on the traditional responsibilities of the Chapter. No cases of the breach of college discipline by undergraduate Students occur in the Chapter Books after the appointment of Jackson, and it is probable that except in the most heinous cases they were dealt with by the Censors.

As the importance of the Censors increased, they tended to hold office for longer periods. Under Dean Fell, the average tenure of both Censors was about a year and a half, and it was not uncommon for them to serve for a single year. In the eighteenth century, however, the Senior Censor was appointed for an average of three and a half years and the Junior Censor for about two and a half years. Some held office for much longer. The longest-serving Senior Censor was Phineas Pett, who held office from 1783 to 1792, and the longest-serving Junior Censor was Charles Sawkins, who held office from 1783 to 1790. The Censors also tended to be appointed increasingly from more experienced Students. Under Fell, some of them had no previous experience of college office, apart from the lectureships in logic, and less than half of the Senior Censors had been Junior Censors beforehand. In the eighteenth century it was usual to progress from one office to the other, and from 1779 it was customary for both Censors to have held either or both of the lectureships in Greek and rhetoric prior to their appointment. At least one of the Censors was usually a Westminster Student.

Early in December, when the Censors were nearing the end of their year of office, the fiction that they then 'died' was commemorated by the ceremony known as Burying the Censor. When George Smalridge was reaching the end of his term as Senior Censor in 1696 he wrote to a friend, 'My thoughts were in such a hurry about preparing for *dying,* as the cant of this place runs, that till that was over I had not leisure to write'.[1] Originally it

---

[1] Nichols, *Illustrations,* iii, 247.

was the practice for the Sub-Dean to appoint four Bachelor Students to dispute in the Hall on the last Wednesday and Saturday of Michaelmas term, and those who did so were subsequently excused disputations the first time it was their turn to respond. By the middle of the eighteenth century the exercise had become an occasion for the delivery of speeches of compliment to the Censors. It was a serious and solemn event, and failure to perform the exercise satisfactorily incurred the wrath of the Chapter. In 1790 J. F. Edgar was rusticated and put back from taking his MA for a year because of 'the indecent and improper manner in which he performed the exercise'.[1] After the Bachelors' speeches, the Senior Censor gave a Latin oration in which he commented on the events which had occurred during his year of office. 'The subject matter', Gladstone wrote to his mother in 1828, 'is anything that has happened during the year in any way interesting to the members of Christ Church: any of its distinguished members having been removed or exalted, or those who have died.'[2] There were, however, limits to what the Censor might touch on. When Francis Atterbury delivered his speech as Senior Censor on 10 December 1768, he made some remarks critical of the Visitor. Although those present heard only indistinctly what was said, they heard enough to cause the Dean and Chapter to assemble on the following day to discuss it. Their deliberations were curtailed by the news that Atterbury had burnt the offending speech, whereupon Dean Markham delivered a magisterial rebuke in the following words:

Dr. Atterbury

When your speech was demanded your answer was that you had burnt it. If the speech had been before us we should have been better able to judge what notice should be taken of it, but tho we have but an imperfect

---

[1] Chapter Act Book, 1 Feb. 1790.

[2] Hawarden Letters, W. E. Gladstone to his mother, 4 Dec. 1828. For a specimen of a Censor's oration see Osborne Gordon's on the death of Fynes Clinton, spoken in Latin on 4 Dec. 1852, printed in C. J. Fynes Clinton (ed.), *Literary Remains of Henry Fynes Clinton* (1854), 361–3.

apprehension of it as you was not distinctly heard, we are all of opinion that there were some expressions in it which seemed to reflect on the proceedings of our Visitor. It was at best very indiscreet to meddle with matters which were foreign to the business of your speech and no way subject to your cognizance.

You are to understand therefore that we consider that part of your speech as very disrespectful to the Chancellor, as very offensive to your hearers, and in every view highly improper. I am now in my own name and that of the Chapter to express our strongest disapprobation of what you have done and you are to consider what I have said as a censure.[1]

The indignation of the Dean and Chapter may not have been unconnected with the Dean's failure to whip up the Christ Church vote on behalf of the court in the election of 1768. The Poll Book shows that Markham voted for George Hay and Charles Jenkinson, but Atterbury for the successful candidates Sir Roger Newdigate and Francis Page.[2]

Next in order of seniority to the Censors was the Catechist, and an important part of his duties was to prepare candidates for ordination. Originally it was his duty to deliver a catechetical lecture once a week in the North Chapel, but in 1761 he was required to give a lecture in the Latin chapel once a term, except in Easter term when he gave a sermon on Easter Day instead. From 1768 the office was held with the lectureship in theology established by the bequest of Robert Challoner. The two offices were first held jointly by James Chelsum, a distinguished Student who wrote two pamphlets on Gibbon's treatment of Christianity and a history of mezzotint engraving. In 1773 the Chapter took the unusual step of allowing him to keep his Studentship with

[1] Chapter Act Book, 13 Dec. 1768. The rebuke given to Atterbury was not the only occasion when a college officer was called to account by the Dean and Chapter. In 1706 the lecturer in rhetoric was accused of having spoken in public 'scandalous words' about the Bishop of Worcester. He was ordered to beg the bishop's pardon on pain 'of the most severe punishment that the Dean and Chapter could inflict in such a case' (Chapter Act Book, 20 Dec. 1706).

[2] For the subsequent history of the ceremony of Burying the Censor see Thompson, *Christ Church*, 137–9.

any benefice not in their own patronage as an encouragement for 'having begun to execute a very useful plan of lectures in divinity for the instruction of youth in this college with a declared purpose of continuing to read once a week in full term'.[1]

By means of the college offices, the Students exercised considerable influence on the education of undergraduates, but their powers were limited by their exclusion from the Governing Body, and matters such as the appointment of tutors, the drawing up of the curriculum, and the regulation of Collections, at Christ Church were discharged by the Dean and the Sub-Dean.

The Sub-Dean had certain specific duties, but his title belied his authority. Nominally the Dean's deputy, he had as much or as little power as the Dean allowed him. At the time of his appointment he was rarely the senior Canon, though, because the office was difficult to get rid of, once appointed to it he might become so by dint of lengthy tenure. The practice of appointing a junior Canon arose because it was necessary for the Sub-Dean to reside during term, and residence was more easily required of junior than of senior members of the Chapter. Moreover, the Brethren may have thought it expedient for newly appointed Canons to discharge their share of capitular duties before death or preferment intervened. It is hardly surprising that the office of Sub-Dean was not keenly sought. In 1759 William Freind wrote to the Duke of Newcastle that 'The burthensome office of the sub-deanery of Christ Church, likely soon to devolve upon me and, if it does, to become my certain destruction, will I trust plead my excuse for petitioning for the earliest relief your Grace shall judge most expedient'.[2] The Duke, who exaggerated the political importance of the office, heeded the plea and persuaded the existing Sub-Dean, Edward Bentham, to stay on for a further year. After the election of officers in the following January, Bentham wrote to tell him that 'Your Grace having been pleased at Newcastle-house to give me your injunction not to decline the Sub-

---

[1] Chapter Act Book, 6 Jan. 1773.
[2] BL Add. MS 32889, fo. 457.

deanery, I beg leave to inform you that I have accepted of a designation to that office for the sixth year'.[1]

The office of Sub-Dean was described by John Fell as one 'to which belongs much of the Scholastick government of the College'.[2] In the majority of cases it was held by Canons who not only had been Students but had also held one or other of the college offices and had been tutors. Most of the Sub-Dean's duties were concerned with the exercises of Masters and Bachelors. As Censor Theologiae he attended the theological lectures and disputations of the Masters, and as Sub-Dean the declamations and disputations of the Bachelors. He appointed the Students who were to perform the exercise of Burying the Censor. But he also had duties in regard to the undergraduates. When Hammond was Sub-Dean, he occupied himself 'not onely in moderating at Divinity-disputations, which was then an immediate part of his Task, but in presiding at the more youthful Exercises of Sophistry, Themes and Declamations'.[3] In the absence of the Dean, he heard themes in Hall with the Censor and lecturer in rhetoric. He was present at Collections, and until 1774 took the Collections and themes of Noblemen and Gentlemen Commoners separately from the rest of the college. He was a judge in the Lee Certamen. When eventually the residence of Masters and Bachelors declined, the Sub-Dean's duties diminished, and as they did so the Chapter's tenuous link with the educational work of the college weakened further.

In addition to the offices established at the foundation, several lectureships were created at Christ Church by benefaction. With them may be included the lectureships in mathematics and Hebrew which Richard Busby intended to found in the Senior Common Room, though there is considerable doubt whether the foundation took effect. On 9 June 1667, the Chapter decreed that 'the new low room beneath the west end of the Hall be for euer set apart and applied to the use of the Mathematick and Oriental lectures

---

[1] BL Add. MS 32901, fo. 100. Bentham's compliance was rewarded when he became Regius Professor of Divinity in 1763.
[2] J. Fell, *Life of Hammond* (1662), 48.
[3] Ibid., 49.

to be founded by the reuerend Dr. Busby; as also to the use of the Masters, Students and others of this house for their publick fires and such like occasions'.[1] Both lecturers were to give twenty-five lectures a year, and all undergraduates were required to attend. The lecturer in mathematics gave his at 9 a.m. on Mondays, or if necessary on Saturdays at the same time. The Hebrew lecturer gave his on Saturdays 'immediately after the undergraduates coming from corrections in the Hall', or on Mondays at 1 p.m. The foundation of the Senior Common Room has endured, but nothing is heard of the lectureships, unless perhaps the lectureship in mathematics was that held by John Keill, whose appointment at Christ Church early in the eighteenth century is clouded in obscurity, or the lectureship in Hebrew was that held by Humphrey Prideaux, who was described in a letter in 1677 as 'Hebrew reader of our College'.[2]

The lectureship in divinity founded with a bequest by Robert Challoner was not constituted until 1750. In that year the Chapter, 'upon lately looking into some of the old evidences of this cathedral church', discovered that Challoner had bequeathed an estate at Garsington near Oxford for a divinity lectureship by the terms of his will, which was dated 20 June 1620. The property did not come into the possession of Christ Church until 1638, but its value was small and for many years the rents were paid to Domus. In 1750 it was resolved that the lecturer should be appointed annually at Christmas with the other college officers. Each term he was to read two lectures in English in the Latin chapel on the Thirty-nine Articles. All Bachelors and undergraduates were ordered to attend.

By the will of Dr Matthew Lee, lectureships in mathematics and anatomy were founded, and are considered later.[3] All the Lee lecturers in mathematics were subsequently Junior Censors, a connection which suggests that the Censorship had not lost its ancient association with natural philosophy.

---

[1] Ch. Ch. Archives, Royal Letters.
[2] BL Add. MS 46954A, fo. 286.
[3] See pp. 272, 314

(*b*) THE TUTORIAL SYSTEM

Between the middle of the seventeenth century and the end of the eighteenth, important changes occurred in the tutorial system. At the beginning of the period the tutor occupied a relatively subordinate role, but by the end he was the principal instrument of education.

The Laudian statutes required every student to have a tutor from the time of his arrival in Oxford.[1] It was laid down that the tutor must be a graduate and a man of virtue, learning, and religion. He was required to instil virtuous morals, and to give instruction in approved authors and in the rudiments of religion. The organization of studies in university and college alike, however, pre-dated the advent of the tutor, and the Laudian statutes accordingly envisaged him as one whose task was to *prepare* his pupils for the public lectures and exercises of the university. Candidates for degrees were examined in the subjects on which they had attended the university lectures and on the authors which the university professors and lecturers were required by statute to read.[2] At Christ Church the organization of studies mirrored that in the university, and the Censors and lecturers gave lectures and managed disputations similar to those provided by the university teachers or administered in the Schools. Even the most ardent reformers did not question the basis of teaching as it had developed. In 1659 the anonymous author of *Sundry Things from Several Hands concerning the University of Oxford* proposed that most of the canonries should be converted into professorships of secular studies. Teaching, he maintained, was to be placed in the hands of these professors, and the tutors were required only to prepare their pupils for the professorial lectures and to examine them afterwards. College teaching supplanted university teaching because it was more efficient, but its efficiency was not due to the tutorial system, which was a characteristic feature of the colleges but not of the university. Until the traditional organization of studies at Christ Church broke down, as

[1] Tit. iii, 2.
[2] Tit. ix, 2. 1.

the university organization of studies had done previously, the position of the tutor as a teacher was subordinate to that of the college officers.

Although the tutor's duties in teaching remained comparatively small while the spread of classical studies envisaged by the Laudian statutes developed, his responsibility for the moral education and pastoral welfare of his pupils was very great. He stood to them, in the words of Richard Newton, who had been a tutor at Christ Church, 'in the room of Parents and Guardians'.[1] Tutors, remarked Humphrey Prideaux, who tutored at Christ Church from 1673 to 1680, ought to take special care to form the morals and principles of their pupils.[2] The pastoral nature of the tutor's duties was particularly important when undergraduates often came to the university at a tender age, but as late as the middle of the eighteenth century Edward Bentham described the tutor as one 'to whom the care of your health, your morals, your oeconomy, your learning, indeed your whole interests in this place are immediately consigned'.[3]

By the beginning of the eighteenth century several factors were causing significant changes in the tutorial system. Amongst them were the improved availability of cheap printed texts, which reduced the importance of oral instruction, and the steady rise in the average age at matriculation, which was accompanied by a higher level of attainment in the best of the public schools though not always in the grammar schools. Such developments eventually undermined the large *Classis* and even the public lectureships, and paved the way for the small tutorial class, which in turn allowed the expansion and enrichment of the curriculum to an extent not previously possible. At Christ Church the introduction of Collections reflected and eventually accelerated change.

In origin, 'Collections' were simply the notes compiled by undergraduates on the authors they read or the lectures they attended. The term was widely used in this sense. John Wesley, for example, noted in his journal on several occasions that he

[1] R. Newton, *University Education* (1726), 88.
[2] *Life of Humphrey Prideaux* (1748), 228.
[3] Bentham, *Advices to a Young Man ... upon his Coming to the University,* 19.

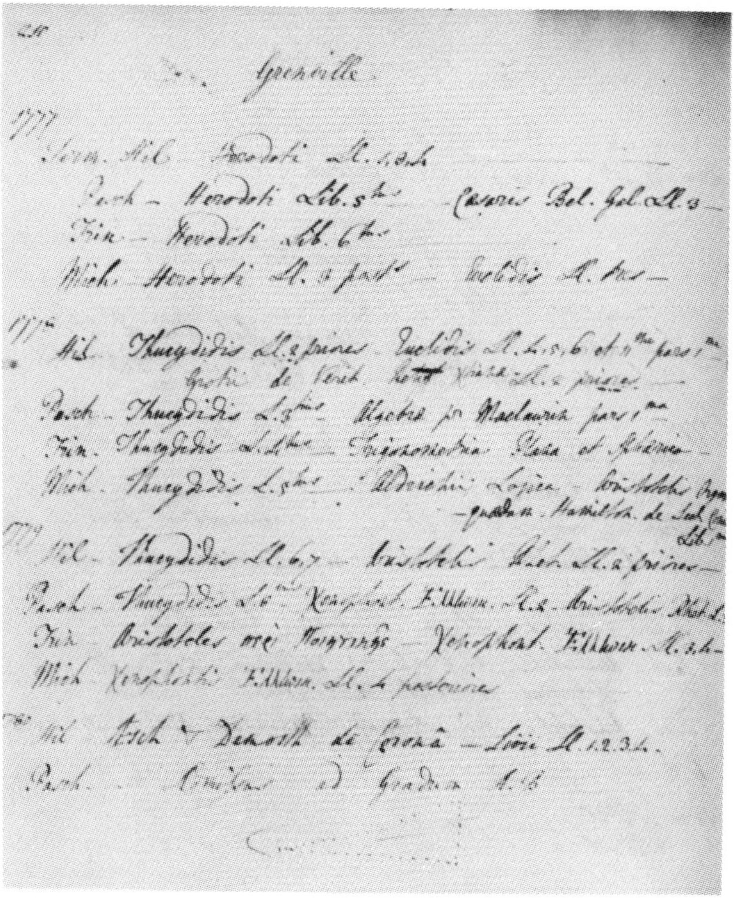

The reading of William Wyndham Grenville, 1777–80

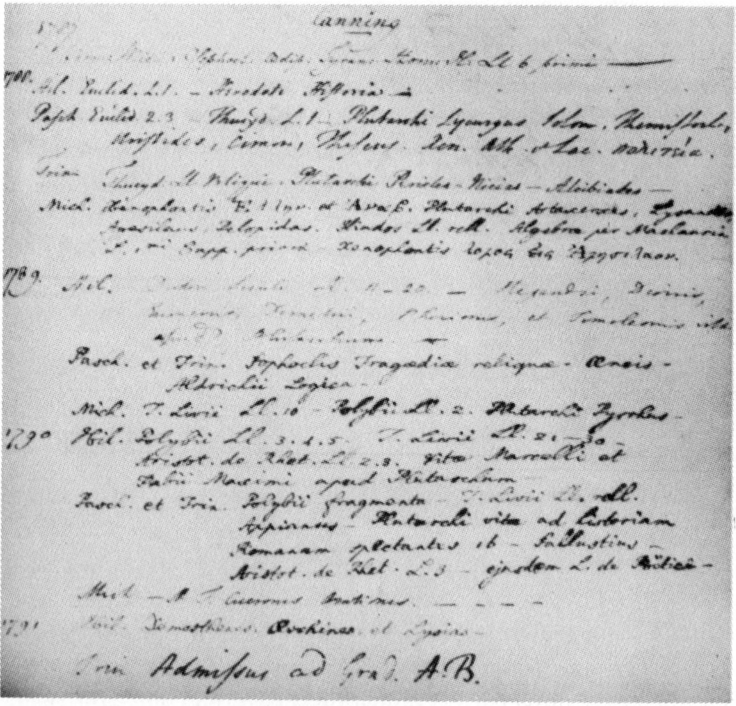

Canning

Admissus ad Grad. A.B.

The reading of George Canning, 1787–90

'collected Dr. Bennet'.[1] At Christ Church in the eighteenth century, Collections retained their original connotation but also acquired a specialized meaning to describe the college examinations at which the notes were produced for inspection, not to the tutors, but to the Dean and the college officers. The earliest use of the term in this sense known to the *Oxford English Dictionary* occurs in 1799 in a letter by Charles Kirkpatrick Sharpe, then an undergraduate at Christ Church, but records of Collections survive at Christ Church from the year 1700, and the term first appears in the records in 1726 in the Latin form *Collectanea*. The idea of Collections as an occasion when undergraduates produced their notes—the almost incontrovertible evidence of some kind of intellectual activity—continued throughout the eighteenth century. In 1726 it was noted that several students 'collectanea sua in aula monstrarunt', or 'collectanea ad aulam attulerunt', and in 1765 it was noted that one of them 'collectanea exhibuit'. In 1762 Arthur Palmer produced '2 years notes' at Collections, and in 1767 it was recorded that 'Mr. Shipley has given up his notes on the Cyropaedia to the Dean'. As late as 1809, by which time Collections had become more inquisitorial, George Chinnery was instructed to take up abstracts of the logic and rhetoric lectures he had attended.

The date when Collections were introduced at Christ Church is uncertain. As early as 1638 a proposal was made that there should be an examination for 'the younger sort before they take their degrees'. It probably arose from a wider dissatisfaction with the university examinations which in the following year earned a strong rebuke from Laud, who wrote to the Dean, Samuel Fell, 'After the university examination is past, you will have them examined again in the college, which is to put a scorn and disrepute upon the regents for their pains, and utterly to disparage the examinations, as if you in Christ Church were able to do more than the whole university in that point.'[2] Nothing is known of the examinations which caused the Archbishop so much annoy-

---

[1] J. Wesley, *Journal*, ed. N. Curnock (n.d.), i, 59.
[2] Laud, *Works*, v, 204, 220.

ance, and whatever their nature they seem to have been speedily discontinued. A good deal is known on the other hand about education at Christ Church after the Restoration, but neither the college records nor the writings of contemporaries refer to Collections. In the eighteenth century, an unnamed Canon of Christ Church informed Archbishop Secker that 'Bp Fell used to examine the Tutors, what they taught their pupils and what they studied themselves',[1] but this examination was not identical with Collections, for the tutors, who were graduates, were never examined at Collections, and if Collections had indeed existed in the time of Fell it is most unlikely that the tradition would have been lost so completely.

The only indisputable evidence for the origin of Collections is contained in the format and content of the Collections Books themselves. On the evidence of the earliest of them, the introduction of Collections may be assigned to the end of the seventeenth century. The volume begins with a list in the hand of Dean Aldrich, written in January 1700, of the authors to be studied during the ensuing twelve months by each of a total of eighteen Students, Commoners, and Servitors. It is followed immediately on the same sheet of paper by a similar list, which is not in the Dean's hand, written in January 1703. There is no list for 1701 or 1702. Subsequently entries were made at yearly intervals, except in 1708 when there was none. Up to the year 1737, the entries appear to have been written for each year separately on loose sheets of paper, which show signs of having been folded. In 1738 they were flattened and bound with additional blank unfolded sheets of paper to form the present book. It seems probable, therefore, that the folded sheets were initially kept in a bundle and only bound when they were considered to be sufficiently important for permanent preservation. The lists for 1701, 1702, and 1708 may have been lost before binding took place. Unless the early records were kept so negligently that even greater losses occurred before 1700, it is a reasonable assumption

[1] Lambeth Palace Library, MS 2564, fo. 325.

that when binding occurred all the records surviving from the introduction of Collections were included.

The view that the volume is not by the accident of history merely the earliest record to survive, but that in fact it dates from the beginning of Collections, is confirmed by the pattern of attendance between 1700 and 1717, when Dean Smalridge reorganized the system. The majority of those who took up Collections were Westminster Students or Servitors. Of the seventy-six Westminster Students elected between 1700 and 1716, thirty-three submitted Collections in three or more consecutive years, and a further eight submitted three Collections but not in consecutive years. Seventeen submitted two Collections but in six cases these were spread over three years. Fifteen submitted a single Collection, and of this number five went down without a degree. Only three Westminster Students, one of whom died prematurely, submitted no Collections at all. In the case of the Canoneer Students a different picture emerges. During the same period only eight of them submitted three or more Collections in consecutive years, and the first of them did not do so until 1707. Sixteen submitted two Collections, and fifteen a single Collection. Eighteen Canoneers submitted none at all, though most in this group took a degree. Of the Commoners and Servitors, eleven and seventeen respectively submitted three or more consecutive Collections; forty-one Commoners and twenty-three Servitors submitted two; forty-five Commoners and twenty-two Servitors submitted one. Many undergraduates submitted none at all.[1] The records also show that there was a steady increase between 1700 and 1717 in the total numbers taking Collections. The evidence of attendance suggests that in the early eighteenth century Collections, despite increasing frequency, were not compulsory for all Students, Commoners, and Servitors, that those who submitted them were not required to do so regularly year by year, and that Collections were not necessary for a degree. It thus seems to indicate that

---

[1] Noblemen and Gentlemen Commoners took up their Collections separately from the rest of the college until 1774. No records of their Collections survive at Christ Church prior to that date.

Collections were gradually being introduced at Christ Church during these years, and that they were then in their infancy.

It is also in the records themselves that the reasons for the introduction of Collections are most likely to be found. An indication of the origin of the institution is to be found in the high proportion of Westminster Students and Servitors present at the early Collections. Disparate in so many respects, the Westminster Students and Servitors shared one important common factor, namely that the Censors were tutors to both groups. The Censors and ex-Censors were also often tutors to the Canoneer Students and Commoners present. Thus it may be that Collections began when the Censors' pupils were required to produce evidence of their studies to the Censors, who were joined on the occasion by the Dean and two other senior college officers, the lecturers in rhetoric and Greek.[1]

The question then arises why Collections were introduced at this particular time. It seems unlikely that a general reform of education was intended, for their introduction passed unobserved by contemporaries, and at least fifteen years elapsed before they were deemed sufficiently important to be made compulsory for all Students, Commoners, and Servitors. The answer perhaps lies in the distinguishing characteristic of Collections which was that their organization and administration was in the hands of the Dean and the college officers. They may therefore have arisen as a means of regulating the tutorial system and the curriculum.

This is supported by the nature of the studies revealed in the earliest records. Collections, as the name suggests, were not concerned with the traditional exercises administered by the college officers, such as themes, disputations, and declamations, but with classical and other authors in the teaching of which the tutors took part. The records show the transition from oral to written studies based on the printed book. They show that at the end of the seventeenth century the written exercises taken up to Collections were of two kinds. In the first category were notes on

---

[1] They were joined by the lecturers in logic and mathematics in the time of Cyril Jackson. The ex-Censors seem to have taken their pupils initially when they were reigning Censors.

authors, mainly writers on divinity and philosophy, whose works had originally been published in the first half of the seventeenth century, and in some cases even earlier. Some of these authors had been reprinted, but others were long out of print, and the question arises how in such instances the notes taken up to Collections came to be made, for undergraduates were excluded from the college and university libraries, and it is not conceivable that sufficient second-hand copies were in circulation—even if they had been, the Servitors, who were the poorest of all undergraduates, would probably have been unable to purchase them. Collections in these circumstances are unlikely to have been based directly on the printed texts but rather on manuscript copies or notes, handed down from one generation of undergraduates to the next in the same way that 'strings' of arguments in disputations were handed down, or on the notes taken at lectures. They were thus essentially the product of an oral system of teaching.

In the second category were the written notes taken from printed texts, particularly classical texts. The Westminster Students, who were so conspicuously present at the early Collections, were familiar with the editions of classical authors published for Westminster School. Dean Aldrich's New Year Books, in contrast with Dean Fell's, were almost invariably editions of classical authors, and a number of them were undoubtedly the source of Collections.[1] As classical authors became more easily available they were read more often, and as the range and variety of authors increased there was a need to stipulate which authors should be read and in what order this should be done. It was in fact necessary to define a plan of study spread over the whole period of preparation for a degree. The traditional organization of studies based on the *Classes* was not suitable for solving these problems. It was designed for the performance of themes, verses, and disputations, and for the delivery of lectures. The college lecturer, presented with a class of differing ages and attainments,

---

[1] The supply of classical texts increased considerably in 1713, when Michael Maittaire, who had been Under Master at Westminster School, commenced the publication of a series of Latin classics which by 1722 numbered no less than nineteen authors.

might teach a limited number of authors, but not the increased number suddenly placed in the hands of students. The spread of classical texts thus made the tutor a more important person in education, and this appears to be reflected in the remarkable statement made in 1685 by Robert South, who had been a Westminster Student, that college tutors were 'a thing lately much in fashion'.[1] The tutors, however, although appointed by the Dean, were not officials of the college and were employed privately by their pupils. The introduction of Collections may thus have served the dual purpose of defining the curriculum and thereby regulating the tutorial system.

That a plan of study for reading classical texts existed by the early eighteenth century is apparent from the earliest records of Collections. In 1707, for example, a student compared Virgil with Theocritus. The words used are 'comparare Virgilium cum Theocrito'. They indicate an exercise to be completed in the future rather than one already executed and so imply a previous plan of study. Occasionally a book or author has been deleted from the record of an under-graduate's Collections, but such deletions would be incomprehensible if made *after* the Collections in question had been submitted and must therefore have been made beforehand. Again a future plan of study is implied. But the structure of the plan is often unclear and the presence of unusual works, of which the appearance of the Koran in 1703 is the most remarkable, indicates that it was less precisely defined than it became later. Its consolidation was the work of Dean Smalridge.

Smalridge drew up a list of books to be read in each of the four years necessary for a degree. It was an administrative rather than an educational reform, and was caused by the yearly increase in the numbers taking Collections and by the growing practice of submitting them in three or four consecutive years. Smalridge made Collections compulsory for Students, Commoners, and Servitors almost immediately after his appointment, and in 1717 the pressure of numbers caused him to revise and simplify the

---

[1] R. South, *Twelve Sermons and Discourses on Several Subjects and Occasions* (1717), v, 26.

curriculum. For each *Classis* he compiled a list of books entitled 'libri legendi a discipulis primae classis', and so forth. The term 'libri legendi' implied that the books were mandatory and also that they were to be read in the future. In fact the lists were compiled in January each year, and it was expected that the prescribed books would be taken up to Collections by the following January. Smalridge laid down the curriculum within the traditional organization of the *Classes,* but in enforcing it he had the great advantage over his predecessors that the institution of Collections provided the means of administering it by calling each undergraduate to account for his studies during the previous twelve months. Although the curriculum was defined, Smalridge made no attempt to change the tutorial system itself.[1]

---

[1] Until 1767, after the Dean had entered the lists of 'libri legendi' for each of the four *Classes,* the names of the undergraduates who formed those *Classes* were added below at the time of their admission to the *Classis* in question. Often they signed their names, but at other times these were entered by the college officers. The entry of an undergraduate's name, whether in his own hand or not, served several purposes. It signified the act of enrolment in a *Classis,* it provided a record of the progression of an undergraduate from one *Classis* to another, and it enabled undergraduates to take note of the books they were required to read for Collections. The entry of an undergraduate's name is not evidence that he submitted Collections, nor, therefore, of the frequency of Collections, for it may be shown that undergraduates were placed in a *Classis* (usually the 1st *Classis*) immediately after matriculation and thus too soon after their arrival at Christ Church to enable them to submit Collections. Evidence of the frequency of Collections may perhaps be found in the addition of a cross against many names. This is not found in every year, nor where it is found does it always appear against the name of every undergraduate in a *Classis*. Until 1767 there is never more than one cross against a name, but in that year the books for each *Classis* were for the first time listed separately under each of the four terms, and for the first time four crosses were placed against the names of undergraduates. At the same time the Westminster Students were placed in a separate *Classis* for a single term and against their names a single cross was placed. The crosses seem to indicate that until 1767 Collections were held annually, and thereafter terminally. Such an interpretation removes what is otherwise a difficulty in understanding how the course of study was pursued, for when the lists of 'libri legendi' were drawn up once a year and were not divided into terms, it is not apparent how books prescribed in January were subsequently studied term by term. Although Collections appear to have occurred annually until 1767, they did not always take place at the same time of year, for there are many examples of them being

Although well attended from the time of Smalridge, Collections were not an occasion for the rigorous scrutiny of studies. In 1737 the Bishop of Oxford, Thomas Secker, was informed that at Christ Church

the young people in their first years make what they call Collections: i.e. observations upon such parts of Homer, Virgil, Pearson on the Creed etc. but these they transcribe from one another. They are also examined in these books by the Dean, Subdean, Censors, and two or more persons, but perhaps 40 are examined in a morning.[1]

Collections, which had been introduced not to stimulate competition between undergraduates but to regulate and rationalize studies, thus continued to serve their original function. The notes produced at Collections reflected the appearance rather than the reality of study, and the examination to which undergraduates were subjected was no more than perfunctory. Conducted in this fashion, Collections imposed a minimum level of attainment but had little effect in raising standards at Christ Church. In these circumstances the curriculum ossified and underwent little change. By the middle of the century it was becoming apparent that classical studies could not be taught adequately through the *Classes,* and that the more active participation of the tutors was needed.

Signs that the organization of studies represented by the *Classes* was not functioning smoothly appeared within a decade of the introduction of compulsory Collections, when wide fluctuations occurred in the size of *Classes* between one year and the next. It was the usual practice for undergraduates to be placed in the first or junior *Classis* at the time of matriculation. The expectation was that after a year they would move into the second *Classis,* and subsequently into the third and fourth. It is evident that this did not take place, for large differences arose between the size of the first and second *Classes* in consecutive years, or between the second and third, or the third and fourth. The examples in Table IV.1,

submitted at different times, but whenever this occurred Collections for more than one year were presented.

[1] Lambeth Palace Library, MS 2564, fo. 319.

taken at random, are typical of the situation before Markham. The fluctuations are too great to be explained by the erratic pattern of matriculation (which the *Classes* were well able to absorb), or by absence or departure from the university, and it is found that only about half the undergraduates who took a degree passed through all four *Classes*. Of those who did not progress through all four, some were older than average or migrated to Christ Church from other colleges, and these were often placed in the third or even the fourth *Classis*. Others jumped a *Classis*. In 1737, for example, John Henchman and Israel Vander are noted as 'e prima in tertiam classem per saltum admissus'. Some undergraduates were held back in the same *Classis* for a second year, while others passed from one *Classis* to a higher within the same year. In the absence of any signs of an improvement in the curriculum itself, such divergences from the original pattern of the *Classes* are a sign not of its flexibility but of its gradual decline. They were caused by the rise in the age at which undergraduates came to the university and the higher level of attainment they brought with them.

If the *Classes* were in decay, so also were the traditional oral exercises performed at Christ Church. The frequency with which the Chapter sought to tighten up the regulations indicated their neglect. Many of the exercises required the presence of graduates, and a decline in the number of resident Masters and Bachelors

TABLE IV. 1. Size of *Classes*

	Classis 1[a]	Classis 2	Classis 3	Classis 4
1730	35	38	20	13
1731	19	17	12	14
1740	21	14	13	4
1741	18	23	15	9
1746	13	16	12	22
1747	19	7	9	7
1753	9	16	13	10
1754	23	11	13	17
1763	3	12	12	
1764	17	15	27	

[a] Figures for *Classis* 1 in 1730, 1740, 1746, 1753, and 1763 should be compared with those for *Classis* 2 in the following year, and so on.

hindered their performance by undergraduates. In 1706, when the fines on Masters were trebled, it was noted that 'for some years past there has bin a great neglect in the performance of divinity exercises both in lectures and disputations'.[1] In 1738 laxity in the performance of exercises by Bachelors and undergraduates was the subject of a stern warning. But the tide was running too strongly to be stemmed by fine or admonition. The college archives contain an account of the Sub-Dean's duties drawn up by Thomas Hunt, who held the office from 1751 to 1753, with annotations by his successor Edward Bentham. It shows that the Bachelors then declaimed only once a week, whereas in the previous century they had done so twice a week. The Senior Censor lectured the Bachelors once a week instead of twice, and the Junior Censor once a week instead of three times as formerly. Bentham noted that Junior Masters only disputed and Senior Masters only read lectures.[2]

By the time of Dean Gregory's appointment in 1756, the reform of the educational system was long overdue. The plan of study was ossified, the organization of the *Classes* was inefficient, the ancient exercises were no longer carefully observed, Collections were a formality, and the tutorial system stagnated. But first under Gregory and Markham, and later under Cyril Jackson, sweeping reforms were made which revitalized and restored education at Christ Church. Through their efforts the natural tendencies of youth to indolence and excessive physical exertion occasionally surrendered to the abrasive charms of classical literature and philosophy. 'Learning', wrote Gibbon of Christ Church, 'has been made a duty, a pleasure, and even a fashion'.[3] Of Markham's reform of the curriculum he wrote that 'a more regular discipline has been introduced, as I am told, at Christ Church: a course of classical studies is proposed and even pursued in that numerous seminary'.[4]

The reform from which all others followed was the reform of

---

[1] Chapter Act Book, 24 Dec. 1706.
[2] Ch. Ch. Archives, liii. b. 4.
[3] J. Murray (ed.), *The autobiographies of Edward Gibbon* (1896), 94.
[4] Ibid.

Collections. From it followed the reform of the plan of study and the tutorial system. So thorough was the reform of Collections in the second half of the eighteenth century that contemporaries came near to believing that a new institution had been created. There was, however, some disagreement as to where the credit for this achievement lay. When Cyril Jackson died in 1819, a correspondent wrote to the *Gentleman's Magazine* to attribute it to him, but he was almost immediately contradicted by another correspondent who declared that 'the credit of putting everything in excellent order is due to Bagot', while yet another authority recorded his conviction that Collections had been invented by Markham.[1] In fact all of them made notable contributions, and to them should be added Dean Gregory, in whose time terminal Collections seem to have begun.

Markham enforced Collections vigorously, using them as the means for introducing the vast changes in the curriculum which are discussed in later chapters. From 1768 the records contain the books actually taken up by each Student, Commoner, and Servitor, and not simply those which they were supposed to have read. In 1769 for the first time an undergraduate was punished for not giving up Collections. The offender was Edward Wortley Montagu, the grandson of Lady Mary. Collections became, at least for Students, the essential preliminary for a degree when the Chapter required Students, when applying for a grace for BA, to produce a copy of the Censors' Book certifying what Collections they had given up from the time of their first entrance to the college.[2] Markham's most important reform occurred in 1774 when Noblemen and Gentlemen Commoners, whose separately presented Collections perhaps indicated a more tenuous connection with the curriculum than that of other undergraduates,

---

[1] *Gentleman's Magazine* (1819), 460; (1820) (1), 393, 504.

[2] Chapter Minute Book, 2 Nov. 1775. The description of the Collections Book as the 'Censors' Book' is an interesting confirmation of the suggestion advanced earlier that Collections originated with the Censors. The production of satisfactory Collections remained a condition for a degree. In 1783 an undergraduate was admonished in the following terms: 'Monitus interclusum ei gradus A B ambitum donec ulterius de collectaneis satisfecit' (Ch. Ch. Archives, Collections Book, 1772–89, li. b. 2, p. 322).

were required to take up their Collections with the rest of the college. This achieved a long-standing ambition. In 1768 Markham had written to Charles Jenkinson, 'My great object is to bring the Noblemen and Gentlemen Commoners to the same attendance on college duties and the same habits of industry with the inferior members'.[1] The Noblemen and Gentlemen Commoners had never been taught in the *Classes,* and the sudden increase in the number of undergraduates receiving a common education, coupled with a simultaneous rise in the rate of matriculation, proved too much for the ancient organization of studies to withstand. From 1776 undergraduates ceased to be entered in *Classes,* and annual lists of prescribed books, the 'libri legendi', ceased to be entered in the Collections Book.[2]

Bagot consolidated the achievements of his predecessors,

---

[1] BL Add. MS 38457, fo. 11ᵛ.

[2] The collapse of the *Classes* had long been heralded under Markham. Although annual reading lists continued to be prescribed, the preferences expressed for particular authors, under the influence of the tutors, were often divorced from them. Sallust, for example, was the most popular prescribed author in the 1st *Classis* in 1768, but in the following year he dropped to 5th place, and Caesar's *Commentaries* fell from 2nd to 10th. In the same year Livy dropped from 2nd to 3rd in the reading of the second *Classis,* but Quintilian climbed from 7th to 2nd, and in the 3rd *Classis* Xenophon's *Hellenica* rose from 6th to 3rd. The question arises whether books on the prescribed lists were in fact read by the *Classes* but not taken up to Collections (in which event there would of course be no record of them having been read). This does not appear to have been the case. George Chinnery records that in Act term 1808 he prepared and took up the *Iliad,* Keill, logarithms, two books of conic sections, and some Horace. 'The Dean', he wrote, 'said that he had not time to examine me in logarithms, or conic sections or Horace, but that Lloyd had told him I knew them very well. He told me I was improved in Greek and said that he knew no man worked harder than I do. Instead of examining me in trigonometry according to the book he made corollaries and deductions of his own in which he questioned me ... He told me to bring up next Collections what he had not examined me in this term, in addition to anything else. He told me that Lloyd thought I was very quick at calculating and that he had purposely put these difficult questions to me' (Ch. Ch. Archives, xlviii. a. 44, fo. 104). The formal record of Chinnery's Collections on this occasion relates that he took up the *Iliad,* the *Satires, Epistles,* and *Ars Poetica* of Horace, two books of conic sections, plane trigonometry, and logarithms, and thus seems to establish that the Collections Books register what was actually read, though not necessarily everything on which an undergraduate was examined.

though not without occasional alarms and excursions. Richard Polwhele recalled one such when he wrote that

At Collections, I was myself under examination at the high-tribunal, where Bagot sat, and Smallwell, Randolph, and Jackson ... when one of our gold-tufts was called up to answer to some question which had been omitted. The question put to him I do not remember: but I remember his answer,—'I neither know, nor care'. Bagot's 'hasty conscience' could not brook such insolence. 'My Lord', said Bagot, 'go down; we have done with you'. My Lord sneered. 'Rascal!' cried the Dean. His lordship turned upon his heel, and walked down the hall with affected indifference. My examination was resumed. But Bagot uttered not a word. In the evening he wrote a note of apology to his lordship,— a note sufficiently humiliating; with which it was his wish that the whole college should be acquainted. So quick was his sensibility, that he could not on all occasions command it.[1]

Nevertheless, under Bagot, Collections were kept carefully and systematically. The numbers attending them increased dramatically, as a result of Markham's reforms. In 1777 John Randolph, who was then Junior Censor, began the practice of compiling terminal statistics, and for the first three years the figures were as shown in Table IV.2.[2]

It was under Cyril Jackson, however, that Collections perhaps reached the zenith of their importance. Whereas Fell presided at

TABLE IV. 2. Totals Attending Collections 1777–1779

Year	No. attending Collections			
	Hil.	Pasch.	Trin.	Mich.
1777	71	64	70	76
1778	83	79	85	91
1779	101	105	104	105

[1] Polwhele, *Reminiscences,* ii, 5.

[2] From 1784 the numbers never fell below 100 in any term, and in 1800 they reached a total of 123. From Michaelmas 1779 separate statistics were kept for Students, Noblemen, Gentlemen Commoners, Commoners, and Servitors.

disputations, Dean Jackson presided at Collections. Under his watchful eye Collections became an impressive and searching occasion. Whereas Bishop Secker was informed that forty students were examined in a morning, George Chinnery noted in 1808 that four were examined in an hour.[1] So lengthy were the proceedings that they were spread over several days, and a trade developed in the sale of turns, for undergraduates were examined in order of seniority, Students and Noblemen having precedence over all others. In 1830 Gladstone wrote to his father that James Gaskell, a Gentleman Commoner, had taken his Collections 'in a Servitor's turn, which a friend of his bought for a guinea and afterwards finding he did not want it made over to him at half price'.[2] Shortly after Jackson's appointment, comments, always critical and never commendatory, began to appear in the Collections Books. The most frequent comment on classical collections was 'minus accurate', and in mathematics 'ulterius satisfaciendum'. Comments on mathematical studies were made almost twice as often as those on all other studies, and reveal the importance which Jackson attached to proficiency in the subject and the difficulty often experienced in obtaining it.[3]

Under Jackson, Collections were not a formal occasion: undergraduates were questioned by him and were expected to satisfy him. When Chinnery proposed to take up the *Georgics* he wrote, 'It is reckoned a very handsome Collection, for the Dean is not satisfied if you can construe it. You must know where each town is to found which the poet mentions, and be acquainted with the pedigree of each hero or personage etc—besides Georgics are full of technical terms and difficult botanical names.'[4] The college library contains an evocative relic of such Collections in a well-

---

[1] Ch. Ch. Archives, xlviii. a. 43, fo. 87ᵛ.

[2] Hawarden Letters, W. E. Gladstone to T. Gladstone, 24 June 1830.

[3] Occasionally the dry records are illuminated by expressions of joy and relief. When Charles Collins left Christ Church for St Mary Hall in 1795, his departure was hailed with the remark, 'Cum magna omnium laetitia migravit' (p. 131), and when at last one Kennedy struggled through a particular author his success was welcomed with the words 'Diodori Siculi opus scilicet cum magna omnium laetitia demum ad finem productum' (p. 177).

[4] Ch. Ch. Achives, xlviii. a. 42a, fo. 144v.

worn copy of D'Anville's *Complete Body of Ancient Geography* (1785), inscribed on the cover 'For Collections'. To obtain the Dean's approval and commendation was the acknowledged ambition of many undergraduates. In a letter written on 9 December 1808 Chinnery made no effort to disguise his pleasure in presenting a good Collection.

I at last walked up to the table, and was made to construe some of the Homer. Goodenough said, 'That is very accurately construed', and the Dean added, 'he is wonderfully improved'. After construing the Euripides, the Dean told me 'that is equally well construed'. I felt myself so perfectly at home with the Satires of Juvenal that I could not fail doing those with perfect satisfaction to myself . . . The Dean was much pleased with the Conic Sections, for having asked several questions, all of which I was fortunate enough to answer very readily, he said, 'All your answers have been uncommonly clear and correct', and last of all by way of a finale he sent me away with these words, 'Very well, Sir, you have pleased me much: these are very good—most excellent Collections'.[1]

How different was W. F. Hook's experience in 1818 when 'Dean Hall came over from his side & asked what kind of an examination I had passed, but of course, as is his custom, did not wait for an answer',[2] or Ruskin's famous account much later of Gaisford at Collections, 'Scornful at once, and vindictive, thunderous always, more sullen and threatening as the day went on'.[3] In the time of Cyril Jackson, Collections at Christ Church provided the effective examination which the university failed to do.[4]

---

[1] Ch. Ch. Archives, xlviii. a. 45, fo. 139ᵛ.
[2] Ibid., Letters, W. F. Hook to his mother, 16 Mar. 1818 (copy).
[3] J. Ruskin, *Works,* ed. E. T. Cook and A. Wedderburn (1903–12), xxxv, 193.
[4] Despite occasional mutterings by Wood, there is little evidence of serious disarray in the university examinations until the middle of the eighteenth century. By then disputations had fallen into decay, and the enlarged curriculum adopted in the colleges was not reflected by a corresponding reform of the public examinations. The experience of Lord Eldon has often been quoted. When he took his degree in 1770, he wrote, 'I was examined in Hebrew and History. "What is the Hebrew for the place of a skull?" I replied, "Golgotha". "Who founded University College?" I stated . . . "that King Alfred founded it". "Very well, Sir", said the Examiner, "you are competent for your Degree"' (H. Twiss, *Life of Lord Eldon* (1844), i, 57). One of the questions, however, may have been

Markham's reform of Collections was followed by the reform of the college lectures. Although reform occurred when he was Dean, it seems not to have been initiated by him but by the Censors and the lecturer in rhetoric. On 24 December 1777 the Dean and Chapter took the unprecedented step of voting £50 each to Thomas Pettingal, the Senior Censor, John Randolph, the Junior Censor, and William Jackson, the lecturer in rhetoric, 'in recognition of their extraordinary services to the college in first contributing to promote the establishment of the public lectures and since in carrying on their respective courses with uncommon diligence and ability'.[1] Of Thomas Pettingal little is known. He was a Westminster Student and after his degree returned to the School as an usher. He was a lecturer in logic at Christ Church for two years and Senior Censor from 1774 to 1779. In 1782 he retired to enjoy the bucolic pleasures of the college living of Easthampstead and was heard of no more. William Jackson, brother of the Dean, was also a Westminster Student, and served as lecturer in Greek and rhetoric and eventually as Junior Censor. From 1769 to 1783 he also held the mathematical lectureship founded under the will of Matthew Lee. Of the three Students, John Randolph was without doubt the most distinguished. He was the son of the President of Corpus Christi College, Oxford, and came up as a Westminster Student in 1767. He was lecturer in Greek in 1774, Junior Censor from 1775 to 1778, Senior Censor from 1779 to 1782, Canon of Christ Church and Regius Professor of Divinity in 1783, and Censor Theologiae almost continuously from the following year until he became Bishop of Oxford in 1799. He was in addition at various times Professor of Poetry, Regius Professor of Greek, and Professor of Moral Philosophy. Randolph was a man of great learning and ability, but he was not able to fire the enthusiasm of his pupils. One of them, Edward

---

an example of the 'wit and jocularity' to which, according to Vicesimus Knox, examiners were prone (*Essays Moral and Literary* (1785), i, 334), for according to Nicholas Amherst the Clarendon Building was 'by the idle wits and buffoons nick-named Golgotha, that is, the place of Skulls or Heads of colleges and halls, where they meet and debate upon all extraordinary affairs' (*Terrae Filius*, 53).

[1] Chapter Act Book, 24 Dec. 1777.

Nares the historian, described him as 'too reserved to give me the encouragement of which I stood in need'.[1] Lord Holland, attempting to be fair but succeeding in being unkind, said of his divinity lectures that they

were probably distinguished by more talent, and certainly possessed learning seldom found and perhaps not often sought for out of the walls of a college. Yet they were no favourites with the public, nor even those young men who were destined to Holy Orders. This was owing to the slovenly delivery, awkward and obscure phraseology, and rude, unpolished manner of the lecturer. Under that exterior, however, the ungraceful and ungracious priest, narrow-minded Tory as he was, concealed a kind heart and a disinterested, compassionate, and generous disposition.[2]

The reform of the public lectures, for which Pettingal, Randolph, and Jackson were so handsomely rewarded, was described in the *Gentleman's Magazine* in 1820 by an anonymous contributor who had been an undergraduate at Christ Church in the time of Dean Bagot. He wrote,

The Public Lectures are classed in three departments; Divinity, pure Mathematics, and Logic, with its kindred subjects. The establishment of a Lecture in Divinity is perhaps coeval with the foundation of Christ Church. For the last fifty years, at least, it has (except with accidental intermissions) been read constantly during every term, and attended regularly ... The two other departments of the Public lectures were established under the auspices of Dean Markham, and had become (in addition to the Tutor's usual courses of private instruction) an effective part of the general system in 1774. From that time to the present, they have gone on with little variation. They have always been delivered, one or other of them, daily, during Term; the attendance of the young men,

[1] G. C. White, *A Versatile Professor* (1903), 17.

[2] Holland, *Further Memoirs of the Whig Party*, 338–9. Cyril Jackson once remarked that Randolph had read much more than he had thought (Lambeth Palace Library, MS 2186, fo. 32); and in 1812 a critic noted that his sermons lacked eloquence and were directed to the head rather than to the heart: 'Learning has rendered him both thinking and argumentative; but nature seems not to have vouchsafed to him the power of animating the mind, and electrifying the feelings' (Onesimus [Garnet Terry], *The Pulpit or a Biographical Account of Eminent Popular Preachers* (1812), ii, 18).

according to their standing, having been constantly required, and their progress, from time to time, the subject of regular inquiry.[1]

In order to accommodate the lectures, the Chapter ordered that a bequest by Dr Daniel Burton should be applied to the fitting up of two lecture rooms in the Old Library.[2]

The reform of Collections and college lectures, and the collapse of the ancient organization of studies by the *Classes,* paved the way for developments in the tutorial system.

Tutors were appointed by the Dean, but had no official standing in the college, and their existence was not formally recognized by the Governing Body, which appointed the Censors and other educational officers of Christ Church. Until the nineteenth century no record was kept of their appointment nor of the allocation of pupils to them.[3] The right to appoint them was a prerogative much prized by the Deans and seldom shared. Occasionally the wishes of a parent might be considered. Dr Stratford relates that Lord Glenorchy appointed Noel Broxholme tutor to his son in 1711 and arranged for him to live in his son's chambers.[4] Even more rarely the preferences of a particular undergraduate might be consulted, for in 1806 B. C. Roberts reported that, during a discussion with the Dean about his tutor, Jackson 'seemed to say that I should have some choice in the matter, asking me who I should like best'.[5] The young William Wake's account of his arrival in the university is perhaps more representative of the manner in which matters were conducted. He relates that in 1673 his father took him to Oxford intending to enter him at Trinity, but 'the very next morning going to see one of his old cavalier

---

[1] *Gentleman's Magazine* (Jan. 1820), 4.

[2] Chapter Act Book, 2 Jan. 1776. The college lectures are not entered as such in the Collections Books until the very end of the century, but their existence may be inferred after the abolition of the *Classes* by the submission of identical or similar Collections by large numbers of undergraduates in the same term. In 1777, for example, classes averaging about fifteen and on one occasion rising to about thirty submitted identical or similar Collections in logic, Euclid, algebra, trigonometry, and various works by Aristotle.

[3] See app. ii below for the identification of tutors.

[4] HMC, *Portland* (1901), vii, 54.

[5] *Letters and Miscellaneous Papers by B. C. Roberts* (1814), 16.

friends at Christ Church, the Dean met us in quadrangle, took us to his lodgings, and immediately entered me into that college, and assigned me the Reverend Mr. Wheeler, then one of his chaplains, to be my tutor'.[1] The Dean's right to appoint tutors strengthened his control of the educational arrangements at Christ Church. In 1725, for example, Stratford, unable as ever to resist a discreditable anecdote, recorded that Dr Terry, the Sub-Dean, 'begins to closet young men, and to tell them if they expect to be trusted with pupils they must give proofs of their affection to the Governor [i.e. the unpopular Bradshaw]', and that he asked them, 'will you do as you are directed? Will you choose such *Parliament men* as you shall be directed?'.[2] It established a powerful interest between the Dean and the Students, for the ability to appoint a tutor to a wealthy and potentially influential undergraduate was a form of patronage not lightly to be dismissed. For Dean Fell the right to appoint tutors was an instrument for achieving his social and political ambitions at Christ Church. It enabled Cyril Jackson to organize the tutors into a band of willing informers ever ready to pour tidings of their charges into the Dean's retentive ear.[3]

At Christ Church the tutors were intellectually and socially a cross-section of the college. What is known of their background does not lend support to the denigration to which tutors in the university were frequently subjected. Indeed the aristocracy and gentry would not have committed their sons to such an intimate relationship as that which existed between tutor and pupil had the college tutor failed to realize their educational and social aspirations.

They were recruited, with a few exceptions, from amongst the

[1] Quoted in N. Sykes, *William Wake* (1957), i, 9.
[2] HMC, *Portland* (1901), vii, 396.
[3] Apart from Aldrich, only Smalridge and Markham had much direct experience as tutors at Christ Church. The only pupils who may be assigned with certainty to Atterbury are Henry Chester, whose caution was repaid to Atterbury on 20 Jan. 1686/7, and Charles Boyle, whose caution was paid to him on 25 June 1690. Bagot's only pupil seems to have been his younger brother Thomas, whose caution he paid on 21 Oct. 1763, though when Thomas Bagot was elected to a Canoneer Studentship in the following Dec. his tutor was Henry Courtenay. Cyril Jackson, unlike his brother William, was never a tutor at Christ Church. Bradshaw and Conybeare were tutors but not at Christ Church.

Students. These exceptions occurred almost entirely in the time of Fell and Aldrich, when a few chaplains were appointed. One of these was Wake's tutor Maurice Wheeler, who was tutor between 1671 and 1675 to at least two Students and seven Commoners.[1] The former Presbyterian Peter Birch, who was a protégé of Fell, was also appointed to a chaplaincy and a tutorship. Between 1674 and 1678 he received as pupils some five Commoners, a Gentleman Commoner, and a Nobleman. In 1706 and 1715 two other chaplains, Sampson Estwick and Thomas Lamprey, were employed.[2] Thereafter it has been possible to find only one tutor in the eighteenth century who was not also a Student. He was Christopher Pegge, who tutored Edward Ash in 1791. Although never a Student, Pegge was Lee lecturer in anatomy at the time.

The social background of the tutors, although similar, was not identical to that of the Students as a whole. Not only were they, with few exceptions, themselves in holy orders but an increasing proportion of them were also the sons of clergymen. Until the middle of the eighteenth century almost 40 per cent of tutors described themselves in the university registers at matriculation as the sons of clergymen, but in the second half of the century the proportion increased steadily and under Cyril Jackson exceeded 60 per cent. The tendency reflected the rising prosperity of many of the parochial clergy as the enclosure movement increased the value of tithes and land. Clergy who in earlier times had been obliged to send their sons to Christ Church as Servitors, who were ineligible for Studentships and therefore for appointment as tutors, now sent them as Commoners eligible for Canoneer Studentships. It also reflected the changing fortunes of Westminster School in the late eighteenth century. The Westminster Students provided about two-thirds of all the tutors, and under Dean

[1] He was employed by Fell to make the drawings for the Coptic type which the Dean caused to be made for the university press (Morison, *John Fell, the University Press and the 'Fell' Types,* 159). He was subsequently a schoolmaster in Gloucester.

[2] Estwick was a crony of Aldrich, and was described by Hearne as 'reckon'd to understand Musick as well as any Man in England'. His only pupil was his nephew Francis Fysher, whose brother Robert was appointed Bodley's Librarian in 1729 (Hearne, *Collections,* iii, 8; xi, 81.)

Fell considerably more.[1] Towards the end of the century the school lost much of its popularity with the aristocracy and gentry, and a higher proportion of Studentships were then filled by sons of the clergy. The clerical background of the tutors was further strengthened by the recruitment of tutors from amongst the sons of Canons, a practice hallowed by tradition, and by the emergence of clerical dynasties of tutors who were the sons of tutors.[2]

After the clergy, a substantial proportion of tutors were the sons of gentlemen or professional men, and some of these proved popular tutors to the Noblemen and Gentlemen Commoners. One of them was Aldrich, who was described in 1679 by John Perceval as 'a gentleman born, well bred himself, and tho excellent both in ancient and modern learning yet wholly free from all yt can be interpreted as Pedantry, [which] makes me think him ye fittest man to beare ye office of a Tutor'.[3] Another example was George Butt, the son of a surgeon, and father of the novelist Mary Sherwood, whose biographer observed that Noblemen and Gentlemen Commoners found his society agreeable 'on account of that sportive wit and humor which enlivened, and that genuine

[1] At the Restoration remarkable preference was given to the Westminster Students in the appointment of tutors. Of ten tutors identified between 1660 and 1662, all but two were Westminster Students. All of them had matriculated before the Restoration and many had taken their first degree and in some instances their Master's degree before 1660. Of the Students restored to their places at the Restoration, only two Westminster Students, Richard Hill and David Whitford, and one Canoneer Student, Ralph Tounson, were employed as tutors. No serious attempt was made to entrust the educational work of the college to the restored Students, many of whom, if the truth were known, had probably forgotten much of their learning during the troubled years of civil war and revolution. During the Commonwealth, Westminster School had been such a centre of loyalty to Church and King that Dean Owen was heard to say on more than one occasion that 'it would never be well with the nation till this school was suppressed' (*Sermons Preached upon Several occasions by Robert South* (1865), i, 431).

[2] Amongst those whose fathers before them were tutors may be accounted Edward Blakeway (1713), son of Richard Blakeway (1676); John Whitfeld (1722), son of William Whitfeld (1677); Thomas Hind (1772), son of Richard Hind (1730); Richard Slade (1783), son of another Richard Slade (1729); William Page (1795), son of William Page (1755). Richard Le Hunte (1742) was nephew of William Le Hunte (1710).

[3] BL Add. MS 49956A, fo. 36.

taste and manly sense which dignified his conversation'.[1] For scions of the aristocracy and gentry, many of whom were Students in the eighteenth century, tutorships possessed few attractions, but Henry Courtenay, who was a tutor from 1763 to 1767, was the grandson of a baronet and the nephew of a viscount. Occasionally the son of a bishop was appointed. Ralph Tounson and David Whitford were the sons respectively of the Bishops of Salisbury and Brechin. In 1696 William Stratford, the son of the Bishop of Chester, was made a tutor, and in 1783 Charles Moss, son of the Bishop of Bath and Wells took as his pupil Lord Frederick North, the distinguished philhellene.

Until late in the eighteenth century, when the status of tutors improved, the attractions of a tutorship were seldom financial. William Taswell, who came up to Christ Church as a Westminster Student in 1670, paid his tutor £4 a year, and this sum was recommended for tuition by Matthew Poole in *A Model for the Maintaining of Students ... at the University,* published in 1658.[2] Noblemen and Gentlemen Commoners paid £20 a year.[3] A tutor could augment his income by writing verses and exercises for his pupils. Of Richard Peers, Anthony Wood wrote that, ' 'twas usual with him to make the exercise of idle scholars, either for money or something worth it from the buttery book'.[4] In 1700 Anthony Alsop received £3. 4s. 6d. for 'making publick verses on the death of the Duke of Gloucester' published under the name of Sir Bourchier Wrey.[5] Some Students made the writing of verses almost a cottage industry. James Harrington, although not a tutor, wrote in 1688, 'Congratulatory Verses are making ... I shall furnish a Gentleman or two with an empty set of distichs'. He also composed speeches for undergraduates to deliver when seeking their degrees.[6] In 1677 John Perceval paid Charles Allestry, a tutor but not his own, the sum of £2. 3s. 0d. for

[1] R. Valpy, *Poems Spoken on Public Occasions at Reading School* (1804), 231.

[2] Camden Society (1853), 18; Bodl. Wood 515 (19).

[3] Ch. Ch. Library, MS 427, fo. 7; BL Add. MS 46955A, fo. 106; HMC, *Finch* (1913), i, 237.

[4] Wood, *Athenae,* iv, 853.

[5] HMC, *11th Report,* app. vii (1888) (Bridgwater), 155.

[6] BL Add. MS 36707, fo. 36.

'making my verses at ye Act'.[1] Such odd sums suggest that sometimes the writing of verses was paid for as piece-work, line for line. In 1708 Edward Harley informed his father that he had given Noel Broxholme two guineas 'for the Ode that is printed in the Oxford verses with my name'.[2] The Censors received certain payments for tuition in addition to their stipends and any emoluments arranged with their pupils privately. A Chapter order on 24 April 1637 directed that the fines levied on Bachelors for absence from disputations or morning lectures, or for omitting to declaim, should be divided into three parts, of which one was to go to Domus and two were to be divided between the Censors. In 1660 the Chapter granted the Censors an allowance of £5 'in consideration of their reading night prayers and taking care of ye servitors'.[3] From the tuition of the Westminster Students, the Censors derived a not inconsiderable income, which was increased to eight guineas a year for each pupil in 1799.[4]

During the latter part of the eighteenth century tutorships became more valuable, as the number of tutors was reduced and the rate of matriculation increased. By then Gentlemen Commoners paid £20 or £30 a year to their tutor, and Noblemen perhaps £100. It was said that in 1754 Edward Smallwell 'hath 400[li] a year from pupils'.[5] The extent to which the income and prospects of a leading tutor had improved by the beginning of the following century is shown by a letter written in 1819 by C. T. Longley, who had taken his MA in the previous year.

I am [he wrote] in receipt of a salary of £450 a year, besides having apartments and a table throughout the year. This salary in the course of five years I might consider as certain of augmenting to between £700 and £800. In the mean time I should by my exertions in my profession, and in the occupation of public tutor, be making myself known to those whose good-will and esteem it is of importance to persons in every situation to deserve; and if I conducted myself in such manner as to

[1] BL Add. MS 46954B, fo. 90.
[2] HMC, Portland, *15th Report,* app. iv (1897), 516.
[3] Chapter Act Book, 24 Dec. 1660.
[4] Chapter Act Book, 26 Jan. 1799.
[5] Lambeth Palace Library, MS 2564, fos. 315–16.

merit their approbation I should be securing a degree of connexion and interest as must ultimately prove beneficial to me.[1]

Longley expressed what for perhaps the majority of tutors was a more important inducement than the financial rewards of a tutorship, namely the opportunity of obtaining preferment through the family and connections of pupils. The evidence on this head is not less convincing for often being circumstantial. Some random examples may be given. Thus in 1702 Edward Wells was appointed to the living of Cotesbach in Leicestershire by the patron St John Bennett, to whose son Thomas Bennett he had been tutor from 1693 to 1696, and in 1716 he was appointed to the rectory of Bletchley in Buckinghamshire by his old pupil Browne Willis, who held the patronage. In 1705 George Bull was made Rector of Tavistock, of which the Wrey family was patron, having taken Sir Bourchier Wrey as his pupil in 1700. Charles Tryon came up to Christ Church in 1717, and two years later his tutor Richard Foulkes was appointed to the family livings of Bulwick in Northamptonshire and Seaton in Rutland. Christopher Haslam was tutor to John Trevelyan from 1720 to 1724. Sir John Trevelyan of Nettlecombe in Somerset, his pupil's father, presented him to the living of Nettlecombe in 1725. In 1742 Haslam was presented to the living of Kentisbeare in Devon by Sir William Wyndham, the father of another pupil, Charles Wyndham, who matriculated in 1725. George Wigan included Thomas Foley (matric. 13 Nov. 1719), the eldest son of Lord Foley, and Strode Talbot Foley (matric. 4 July 1722) amongst his pupils, and in 1722 was presented to the living of Old Swinford, of which Lord Foley was patron. In 1731 William Le Hunte was made rector of Oxhill, the patronage of which was in the Bromley family of Bagginton in Warwickshire; William Bromley had been tutored by him between 1717 and 1721. Euseby Cleaver began a long and distinguished career in the Church by taking the Earl of Egremont as a pupil in 1767. He became rector in 1774 of Spofurthe in Yorkshire, and in 1783 of Petworth, both livings in the

---

[1] Lambeth Place Library, MS 1841, fo. 110.

gift of the Earls of Egremont. In 1799 Lord Liverpool wrote to Archbishop Markham,

I have given ... to one gentleman who had some share in the education of Lord Hawkesbury [his eldest son] and who under my eye now devotes the whole of his time to the education of my second son and with great success, the living of Barwick in Elmet, and I have authorised Lord Hawkesbury to offer the living of Kirk Bramwirth to Mr. Hall, who was his tutor at Oxford.[1]

The Hall referred to in this letter was Charles Henry Hall, who succeeded Jackson in the Deanery in 1809 largely owing to the interest of Lord Liverpool.

The picture that emerges of the tutors of Christ Church is of a body of well-educated young men whose average age was about thirty. The majority of them came from the middle ranks of society, mainly from clerical families, and many had received their earlier education at Westminster School. They were a homogeneous group, sharing a similar social and educational background and united by many common assumptions. Most still looked to a career in the Church rather than in the university. Few then or later produced works of scholarship.

During the eighteenth century, education at Christ Church passed more and more into their hands. The college officers, who administered exercises such as verses, themes, and disputations, and were traditionally tutors to the Westminster Students and the Servitors, constituted what were known as the public tutors. But when undergraduates matriculated at an early age and tutors were responsible for their morals and behaviour, a large number of tutors was required in addition to the public tutors. For the period 1660–1700 the names of more than a hundred tutors may be identified, and until the rate of matriculation declined in the 1720s an average of nine or ten tutors were appointed each year, and in 1675, 1679, and 1680 the number rose to sixteen. Many of these tutors, who like the public tutors were appointed by the Dean, took very few pupils, sometimes no more than one or two, and held their tutorships for correspondingly short periods of time.

[1] BL Add. MS 38311, fo. 2ᵛ.

The need for so many tutors meant that a high proportion of the resident graduate Students, then more numerous than they became in the eighteenth century, was engaged in tuition. Perhaps as a consequence of the pastoral nature of tutorships and of the large complement of tutors which this involved, the office of tutor in the seventeenth century and for much of the eighteenth was not always highly regarded. A tutorship was not the indispensable preliminary to one of the college offices until the mid-eighteenth century. The Censors generally took pupils in addition to the Westminster Students and Servitors, but many of the lecturers in rhetoric and Greek were never tutors, and conversely some of the most successful tutors, such as Joseph Gascoigne and William Levett in the seventeenth century, and Edmund Bateman, George Butt, and Robert Jenner in the eighteenth, never held any major college office.

When the pastoral nature of the tutorship diminished, fewer tutors were needed and one of the motives for Students to reside after graduation was removed. The public tutors remained, reinforced by one or two promising Bachelor Students who might eventually succeed to college office. The number of tutors appointed annually in the late eighteenth century thus fell to about six. The proportion of Bachelor Students greatly increased at this time. Whereas between 1660 and 1700 about one tutor in seven was a Bachelor when first appointed, the proportion rose to about one in five in the first half of the following century, and under Cyril Jackson was not less than two out of three. Most of the tutors in the later period—John Randolph, William Jackson, Phineas Pett, C. H. Hall, Samuel Smith, James Webber, and William Wood—were Bachelors when they received their first pupil. With fewer tutors, the average length of tutorships increased. If those are excluded who tutored for less than three years (of whom there were very few after 1770), the proportion of tutors active for ten years or more in the second half of the eighteenth century was double that in the first half. The length-ening of tenure meant that on the whole tutors were more experi-enced than their predecessors. The appointment of younger tutors, who acted for longer periods, who taught the reformed curriculum, who were largely relieved of the task of policing the manners and morals of their pupils, and who had good prospects of succession to one of the senior college offices, heralded the idea that a career in the university was an alternative destiny to a career in the Church.

The number of pupils allocated to individual tutors depended on the number of tutors appointed. When the college supported a large number of tutors each of them had a small number of pupils, and vice versa. But there was no simple mathematical equation, and the number allotted to a tutor varied greatly between one period and another, between one tutor and another, and between one year and another for the same tutor.[1] Between the seventeenth century and the end of the eighteenth, the average number of pupils taken by established tutors had roughly doubled from three or four new pupils a year to six or seven. There were always exceptionally active tutors who exceeded the average, and in the late eighteenth century John Randolph and Phineas Pett took fifteen or more pupils in some years.

The large increase in the number of pupils allocated to the

---

[1] Precise figures are not easily obtained because the records do not distinguish every tutor appointed, nor, except in the case of Students, changes of tutor. Despite such limitations, the Caution Books often confirm the number of pupils a tutor is known from other sources to have had. In Nov. 1679, for example, Nicholas L'Estrange remarked that since the previous Mar. Roger Altham had taken two more Gentlemen Commoners as pupils (BL Add. MS 46956B, fo. 84). This is confirmed by the Caution Book, which shows him in receipt of the caution of Charles Cleaver and Robert Osbaldeston. In 1768 Dean Markham informed Charles Jenkinson that he had appointed William Conybeare tutor to Lord Bute's son Frederick Stuart. Conybeare, he wrote, 'has for some time declined taking pupils and has now only one, Lord Trevor's younger son whom he took only because asked by the Bishop of Durham. He has consented to undertake the case of Mr. Stuart and at my persuasion agrees to take two or three more, enough to make a class and support an emulation among those who are lectured together' (BL Add. MS 38457, fo. 11). The Caution Book confirms that at the start of 1768 Trevor was Conybeare's only pupil and that during the year he took a further three pupils including Frederick Stuart. In addition to John Trevor, second son of Lord Trevor, who was a Commoner, the class consisted of Frederick Stuart and William Wrightson Battie, Gentlemen Commoners, and Henry Gregory, son of the Dean, who entered as a Commoner and was elected to a Canoneer Studentship in 1769.

public tutors under Bagot and Jackson was caused by the rise in matriculations. The problems which it caused were not confined to Christ Church, and as early as 1781 Vicesimus Knox remarked that college tutors in general had too many pupils and that private tutors should be appointed.[1] The private tutor, as he developed in this period, differed in many respects from the private tutor in earlier times or as he became in the nineteenth century. Until the time of Dean Markham, it was not uncommon for Noblemen to be attended at the university by their private tutors. When Lord James Butler came up he was accompanied by a private tutor named Peter Drelincourt, and both pupil and tutor matriculated on 23 February 1679. The Ormonde Papers, however, show that Butler's tutor at Christ Church was Henry Aldrich, and the Caution Book shows that Aldrich received and subsequently repaid the cautions of both Butler and Drelincourt. It is thus apparent that there was a distinction between the private tutor and the college tutor, and that even if an undergraduate brought a tutor with him he was obliged to receive a tutor appointed by the Dean.[2] The college tutor was appointed by the Dean from the roll of Students and, within the limitations already described, was

[1] Knox, *Liberal Education*, 328.

[2] The Caution Books appear occasionally to identify private tutors. For example, Sir Robert Worseley matriculated as a Nobleman on 22 Nov. 1684, and on the same day John Michel was incorporated as a Commoner Master. Michel paid his own caution money and also that of Worseley on the following 12 Dec. and later received the repayment of Worseley's caution and his own on 13 Sept. 1685. A further example is provided by J. M. De L'Angle, who entered as a Commoner and left without a degree in 1685. On 6 Apr. 1691 he re-entered and paid his caution as a Commoner and also that of Philip Stanhope as a Nobleman. He signed for the repayment of both cautions on 5 Feb. 1692. The Earl of Salisbury in 1705 and the Earl of Warwick in 1713 seem on the evidence of the Caution Books to have been accompanied by private tutors, the former by John Savage and the latter by John Pountney. In the 18th cent. such instances became rare, but until 1773, when the practice was abolished, it was not uncommon for Noblemen and Gentlemen Commoners to bring their personal servants and chaplains to Christ Church, and some of these were certainly private tutors. Samuel Horsley, a graduate of Trinity Hall, Cambridge, and later Bishop of St Asaph, resided on Peck. 7 with his pupil Heneage Finch, Lord Guernsey, later 4th Earl of Aylesford, from 1767 to 1771, and William Cleaver, a graduate of Magdalen and later Bishop of St Asaph in succession to Horsley, resided in Christ Church on Peck. 1 with his pupil Thomas Grenville from 1773 to 1775.

responsible for the moral and academic education of his pupil, but the Nobleman's and Gentleman Commoner's private tutor was not appointed by the Dean, was not a Student, and although he may have assisted in the moral and academic education of his charge was mainly responsible for his social education.

The private tutor in the time of Cyril Jackson differed from the private tutor in the entourage of the Nobleman or Gentleman Commoner. He also differed from the public tutor and the numerous tutors in the seventeenth and eighteenth centuries who took no more than one or two pupils. Unlike the latter, he was not appointed at matriculation but later in his pupil's career and often much later. He was thus a second tutor appointed in addition to the official tutor. He also differed from the private tutor in the nineteenth century. At Christ Church he was appointed by the Dean from amongst the Students, and took only pupils given to him by the Dean from the members of his own college; he did not specialize in any branch of the curriculum but taught the whole of it in close co-operation with the Dean and the public tutor; if he was successful as a private tutor, his reward was not an increase in the number of his pupils but rather appointment to one of the public tutorships.

The nature of the private tutor in the time of Cyril Jackson is well illustrated by the appointment of Charles LLoyd to be George Chinnery's private tutor in 1808. When Chinnery came up to Christ Church, Jackson refused to allow him to be taught by John Mullens, a graduate of Exeter College, under whom he had studied before coming to Oxford. He was placed instead under William Corne, one of the public tutors, and when he had resided at Christ Church for almost a month, during which time he was examined by Corne in mathematics, Greek, and Latin, he was summoned to the Deanery. Jackson spoke to him in the following vein:

Sir, I have had a great many serious thoughts about you, and I never was more puzzled about any man to know how I should direct his studies ... Mr. Corne and I have had much conversation about you. He says he is persuaded that you would do anything that was desired of you, and that you would work indefatigably. But, Sir, it depends very much upon the turn which is given to that assiduity. Mr. Corne has not time to be with you sufficiently. You want a man who can be with you oftener, who can retravel over the ground which you have been over, and fill up every chink ... Now, Sir, the man I want is Mr. Lloyd. Had I created a man for the purpose I could not have made a better one than he is.[1]

Jackson's remarks show that the private tutor was appointed to improve the able student rather than to cram the idle and incompetent. Every undergraduate had a public tutor, for the public tutor was required by the university statutes, but he only had a private tutor if the Dean thought he should and he could afford one.

It is probable that undergraduates saw their tutors less frequently as the eighteenth century advanced, although evidence on this as on other aspects of the tutorial system is scanty. When they came to the university at a tender age, and tutors were responsible for their moral education and pastoral welfare, they inevitably saw their tutors regularly. When the average age at matriculation rose the duties of the tutor diminished, and it was expected that undergraduates should do much of their reading in private because, as James Hurdis put it, young men came to the university with habits of application and of an age to continue their studies without compulsion.[2] Throughout the period the tutor was expected to provide instruction in all aspects of the curriculum, and it is in the nature of tutorial teaching that the key to the frequency of tutorials is probably to be found. To have given detailed instruction in the whole curriculum would have made life for tutor and pupil alike almost a continuous tutorial. Not the least difficulty was the number of pupils. In the early eighteenth century the tutor might expect to receive five or six new pupils a year, so that over a period of three years he might have almost twenty pupils. By the end of the century he might have between twenty-five and thirty on his list. To have taught so many pupils Greek, Latin, logic, mathematics, and divinity was not possible within the framework of the tutorial class. In fact a considerable amount of teaching was taken off the shoulders of

---

[1] Ch. Ch. Archives, xlviii. a. 42a, fos. 76ᵛ–77.
[2] J. Hurdis, *Word or Two in Vindications of the University of Oxford* (c. 1800), 24.

the tutors by the college lecturers and by the *Classes*. The lectures were occasions when undergraduates construed or copied out notes, and in the *Classes* public exercises such as declamations and disputations were rehearsed. When the *Classes* eventually collapsed the vacuum was filled, as has been shown, by the emergence of the private tutor. In these circumstances the function of the public tutor was to define the curriculum, to explain difficult passages, and to examine students on what they read. Gibbon's complaint at Magdalen was not that his tutorials were infrequent but that his tutor failed to give him a plan of study.

It is in the composition of the tutorial class that important social and educational changes are found. In size the tutorial class probably changed very little. In the seventeenth century, when the college possessed a large number of tutors, many of whom had very few pupils, and when there was a great discrepancy in the age and attainments of undergraduates at matriculation, tutorial classes were often very small, and in some cases no doubt consisted of a single individual. This continued to be the case, but there were also larger classes, and in the middle of the eighteenth century Markham was of the opinion that a class of four was enough to 'support an emulation'. However, the classes, sometimes differed considerably in character and composition. In the seventeenth and eighteenth centuries some tutors seem to have taken their pupils principally, and on occasion entirely, from particular social groups to the exclusion of others. Thus some took only Noblemen or Gentlemen Commoners, others only Commoners, some only Students, and some combinations of these[1]. The choice of certain tutors to take most or all of their pupils from the Noblemen and Gentlemen Commoners almost certainly reflected deliberate policy on the part of the Dean who appointed tutors. Fell, as has been shown, used the tutorial system to educate the aristocracy and gentry in sound Protestant principles, and employed for the purpose not only Aldrich but George Hooper and Thomas Newey, who between them covered almost the entire period of his tenure of the Deanery. Nearly all John Fanshawe's pupils were Noblemen or Gentlemen

[1] For some examples see Table IV. 3.

TABLE IV. 3. Specialized Tutorships

Year	Tutor	No. of known pupils	Social group of pupils
1662	T. Martin	18	No Nobs. or GCs
1664	G. Hooper	20	9 GCs but only 2 Cmrs.
1666	W. Levett	13	No Students
1670	H. Aldrich	16	Only Nobs. and GCs
1675	D. Hill	18	13 Students
1676	J. Gascoigne	25	13 Cmrs., 11 Students
1678	W. Taswell	23	No Nobs., only 1 GC
1680	W. Breach	16	No Nobs. or Cmrs.
1682	T. Newey	26	Only 2 Cmrs.
1688	W. Ellis	7	No Nobs. or GCs
1705	R. Frewin	10	Only 1 Cmr., no Students
1711	C. Fairfax	9	No Students
1713	H. Gregory	55	Only 3 Nobs. and 4 GCs
1723	J. Fanshawe	25	Only 1 Cmr. but 10 Nobs.
1737	T. Burton	14	No Nobs. or GCs
1740	W. Lewis	15	All GCs except 6
1742	W. Markham	28	17 Students and 9 GCs
1753	T. Skynner	12	No Cmrs.
1764	F. Atterbury	46	No Nobs., only 5 GCs
1767	W. Conybeare	19	1 Cmr.
1777	T. Hind	16	All Cmrs., except for 2 GCs and 1 Student

Dates indicate only the first appearance as a tutor, but totals of pupils cover the whole period for which each tutor acted.

Commoners, and Markham took only Noblemen, Gentlemen Commoners, and Students. Apart from reasons of policy, there were other reasons for teaching the aristocracy and gentry separately from other undergraduates. Until late in the eighteenth century they were often younger than other students at matriculation. The statutory provision for them to take a degree after a shorter period of residence than was required of other undergraduates, and the practice of submitting their Collections separately, also tended to distinguish their tutorial arrangements from the rest of the college. But they were not segregated because of differences in the formal curriculum, for, despite minor differences in emphasis between, for example, the studies of Noblemen and Servitors, all undergraduates received essentially the same education. Nor were they segregated because of the barriers of rank, since these were taken for granted and often merged so imperceptibly that they were incapable of rigid definition.[1]

When in 1774 Noblemen and Gentlemen Commoners began to take up their Collections with the rest of the college, the tutor who took his pupils mainly or exclusively from the aristocracy and gentry disappeared. In his place, owing to the simultaneous extinction of the old *Classes,* and the increase in the undergraduate population and its greater maturity, there appears to have been a degree of specialization in the tutorial system, based perhaps on the differing aptitudes of pupils. It seems to have been specialization within the curriculum as a whole rather than by subject. That is to say, there were not separate tutors for Greek or Latin or logic, but these and other subjects were taught to a higher level in some classes than in others. In the case of the college lecturers in logic, mathematics, rhetoric, and Greek, specialization was more apparent than real, for they were recruited from the generality of tutors and were not appointed because of particular aptitude. The tutors were still responsible for the whole curriculum. It was a

---

[1] It is noteworthy that although Noblemen and Gentlemen Commoners had separate tutorial arrangements, and distinctions of rank were observed by dress and in other ways, undergraduates were not strictly segregated in their residential arrangements, for by its nature the quadrangle, and especially the individual staircase on which students of different standing were lodged in rooms adjacent or in close proximity, tended to reduce social exclusiveness. The chamber rents for Peckwater after the rebuilding show that from 1715, when it came into occupation, Noblemen, Gentlemen Commoners, Students (including graduate Students until Markham), Commoners, and Servitors usually had rooms on the same staircase. Propinquity mitigated but did not abolish social distinctions, for the Noblemen and Gentlemen Commoners tended to occupy the best rooms, which were on the first floor, while Students and Commoners had those on the ground floor, and Servitors had the garrets, though it was not unknown for rooms occupied by Students, Commoners, and Servitors to be interchangeable. The youthfulness of many undergraduates made it necessary for their tutors to live nearby—hence the presence of graduate Students. When the average age rose, the tutors had rooms elsewhere, and the Noblemen and Gentlemen Commoners tended to be concentrated in Canterbury quadrangle. Private tutors continued to reside until the 1770s, when the practice of bringing personal servants into residence (often the cause of wealthier undergraduates taking two or more sets of rooms) was stopped.

practice which reflected some fundamental premises of liberal education but one which Gibbon did not allow to go unscathed.

> Instead [he wrote] of confining themselves to a single science which had satisfied the ambition of Burman or Bernouilli, they teach, or promise to teach, either history, or mathematics, or ancient literature, or moral philosophy; and as it is possible that they may be defective in all, it is highly probable that of some they will be ignorant.[1]

At Christ Church evidence of variations in the studies of the pupils of some tutors compared with those of others is to be found in the Collections Books. In 1777, for example, the most active tutors were John Randolph and Thomas Hind. Most of Randolph's pupils took up trigonometry, and the Commoners algebra, but few of Hind's pupils took up any mathematics at all. Randolph's pupils frequently read Aristotle's *Organon,* but Hind's rarely did so. The Commoners tutored by Randolph read a great deal of Xenophon and Demosthenes, but those taught by Hind read little of either author except the *Memorabilia* of Xenophon. It would appear, therefore, that Randolph's pupils read appreciably more mathematics, logic, and Greek than did Hind's. Similar differences may be found between the pupils of Pett and Barker in 1785. Pett's pupils often read Polybius: not so Barker's. Of the Latin historians, Caesar and Livy were much read by Pett's pupils but very little by Barker's. All Pett's Student pupils and most of his Commoners read Euripides, Sophocles, and Aeschylus, whereas the Greek dramatists fared badly with Barker's pupils. Again, Pett's pupils studied more mathematics than Barker's, and Aristotle's *Ethics* were taken up by his Student pupils but by hardly anyone else. On the other hand, Barker's pupils read much Cicero, and most of them included some of the *Orations* in their

---

[1] Murray, *Autobiographies of Edward Gibbon,* 77. Specialization of tuition was not fully adopted at Christ Curch until the following century when the public examinations were reformed, but in 1853 Pusey referred to what may have been an early manifestation of it when he wrote that 'There was of old an understanding that the pupils of one tutor might attend the lectures of any other in any branch in which he was understood to excel' (*Report and Evidence ... presented to the Board of Heads of Houses and Proctors* (1853), evidence, 79).

Collections. In 1796 Barker was still tutoring. His pupils were then as weak in mathematics as they had been a decade earlier, but they paid more attention to the Greek dramatists, particularly Euripides. Horace was read by most of his pupils and also by those of two other tutors, Slade and Wood, but seldom by the Commoners tutored by Illingworth. In this year also, Polybius was often read by Illingworth's pupils, but was still neglected by Barker's, and although Aristotle's *Rhetoric* was widely read it was taken up with particular frequency by Illingworth's pupils.

George Chinnery's letters to his mother give the best account of the way in which the tutorial system worked under Cyril Jackson. They show not only what Chinnery studied, and how Collections were conducted, but also the relationship between his public and private tutors. He matriculated in 1808 and was immediately placed in the charge of William Corne, one of the public tutors. Corne examined him without delay in algebra, trigonometry, Homer, and Virgil, and on the basis of his report the Dean decided that Charles LLoyd should be Chinnery's private tutor. Chinnery saw LLoyd almost daily for about an hour until he took his degree. He saw Corne only about once a month until his first examination approached, when he saw him daily for logic. After the examination, monthly tutorials were resumed with Corne until January 1811, when they were increased to twice a week, and from October until the final examination they took place daily. Chinnery spoke ungratefully of the benefit he had received from Corne, and towards the end of his time at Christ Church he wrote, 'Corne has done mightily little for me since I have been in College: the tutorage has devolved almost entirely on LLoyd'.[1] Although he occasionally construed for Corne and in 1810 read Herodotus with him, it seems that the principal purpose of Corne's tutorials, apart from instruction in logic, was to enable Chinnery's progress to be monitored and his studies directed.

The conduct of affairs had not changed when W. F. Hook went up in 1817. He appears not to have had a private tutor at first, and was put in the charge of Edmund Goodenough, one of

---

[1] Ch. Ch. Archives, xlviii. a. 55, fo. 117.

the public tutors. In January 1818 he wrote to his father that Goodenough had seen him twice during the term, which 'is generally as often as he sends for a man in one term'. His tutor, he remarked, was not popular either with the reading men or with the idle. 'The former do not like him because by his sending for them so seldom they cannot have the passages explained to them which they cannot make out till they almost forget what they are about, and the latter because though he sends seldom yet he expects a very great deal to be done.'[1] A year later Hook was going to Goodenough about once a fortnight and sometimes once a week, 'which for him is reckoned a very great deal'.[2] By this time Goodenough was Senior Censor, and tutorials were often frustrated by the arrival of the manciple or the Dean on college business. Eventually Hook became so discouraged that he wrote to his father, 'I shall save money this year and next and sport myself a private tutor in my last year'.[3] As the time for taking his degree approached he saw Goodenough with greater regularity, and in May 1819 his tutor gave him three hours a week for Thucydides with three other men, and offered him one hour a week for Aeschylus. Both Corne and Goodenough, as public tutors, saw their pupils infrequently for most of their undergraduate careers, but they directed their studies, and as the final examination approached increased their tutorial supervision. If an undergraduate could afford a private tutor he might study with him daily. If he could not afford one he was dependent on the public tutor and the college lectures. The public tutor for his part was no longer the subordinate who prepared his pupils for the public exercises and guarded their morals and manners, but was an august figure who regulated the plan of study of his pupils, and intermittently resolved their difficulties, but did not regard it as his function to give close and frequent attention to their instruction. As a system of tuition it suited equally those who needed little help from their tutor and those who did not want any.

---

[1] Ch. Ch. Archives, Letters W. F. Hook to his father, 26 Jan. 1818.
[2] Ibid, W. F. Hook to his father 21 Mar. 1819.
[3] Ibid.

V

Undergraduate Studies

(*a*) EXERCISES

THE course of study for the degree of BA embraced, in theory if not always in practice, logic, mathematics, natural and moral philosophy, the elements of religion, and prescribed classical authors. Many of these studies were constantly rehearsed by means of exercises such as the composition of verses and themes in Latin and Greek and the performance of public disputations. Often the exercises were of great antiquity, and because they were originally administered by the Censors and college officers they appear to pre-date the introduction of the tutorial system. Many, notably verses and themes, had probably been oral exercises, and, although in the course of time they became written, they retained vestiges of their ancient derivation by continuing to be read out in Hall well into the nineteenth century.

Disputations developed in the medieval universities as a method of resolving questions left in doubt by the best authorities, and of reconciling conflicting opinions and conclusions. A controversial question in grammar, logic, rhetoric, or philosophy was posed in the form of a question which could be argued by the canons of Aristotelian logic. The respondent first offered an answer to, or interpretation of, the question and advanced arguments in support of it. The opponent then stated contradictory propositions and attacked flaws in the respondent's reasoning. The determiner finally summed up the arguments, pointed out the fallacies in the reasoning of the participants, reconciled the differences, and pronounced a decision or determination. By the seventeenth century disputations had ceased to be valuable as a method of advancing knowledge. They were attacked by Francis Bacon as inferior to experimental evidence in natural philosophy, and by divines who felt that religious truth suffered from such logical analysis, and indeed, according to Obadiah Walker, they had sometimes been forbidden where religious truth 'was of concernment'.[1] Such difficult philosophical questions as 'An anima sit in toto corpore' or 'An natura sit perfectior arte' were incapable of solution by syllogism, and scientific questions such as 'An imago rei in mente conveniat cum objecto extra mentem' or 'An quicquid sit in intellectu prae-existat in sensu' were insoluble by the authority of Aristotle or of the scientific knowledge of the time, and so remain. Having thus outlived their original function, disputations were defended in the latter part of the seventeenth century as exercises for training the logical faculties. Students, wrote Walker, were put

upon a continual stretch of their wits to defend their cause, and it makes them quick in replies, intentive upon their subject; where the opponent useth all means to drive his adversary from his hold; and the answerer defends himself with the force of truth, sometimes with the subtility of his wit; and sometimes he escapes in a midst of words, and the doubles of a distinction, whilst he seeks all holes and recesses to shelter his persecuted opinion and reputation.[2]

The disputation was no longer a quest for truth but a 'dispute for victory'. The opponent who argued against the tenets of religion was not esteemed a worse Christian, for, said William King, 'he believes nothing he asserts, and is ready at any time to take the contrary part, and to contradict and confute whatever he said before'.[3]

In the eighteenth century, the author of *Terrae Filius* complained that disputations in the Schools had degenerated into the repetition of syllogisms by rote, and that sets of syllogisms, known as 'strings', were handed down from one generation of undergraduates to the next. By that time disputations had become formal exercises, but the theses or propositions for debate survived

[1] Walker, *Of Education*, 125.
[2] Ibid., 124.
[3] W. King, *Works* (1776), i, 272.

as the subjects for Latin verse and written composition and so continued to discharge a useful function in the teaching of logic.

The ability to write Latin verse was a highly prized accomplishment at Christ Church. When Samuel Palmer came up in 1709, he had hardly set foot in the college before he was made to compose verses. 'I have', he noted within a week of his arrival, 'made two themes ... and six verses on one of them.' His tutor, he added, advised him to read the Latin poets 'that I may the better compose verses myself, without which there is no living here'.[1] Not every undergraduate was capable of excellence, but in Lent, the traditional season for amendment and reformation, every undergraduate was obliged to make the attempt. He was then required to write Lent verses, which were compositions in Latin elegiacs of six or more lines modelled on the epigrams of Martial. When this exercise began is not known, but William King believed it to be of considerable antiquity when he entered Christ Church as a Westminster Student in 1681.[2] In the nineteenth century, Charles Wordsworth, who was a tutor in Gaisford's time, explained its origin. For part of Lent, he wrote, the weekly themes were replaced by 'compositions of the nature of epigrams in Latin elegiacs. The custom had come down from the time when disputations were held upon questions proposed in certain well-known *formulae,* and admitting of a negative or of an affirmative answer'.[3] The derivation of the Lent verses from the theses debated at disputations is amply confirmed by the exercises of the Determining Student Bachelors published in 1723 in *Carmina Quadragesimalia ab Aedis Christi Oxon. Alumnis Composita et ab ejusdem Aedis Baccalaureis Determinantibus in Schola Naturalis Philosophiae Publice Recitata.* Hearne reported that the volume contained, 'all the considerable Verses at our Ashwednesday's Exercises, that have been made by the Christ-Church Gentlemen, wch, indeed, have been remarkable for their Excellency'.[4] Other editions were published in 1741, 1748, 1757, and 1761. Each set of verses in

---

[1] BL Add. MS 35584, fo. 101ᵛ.
[2] King, *Works*, i, 237.
[3] Wordsworth, *Annals of my Early Life,* 50.
[4] Hearne, *Collections,* vii, 337.

Carmina Quadragesimalia was written for or against a thesis. There are verses on 'An aliquid producatur ex nihilo. Neg.', 'An omnia agant propter finem. Aff.', 'An natura sit perfectior arte. Aff.'. There are verses on 'An luna sit habitabilis', which was also a thesis affirmed in Charles Potter's *Theses Quadragesimales* in 1651, and the verses on 'An idem semper agat idem' are not dissimilar in subject to those written by Gladstone in 1829 on 'An aliquid sit immutabile. Aff.'.[1]

The writing of epigrammatic Latin verses was an exercise especially associated with Westminster School, and was one of the most striking examples of the influence of Westminster on the studies pursued at Christ Church. The nominal editor of *Carmina Quadragesimalia* was Charles Este, a Westminster Student Master, but the true editor was Robert Freind, the Headmaster of Westminster. According to Hearne the book was revised by him, and 'nothing was taken into it but with his Approbation'.[2] Although the verses are anonymous, their authors in the early part of the eighteenth century may be identified from a manuscript in the Bodleian Library containing a collection of Lent verses dated between 1714 and 1718 made by William Davis, who was elected to a Westminster Studentship in 1714.[3] The extent of the contribution by the Westminster Students is immediately apparent, for, of the thirty-eight authors represented, all but four were Westminster Students or had been educated at Westminster. Davis himself wrote four sets of verses in 1715, and in the same year a further four sets were made by Matthew Lee, the physician and benefactor of Christ Church, who determined in 1717. Even after they had ceased to be published, the best of the Lent verses were handed down as models. The papers in the Public Record Office of Charles Abbot, first Baron Colchester, who matriculated in 1775, contain a collection of them for the years 1766 to 1776, amongst which are two sets of verses composed by Cyril Jackson.[4] At Westminster the exercise went back at least to the time of

---

[1] J. Morley, *Life of Gladstone* (1903), i, 63.
[2] Hearne, *Collections*, viii (1907), 94.
[3] Bodl. MS Eng. Misc. e. 183. Davis died in 1790 aged 105.
[4] PRO 30/9/3/31.

Busby, whose 'old rule to write his invention in English' is mentioned by Matthew Prior in a discussion of Latin verses.[1] From Westminster it spread to other schools. When Roundell Palmer went to Winchester in 1825, he found that *Carmina Quadragesimalia* was used as a model for the Vulgus.[2]

The Lent verses represented many of the most characteristic aspirations of education at Oxford in the seventeenth and eighteenth centuries. They encouraged clarity of thought, elegance, eloquence, brevity of expression, versatility, and quickness of wit, but seldom substance or originality. They valued form and discipline more highly than imagination or mental curiosity. They inculcated the virtues of the pulpit, the bar, and the legislature, and most of those who laboured to perfect them followed careers in the Church, the law, or government. Locke condemned the writing of verses as 'a sort of Aegyptian tyrany, to bid them make bricks who have not yet any of the materials',[3] but, as Copleston noted in 1810, the intention was not 'to stock the world with new poems'.[4]

Like the Lent verses, the theme, which was the distant but direct ancestor of the essay, was an exercise designed to develop logical thought and gracefulness of expression. 'I know of no practice in the Schools more judicious, pertinent, or useful than this,' wrote the Revd Roger Pickering in 1749. 'This gradually introduces Youth to think, reason, and judge from their own fund upon men and things.'[5] The themes were submitted to the lecturer in rhetoric and read in Hall on Saturdays, a practice which was still observed when Charles Wordsworth came up in 1825.[6]

> Whether the Strife of Declamation blew
> The Sparks of young Invention into View;
> Or, as the Flame our weekly Theses fann'd,
> We tremulously join'd the Theme-struck Band,

[1] HMC, *Bath* (1908), iii, 423.
[2] R. Palmer, *Memorials Family and Personal* (1896), i, 101.
[3] J. Locke, *Some Thoughts Concerning Education* (1693), para. 171.
[4] Copleston, *Reply to the Calumnies*, 129.
[5] Nichols, *Literary Anecdotes*, ix, 332.
[6] Wordsworth, *Annals of my Early Life*, 50.

Where the long Hall, with hoary Portraits hung,
Its iron wreathed Gate far open flung.[1]

The convention that the public tutors were not permitted to
approve themes before they were submitted to the lecturer in
rhetoric is perhaps an indication that the exercise was of such
antiquity that it preceded the tutorial system. In 1809 George
Chinnery noted that one of the advantages of a private tutor was
that themes could be shown to him in advance, whereas it was
not allowed to show them to a public tutor before giving them
up in Hall.[2] When themes were submitted to the lecturer in
rhetoric, the proceedings were in Latin well into the eighteenth
century. In 1725 Dr Stratford recounted the discomfiture of
Robert Foulkes, the son of a Canon of Christ Church, and a
recently appointed Canoneer Student, when he sought unsuc-
cessfully to submit his theme to the lecturer in rhetoric, George
Wigan.

On Saturday last the boy offered his theme again to Wigan in the hall.
Wigan said, 'Non est mei ingenii judicium ferre de tuis scriptis'. The
boy began to say, 'the Dean'—Wigan interrupted him, 'Quid vis tibi
loquere Latine si Decanus jussisset te mandata sua ad me deferre, jussisset
te etiam ea Latino sermone exprimere'. The boy began 'Decanus,
Decanus', but could get no further. Wigan said 'Abi et disce Latine
loqui, non est meum in hoc loco audire aliquem nisi Latine loquentem'.[3]

Many examples of themes survive. It is probable that some of
the specimens in John Locke's herbarium in the Bodleian Library
were mounted on the back of themes submitted to him after his
appointment as lecturer in rhetoric in 1662.[4] George Chinnery
frequently noted the subjects of his themes in the early nineteenth
century. In his correspondence he mentions themes 'on the punishment of death', 'on the search for truth', and on the proposition
'if once we suffer ourselves to break through the rules or laws

---

[1] R. Polwhele, 'Epistle to a College-friend', in *Poems* (1788). Polwhele matriculated at Christ Church in Mar. 1778.
[2] Ch. Ch. Archives, xlviii. a. 46, fo. 96.
[3] HMC, *Portland* (1901), vii, 409.
[4] Bodl. MSS Locke c. 41 and b. 7.

prescribed to us, all sense of shame and fear will soon vanish from our hearts'. On other occasions he noted Latin themes on 'Verba provisam rem non invita sequentur', which he translated as 'Things being provided words will follow uninvited', and on 'Naturale est magis nova quam magna mirari', which he rendered as 'It is natural that surprise should be excited more by the novelty than by the greatness of things'.[1] The form of the theme underwent little change. In 1808 apropos a Latin theme, Chinnery's tutor Charles LLoyd told him that 'the theme itself, being in Latin, need not fill up two pages, but that I must write some Latin verses at the end of it, which is the principal object, and in which he has promised to help me'.[2] LLoyd's prescription would equally well have applied to the Latin exercise which John Locke, then a schoolboy at Westminster, submitted to the electors when seeking a Studentship in 1652. In it, after comparing himself to Ulysses returning to Penelope, he says that he has studied grammar and mastered Homer, and now seeks admittance to the fatherland of all men of learning. The exercises concluded with eight lines of Latin verse.[3]

Themes differed in intention and in manner of composition from the essays of more recent undergraduates. They were not concerned with the analysis of facts but with the best way of saying things, the most persuasive, the most eloquent. Cyril Jackson described some of the qualities of a good theme when, in 1808, he encountered George Chinnery while taking his favourite walk with James Webber in Christ Church Meadow. 'The Dean stopped to speak with me', Chinnery wrote. 'He said that I had read my theme very well, but that there was a little sharpness which he wanted me to correct. As to the theme itself he wished to *prune me down*: there were several excrescences in it.'[4]

It was an advantage of oral exercises that they were performed

---

[1] Examples of a Latin and an English theme by Chinnery are to be found in Ch. Ch. Archives, xlviii a. 49, fos. 39, 42[v].

[2] Ch. Ch. Archives, xlviii. a. 45, fo. 21.

[3] Locke, *Correspondence,* i, no. 5.

[4] Ch. Ch. Archives, xlviii. a. 45, fo. 136[v]. *A View Taken from Christchurch Meadows Oxford* was published in May 1807 (M. D. George, *Catalogue of Political and Personal Satires* (1947), no. 10780).

in public, and so provided an opportunity for undergraduates to distinguish themselves in the eyes of their contemporaries to an extent that ceased to be possible when the private tutorial essay dominated the educational system. Verses, especially an oral exercise, continued to be read in Hall before the whole college. In 1818 W. F. Hook wrote that he was to read out his verses, 'which is a great honour but a very troublesome one'.[1] A day or two later he remarked that 'the reading of them is little more than a Form as nobody attends, and as they are never read loud enough to be heard, the only use of reading them is to let men know that you are chosen out as one of the best'.[2] When the traditional exercises either lapsed or assumed written form, new exercises and prizes, which formed no part of the curriculum, were established and offered a forum for public acclaim.[3]

Amongst these exercises were the Certamen Poeticum and the Lee Certamen. The former appears to have been founded by Atterbury in 1712. Although John Pointer spoke of it as still in existence in 1749,[4] there is no evidence that it was held on more than one occasion, and the probability is that it was founded to celebrate the rebuilding of Peckwater. Dr Stratford complained to Harley that it was characteristic of the Dean 'to design to divert to so ridiculous a use the chief fund we have had for fifty years past for our building, and the only fund we have any prospect of now, for paying that which is still due for the third side of Peckwater, and for finishing the inside of it'.[5]

Pointer printed the announcement of the prize as follows:

CERTAMEN POETICUM:
cujus hae Leges sunto,
Fas sit omnibus ex hac Aede Non-graduatis, sive

---

[1] Ch. Ch. Archives, Letters, W. F. Hook to his mother, 4 Mar. 1818 (copy).

[2] Ibid., W. F. Hook to R. Hook, 8 Mar. 1818.

[3] It is worth noting that the Chancellor's Latin and English verse prizes, the first of the great university prizes, were founded in the late 18th cent. when the public exercises such as disputations were obsolescent.

[4] J. Pointer, *Oxoniensis Academia* (1749), 84.

[5] HMC, *Portland* (1901), vii, 91.

Alumni fuerint sive Commensales, Experiri quid
possint in Carmine Heroico.

Argumentum Carminis sit

ATRIUM PECKWATERIENSE,

Numerus Versuum circiter 80.

Exhibeantur Poemata 4to Id. Novembris,
Propria cujusque Authoris Manu descripta, celato
tamen Nomine.

Judices Certaminis sint Decanus, Sub-Decanus,
Cathechista, Uterque Censor, Rhetorices & Graecae
Linguae Praelectores.

Qui in hoc scribendi genere caeteros omnes anteiverit,
Praemium ferat

Platonis Opera, a Serrano; &

Demosthenis Opera, Lutetiae edita.

Primo-proximus

Dionysii Halicarnassei Opera, ab Hudsonio.

Livii Opera, ab Hearnio edita.

Tertius

Homeri Opera a Barnesio edita.

Qui Praemia tulerint, sua quisque publice recitet
Poemata.

Victorum Nomina una cum Poematis inserantur Registro in
Ecclesiae hujusce Archivis asservando.

Sept. 13. 1712. F. A. Decanus.

There were accusations of foul play, and it was alleged that some
had notice of the theme beforehand, and others had verses written
for them,[1] but eventually the prizes were awarded to a Westminster
Student, a Canoneer Student, and a Commoner named William
Le Hunte.[2]

Amongst the many benefactions made to Christ Church by
Matthew Lee were a Latin verse prize for undergraduate Students
and Commoners, and a Latin prose prize for Student and Commoner Bachelors. They were held in alternate years, and were
judged by the Dean, the Sub-Dean, the Catechist, the Censors,

---

[1] HMC, *Portland* (1901), vii, 110.

[2] Atterbury, *Epistolary Correspondence,* iii, 305.

and the lecturers in rhetoric and Greek. There were four prizes in books worth altogether £50, the first prize being of the value of £18, and the successful compositions were read in Hall. It appears from an anonymous pamphlet entitled *Comparative Observations on two of the Poems . . . in a Late Certamen,* published in 1767, that the examiners were in the habit of stating publicly the reasons for their choices in awarding the prizes. The pamphlet was a sarcastic attack on the partiality and competence of the judges by a disappointed competitor named William Davis Shipley, who was an undergraduate Westminster Student. When it became known that Shipley was the author he was summoned before the Chapter, charged with publishing a libel, and promptly expelled from his Studentship without being given an opportunity to defend himself. He thereupon appealed to the Visitor, who ordered that he should be restored to his Studentship on the ground that expulsion was too severe a punishment for his offence, but that he should be set back for six months from taking his degree for publishing a libel. The prizes continued to be awarded regularly until 1788, but in 1789, 1792, 1795, and 1797 none was awarded. In 1790 and 1800 prizes of only £25 and in 1799 prizes of only £18 were given.

Little is known about the exercises performed by graduates at Christ Church, but disputations by Bachelors continued to be held in some form throughout the eighteenth century. The exercises for MA, on the other hand, were neglected because of the discontinuance of the university Act, to which they were supposed to lead, and the few Masters in residence after the disappearance of the residence qualification. Those who remained, however, performed some of the extra-curricular exercises established at Christ Church. Of these the earliest was an annual oration founded by the will of John Cross, one of John Fell's executors. He bequeathed the sum of £5 a year out of his estates at Ampthill and Millbrook in Bedfordshire for a Student Master of Christ Church to deliver an anniversary oration in Hall on All Saints Day in memory of Fell, 'for exciting the members of that Society to study of piety and virtue of which he was so great a pattern and example'. Anthony Wood heard Edward Wells deliver the oration in 1694,[1] and Hearne noted it in 1719,[2] but in 1872 Dean Liddell informed the Universities Commission that it had 'for many years been discontinued' and the funds applied to the hospital at Ampthill.[3] More enduring was the Commemoration Speech, now known as the Gaudy Oration, founded in 1754 by the will of Richard Russell Nash, a former Westminster Student who had been Junior Censor in 1739 and 1740 and a tutor for several years.[4] Nash endowed the speech with the sum of £10 a year and directed that it should be given by a Student Bachelor in Hall in Act term in order to celebrate 'the life and character of the Founder or some principal benefactor or other eminent persons educated at the said college'. The bequest was found to be charged on estates which were in strict settlement and thus not chargeable as Nash had supposed, but his brother paid the sum of £300 to the Dean and Chapter to fulfil the intentions of the bequest. The capital was added to the Lee trust in 1777, and two years later in 1779 Thomas Bentham delivered the first Commemoration Speech. Many of the speeches are preserved in the library at Christ Church. Up to the end of the eighteenth century they were delivered as listed in Table V.1. During this period, and indeed in subsequent years, admission to the Christ Church pantheon often depended on eccentric credentials. Wolsey had to wait until 1925. Henry VIII is waiting still.

The famous New Year Books were neither exercises nor prizes, but some of them were undoubtedly conceived as a means of encouraging young scholars at Christ Church. Their origin was described by Dean Fell in 1669 in the preface to his edition of Clemens Romanus. He stated that he was ashamed that the young scholars of Christ Church should greet him with a congratulatory epistle on New Year's Day and he make no return or acknowledgement. Therefore, he declared, he had determined to give to

---

[1] P. Bliss, *Life* (1813), i, cxix.

[2] Hearne, *Collections*, vii, 63.

[3] *Report of the Universities Commission on Property and Income* (1874), ii, 712.

[4] He was described as one for whom Harley was concerned at Auditor Foley's desire (HMC, *Portland* (1901), vii, 281). His brother was Treadway Russell Nash, the historian of Worcs.

TABLE V. 1. Commemoration Speeches

YEAR	SPEAKER	SUBJECT
1779	Thomas Bentham	*speech missing*
1780	Phineas Pett	*speech missing*
1781	James Harwood	*speech missing*
1782	George Drummond	*speech missing*
1783	C. T. Barker	Edward Littleton
1784	C. H. Hall	Richard Hakluyt
1785	C. Moss	*speech missing*
1786	J. Erskine	Bennet, Earl of Arlington
1787	W. Garthshore	Sir Dudley Carleton
1788	J. R. Hall	Heneage Finch, Earl of Nottingham
1789	G. Illingworth	Samuel Fell
1790	J. Bruce	Humphrey Prideaux
1791	*not awarded*	
1792	G. Canning	Daniel Finch
1793	C. B. Agar	Lord Lyttelton
1794	W. E. Taunton	Thomas Randolph
1795	W. Carey	*speech missing*
1796	F. Barnes	Henry, Earl of Surrey
1797	R. H. Peckwell	John King, Bishop of London
1798	R. P. Goodenough	*speech missing*
1799	J. Kidd	Archbishop Robinson
1800	W. T. Roe	W. Pulteney, Earl of Bath

each of them a book every year 'pro recepto apud me more'. Wood dated the commencement of the practice to 1661 but confessed that he had been unable to collect all the titles. The earliest known example is the edition of the *Epitome* of Aristotle's *Organon* by the Byzantine historian and philosopher Georgius Pachymeres printed in 1666 at the Oxford University Press, where all the New Year Books were printed. Where Wood failed, posterity has been more successful, for, through a combination of historical evidence and Madan's bibliographical intuition, most of the volumes may be identified with reasonable certainty for every year up to Fell's death, except 1673. Most of the books given by Fell were edited by him, though Thomas Sparke, a Student of Christ Church, assisted with three of them, and it is very likely that other members of the college were employed to collate or prepare texts. Whatever assistance he received, however, all Fell's New Year Books bear the imprint of his own editorial method. As an editor, Wood remarked, 'he neither put an epistle, or running notes, or corrections'.[1] In the preface to his Epictetus in 1670, he condemned pointless and wordy notes with severity. His object was to produce a plain edition of the text, usually with a Latin translation where the original was in Greek. In the preface to the Nepos of 1675 he stated his editorial principles clearly: 'purum putum Autorem nostrum exhibeo, nec notarum sarcina oppressum, nec frigidis conjecturis interpolatum, sed duntaxat ad MSS. codicum fidem diligenter recognitum'. For the text he generally went back to earlier editions, or collated the manuscripts available to him, or printed the notes made by other scholars. Fell printed few classical texts, and with one exception all the New Year Books from 1677 to the end of his life were patristic texts.

Dean Aldrich continued the practice of giving New Year Books, but, in contrast to Fell's preference for patristic texts, all but three of the volumes which have been identified between 1690 and 1710, when he died, were editions of Greek or Latin classical authors. Some of these editions seem to have found their way into the curriculum at Christ Church. It is surely no accident that in 1707 an undergraduate took up to Collections the commentary by Grotius on the Sermon on the Mount which Charles Aldrich edited as a New Year Book in the previous year. Similarly the editions of Homer's *Odyssey* in 1705 and of the letters of St Ignatius in 1708 were both followed by an increase in the number of undergraduates to take these works up to Collections. The New Year Books were more than graceful compliments: to Fell they were in addition a contribution to his ideal of a learned clergy, and to Aldrich a means of encouraging classical studies by making the texts available to undergraduates. This was not the only difference between the New Year Books of Fell and those of Aldrich. Aldrich made greater use than did Fell of graduates and undergraduates as editors. His nephew Charles Aldrich edited no fewer than four New Year Books.[2] Most of the editors were

[1] Wood, *Athenae,* iv, 198.
[2] Since, according to Stratford, the Dean for many years had 'an aversion' for his nephew, perhaps the invitation to edit a New Year Book contained in this instance a penal element (HMC, *Portland* (1901), viii, 85).

graduate Westminster Students, but when Peter Foulkes and John Freind produced their edition of Aeschines and Demosthenes in 1696 both were still undergraduates. Fell's New Year Books were straightforward texts and some of them were works of considerable scholarship. By using young and inexperienced Students as editors, Aldrich also produced straightforward texts, but it could not be claimed that his intention was to produce scholarly editions as well. This distinction may be kept in mind when considering the most famous of all the New Year Books, the ill-fated edition of the *Letters of Phalaris* edited by Charles Boyle in 1695.

Charles Boyle was the brother of the Earl of Orrery, and came up to Christ Church in 1690 as a Nobleman when he was fifteen years old. He was a gifted young man, and, according to Budgell, 'applied himself so closely to his Studies as made all his Friends apprehend that he would injure his Constitution'.[1] In 1694 he took his degree of BA. Although Noblemen were sometimes awarded honorary degrees, it was rare indeed for them to take a degree by examination, and between the Restoration and 1694 only three other instances are on record.[2] Aldrich, who had written his famous compendium of logic for one of his aristocratic pupils, persuaded Boyle to undertake an edition of Phalaris as a New Year Book. It is inconceivable that he envisaged Boyle making an original contribution to classical scholarship. Rather he sought to encourage a promising young man and perhaps through him the academically intractable social order he represented. Boyle's edition was in fact a typical New Year Book, and consisted of the Greek text with a Latin translation, a preface, and a short apparatus of notes.

The preface shows that Boyle was aware of the attribution of the letters to Lucian by some scholars, including Politian, but he accepted that they were genuine on the strength of the opinion which Sir William Temple had expressed as recently as 1692 in

---

[1] E. Budgell, *Memoirs of the Earl of Orrery* (1732), 156.
[2] See p. 177.

his *Essay upon Ancient and Modern Learning*. Temple argued for the genuineness of the letters on the ground that the sentiments in them 'could never be represented but by him that possessed them'. Lucian, he said, was no more capable of writing them than he was of performing the acts attributed to Phalaris. 'In all the one writ you find the scholar or the sophist; and in all the other the tyrant and the commander.' Arguments such as these reflected what was then considered polite scholarship. The criteria adopted by Temple were not historical or analytical but stylistic and literary. He himself used the metaphor of art when he remarked that 'he must have little skill in painting that cannot find out this to be an original'. In contrast Richard Bentley demonstrated in his *Dissertation upon the Epistles of Phalaris* that the letters were spurious by pointing out anachronisms such as the reference to cities founded long after the death of Phalaris, expressions derived from later authors such as Herodotus, and above all the date of the dialect in which they were written. Bentley's attack on Boyle was thus also an attack on some of the basic assumptions of liberal education. The intention of liberal education was to train not scholars but citizens. Scholarship, with its laborious pursuit of facts, was as much a form of specialization as professional singing was to Obadiah Walker, and equally to be avoided in education.[1] It was small wonder in these circumstances that the dons of Christ Church rallied in force to Boyle's defence. Francis Atterbury and Robert Freind, who as Boyle's tutors had contributed to the edition in much the same way as tutors sometimes wrote the verses published in their pupils' names, were joined by George Smalridge, Anthony Alsop, and William King, who, as Pope told Warburton, was the author of the ingenious argument that just as Phalaris was said by Bentley not to be the author of the *Letters,* so Bentley himself was not the author of the *Dissertation upon the Epistles of Phalaris*.[2] Opinion was divided whether Bentley or Boyle had the better of the argument, and as late as 1748 the author of the life of Bentley in *Biographia Britannica* implied that

---

[1] O. Walker, *Of Education* (1677), 115.
[2] J. Nichols, *Literary Anecdotes,* v, 86; *Short Review of the Controversy* (1701).

the letters were not universally believed to be spurious. But gradually the view prevailed that, in Johnson's words, Atterbury and his allies had tried 'what Wit could perform in opposition to Learning, on a question which Learning only could decide'.[1] If Lord Holland is to be believed, the eventual realization of the magnitude of its defeat at the hands of Bentley had a profound effect at Christ Church. Writing more than a century after Boyle published his edition, Lord Holland remarked that in its dealings with Samuel Parr the college was 'wonderfully cautious not to offend', and he attributed its caution to the rebuff received from Bentley.[2] The dispute did not affect the nature of liberal education, but it may well have contributed to the sparseness of classical scholarship at Christ Church in the eighteenth century.

The New Year Books are as follows (in some instances identification remains conjectural):

1666 Georgius Pachymeres, *Epitome Logices Aristotelis,* editing attributed to Fell (Madan, *Oxford Books,* no. 2753; Morison,[3] 12).

1667 Albinus, *In Platonicam Philosophiam Introductio,* editing and preface attributed to Fell (Madan, 2762; Morison, 13).

1669 Clement I, *Epistola ad Corinthios,* edited by Fell (Madan, 2822; Morison, 14).

1670 Epictetus, *Enchiridion*; Cebes, *Tabula*; Theophrastus, *Characteres Ethici,* edited by Fell (Madan, 2853; Morison, 19).

1671 Nemesius, *De Natura Hominis,* editing attributed to Fell (Madan, 2891; Morison, 21).

1672 Aratus, *Phaenomena & Diosemia,* edited by Fell (Madan, 2919; Morison, 22).

1674 Justinus, *Historiarum ex Trogo Pompeio libri 44,* editing attributed to Fell (Madan, 3014; Morison, 27).

1675 Nepos, *Vitae Excellentium Imperatorum* ..., edited by Fell (Madan, 3066; Morison, 32).

---

[1] S. Johnson, *Works* (1787), iii, 2.
[2] Holland, *Further Memoirs of the Whig Party,* 326–7.
[3] Morison, *John Fell, the University Press and the Fell 'Types',* app. i.

1676 Suetonius Tranquillus, *Opera Omnia* or *Idylls and Epigrams of Theocritus,* editing in both cases attributable to Fell (Madan, 3123–4; Morison, 39–40).

1677 Clement I, *Epistola ad Corinthios,* edited by Fell (Madan, 3138; Morison, 41).

1678 Faustinus Presbyter, *Opera,* preface and notes attributed to Fell (Madan, 3174; Morison, 43).

1679 Zosimus, *Historiae Novae libri sex,* editing attributed to Fell, notes by Thomas Sparke (Madan, 3242; Morison, 48).

1680 Lactantius, *De Mortibus Persecutorum liber,* edited by Fell, perhaps sub-edited by Thomas Sparke (Madan 3269; Morison, 50), or (less likely) Epictetus, *Enchiridion,* edited by Fell (Madan, 3264; Morison, 49).

1681 Cyprian, *Of the Unity of the Church,* translation attributed to Fell (Madan, iii, 521; Morison, 52).

1682 Athenagoras, *Opera,* editing attributed to Fell (Madan, iii, 521; Morison, 53).

1683 Clement of Alexandria, *Liber Quis Dives Salutem Consequi Possit,* editing attributed to Fell (Madan, iii, 521; Morison, 56).

1684 Lactantius, *Opera,* editing attributed to Fell, but described as 'illustrata a Tho. Spark' (Madan, iii, 521; Morison, 62).

1685 St Barnabas, *Epistola Catholica,* editing attributed to Fell (Madan, iii, 521; Morison, 66).

1686 Origen, *Treatise on Prayer,* editing attributed to Fell (Madan, iii, 521; Morison, 67).

1690 Xenophon, *Memorabilia,* edited by H. Aldrich (Madan, iii, 521).

1691 Xenophon, *Agesilaus, Spartan Polity, Symposium etc.,* edited by E. Wells (Madan, iii, 521).

1692 Aristeas, *Historia LXXII Interpretum,* edited by H. Aldrich, H. Hody, and E. Bernard (Madan, iii, 521).[1]

1693 Xenophon, *De Re Equestri etc.,* edited by E. Wells (Madan, iii,

---

[1] Bentley's copy of this work annotated by him is BL IIII f. 16.

521), or Velleius Paterculus, edited by H. Dodwell (Wood, *Athenae,* iv, 452). A Charlett book.

1694   Plutarch, *De Audiendis Poetis,* edited by J. Potter (Carter,[1] i, 424). A Charlett book.

1695   Phalaris, *Epistolae,* edited by C. Boyle (Madan, iii, 521).

1696   Aeschines and Demosthenes, edited by P. Foulkes and J. Freind (Bodl. MS Rawlinson J. fol. 2, fo. 16).

1697   Nepos, *Excellentium Imperatorum Vitae,* edited by W. Adams (Bodl. MS Rawlinson J. fol. 2, fo. 16).

1698   *Fabularum Aesopicarum Delectus,* edited by A. Alsop (Madan, iii, 521; Bodl. MS Rawlinson J. fol. 2, fo. 16).

1699   Theocritus, edited by R. West (Madan, *Chronological List*[2]), or Herodian (Madan, *Chronological List*).

1700   Tatian, edited by W. Worth (Madan, *Chronological List*).

1701   Sallust, edited by W. Ayerst (Madan, *Chronological List*). ? A Charlett book (Ayerst of Univ.), or Marcus Hieronymus Vida, *Poeticorum libri tres* (Madan, *Chronological List*).

1703   Justin Martyr, *Apologiae,* edited by H. Hutchin (Madan, iii, 521; HMC, Portland, 15th *Report,* app. iv (1897), 93), or Eutropius, *Historiae Romanae Breviarium,* edited by T. Hearne (Madan, iii, 521).

1704   Marcus Aurelius Antoninus, *Eorum Quae ad Seipsum libri XII,* edited by R. Ibbetson (Madan, iii, 521). ? A Charlett book (Ibbetson of Univ.).

1705   Homer, *Odyssey,* edited by C. Aldrich (Bodl. MS Rawlinson J. fol. 2, fol. 16; Carter, i, 147; Madan, iii, 521).

1706   Grotius, *Baptizatorum Puerorum Institutio,* edited by C. Aldrich (Bodl. MS Rawlinson J. fol. 2, fo. 16; Carter, i, 147; Madan, *Chronological List*).

1707   Epictetus, *Enchiridion*; Theophrastus, *Characteres Ethici,* edited

---

[1] H. Carter, *History of the Oxford University Press* (1975).
[2] Madan, *Chronological List of Oxford Books 1681–1713,* ed. J. S. G. Simmons, 1954.

by C. Aldrich (*et al.*) (Bodl. MS Rawlinson J. fol. 2, fo. 16; Carter, i, 147; Madan, *Chronological List*).

1708   St Ignatius, of Antioch, *Epistolae,* edited by C. Aldrich (Bodl. MS Rawlinson J. fol. 2, fo. 16; Carter, i, 147; Madan, *Chronological List*).

1709   Palladio. *Antichità di Roma di M. Andrea Palladio,* edited by C. Fairfax (Bodl. MS Rawlinson J. fol. 2, fo. 16; Carter, i, 147; Hearne, *Collections,* viii, 103; Madan, *Chronological List*).

1711   *Plato (Symposium) etc.,* edited by C. Fairfax (Bodl. MS Rawlinson J. fol. 2, fo. 16; Madan, iii, 521; Hearne, *Collections,* xi, 278).

1714   Homer, *Iliad,* edited by C. Fairfax, T. Fenton, and L. Stephens, promoted by Atterbury (Bodl. MS Rawlinson J. fol. 2, fo. 16).

1715   Epictetus, *Enchiridion Versibus Adumbratum,* edited by E. Ivie (Bodl. MS Rawlinson J. fol. 2, fo. 16).

(*b*) LOGIC

The study of logic[1] was an important element in liberal education. At Christ Church, from the foundation until late in the eighteenth century, each of the four *Classes* had its own lecturer in dialectic or logic, whose duty was to moderate at disputations and to deliver lectures in logic. Neither the lecturer in rhetoric nor the lecturer in Greek was assigned to a particular *Classis*: only logic was deemed to require such extensive provision. Disputations were the most important logical exercises, but when written replaced oral exercises their place was taken by the needs of composition. Logic then tended to be pursued more intensively in the latter part of an undergraduate's career. Until 1775 Collections in logic were taken up in the first year, but after the revival at that period in the study of mathematics logic was moved to the second year, and in the closing years of the eighteenth century, perhaps under the shadow of the approaching reform of

[1] See J. Yolton, 'Schoolmen, Logic and Philosophy', in Sutherland and Mitchell, *History of the University of Oxford,* v, 566–91.

the university examinations, it became predominantly a study for the final year.

By the sixteenth century, the textbooks most commonly used were encrusted with what Edward Bentham disparagingly termed the 'abstruse Scholastick Language' of former ages.[1] The esteem in which Aristotle was held at Oxford did not extend to his commentators and interpreters, and attempts were made to purge the glosses and to produce a textbook suitable for the times. Amongst those who sought to do this was John Fell, who wrote in the preface to his *Grammatica Rationis, sive Institutiones Logicae,* published in 1673, that he considered the existing handbooks on logic uninteresting to students. Other editions of this work appeared in 1675, 1685, and 1697, and it was probably used at Christ Church, but it eventually gave way to Aldrich's *Artis Logicae Compendium,* which was published at the university press in 1691, and became the principal textbook in logic not only at Christ Church but throughout the university until the publication of Whately's *Logic* in 1826.[2] The remarkable popularity of the compendium was due not only to its commendable brevity but to the clarity and simplicity with which Aristotle's ideas were presented. It was, wrote one commentator, relieved of the tedious explanations and subtleties of the *Organon,* 'and totally free from the barbarous jargon with which the later Schoolmen had over-loaded and corrupted it'.[3] It did not immediately rout all rivals, and several other treatises on logic are mentioned in the Collections Books, mostly during the early eighteenth century. The following textbooks based on traditional logic have been noted:

Samuel Smith, *Aditus ad Logicam* (1613); read in 1714–15.
Robert Sanderson, *Logicae Artis Compendium* (1615); read in 1704, 1712–16.
Obadiah Walker, *Artis Rationis* (1673); read in 1712.
John Wallis, *Institutio Logicae* (1687); read in 1713–16.

---

[1] E. Bentham, *Reflections upon the Nature and Usefulness of Logick* (1740), 6.
[2] E. J. Whately, *Life and Correspondence of Richard Whately* (1866), i, 49.
[3] Copleston, *Reply to the Calumnies,* 22.

Locke was studied at Christ Church in the eighteenth century,[1] but mainly as a replacement in the third or fourth year for the *Institutiones Metaphysicae* of Burgersdicius. Nevertheless, in 1703 the *Logica* of Jean Le Clerc, a follower of Descartes and Locke, was taken up to Collections, and in 1809 George Chinnery noted in one of his letters the use of Isaac Watts's logic,[2] which was much influenced by Locke. Thus, although Locke exerted some influence, the evidence suggests that in the teaching of logic Christ Church was conservative.

In addition to textbooks on logic, Aristotle's writings on logic were also sometimes studied. In 1654 Seth Ward declared that the *Organon* was not read at Oxford,[3] but it is perhaps worth noting that the first of Fell's New Year Books was an edition of the *Epitome of the Organon* by Georgius Pachymeres published in 1666. The *Categories* was taken up to Collections in 1704, and the *Organon* in 1714, but these were isolated instances, and Aristotle's logical writings, although perhaps the subject for lectures, appear not to have received much attention until the study of Greek had made considerable progress. In 1776 the *Prior Analytics* and *De Interpretatione* were prescribed reading in conjunction with Aldrich, and there is evidence that other works were read at this time. Thomas Grenville's interleaved copy of Aldrich's *Compendium,* now in the British Library, for example, contains annotations on the *Posterior Analytics* and the *Topics,* and on Porphyry's commentary on the *Categories.* Grenville matriculated in 1771. Eventually there developed the need for a textbook containing relevant extracts from Aristotle, not to supplant Aldrich but to be read with the *Compendium,* and on 8 December 1789 the Treasurer of Christ Church was empowered to pay the sum of twenty guineas to George Illingworth, a Student and tutor, 'for the trouble which he has had in preparing for the Press under the Dean's direction certain extracts from Aristotle and others for the use of the Logical

---

[1] See p. 300.
[2] Ch. Ch. Archives, xlviii. a. 46, fo. 62ᵛ.
[3] S. Ward, *Vindiciae Academiarum* (1654), 25.

Lectures'.[1] No trace has been found of this publication, and it may have taken the form of fly-sheets rather than a book.

From the time of Francis Bacon, critics complained that the university paid excessive attention to the study of Aristotelian logic. The clamour grew in intensity towards the end of the eighteenth century, at precisely the time that logical studies at Christ Church were pursued with greater energy than before. The main charge was that the study of logic stifled free inquiry and was responsible for the decline of scientific studies at Oxford because syllogistic reasoning was based on deduction whereas scientific discovery was founded on induction. In fact this argument was well understood in the university in the early eighteenth century, when logic was recognized to be an unsuitable instrument for the advancement of science. Although mathematics depended on deduction, critics also alleged that the dictates of Aristotle prevented students from progressing beyond the elements of geometry.[2] Defenders of the university retorted that undergraduates often studied plane and spherical trigonometry and conic sections—a claim largely substantiated at Christ Church by the Collections Books—and that Aristotelian logic was so far from being harmful to mathematics that John Wallis, the greatest mathematician in the university during the seventeenth century, wrote a standard textbook on logic which was often used in place of Aldrich.

The main defence of logic was that it trained the mental faculties. Edward Bentham, who had been a tutor at Oriel before becoming Regius Professor of Divinity in 1763, wrote that it enabled a man to view a subject in all its branches, to judge which parts deserved to be considered more minutely, to consider the arguments of opponents, and to determine whether they proved their conclusions.

Let a Young Gentleman consider Logick as part of his Education not as his Profession: if it makes him acquainted with the instruments of reasoning and puts his natural faculties into a regular disposition, it fully

---

[1] Chapter Minute Book.
[2] Copleston, *Reply to the Calumnies*, 15.

answers its purpose. His real improvement in the art of Reasoning will all along be proportioned to the progress which he shall make in Science'.[1]

To Edward Copleston, writing more than fifty years later, logic gave the habit of discrimination, the power of stating a question distinctly and of arguing it with perspicuity.[2]

The deductive methods of logic, unlike the inductive methods of scientific inquiry, were especially suited for reasoning on matters of law, morals, and divinity, where the premises were provided by the unquestionable texts of statutes, classical authors, or the Scriptures. Logic was thus concerned with words and ideas rather than with the observation of nature or of fact. It was in the definition of the premises and in particular in the close attention paid to the meaning of words that traditional logic was influenced by the criticisms made by Locke. The logic taught at Christ Church in the latter part of the eighteenth century was defined by Cyril Jackson in some lecture notes in his hand amongst the papers of Charles Abbot in the Public Record Office.

A Syllogism [he wrote] is compos'd of Propositions—a Proposition of words. Words, Propositions, Syllogisms are the subject of Logic. Words express Ideas, and hence the first Part of Logic is said to treat of simple Ideas. Propositions express a decision of the mind concerning the agreement or disagreement of two Ideas. Hence the second part of Logic is said to treat of Judgment. Syllogisms express a decision of the mind &c deduc'd from other previous ones. Hence the third part of Logic is said to treat of Reasoning. Words then are the basis of the whole superstructure. If these are false or fallacious, the whole will necessarily be so ... It shd. seem therefore that it wd. be necessary to enquire into the nature of words. Are they all of one sort or different? If the latter can they be reduc'd into classes? If so what are those classes?[3]

The study of logic was an important factor in causing liberal education to develop its literary character. The methods of natural science were as suitable as those of logic for training the mind,

---

[1] Bentham, *Reflections upon ... Logick,* 10.
[2] Copleston, *Reply to the Calumnies,* 176.
[3] PRO 30/9/3/31.

but science applied its disciplines to practical ends and particularly to the specialization of function required in an industrial society. Logic on the other hand being concerned with words and ideas, with the formation of judgement, and with the perception of rational truth, its disciplines were more fittingly exercised through the literature of classical antiquity.

(c) MATHEMATICS

Mathematics was studied by undergraduates at Christ Church mainly as an exercise in logic and as an introduction to sciences, such as astronomy and optics, which depended on deduction. In such circumstances mathematics was slow to develop as an autonomous discipline, for its use in the study of logic was limited, and natural science was seldom taken beyond a fairly elementary level. A further restraint on the development of mathematical studies was imposed by the lack of adequate teaching, which was partly remedied by Dean Gregory.

For the second half of the seventeenth century, the evidence at present is too fragmentary to allow the course of mathematical studies at Christ Church to be reconstructed with any degree of certainty, but it is sufficient to suggest that mathematics was far from neglected. The Duke of Ormonde's grandson, Lord James Butler, for example, read some arithmetic, and in 1676 John Perceval spent his afternoons studying 'Mathematics and Arithmetick and Latin Orations as Tully or Quintilian'.[1] Charles Boyle, the editor of the *Letters of Phalaris,* read Euclid and works by William Oughtred with his tutor Francis Atterbury.[2] The early records of Collections in the eighteenth century include such works as Gassendi's *Institutio Astronomica,* Blaeu's *Institutio Astronomica de Usu Globorum,* and Keill's *Introductio ad Veram Physicam,* which presuppose a familiarity with elementary geometry, and some of these works were very probably read in the previous century as well. Perhaps above all the Deans of Christ Church

---

[1] HMC, *Ormonde,* NS (1899), v, 141, 156; BL Add. MS 46953, fo. 74.
[2] Atterbury, *Epistolary Correspondence,* ii, 1–16 *passim.*

encouraged the study of mathematics. John Fell, though not generally reputed a mathematician, contributed a preface in 1676 to John Wallis's edition of Archimedes and Eutocius in which he spoke of the disappointing reception of the proposal to issue an edition of *Veteres Mathematici*. His successor Aldrich was described when a tutor as 'a great mathematician of our house',[1] and at the time of his death had an edition of Euclid in the press, though, according to Hearne, not more than a dozen copies were printed because 'this Book being not quite finish'd (ending at Propos. LXXVI of the IVth Book) it was never publish'd'.[2]

Although through their reference to works by Gassendi, Blaeu, and Keill, the early records of Collections provide indirect evidence of the study of mathematics in the eighteenth century, no purely mathematical work was taken up to Collections until 1763. During this period, however, it is probable that undergraduates studied mathematics with logic, and were taught by the lecturers in logic with the *Classes* into which they were distributed. They also learnt mathematics by attending university lectures. Attendance at lectures in natural science was compulsory at Christ Church from the early years of the eighteenth century,[3] and it is apparent that such lectures required, and seem to have included, knowledge of mathematics. For example, in 1703 David Gregory, the Savilian Professor of Astronomy, issued the prospectus of a course of lectures in the *Oxford Almanac*. It embraced the following topics:

I. The First Six Books, with the Eleventh, and Twelfth Books of *Euclid's* Elements.

II. The plain Trigonometry; where is to be shewed the contraction of natural Signs, tangents, and Secants, and the Table of Logarithms, as well as natural Numbers as of Signs &c. the practical Geometry, comprehending the Description and use of Instruments, and the manner of measuring Heighth, Distances, Surfaces and Solids.

[1] HMC, *Egmont,* ii (1909), 38.
[2] Hearne, *Collections,* iii, 363; Carter, *History of the Oxford University Press,* i, 148.
[3] See p. 311.

III. *Algebra,* wherein is taught the method of resolving, and contracting plain and solid Problems; as well Arithmetical as Geometrical, or Diophantaean Problems.

IV. Mechanicks, wherein are laid down the Principles of all the Sciences concerning motion, the five Powers (commonly so call'd) explain'd, and the Engines in common use, reducible to those Powers describ'd.

V. Catoptricks and Dioptricks; where the effects of Mirrors and Glasses are shewed, the manner of Vision explain'd, and the Machines for the helping and enlarging the Sight (as Telescopes, Microscopes &c.) describ'd.

VI. The Principles of Astronomy, containing the Explication of all the most obvious Phaenomena of the Heavens, from the true System of the World, and the Generation of the Circles of the Sphaere thence arising. Here also is to be taught the Doctrine of the Globes, and their Use; with the Problems of the first motion by them resolved. After this to be demonstrated the Sphaerical Trigonometry, and the application thereof to Astronomy shewed, in resolving the Problems of the Sphaere by calculation, and the contraction of the Tables of the first motions depending on this.

VII. The Theory of the Planets, where the more recondite Astronomy is handled, that is the Orbits of the Planets determin'd by observation: the Tables of Motions describ'd; the methods of constructing them taught; and the Use of these Tables shew'd; as finding the Planet's places, the Eclipse of the Luminaries &c. Many of these Courses may be farther carried on, as the particular Inclinations of a Classe lead them. For example, subjoin'd to the practical Geometry may be a Lecture of Fortifications, so far as it is necessary for understanding it, without actual serving in an Army, or Fortifying a Town or Camp. Under the head of Mechanicks, there may be (if desired) colleges of Hydrostaticks, with all the experiments thereunto belonging; of the Laws of Communication of Motion, whether the Bodies be hard or elastick; of the Gravity of the Bodies, lying on inclin'd plains; of Ballisticks, or the Doctrine of Projecticks, as Bombs &c. of the Doctrine of Pendulum's and their application to the measuring of Time (after the principles of Astronomy or the sixth college) may be prosecuted, the Doctrine of the Sphaere projected *in plano,* or the Analemma or Astrolabes and Dialling; as also Navigation, and so of others.[1]

Later on in the eighteenth century, however, it became less common for courses of lectures in natural philosophy to include instruction in mathematics.

A significant improvement in mathematical studies at Christ Church occurred under Dean Gregory. In 1763 he included amongst the prescribed books for that year the first six books of Euclid, which eventually became the most frequently read of all books studied at Christ Church. In 1767 he added Colin Maclaurin's *Treatise of Algebra,* first published in 1748, and in 1775 his successor, Markham, made John Keill's *Elements of Plane and Spherical Trigonometry* a set book.[2] By the introduction of new works, Gregory gave greater emphasis to mathematics and sought to raise the level of attainment. In order to raise the level of attainment, however, it was not enough to introduce new works to the curriculum unless the teaching of mathematics was improved. When tutors taught every subject in the curriculum and mathematics was merely one subject amongst many, the possibility of a sustained improvement was slight. Although the college lectureships in logic, Greek, and rhetoric established at the foundation of Christ Church were not paralleled by a lectureship in mathematics, and the Junior Censor, or to give him his correct designation, the Censor Naturalis Philosophiae, is not known to have lectured on the subject, it was recognized as early as the seventeenth century that a lectureship in mathematics was needed. In 1667 Richard Busby, who had taught Euclid to Robert Hooke at Westminster, proposed to found such a lectureship. It was intended that the lecturer should deliver twenty-five mathematical lectures a year to undergraduates. They were to be given on Mondays at nine o'clock, or, if prevented, at the same time on Saturdays, but nothing seems to have come of the scheme. A

---

[1] *Oxford Almanac* (1703), 2–4.
[2] Keill's *Elements* was first printed in English in 1723 with an edition of Euclid. The first separate English edition seems to have been printed in Dublin in 1726.

similar intention perhaps lay behind the admission of John Keill to Christ Church in the following century.[1] It was left to Dean Gregory to establish a lectureship in mathematics. He did so by altering one of the provisions in the will of Matthew Lee. By his will, Lee, who died in 1755, provided for four undergraduate Westminster Students to learn mathematics and attend lectures on natural philosophy. To this end he bequeathed the sum of £30 a year to be divided equally amongst the four Students. When the bequest was finally placed at the disposal of the Dean and Chapter in 1765, £20 was applied to the salary of a mathematical lecturer, and only £10 was distributed according to the original intention of the will. The Lee mathematical lecturers during the eighteenth century, all of whom at some time held the office of Junior Censor, were:

Samuel Wells Thomson (1766–8)
William Jackson (1769–83)
Charles Sawkins (1784–94)
William Wood (1795–9)
Frederick Barnes (1800–3).

Between 1768 and 1775 only a minority of undergraduates took up the recently introduced Euclid to Collections, and none took up algebra until 1774, but the foundation of the Lee mathematical lectureship led to a gradual improvement. There are no formal records of attendance at the lectures, but the Collections Books show that from 1776 a sufficiently large number of undergraduates to imply the existence of a lecture took up almost identical mathematical Collections simultaneously. The existence of these lectures reveals an orderly progression from Euclid to algebra and finally to trigonometry. Thus in 1776 a substantial number of undergraduates presented the first book of Euclid at Collections in Easter term, followed by Books 2–4 in Trinity term, and Books 5–6 at Michaelmas. In the following year there was a mathematical lecture only in Michaelmas term when Books 1–3 were taken up. In 1778 two classes were held in Euclid. One of them took up Books 1–3 in Michaelmas term, and the other Books 4–6 in

[1] See p. 311.

Hilary term. The course in geometry was thus completed in two consecutive terms, and this remained the practice for the rest of the eighteenth century. Algebra was completed in a single term, apparently up to quadratic equations, and trigonometry in one term or sometimes two consecutive terms.

These improvements in the teaching of mathematics took place after the great advance in classical studies in the middle of the eighteenth century. Mathematics then became even more closely integrated with the study of logic, to which it was preparatory. When Euclid was introduced as a book for Collections it was for the second year. In 1768, after the introduction of Maclaurin's *Algebra,* Books 1–4 of Euclid were prescribed for the first year, and Books 5 and 6 and 11 and 12 for the second. Algebra, which had originally been read in the first year, was at the same time moved to the second year and studied with the later books of Euclid. After the introduction of trigonometry the plan of study was altered yet again. Euclid and algebra were then read in the first year and were followed by trigonometry in the second. In all these changes care was taken that the study of mathematics should be completed by the second year, when the serious study of logic began.

By about 1776 the Lee mathematical lecturers seem to have been moderately successful in introducing a course of mathematics which consisted of Euclid, algebra, and trigonometry. Its study reached a peak under Bagot, but thereafter, although the proportion of Westminster Students and Servitors to read the full course remained fairly steady, it declined for other groups. Those who did not take up the full course to Collections usually took up either Euclid or algebra, and a not inconsiderable proportion took up both of these, but in the last quarter of the eighteenth century about 10 per cent of Students, Commoners, and Servitors seem to have graduated without any mathematical Collections, and in the case of Gentlemen Commoners the percentage was even higher. In some cases the omission of mathematics is probably to be explained by proficiency in logic. In other cases it is apparent that undergraduates of exceptional ability were spared the rudiments. When George Chinnery came up, his tutor said to him,

'You know abundantly to omit all mathematical lectures', and when a few days later Chinnery saw the Dean, Jackson remarked, 'Mr. Corne tells me, Sir, you are out of the mathematical lecture'.[1] Peter Elmsley, the classical scholar, who matriculated in 1791, perhaps for the same reason read only conic sections, and Henry Hallam, who matriculated in 1795, read only algebra and trigonometry in his first year and conic sections in his last. Chinnery's experience shows that the Dean, in consultation with the tutors, decided whether an undergraduate should attend the mathematical lectures, and that this decision was made at the time of matriculation. It thus indicated the level of teaching in the school from which that undergraduate came.

The omission of mathematical Collections is not the only evidence of the existence at Christ Church towards the end of the eighteenth century of a minority of undergraduates of relatively exceptional ability in mathematics. In the 1790s, perhaps influenced by Cyril Jackson's enthusiasm for the subject, there appeared a small number of undergraduates who read more advanced mathematics, notably integral calculus, or 'fluxions' as it was called, and early in the next century mechanics. The principal works on fluxions were Benjamin Robins, *Discourse Concerning ... Fluxions* (1735), John Rowe, *Introduction to the Doctrine of Fluxions* (1751), and works by Bishop Horsley and Samuel Vince. In 1780, a Canoneer Student named John King took up Newton's *Principia Mathematica* to Collections, and others did so in 1789, 1796, and 1798. From 1790 Hugh Hamilton's *De Sectionibus Conicis* (1758), was read with frequency, and was joined in 1794 by Abraham Robertson's *Sectionum Conicarum Libri.*[2] Between 1790 and 1800 only about a score of undergraduates read any of these works, but the existence at Christ Church of a minority of undergraduates whose mathematical attainments greatly exceeded those needed for the study of logic, and the simultaneous emergence of a parallel minority whose attainments in classical studies outstripped those of their fellows, foreshadowed the eventual division of the public

[1] Ch. Ch. Archives, xlviii. a. 42a, fos. 9ᵛ, 46.
[2] Robertson entered Christ Church as a Servitor in 1775, aged 22.

examinations into two Schools in the following century. At Christ Church the minority capable of studying mathematics as a separate discipline rested on a narrow foundation composed mainly of Commoners, and the failure of Westminster School to nourish mathematical studies helped to ensure that the study of mathematics remained tied to logic and did not achieve parity with the classical tradition.

(*d*) CLASSICS

In the seventeenth and eighteenth centuries, undergraduates studied the literature of ancient Greece and Rome mainly as an instrument for training the mental faculties and as a model for moral and social behaviour. By construing classical authors and by writing verses and themes, they learnt to think logically, to speak and write with fluency, clarity, brevity, and occasionally wit, and to acquire the virtues of moderation, prudence, fortitude, and the rest. These were the qualities prized by liberal education and coveted by those for whom that education existed. Classical authors were widely studied for their substance and style. Students often knew their texts very well, but they seldom read them critically. The unnamed editor of the Oxford Pliny (1677), whom Madan believed to be John Fell, insisted that if possible the classics should be presented in plain texts without notes or display of erudition: 'Ideo nos omne in hoc studium contulimus ut, additis duntaxat quae ad rem facerent, editio nostra praeter Plinium nihil exhiberet'. When Copleston advocated the study of Thucydides and Xenophon, he did not mention their importance for classical scholarship but for contemporary affairs.

From no study [he wrote] can an Englishman acquire a better insight into the mechanism and temper of civil government: from none can he draw more instructive lessons, both of the danger of turbulent faction, and of corrupt oligarchy: from none can he better learn how to play skilfully upon, and how to keep in order, that finely-toned instrument, a free people.[1]

---

[1] Copleston, *Reply to the Calumnies,* 160.

The approach to classical literature was much influenced by the fact that Latin was the lingua franca in which the university conducted all its affairs until the end of the eighteenth century, and in some areas for even longer. Not until 1854, when it had ceased to be a living language, was a Professorship of Latin considered necessary at Oxford. Latin was not only the language of formal and ceremonial occasions but often of teaching also. It was the language used by the university professor and the college lecturer; disputations and even tutorials were in Latin. It was the language of many of the textbooks in philosophy, religion, mathematics, science, and logic, which filled the curriculum. John Keill's book on plane and spherical trigonometry first published in 1715 continued to add to the natural complexities of its subject by appearing in Latin into the nineteenth century, and Aldrich's compendium of logic was printed in its original Latin even longer. The records at Christ Church rarely indicate which editions of classical authors were studied,[1] but editions of Greek authors for the use of undergraduates were usually published with Latin translations.[2] Rarely were the adulatory verses contributed to the numerous volumes commemorating royal births, marriages, and deaths composed in anything but Latin. Because Latin was the ordinary and familiar language in which education was conducted, students tended to approach classical authors such as Virgil and Horace in much the same way as they would have read Milton or Pope.

The Greek and Latin classics were not an unchanging and rigidly defined body of authors. Certain works were read frequently throughout the period (Cicero's *De Officiis* was perhaps the most outstanding of these), but the authors popular at the end of the eighteenth century often differed from those read at the

[1] On this subject, see especially P. Quarrie, 'The Christ Church Collections Books', in Sutherland and Mitchell, *History of the University of Oxford*, v, 493–506.

[2] Although the use of such cribs declined from Markham's time, Fynes Clinton, who matriculated in 1799, noted that on his arrival at Christ Church he aimed to have Greek texts 'without the encumbrance of Latin versions' and had to mutilate his books to obtain them (C. J. Fynes Clinton ed, *Literary Remains of Henry Fynes Clinton* (1854), 9).

beginning, and these in turn were not identical with those favoured in the previous century. Such preferences, although not immune from the vagaries of fashion and the availability of published editions, in general reflected the aspirations of those sections of society which attended the university—aspirations which were themselves moulded by political and social change—but were also greatly influenced by the spread of Greek and by the study of ancient history, which transformed the cultural and intellectual assumptions of the educated man in the eighteenth century.

For almost a century after the Restoration, Latin authors dominated the curriculum. Greek was studied, especially at Westminster, but on the whole lost ground. A revealing anecdote concerning David Jones, who was elected to a Westminster Studentship in 1681, is recorded by Hearne, who relates that he 'would frequently baffle even the Proctors themselves in the publick University Schools by his ready citing of Greek Authors, & speaking in that language'.[1] Even so it was not for Greek but for Latin that Westminster gained admission to the *Dunciad*:

Let Freind affect to speak as Terence spoke,
And Alsop never but like Horace joke.[2]

The account book which John Locke kept for his pupils (except the Westminster Students) mentions Juvenal, Ovid, Suetonius, Persius, Horace, Justin, and Velleius Paterculus, but Greek writers are notably absent. In the time of Dean Fell, Livy and the ubiquitous Cicero were much admired. When Justinian Isham came up to Christ Church in 1674, his cousin and tutor Zaccheus Isham wrote to his father recommending the study of Livy 'because the knowledge of the Roman History is so necessary, and his style and manner of writing is generally commended by all men ... That he should never lay Tully out of his hands I acknowledge to be excellent advice.'[3] It is not until the records of Collections begin early in the eighteenth century, however, that the reading

[1] Hearne, *Collections,* viii (1907), 249.
[2] A. Pope, *Dunciad,* iv, 224–5.
[3] Northants. Record Office, I.C. 862.

of more than isolated individuals can be ascertained. They show that between 1700 and the death of Queen Anne the most frequently read Latin authors were in order of popularity:

Virgil, *Aeneid*	Caesar, *Commentaries*
Cicero, *De Oratore*	Horace, *Satires*
Sallust	Virgil, *Georgics*
Cicero, *De Officiis*	Cicero, *Tusculanae Disputationes*
Horace, *Ars Poetica*	Horace, *Epistles*.
Cicero, *Orator*	

Of these, the first five were read much more frequently than the remainder. As befitted the Augustan Age, much store was set on Latin verse, where Virgil and Horace led the field. Juvenal and Ovid followed at a distance. Cicero as usual was always read. Among the Latin historians, Livy, Nepos, Florus, Suetonius, Tacitus, Velleius Paterculus, and Eutropius followed occasionally in the wake of Sallust. Of the Greeks, the *Iliad* exceeded all other Greek works in popularity, and a common exercise was to compare it with the *Aeneid*. Longinus, a key book for eighteenth-century taste and culture, was popular, and Theocritus, Andronicus Rhodius, Xenophon's *Cyropaedia* and *Memorabilia,* Epictetus, Demosthenes, and Isocrates were read from time to time. Herodotus and Thucydides were almost entirely neglected.

The introduction of compulsory Collections under Smalridge did not improve classical studies at Christ Church, and the period from 1719 until the appointment of Dean Gregory in 1756 was one of stagnation. In 1735 Richard West wrote that at Christ Church 'Horace and Virgil are equally unknown'.[1] Unknown to West they may have been, but only Horace was more generally assured of this fate, for he ceased to be read for forty years from 1716 to 1756. Virgil, on the other hand, retained his pre-eminence and with Cicero was the most commonly read of all authors at this time. Between 1717 and 1754 the only Greek work read at Christ Church was the *Iliad,* which was spread over three years. The amount of classical literature, in fact, which undergraduates

---

[1] P. Toynbee (ed.), *Correspondence of Gray, West, and Ashton* (1915), i, 51.

were required to read during this period was small. Apart from the *Iliad* and *Aeneid,* they were expected to read Lucretius, and Cicero's *Brutus, De Officiis, De Oratore, Orator,* and *Tusculanae Disputationes.* They read no history or drama, nor the great political orations of antiquity. The model to which classical education at Christ Church aspired was represented by William Conybeare, the son of Dean Conybeare, who matriculated in 1757. He was, wrote his son, a 'perfectly trained Oxford scholar of that day ... really an elegant Latin scholar, struck with horror at any phrase or idiom which could not vouchsafe Ciceronian authority, and a great reader of Clarendon, with little Greek and no mathematical or physical science'.[1]

The renaissance in classical studies began under Dean Gregory. The prescribed books were changed, often yearly, and as new works appeared for the first time the curriculum was infused with freshness and vitality. Not only was the meagre reading required for a degree expanded, but undergraduates were required to work harder. Whereas in the past the *Aeneid* had been spread over two years, under Gregory it was read in one, and the *Iliad* was read in two years instead of three. Gregory's most important achievements, however, were the revival of ancient history and Greek. In 1763 Sallust, who had not been read since 1716, was restored to the curriculum, and in the same year Greek history made a tentative appearance in the form of Xenophon's *Anabasis,* which quickly established itself in popularity. Homer remained the principal Greek author, but in 1755 Aristotle's *Poetics* and *Rhetoric* and the *De Compositione Verborum* of Dionysius of Halicarnassus were prescribed books, followed a year later by Demosthenes (*De Corona* and *Olynthiacs*) and the *Apologias* of Plato and Xenophon. In the case of the Latin writers, the poets continued to be held in high esteem, and, although Lucretius was dropped, the primacy of Virgil was strengthened by the addition of the *Georgics* and *Eclogues.* Cicero's *De Officiis* and his treatise *De Oratore* continued to be read, but in 1763 five of his great political orations included in *Orationes Quaedam Selectae,* which was originally a Delphin

[1] Conybeare, *Elizabethan Schoolmaster,* 115.

Classic, were added to the curriculum for the first time. From 1763 until Gregory's death in 1767, undergraduates were expected to read the following classical authors:

Cicero, *De Amicitia; De Oratore; De Senectute; De Officiis; Pro Archia; Pro Caelio; Pro Ligario; Pro Marcello; Pro Milone*
Sallust
Virgil, *Aeneid; Eclogues; Georgics*
Homer, *Odyssey*
Theocritus
Xenophon, *Anabasis.*

The continuity and impetus of reform persisted under Dean Markham, who, after his appointment as Headmaster of Westminster in 1753, had been closely involved in Gregory's achievements. Speaking of the new spirit of the youth at Christ Church, Gregory's biographer remarked

This ardor indeed was the less to be wondered at, when we consider that they came mostly out of the hands of one of the most learned men of the age, who had warmed their imagination with the enchanted scenes he had occasionally pointed out to them, and to which he had directed their flight, and given them wings to soar with.[1]

In a footnote this 'most learned man' is identified as Markham. Markham was thus able to continue the work of reform without delay and to introduce at Christ Church studies which he had encouraged at Westminster. The extent and immediacy of his reforming zeal may be seen in the list of prescribed books drawn up for Collections in 1768, less than a year after his installation. It consisted of the following works:

Caesar, *Commentaries*
Cicero, *Brutus; De Natura Deorum; De Finibus; De Oratore; De Officiis; Orator; Tusculanae Disputationes*
Horace, *Ars Poetica; Epistles*
Livy
Lucretius
Quintilian, *De Institutione Oratoria* (ed. Chas. Rollin, 1741)

---

[1] *Essay on the Life of David Gregory*, 18.

Sallust

Tacitus

Virgil, *Georgics*

Aeschines and Demosthenes, *De Corona*

Aeschylus, *Choephori*

Aristotle, *Poetics*

Demosthenes, *Philippica Prima et Tres Olynthiacae* (ed. Ric. Mounteney, 1731).

Euripides, *Electra*

Herodotus

Sophocles, *Electra*

Thucydides

Xenophon, *Anabasis; Cyropaedia; Hellenica; Memorabilia.*

Almost every year some new work was added to the curriculum or restored after long absence. Of all Markham's achievements, however, the encouragement of Greek studies and the emphasis placed on ancient history stand out. So far as Greek was concerned, he revived, and indeed may be said in some instances practically to have introduced at Christ Church Herodotus, Thucydides, Longinus, Demosthenes, and Aristotle's *Poetics, Ethics,* and *Rhetoric,* and he added several works by Xenophon for the first time. Above all he introduced the Greek dramatists to Christ Church. In 1768 the *Choephori* of Aeschylus, and the *Electra*s of Euripides and Sophocles were read. In 1771 the *Oedipus Tyrannus* of Sophocles was added, followed a year later by the *Hippolytus* of Euripides and the *Antigone* of Sophocles, and in 1773 the *Iphigenia in Aulis* of Euripides. In 1774 *Prometheus* and *Seven Against Thebes* by Aeschylus were read, and in 1775 three further plays by Euripides—*Alcestis, Medea,* and *Orestes*—and the *Ajax* of Sophocles. In these developments the influence of the leading public schools, and especially of Westminster, is apparent. Since the seventeenth century the school had published its own classical textbooks. In the time of Dean Aldrich, Westminster Students occasionally took up the *Planudean Anthology* (referred to as *Epigrammata Graeca*) to Collections, and in 1723 Hearne reported that Robert Freind, the Headmaster of Westminster, intended to produce a new edition.[1]

[1] Hearne, *Collections,* viii, 56.

In 1729 Fifield Allen, a former Westminster Student, published an edition of the three *Electra*s of Aeschylus, Sophocles, and Euripides. This edition was used at Westminster School,[1] and may have been the edition in use at Christ Church under Markham, for the three plays it contained were read much more frequently than any others. Another edition of the Greek dramatists in use at Christ Church was John Burton's *Pentalogia,* published in 1758. This was an Eton textbook and included *Oedipus Tyrannus, Oedipus Coloneus, Antigone, Seven Against Thebes,* and *Phoenissae.*[2] Some 65 per cent of Westminster Students under Markham read a play by Sophocles or Euripides, and sometimes more than one, against 40 per cent of Canoneer Students to do so. The study of the Greek dramatists was so well established at Westminster that at the end of the eighteenth century Fynes Clinton remarked that 'the most solid literary advantage that I derived from Westminster was a taste for the Greek tragic poets'.[3]

It was consistent with the renewed emphasis on Greek that in reforming the study of ancient history Markham should have concentrated as much on the Greek as on the Roman historians. In 1768 he added Caesar's *Commentaries* to Sallust as a book for the first year, with Livy and Tacitus as books for the second year, but in the second year he also required undergraduates to commence Greek history with Herodotus, and this was followed in the third year by Thucydides and Xenophon's *Hellenica.* The plan of study was not always strictly observed in practice, and it was not uncommon for the Greek historians to precede the Roman, but on the whole the authors were read in a sequence which reflected the progress made by undergraduates in mastering classical languages and compared favourably with the haphazard manner in which the same authors were read, if at all, in the early eighteenth century. Nevertheless, the records of Collections suggest that, despite Markham's efforts, it was possible for an undergraduate to take a degree without apparently reading any of

---

[1] W. B. Cadogan, *Life of the Revd. William Romaine* (1796), 5.
[2] Collections Book, li. b. ii, fo. 28.
[3] Fynes Clinton, *Literary remains of Henry Fynes Clinton,* 8.

the Greek historians. About a third of the Canoneer Students and Commoners graduated having read only Roman history. Of the Westminster Students only about a sixth omitted Greek history.

The revival of classical studies in the mid-eighteenth century was a European phenomenon, but in England it occurred at a time when the beginnings of empire and the supremacy of Parliament had obvious parallels in the ancient history of Greece and Rome. History was thus a topical study. By including other disciplines, such as geography, numismatics, archaeology, and art, it broadened the intellectual horizon, and fostered a more inquisitive and analytical spirit. The study of ancient history was also, however, a moral study. Markham's conception of history was not unlike that expressed by Charles Thomas Barker, a Westminster Student and subsequently a distinguished tutor and Senior Censor, who won the Chancellor's English Essay prize in 1783 for his essay 'On the use of history'. In it he wrote that 'Of the general uses of history ... the aid which it lends to virtue is the most distinguished and extensive'. History furnished examples of conduct worthy of imitation, and mirrored that experience which otherwise could only be gained from life. It taught prudence and discernment, and disclosed the true motives of human behaviour. It taught fortitude by revealing the painful path trodden by others, and reason by tracing cause and effect. History removed prejudice and expanded the mind, and it revealed the faults which destroyed national greatness. Thus defined, history illustrated and reinforced the traditional values of liberal education.

In addition to enlarging the curriculum by the encouragement of Greek and ancient history, Markham also increased the amount of reading expected of undergraduates. This is shown in the extent of the studies prescribed for each of the three years needed for a degree.

In 1768 he introduced Richard Mounteney's Greek and Latin edition of the *Philippics* and *Olynthiacs* of Demosthenes, first published in 1731, as a book for the first year. It continued to be read under Markham more extensively than at any other time until the closing years of the eighteenth century. Cicero's orations, on the other hand, which Gregory had introduced, were read rarely, but

De Oratore and *Brutus* were required reading for the first year. Also in the first year, in addition to Roman history, undergraduates read Xenophon's *Anabasis* and *Memorabilia,* and either the *Epistles* or *Ars Poetica* of Horace. Homer, who had been one of the sheet-anchors of the curriculum for most of the century, was omitted entirely from the plan of study, though, perhaps owing to the initiative of individual tutors, often taken up to first-year Collections from about 1772.

For the second year, the plan of study included the *Cyropaedia* of Xenophon, two or three Greek plays, and some Herodotus. Undergraduates were also expected to read the *Poetics* of Aristotle, though this was not a work read with great frequency until after Markham. Of the Latin writers, they studied the historians, including Tacitus, and also Cicero's *De Officiis,* and some Virgil and Horace. Not content with deposing Homer, Markham also dislodged Virgil from the position of eminence he had previously occupied, when for more than fifty years the *Aeneid* had been read to the exclusion of nearly all other Latin poets. The *Georgics* was retained as a book for the second year, but Horace replaced the *Aeneid* in the first. Virgil was never without readers, but he did not recover his earlier popularity, and was overtaken by Horace, who perhaps fitted the mood of the times better than the heroic manner of the *Aeneid*. Another casualty to literary fashion was Quintilian, a great favourite in the seventeenth and early eighteenth centuries. After his revival in 1767 Quintilian was read by a minority of undergraduates as a book for the second year, in the edition of Charles Rollin published in 1738 'ad usum scholarum', until 1772 when he vanished from the curriculum almost completely, perhaps to be replaced by the Oxford edition of Aristotle's *Rhetoric* published in 1759.[1] For the rest of the century the *Rhetoric* was widely read.

---

[1] The editor was William Holwell, a Canoneer Student and tutor of Christ Church. Of this edition Edward Harwood wrote, 'One of my friends, who hath known for many years those who have signalized themselves as Scholars at Oxford, acquainted me that the name of this learned Editor was Holwell. His criticisms have poured such distinguished light upon this abstruse and most excellent Treatise, that it gives me singular pleasure in announcing to the reader of this accurate Edition, the name of the Gentleman to whom he is under so

The latter part of the curriculum was by tradition devoted to religious and metaphysical studies as well as to classical, but from the middle of the eighteenth century religious studies became to an increasing extent the province of the divinity lectureship founded in 1750,[1] and metaphysics, which had been studied in the Aristotelian compendiums of Burgersdicius and Eustachius, was dropped from the curriculum prescribed at Collections. By increasing the amount of time for classical studies, the alteration in studies for the third year presaged a significant change of emphasis in the curriculum. When Conybeare died the classical reading for the third year consisted of the *Iliad,* Lucretius, and Cicero's *Tusculanae Disputationes.* From 1763 until Gregory's death undergraduates read eight books of the *Odyssey,* the *Anabasis* of Xenophon, the *Georgics,* and *De Officiis.* Markham increased the classical reading still further. He restored Lucretius and the *Tusculanae Disputationes,* and added Thucydides, Xenophon's *Hellenica,* and Cicero's *De Finibus* and *De Natura Deorum.*

It is tempting to linger on Markham. His achievements were considerable. By encouraging Greek and ancient history, by reorganizing and broadening the plan of study, and by reforming Collections, he gave new vitality to education at Christ Church. He was an excellent administrator and teacher, but not an innovator. He was conservative by instinct and training, and inclined to the caution and prudence which he believed it was the object of education to inculcate. His portrait at Christ Church does him justice. His avuncular features, unravaged by thought, combine urbanity with apprehension. Worldliness is tempered by anxiety as though he expected to be informed that the college was on fire.

Markham's removal to York was followed at Christ Church by a period of consolidation under Dean Bagot. Collections were held with commendable regularity, and the plan of study was carefully observed. Markham had reorganized the curriculum, but he had been less than entirely successful in ensuring that it was

---

many obligations' (E. Harwood, *View of the Various Editions of the Greek and Roman Classics,* 4th ed. (1790), 48). In this edition Holwell dispensed with a Latin version but provided extensive notes explanatory of difficult passages.

[1] See p. 206.

adopted in practice. Bagot had greater success, and whether in mathematics, logic, or classical literature, the curriculum was studied systematically. The study of ancient history received greater attention than ever before. Recalling his time at Christ Church, Richard Polwhele, who matriculated as a Commoner in 1778, wrote that he,

Mus'd o'er the historic Tales that simply tell
Hôw Roman Glory rose, how Athens fell.[1]

His Collections bear out his claim, for he took up thirty-three books of Livy, and the whole of Herodotus and Thucydides. Until 1780 only Books 6–9 of Herodotus were read, but thereafter the whole work except Book 2. Thucydides was read in its entirety. It was usual to read both authors at the rate of one or two books a term, so that Herodotus was spread over at least three terms and Thucydides over four or five. These histories, to which may be added the *Hellenica,* were typical of the Greek history read by undergraduates under Bagot. Of the Latin historians, Caesar's *Commentaries* enjoyed great popularity from about 1779, and Sallust and Tacitus held their ground. The reading of the Greek and Roman historians for a degree increased rapidly under Bagot, and even the Noblemen and Gentlemen Commoners, who previously had seldom done more than dabble in Sallust or Caesar, tended to take up Greek history to Collections. But despite its virtues, the curriculum under Bagot was unimaginative and lacking in freshness or vitality. In his time no new works were added, apart from the *Oedipus Coloneus* of Sophocles, and, fleetingly, Polybius. Even the study of ancient history flourished at the expense of the poets, and the Greek dramatists so recently introduced at Christ Church fell into neglect. From time to time a play of Sophocles was taken up to Collections, but Euripides hardly at all. Homer declined further in popularity except amongst the Servitors. The Latin poets fared no better, and Horace suffered eclipse.

When Jackson arrived at the Deanery in 1783 a new era dawned.

---

[1] Polwhele, 'Epistle to a College-friend', in *Poems.*

As early as 1775, when Markham was still Dean, Jackson had expressed his concern about the curriculum at Westminster in words which applied with equal force to Christ Church. To Charles Abbot he wrote,

You must not forget your Greek, particularly because it is from the Greek authors only that you can learn composition, and it is that alone which will fix your character at Xt.Ch. I think, if you will forgive me the freedom of the remark, that the course of your lessons at Westminster is not at present such a one as tends to improve the imagination so much as it ought and that you want a little addition in that point—Homer and the Greek Tragedies will assist you and so will our own great poet Shakespeare. I need not add that the imagination I speak of is not Ovidean or puerile but the result of the judicium probe subactum.[1]

Jackson lost no time in putting his beliefs into practice. During his regime almost fifty works of Greek classical literature were introduced for the first time, and new ones appeared at Collections in every year up to 1796.

'Homer and the Greek tragedies' was the cornerstone. Homer, whom Jackson revered as the greatest expression of the Greek imagination, immediately became required reading for the majority of undergraduates, despite a perverse tendency for the Westminster Students to prefer Pindar, an author little favoured by others. The Greek dramatists flourished after their recent neglect, and Euripides was established as one of the most popular of all classical authors. After its introduction by Markham in 1768, the *Electra* was for long the only play by Euripides read with any frequency, but between 1783 and 1791, helped no doubt by the publication of Samuel Musgrave's Oxford edition in 1778, a further eleven plays were taken up to Collections for the first time.[2] *Medea* became by far the most frequently read play by Euripides, but *Hecuba,* the two *Iphigenia* plays and *Phoenissae* followed albeit at a distance. Of the remaining dramatists, Sophocles was read a great deal, and Aeschylus, whose *Choephori* appeared

---

[1] PRO 30/9/12/2, pt. 1.
[2] Musgrave's edition is noted in the Collections Book in 1797 (li. b. iii, fo. 219).

occasionally under Markham, achieved great popularity. *Seven against Thebes* was the most often read, followed by *Prometheus* and the *Persae*. Aristophanes was not taken up to Collections until 1791, and was never read by more than a handful of undergraduates. Of other Greek poets, Anacreon and Hesiod were read, and Theocritus, once a popular author, was revived. In 1786 Thomas Tyrwhitt Jones read Moschus on the only occasion the poet is known to have been studied at Christ Church in the eighteenth century.

In addition to restoring the Greek poets and dramatists, Jackson may claim to have revived the study of Plato, which had been greatly neglected throughout the eighteenth century. The *Apology* and *Crito* appear very occasionally in the early records of Collections, and in 1756 the *Apology* was coupled briefly with Xenophon's *Apology* as a book prescribed for the second year. In 1767 Markham introduced Nathaniel Forster's Greek and Latin edition of the *Dialogues,* which had been reprinted two years previously, also as a book for the second year, and between 1772 and 1774 a handful of undergraduates took up one or other of the dialogues at Collections. But in the decade after Jackson's appointment, about a dozen dialogues appeared at Collections, most of them for the first time at Christ Church. The earliest to appear were the *Crito* and *Apology,* together with *Menexenus,* and they were followed in rapid succession by the *Alcibiades* and *Gorgias* (1785), *Euthydemus, Erastae,* and *Phaedo* (1788), *Minos* (1790), *Euthyphron* (1791), *Hipparchus* (1793), and *Hippias* and *Ion* (1794). The most popular were the *Gorgias* and *Alcibiades.* Plato's *Republic* was almost entirely ignored, and one of the few undergraduates to take the book up to Collections was William Wood, who later became Censor and tutor. Plato was no longer read under Jackson as a book for the second year but was usually studied towards the end of the course. Not more than about a tenth of the ablest undergraduates read any of his writings, and in the case of the Westminster Students the proportion to do so was significantly lower.

The supremacy of Greek at the end of the eighteenth century is nowhere better illustrated than in the study of ancient history, which under Jackson assumed even greater importance than it had enjoyed under Markham and Bagot. One of Bagot's achievements, as has been shown, was to ensure that Herodotus was usually read in about three terms and Thucydides in four or five, but within the space of a few years Jackson had concentrated Herodotus into two terms and Thucydides into three and sometimes less. By means of this simple change a considerable expansion of the entire curriculum became possible, enabling new authors to be introduced and familiar authors to be studied more extensively. In Greek history, Xenophon's *Hellenica,* which had been read under Bagot, was now studied with great frequency, as also was Diodorus Siculus, whose history first appeared in the curriculum in 1785. In 1790 Gemisthus Pletho was introduced. Under Markham, Roman history had preceded Greek, and under Bagot the two had been read side by side. Jackson, however, placed the history of Greece at the commencement of the course of studies, and thereby emphasized the chronological connection between Greek and Roman. That this change was possible is a clear indication of the improvement in Greek studies which had taken place since Markham. It meant that almost for the first time the history of Rome could be studied in Greek authors. Amongst these the most important was without doubt Polybius, who for all practical purposes was introduced into the curriculum by Jackson. Appian was also read,[1] and, though less often, the historical works of Dionysius of Halicarnassus, whose rhetorical works alone had been studied earlier in the century. The immense popularity of Polybius suggests that one of the main objects of the study of Roman history was the cause of Roman ascendancy, particularly as it lay in the Roman character and constitution. Thus the study of Roman history was increasingly confined to that of the republic. In 1801 C. H. Hall wrote to Lord Liverpool concerning his son Cecil Jenkinson, 'After he has gone through his classical course I shall with great pleasure read with him the latter part of the Roman History (which is seldom included in the

---

[1] The Amsterdam edition of Appian is mentioned in 1796 in the Collections Book (li. b. iii, fo. 136).

course of reading here, nor can be so indeed excepting with a young man who will make rapid progress)'.[1] Of the Latin historians, Livy remained pre-eminent and was read in whole or in part by most undergraduates. Imperial Rome was largely ignored: Tacitus and Suetonius were seldom studied. Bestriding the history of the ancient world was Plutarch,[2] who enjoyed immense popularity from shortly after Jackson's appointment until the end of the eighteenth century, but the noble Greeks and Romans whose lives offered inspiring examples of patriotism and public service were those who lived before Augustus.

The development of Greek studies at Christ Church, and the improved knowledge of Greek with which undergraduates came to the university, contributed to a decline in the reading of Xenophon, whose simple style had for many years been useful as an introduction to Greek. From 1768 until 1786, when the changes made by Jackson began to be felt, the *Memorabilia, Cyropaedia,* and *Anabasis* were very popular, and most Students and Commoners read all three, but, although the study of ancient history found a place for the *Hellenica,* Xenophon's other works fitted less easily into the curriculum when their utility for learning the Greek language declined. The *Anabasis* kept its place longer than the remaining works and was usually read with the *Hellenica,* but by the end of the century it too had lost favour. The Servitors, who generally had less Greek than other undergraduates, read Xenophon widely until about 1793, when there ceased to be a significant distinction between their classical reading and that of others, perhaps because by that time the level of Greek amongst them had improved.

In the last decade of the eighteenth century there was a notable increase at Collections in the number of histories of the ancient world written in English. Such works had occasionally been read in the early years of the century. Laurence Echard's *Roman History,* for example, was read in 1704 and 1706, Basil Kennett's *Lives* . . .

---

[1] BL Add. MS 38473, fo. 11ᵛ.

[2] Fynes Clinton says that Plutarch was not read in the original (*Literary Remains of Henry Fynes Clinton,* 22).

of the Antient Greek Poets and *Romae Antiquae Notitia* in 1703
and 1704 and in 1713 and 1716 respectively, and John Potter's
Archaeologia Graecae in 1709. These and similar works probably
continued to be studied privately, but they were omitted from the
formal curriculum by Dean Smalridge, and from 1717 to 1789
no secondary work on Greek or Roman history appeared at
Collections. In the latter year Sir Walter Raleigh's *History of the
World* was read, and in 1792 William Mitford's *History of Greece*.
For the rest of the century both works, and especially Raleigh,
were often read. Between 1795 and 1800 other books were introduced, including some in French, though none enjoyed the popularity of Raleigh and Mitford. The following are found in the
Collections Book at this time:

> Temple Stanyan, *Grecian History* (1739); read 1795–1800
> Thomas Leland, *History of the Life and Reign of Philip King of
> Macedon* (1758); read 1795–6, 1800
> Montesquieu, *Considérations sur les causes de la grandeur des romains
> et de leur décadence* (1734); read 1796
> René Aubert de Vertot, *Histoire des révolutions* (1719); read 1796,
> 1798–9
> Adam Ferguson, *History of the Progress and Termination of the
> Roman Republic* (1783); read 1797
> Oliver Goldsmith, *Abridgement of the History of Rome* (1772);
> read 1799
> Nathaniel Hooke, *Roman History* (1738–71); read 1800.

The most notable omission was Gibbon's *Decline and Fall*. Gibbon's religious opinions no doubt contributed to his neglect at
Christ Church, and he had been attacked for them by a learned
tutor named James Chelsum, but they were not the only factor in
a college which had continued to read Locke after the university
had condemned him. Gibbon was also neglected for the more
mundane reason that the study of Roman history at Christ Church
concentrated on the rise and fall of the republic: the rise and fall
of imperial Rome received scant attention.

The appearance at Collections of secondary historical works in
English or French was less an indication of the enrichment of the

curriculum by the fruits of recent scholarship than a testimony to the halting mastery of Latin and Greek possessed by some undergraduates. Thus it is no accident that Raleigh and Mitford were read most frequently by Noblemen and Gentlemen Commoners and seldom by other students. One of the methods adopted by Cyril Jackson for stimulating the enthusiasm of Noblemen and Gentlemen Commoners was to give them modern historical books to read. It was better that they should have a smattering of ancient history than none at all. On the same principle he also introduced them to modern English and European history. In the 1790s undergraduates took up to Collections Robert Henry's *History of Great Britain,* Burnet's *History of his Own Times,* Sir William Temple's *Introduction to the History of England,* William Robertson's *History of the Reign of the Emperor Charles V,* Robert Watson's histories of Philip II and Philip III of Spain, and the histories of Hume and Clarendon. De Lolme's famous study of the constitution was also read from time to time.

In Latin as in Greek, Jackson introduced new authors and works and revived others long neglected. Among the former were the *Epodes* of Horace (1790), Tibullus (1791), Plautus (1792), Quintus Curtius Rufus (1792), Valerius Maximus (1797), the *Epistolae* of Ovid (1799), Catullus (1800), and Propertius (1800). Among the authors and works resuscitated by him were Justin (1785), the *Carmina* of Horace (1785), Florus (1786), Velleius Paterculus (1786), Nepos (1789), Suetonius (1792), and Ovid's *Metamorphoses* (1800). Few of these authors became firmly established at Christ Church, and some were read by a mere handful of undergraduates, but the fact that they were read at all illustrates the vitality of classical studies under Jackson. Juvenal, on the other hand, became a very popular author after 1785, having made a unique appearance in the Collections of Sir Harry Trelawny ten years earlier. Juvenal was read by all groups of undergraduates, and about a third took up some of the *Satires* to Collections. As Juvenal waxed, so Virgil waned. The *Georgics,* which had languished under Bagot, made a slight recovery under Jackson, and the *Aeneid,* which had been ignored by Bagot, stepped timidly back into the curriculum. In Markham's time about half the

Westminster Students read Virgil, but, faced with the delights of Juvenal, only a quarter did so under Jackson. Horace, who had suffered a partial eclipse under Bagot, returned to something approaching the popularity he had enjoyed under Markham. The *Carmina,* which had last been taken up to Collections in 1714, was much read after 1785, but the most popular work by Horace, particularly with the Westminster Students, the Noblemen, and the Gentlemen Commoners, was the *Epistles.* The Canoneer Students and Commoners demonstrated a preference for the *Satires.* About half of all undergraduates, the Servitors excepted, read some Horace.

Like Juvenal, Cicero assumed particular importance under Jackson. Although Dean Gregory's attempt to introduce some of Cicero's orations was short-lived, within a few years of Jackson's appointment the most important of them appeared at Collections. The most popular were the orations against Catiline. In their wake followed the orations for Archias, Milo, and Manilius. The Philippics were read less often. In contrast to the orations, Cicero's treatises on oratory, *Brutus* and *Orator,* which had been held in high esteem in earlier times, fell into neglect, though *De Oratore* continued to be read especially by Commoners. Instead of reading *about* oratory, undergraduates read the great orations of antiquity. The Noblemen and Gentlemen Commoners, who tended to have more Latin than Greek, read Cicero's orations more often than any other group of undergraduates, but in the last decade of the eighteenth century Demosthenes, after a period of oblivion under Bagot, achieved considerable popularity with undergraduates of all kinds. George Colman indicated a compelling reason for this interest in the great orators when he recorded, on hearing Richard Wellesley read Cicero and Demosthenes aloud, 'these were, I presume, self-imposed exercises of a political tyro, training himself for public speaking, and ambitious of the eloquence which he has, since, so happily acquired'.[1] In his last two terms Canning read nothing but the orations of Cicero, Demosthenes, Aeschines, and Lysias.[2]

[1] R. B. Peake, *Memoirs of the Colman family* (1841), ii, 41.

[2] Demosthenes was read in the editions of John Taylor (Greek and Latin), William Allen, and Jacob Reiske's *Oratores Graeci* (Collections Book, li. b. 2, fo. 477).

Although the orations occupied an important place in the curriculum, the most popular of Cicero's works was his *De Officiis,* which was as generally esteemed a cornucopia of practical wisdom under Jackson as it had been under John Fell. It was often read with the *De Amicitia* and *De Senectute.* Of Cicero's writings on speculative philosophy, the *Tusculanae Disputationes,* which was also a favourite of long standing, continued to be read with regularity, but *De Finibus* only seldom, and of his theological works *De Natura Deorum,* which had held a place of honour under Markham and Bagot, was read under Jackson mostly by Servitors.

The quantity of reading undertaken by the generality of undergraduates increased considerably under Jackson. This was the continuation of a tendency which had started with Gregory and Markham. It became common for undergraduates to read not only a larger number of authors than previously but also to read individual authors more deeply. For example, in Greek history many more students took up to Collections the three basic authors, Herodotus, Thucydides, and Xenophon, than had been the case under Bagot, and more took up the whole of the *Hellenica* or the whole of Horace's *Satires* rather than a part of them. This extended not least to the Noblemen and Gentlemen Commoners, and, although there continued to be many who seldom displayed signs of excessive industry, from 1794 about a quarter of them took up for their Collections in ancient history not only Herodotus, Thucydides, and Xenophon but also either Diodorus Siculus or Polybius or both of them. Coupled with this increase in the quantity of reading there was a wide variety in the choice of books made by one undergraduate compared with another. Different groups of undergraduates expressed different preferences. The Westminster Students, for example, were influenced by the studies they had pursued at Westminster School, and were seldom amongst the most academically adventurous undergraduates as the eighteenth century drew to a close. Noblemen and Gentlemen Commoners, many of whom were destined for a career in politics, read the orations of Cicero and Demosthenes more often than did other undergraduates, and the Servitors, who were often deficient in Greek, tended to read Xenophon in preference to more difficult authors. Tutors exercised a great influence on the choice of reading, as has been shown in another chapter. In the face of such diversity it is difficult to generalize about the content of the curriculum at the end of the eighteenth century, but a considerable proportion of those students who were sufficiently industrious to read for a degree took up to Collections logic, mathematics (which included Euclid, algebra, and trigonometry), Greek and Roman history (which included Herodotus, Thucydides, Xenophon, Livy, Polybius), some Greek plays, perhaps Cicero's *De Officiis,* one or two Greek or Latin poets, and Aristotle's *Rhetoric.* The better students took up much more. There is little evidence to show how studies at Christ Church compared with those at other colleges, but in his *Word or Two in Vindication of the University of Oxford,* James Hurdis wrote that at Magdalen Collections during the last thirty years of the eighteenth century had consisted of the following:

First year	Sallust; Theophrastus; Virgil *Aeneid*; Xenophon *Anabasis.*
Second year	Caesar; *Iliad*; Cicero *De Oratore* and *De Officiis*; Dionysius of Halicarnassus *De Compositione Verborum.*
Third year	Livy, Books 1–6; Xenophon *Cyropaedia* and *Memorabilia*; Horace *Epistles* and *Ars Poetica*; Cicero *De Natura Deorum*; Juvenal.
Fourth year	Tacitus *Annals,* Books 1–6; Sophocles *Electra*; Cicero orations (*In Catilinam, Pro Ligario, Pro Archia*); Demosthenes (ed. Mounteney); Plato (ed. Forster); Virgil *Georgics.*[1]

Although the amount of reading required at Christ Church for a degree was more at the end of the eighteenth century than it had been at the beginning, the burden for most students was not heavy, and on the evidence of the Collections Books it was possible

[1] Hurdis, *Vindication,* 14–17.

to proceed to a degree with very little. Even the best students
were seldom stretched, often because they reached the university
having been well grounded at school. When Fynes Clinton, the
classical scholar, came up in 1799 he relates that he was indolent
for two years. 'I wandered from book to book in search of striking
passages, till at the end of term my required portion of reading
was still unprepared; and I was obliged to get through it by a
hasty application of a few days or nights.'[1] The record of his
Collections shows that when he took his degree he had read
Herodotus, Thucydides, Xenophon's *Hellenica,* Livy, the *Odyssey,*
Juvenal's *Satires,* Demosthenes, Aeschines, Lysias, Aeschylus,
Plato and Diodorus Siculus. Yet the attainments of the best
students under Cyril Jackson compared favourably with those of
the best of the candidates for honours in the middle of the
nineteenth century. The Royal Commission on the university
in 1852 noted that the course in classical studies had become
progressively more limited since the reform of the public examinations.

From the year 1807 to 1825, [it declared] the students were encouraged
to study many works which have now almost entirely disappeared from
the university course, such as Homer, Demosthenes, Cicero, Lucretius,
Terence, Plutarch, Longinus, Quintilian. A list of twenty classical
authors was not unfrequent even so late as 1827. At present, fourteen,
thirteen, or even twelve, are sufficient for the highest honours. The
authors now usually studied at Oxford, by the most distinguished
students, are: (1) in Philosophy—Aristotle's Ethics, with his Rhetoric
or Politics, two or three Dialogues of Plato, Butler's Analogy or his
Sermons; (2) in Ancient History—Herodotus, Thucydides, the 1st or
2nd Decade of Livy, the Annals or the Histories of Tacitus; (3) in
Poetry—Aeschylus, Sophocles, Aristophanes, Virgil, Horace, and
Juvenal.[2]

Although classical studies were more varied and more widely
based at the end than at the beginning of the eighteenth century,
they continued throughout the period to be founded securely on
a knowledge of the texts. The advances of scholarship were

[1] Fynes Clinton, *Literary Remains of Henry Fynes Clinton,* 11.
[2] *Report of the Oxford University Commission* (1852), 62.

absorbed slowly. Fynes Clinton complained that as an undergraduate he 'never received a single syllable of instruction concerning Greek accents, or Greek metres, or the idiom of Greek
sentences; in short, no information on *any one point* of grammar,
or syntax, or metre. These subjects were never named to me.'[1]
The severity of Fynes Clinton's judgment on his tutors is perhaps
mitigated by Chinnery's experience at the same time. Chinnery
records that when he read Porson, his private tutor, Charles
LLoyd, made him study Greek accents, 'of which I never heard
a word but from him',[2] and in another letter he remarked that
LLoyd required him to read 'Seale's Greek metres at the same
time that we are going on with the play so that I may acquire some
knowledge of the intricacies of Greek prosody'.[3] It is probably
significant that Chinnery owed his introduction to the subject to
his private tutor.

(e) ETHICS, METAPHYSICS, AND RELIGION

Although Newman argued that there was nothing specifically
Christian about liberal education, religion and moral teaching
were intertwined. Religion gave a sanction to ethics, and ethics
provided a rational interpretation of the principles of religion.
The belief that ethics were based on reason was the main justification for the study of the Greek and Latin moralists of classical,
and pagan, antiquity. Their writings developed the rational faculty
when, as Copleston said, 'Hardly any man but the Enthusiast
contends that the Gospel was designed to supersede moral reasoning'.[4]

The most influential classical authors to write about ethics were
Aristotle and Cicero, whose practical and common-sense codes of
morality were absorbed into the educational fibre of the eighteenth
century. Aristotle's influence on education through his ethical
writings was at least as great as his influence on the study of logic,

[1] Fynes Clinton, *Literary Remains of Henry Fynes Clinton*, 230.
[2] Ch. Ch. Archives, xlviii. a. 42a, fo. 159ᵛ.
[3] Ch. Ch. Archives, xlviii. a. 44, fo. 170.
[4] Copleston, *Reply to the Calumnies*, 179.

and perhaps more enduring. Until Greek was firmly established
in the curriculum, Aristotle was usually studied in commentaries
and textbooks. The most popular of these was the short Latin
treatise by Asseline Eustachius first published in 1658. The first
section of this work discusses the nature of happiness, the second
the principles of human actions, and the third the human passions,
virtues, and vices, including the four cardinal virtues of prudence,
justice, fortitude, and temperance. The book was often taken up
to Collections in the early eighteenth century, and between 1717
and 1743 was a prescribed textbook for the second year. There
were many similar books in use in the early eighteenth century,
though none of equal popularity. Among them were Theophils
Golius' *Epitome Doctrinae Moralis,* and Dionysius Lambinus' *Aristotelis Ethicorum,* both of which were first published in the sixteenth
century, Johann Crell's *Ethica Aristotelica,*[1] Anton Van Wale's
Compendium Ethicae Aristotelicae, and Gerard Langbaine's *Ethicae
Compendium.* Edward Bentham included Wale and Crell among
writers 'who have professedly taken the Christian doctrines of
Morality into their account'.[2] In the same group he also included
Daniel Whitby, whose *Ethices compendium,* published in 1684, was
read at Christ Church.

When Eustachius was dropped from the curriculum in 1743, it
was replaced by an anonymous work described in the Collections
Book as *Ethicae Compendium.* This was probably the Aristotelian
compendium of ethics published at Oxford in 1743 and included
in the list of volumes on moral philosophy published in Bentham's
Introduction to Moral Philosophy two years later.[3] It continued to be
read until 1755 and then intermittently until it was omitted from
the curriculum in 1763. Under Dean Gregory, Pufendorf's *De
Officio Hominis et Civis,* first published in 1673, was prescribed
reading in some years, and between 1757 and 1759 Burlamaqui's

---

[1] The Collections Book does not distinguish which of Crell's ethical works
was used at Christ Church, but the inclusion of the *Ethica Aristotelica* by Edward
Bentham in his *Introduction to Moral Philosophy* (1745) seems to establish the
preference.

[2] Bentham, *Introduction to Moral Philosophy,* 107.

[3] Ibid., 104–9.

Principles of Natural Law,[1] which Bolingbroke described in a letter to the Earl of Huntingdon, then an undergraduate at Christ Church, as containing 'many plain and obvious reflections expressed clearly and methodically, which is just what a book writ on that subject should contain. He has stripped it of much useless matter which swell the writings of Puffendorf and even of Grotius.'[2] The disappearance of the compendium of ethics and of works of a similar character did not indicate that less attention was paid to Aristotle, and the *Ethics,* often in conjunction with the *Politics,* were frequently read during the second half of the eighteenth century. The revival of Greek and the encouragement of ancient history also enabled vice and virtue to be studied in action in the writings of historians such as Plutarch and Thucydides.

Until about the middle of the eighteenth century, an undergraduate was expected to study metaphysics in his third or fourth year. In the early years of the century, the following works were taken up to Collections from time to time:

Robert Baron, *Metaphysica Generalis;* Andreas Frommenius, *Synopsis Metaphysica;* Caspar Bartholinus, *Enchiridion Metaphysicum ex Aristotelis*; Johannes Combachius, *Metaphysica*; Christophorus Scheibler, *Metaphysica.*

More important than any of these was the *Institutiones Metaphysicae* of Franco Burgersdicius, first published in 1653. It was read at Christ Church until 1743, by which time all the other works listed above had long fallen into oblivion. All the textbooks on metaphysics entered in the Collections Books had originally been published many years earlier during the seventeenth century. This was also true of the compendiums of ethics, some of which even dated from the sixteenth century. There is thus a presumption that in ethics and metaphysics the works studied in the eighteenth century were also studied in the previous century.[3] In 1744 Bur-

---

[1] Translated by T. Nugent in 1748.

[2] HMC, *Hastings* (1934), iii, 68.

[3] Evidence to support this view is provided by Francis Vernon, a Westminster Student, who in his poem *Oxonium Poema,* published in 1667, envisaged scholars

gersdicius was replaced in the curriculum by John Locke's *Essay concerning Human Understanding*. This famous work, which established its author as the principal English metaphysician, was first noted at Collections in 1703—the year that the college Heads sought to prevent its study at Oxford—and then in 1707, 1712, and 1714. Since Locke was the philosopher of Whiggism, and Christ Church the most Whiggish college in the university, there may have been political as well as philosophical reasons for adding the *Essay* to the curriculum, but its inclusion marked the decline of the study of Aristotelian metaphysics at Christ Church. Locke retained his place in the curriculum until the appointment of Dean Bagot in 1776, and, although excluded thereafter owing to the pressure of classical studies, he continued to be read at the discretion of the tutors. In 1801 C. H. Hall, the future Dean, wrote to Lord Liverpool, 'Locke's Essays, although frequently recommended and read privately, do not form any part of any public course here'.[1]

disputing as they walked about the college grounds and quoting the authors who besieged their studies.

> Mox Burgersdicius tumidus crepat, hinc Brerewoodus,
> Hinc & Aristotelis tonat Organum, inde fragore
> Insolito Sandersonus diverberat aures,
> Jamque Poloniacis acer Smiglecius armis
> Emicat, oppositus stat Keckermanus atrox vi.
> Nec mora, cum totam videas ardere Conimbram,
> Et Complutenses vibrare incendia Patres.
> Hinc Scote cordigeros animas ad fortia calvos
> Parte alia, nigras longo movet ordine Turmas
> Aspera bella ferens, nec segnior ardet Aquinas.
> Inde Gigantaeus per vasta volumina Suarez
> Sternit in astra viam, ac imponit Pelion Ossae.
> Quem premit assistens praeacuta cuspide Vasquez.
> Dejicit extructos contorto fulmine montes
> Scheiblerus, magnasque quatit moles Herebordus.
> Tandem Combachius furit . . .

A similar continuity is found in the teaching of theology. Pusey relates that when he was in Germany in the 1820s he informed German students that 'in England we studied chiefly old books ... If they asked of me how we studied Theology, they were surprised to hear of standard, solid writers of the seventeenth and eighteenth centuries, as Hooker or Bull, Butler or Pearson' (*Report and Evidence ... to the Board of Heads of Houses* (1853), evidence, 10).

[1] BL Add. MS 38473, fo. 12.

In addition to ethics and metaphysics, undergraduates were
expected to acquire what Edmund Goodenough described in a
letter written in 1815 outlining the course of studies at Christ
Church as an 'intimate acquaintance with the Doctrines and Evidences of the Christian Religion'.[1] A few years earlier, in 1810,
Edward Copleston described in more detail what was then
involved in the university examinations. The candidate for a
degree, he wrote, was first examined in the rudiments of religion.

A passage in the Greek Testament is given him to construe, and he is
tried, by questions arising out of it, whether he has a proper view of the
Christian scheme, and of the outline of sacred history. He is expected to
give some account of the evidences of Christianity, and to shew by his
answers that he is acquainted with the thirty-nine Articles, and has read
attentively some commentary upon them.[2]

The requirements had changed little since the Restoration.

In his *Defence of Humane Learning,* published in 1660, Henry
Thurman claimed that knowledge of Hebrew and Greek was
necessary for an understanding of the Scriptures. This widely held
belief provided a powerful motive for the study of the Bible in
its original languages. In particular the teaching of Greek to
undergraduates owed a great debt to the Greek New Testament.
The method of teaching changed little over the centuries. In 1772
a disgruntled candidate for holy orders complained to the Bishop
of London that the bishop's examining chaplain required him to
construe the Greek Testament word for word from Greek into
Latin and from Latin into English.[3] The chaplain in question was
Richard Hind, who had been an industrious tutor at Christ Church
as well as Senior Censor from 1741 to 1745 and Catechist from
1747 to 1752. Another frequent exercise consisted of translating
passages from the Hebrew Psalms or from the Greek Testament
into Latin or English verse. This exercise was popular at
Westminster School,[4] where Joseph Wilcocks's *Sacred Exercises* ...

[1] Bodl. MS Top. Oxon. d. 156, fo. 3.
[2] Copleston, *Reply to the Calumnies,* 140.
[3] *Letter to the Bishop of London* (1772), 8.
[4] Vincent, *Defence of Public Education,* 33.

for the Use of Places of Education was often used. Wilcocks, who had been elected to a Westminster Studentship in 1740, published his book in 1759, and by 1785 it had reached its fifth edition. In it were arranged passages from the Gospels designed to provide 'a system of the moral virtues' and a scheme of translations and other exercises. It was, Wilcocks wrote, intended to form part of a larger plan of moral education, which included a course of ethical instruction exemplified in the life of Socrates by Xenophon and Plato, and of a moral history of the world 'setting forth the great and beneficent actions of the illustrious men of all ages and nations' (p. vii). In such books Christian and pagan ethical teaching were combined.

There is little evidence that Hebrew was studied by under-graduates at Christ Church much earlier than the Restoration. Although some of them contributed to the volumes of verse published in the years immediately after the King's return, applauding royal births and lamenting royal deaths with impartial facility, none wrote in Hebrew. Hebrew studies at Oxford, however, had been stimulated by the annexation of a stall at Christ Church to the Regius Professorship of Hebrew in 1630 and by the munificent donations to the university by Archbishop Laud. Edward Pococke, the leading oriental scholar of the day, received encouragement from Laud, and, after the disruption of the Civil War, returned to his canonry at Christ Church and to the regius professorship in 1660. From that time the momentum of Hebrew studies quickened. In 1667 at the instigation of Dean Fell, Samuel Clarke edited part of the Mishnah, on which the Talmud is based, 'in usum studiosorum literarum Talmudicarum in Aede Christi'. The text was printed in pointed Hebrew with a Latin translation on alternate leaves. In the same year Richard Busby founded an oriental lectureship at Christ Church at which all undergraduates were required to be present. In 1679, Humphrey Prideaux, a Westminster Student who subsequently declined the chair of Hebrew when Pococke died in 1691, produced an edition of Maimonides with a Latin translation for young students of Hebrew.

Although there were teachers of Hebrew resident in Oxford,

such as John Gagnier and Philip Levi in the early eighteenth century, most teaching at Christ Church was undertaken by the Regius Professors of Hebrew. It owed much to the bequest of John Morris, who was appointed to the chair in 1626. When he died in 1648, Morris provided in his will for seven exhibitions worth up to £3 a year in order to encourage Students of Christ Church to study the Hebrew language and to attend the lectures of the Professor of Hebrew. One each was to be awarded to a senior Student Master, a junior Student Master, and a senior Bachelor Student, and two each to the junior Bachelor Students and the undergraduate Students. The benefaction did not take effect until the death of Morris's widow in 1681, and the exhibitions were first awarded in 1693. They were given in almost equal proportions to Westminster and Canoneer Students until about 1760, but from that date until the end of the century the majority of the exhibitioners came from Westminster. Throughout the period there was a strong tradition of Hebrew studies at Westminster. Busby produced a Hebrew grammar which, 'after it had been handed about in MSS^r. and continually transcrib'd for the use of the Boys at Westminster schoole' was printed early in the eighteenth century and reprinted frequently.[1] The Westminster tradition had considerable impact on Hebrew studies at Christ Church, for only the Westminster Students were positively required to take up Collections in Hebrew. Until 1776 it was the practice for them to take up Collections on the Psalms and on one or two books of the Old Testament, usually from the Pentateuch. In the last quarter of the eighteenth century, as the study of classical Greek increasingly dominated the curriculum, Hebrew Collections became infrequent, but the tradition continued at Westminster School, where the Hebrew Psalter was still read early in the nineteenth century.[2]

Next to the Bible, the most important element in religious education was the doctrine of the Church of England represented by the Articles of Religion. Undergraduates had been required to

---

[1] Hearne, *Collections,* ii, 307. Hearne says it was printed 'at ye Theater', but it is not listed in Carter's *History of the Oxford University Press,* i, 245.

[2] Vincent, *Defence of Public Education,* 33.

subscribe to them at matriculation since the sixteenth century, and the Articles themselves were printed in various editions of the *Parecbolae* from 1671. In the nineteenth century subscription at matriculation was thought to habituate the mind 'to give a careless assent to truths which it has never considered',[1] and the same objection could no doubt have been raised in earlier times, but once in residence undergraduates at Christ Church were required to study the Thirty-nine Articles, whether intended for holy orders or not. It was a requirement which did not sit easily with the enormous popularity enjoyed by the *De Veritate Religionis Christianae* of Hugo Grotius. Nevertheless, from 1717 to 1755 the *Articulorum XXXIX . . . Defensio* by John Ellis, published in 1694, and from 1756 to 1762 the *Articuli 39 Ecclesiae Textibus e S. Scriptura Depromptis* by Edward Welchman, published in 1713, were prescribed reading. Gilbert Burnet's *Exposition of the Thirty-Nine Articles* (1699) is not noted at Christ Church until 1794. Although such commentaries are omitted from the lists of prescribed books after 1762, it is likely that knowledge of the Articles continued to be taught in the lectures on theology founded in 1750 by the bequest of Robert Challoner, and in the lectures given by the Catechist, one of whose functions was to prepare candidates for ordination. In 1801 the Chapter ordered that no Student should have his grace for BA unless he had attended a course of lectures by the Lady Margaret Professor of Divinity on the Articles of Religion and produced a certificate of attendance.[2] Apart from commentaries on the Articles, the most commonly read book on the doctrine of the Church of England was John Pearson's celebrated *Exposition of the Creed,* first published in 1659, and read frequently throughout the eighteenth century. Henry Hammond's *Practical Catechism* (1645) was taken up to Collections on several occasions until 1716, and Fell's association with its author, in addition to the undisputed merits of the book itself, probably ensured that it was also read at Christ Church in the seventeenth century. In the 1790s Alexander Nowell's *Catechism* was taken

---

[1] *Report of the Oxford University Commission* (1852), 56.
[2] Chapter Minute Book, 20 Apr. 1801.

up, perhaps because it had been reprinted in John Randolph's *Enchiridion Theologicum*. Biblical commentaries, although sometimes read privately, were seldom taken up to Collections, and only George Stanhope's *Paraphrase and Commentary on the Epistles and Gospels* is noted in 1711, and John Taylor's *Paraphrase ... on the Epistle to the Romans* in 1799.

The history of the Church of England from the Reformation was seldom studied, though in the time of Cyril Jackson a minority of undergraduates, mainly Noblemen and Gentlemen Commoners, was encouraged to take up Clarendon, Burnet, Hume, or Robert Henry to Collections. Such neglect was due to the belief that the justification of the Church was the purity of its doctrine rather than the fact of its survival or the progress of its development. In the closing years of the eighteenth century, Jewel's *Apology* appeared occasionally at Collections, perhaps because, as with Nowell's *Catechism,* it had been reprinted in Randolph's *Enchiridion*. The English divines of the seventeenth century were almost entirely neglected, but Chillingworth's *Religion of Protestants* was taken up in 1711 and 1713, and Hooker was read on a few occasions. On the other hand, the early years of the eighteenth century were marked by considerable interest in the Fathers and the Primitive Church, on which the Church of England claimed to be founded, and between 1700 and 1716 the following works appeared at Collections:

Athenagoras, *Legatio pro Christianis; De Mortuorum Resurrectione*
William Cave, *Antiquitates Apostolicae* (1676).
Clement I, *Epistola ad Corinthios*
St Chrysostom, *De Sacerdotio*
St Cyprian, *De Idolorum Vanitate*
St Ignatius, *Epistolae*
St Justin Martyr, *Apologia*
Bede, *Ecclesiastical History.*

The patristic tradition represented by such works was perhaps inherited from the time of John Fell, or from an even earlier period, but the rational and self-confident eighteenth century had little time for such matters, and patristics disappeared from the curriculum after 1716 and were not restored.

The contemporary theological preoccupations of the eighteenth century sometimes found their way into the curriculum. In the early years, John Wilkins's *Principles and Duties of Natural Religion* (1675) was often read, though perhaps as much for its value in demonstrating the nature of evidence and the manner of drawing rational conclusions as for an introduction to rational theology. In 1755 the brief appearance as a set book of Henry Stebbing's *Christianity Justified* (1750) recalled, if only indirectly, the stormy controversy over Warburton's *Divine Legation* (1738–41). Bishop Butler's *Analogy of Religion* was not read for more than fifty years after its publication and then only seldom, though it was held in high esteem by Cyril Jackson. The book which more than any other came to represent the tolerant and unenthusiastic religion taught at Christ Church was Grotius' *De Veritate Religionis Christianae,* in which a code of Christianity irrespective of sectarian belief was set out. With Pearson on the Creed, it was among the most commonly read books throughout the eighteenth century, especially during the latter half. At Westminster School, two years were spent on the study of Grotius, and it was, in the words of the Headmaster William Vincent, 'the most laboured lesson of the week'.[1]

From the time of Dean Bagot, and especially after about 1790, religious studies, with the exception of Grotius, were increasingly excluded from the Collections of Students and Commoners. In particular they ceased to take up the New Testament when Greek was studied in classical texts. Religious studies continued to be pursued in the lecture room, and the rudiments of religion were required by the university examinations, but their exclusion from Collections, which by the late eighteenth century had become the intellectual forum of the college, diminished their importance and emphasized the more secular character which education then assumed. Religious studies continued to be appropriate for those intending to take holy orders. This is illustrated by the reading of the Servitors, who took religious works up to Collections more often than any other group of undergraduates, for a higher

---

[1] Vincent, *Defence of Public Education,* 35.

proportion of Servitors than of other groups of undergraduates entered the Church. They were the main readers of Wilkins, Hooker, Butler, Stillingfleet, Nowell, Robert Jenkin's *Reasonableness and Certainty of the Christian Religion* (1698), and Thomas Gisborne's *Familiar Survey of the Christian Religion* (1799). Commoners took up religious works to Collections less often than the Servitors but more often than Students, Noblemen, or Gentlemen Commoners.

(*f*) SCIENCE

The study of natural philosophy was for many years necessary for the degree of BA. During the first half of the seventeenth century science flourished vigorously at Oxford. Chairs of natural philosophy (1621), anatomy (1624), and botany (1659) were founded, and the Royal Society held its early meetings in the Warden's lodgings at Wadham. After the Restoration, however, the intellectual atmosphere in the university became less favourable to science, and nowhere more so than at Christ Church. Science was not thought to be hostile to religion, and in 1658 Edward Reynolds, who was soon to become Dean for the second time, coupled 'philosophical' and mathematical learning as conducive to knowledge of the works of the Creator,[1] but it was thought to be hostile to Aristotle. For this reason it was fiercely opposed by John Fell, the traditionalist and conservative enemy of innovation. In his autobiography, William Wake wrote that it was not until after he had graduated that he read Descartes, 'which Bishop Fell always discouraged, being wholly devoted to the old philosophy',[2] and Wood noted that Fell was 'no admirer' of the Royal Society because 'the members thereof intended to bring a contempt upon antient and solid learning, upon Aristotle, to undermine the Universities, and reduce them to nothing, or at least to be very

[1] E. Reynolds, *Sermon Touching the Use of Humane Learning* (1658), 13.
[2] Quoted in N. Sykes, *William Wake* (1957), i, 10.

inconsiderable ... at long running to destroy the established religion, and involve the nation in popery and I know not what'.[1]

Aristotelian science retained a firm foothold in the curriculum at Christ Church until the time of Dean Gregory, and several works based on the writings of Aristotle were regularly taken up to Collections. Amongst them were the *Epitome Naturalis Scientiae* by Daniel Sennertus and the *Idea Philosophiae Naturalis* by Franco Burgersdicius. The most popular manual in use, and for many years the only one, was the *Enchiridion Physicum* of Caspar Bartholinus, which was a prescribed book from 1717 to 1755 and again from 1760 to 1762. Since many of these and similar works were originally published in the seventeenth century, it is probable that they were read at Christ Church at that time as well as in the eighteenth century, when the records of Collections begin. The study of such books, firmly based on the writings of Aristotle, was not intended to keep abreast with contemporary advances in science but rather to explain the natural order in metaphysical terms. When it ceased to provide a convincing explanation of that order, Aristotelian science lost credibility, and in the middle of the eighteenth century was omitted from the curriculum at Christ Church. It was not, however, replaced by the study of natural science, and scientific studies ceased to be necessary for a degree. The causes of this omission, which was of considerable significance in causing liberal education to be increasingly equated with classical education, deserve explanation.

The decline of scientific studies at Oxford has been attributed to the stifling of free inquiry by veneration for the authority of Aristotle. In particular, the argument went, the deductive methods of Aristotelian logic were inimical to the inductive methods of natural science. At best this is an inadequate explanation. The function of logic was well recognized in the university to be the

---

[1] Wood, *Athenae*, iii, 1071. In 1677 Fell proposed to add 'a tower for astronomical observations' to Tom Tower and only abandoned the idea in the face of Wren's opposition, but he was inspired less by enthusiasm for science than by the belief that it would yield subscriptions for the building itself (*Letters of Humphrey Prideaux*, Camden Society, 2nd series (1875), 61; W. D. Caröe, '*Tom Tower*', *Christ Church, Oxford* (1923), 31–2).

development of the faculty of reason, and not the discovery of new facts on which the advancement of natural science depended. Moreover, if logic had caused the decline of the inductive sciences, by the same token it ought to have caused progress to be made in the deductive sciences, but sciences such as physics and astronomy based on mathematics, which was of all studies perhaps the one most dependent on deduction, failed to continue the progress made in the seventeenth century.

In so far as the authority of Aristotle was a factor in the decline of science, it was not through his writings on logic but through his writings on ethics and politics, which profoundly influenced the idea of liberal education. Here a broad distinction may be drawn between empirical science as an intellectual discipline and its practical application. Liberal education was concerned with the whole man considered as a moral and political animal. Study of the principles of natural science, and especially of mathematically based sciences, was not in conflict with it. But liberal education was opposed to specialization, which distorted and fragmented the intellectual and moral unity of man. By the middle of the eighteenth century, the rapid advance of the Industrial Revolution demanded specialization of function and profession on an increasing scale. A system of education designed for the clergy and a landed governing class was not intended to develop the special skills needed by merchant and manufacturer. The intellectual climate in the university in these circumstances was not favourable to the study of chemistry and other sciences of a utilitarian nature.

Considered solely as an intellectual discipline, the study of natural science was not incompatible with eighteenth-century ideas on the education of gentlemen, and in addition had the undoubted merit of providing an innocent diversion. It was, none the less, excluded from the formal curriculum even on these terms because of the difficulty of providing tuition within the collegiate system. The college tutor taught every subject in the curriculum, but it was not possible to add the teaching of science to this already heavy burden, particularly at a time of considerable scientific advance. Dean Gregory tried to do so but in vain. Between 1757 and 1759 he replaced Bartholinus as a prescribed book for

Collections by John Rowning's *Compendious System of Natural Philosophy* (1735–42) and, after a short interval during which Bartholinus was restored, by Benjamin Worster's *Compendious and Methodical Account of the Principles of Natural Philosophy* (1722). The appointment of separate tutors to teach natural science was not a practical alternative. Not only was specialization in itself viewed with suspicion but college establishments were contained within rigid traditions or statutes, and at Christ Church whenever extra facilities were needed they were created by special endowment as in the case of the Busby mathematical lecture and the Lee lecturer in anatomy. The Faculty Studentships, as has been shown in another chapter,[1] were intended for laymen, and any attempt to divert them to tutorial duties would have been beset with difficulties. The crisis in scientific studies in the mid-eighteenth century coincided with the classical revival, and the vacuum created by the collapse of Aristotelian science was filled not by natural science but by classical literature, which was readily absorbed within the existing tutorial system.

Tuition in natural science, however, was provided by requiring undergraduates of Christ Church to attend professorial lectures. In 1850 Nevil Maskelyne, subsequently professor of mineralogy, stated in his evidence to the Royal Commission on the university that Christ Church was the only Oxford college which obliged its undergraduates to attend a course of lectures on experimental

---

[1] See Ch. III (*c*). Edward Hannes, for example, lectured on chemistry in 1689 (BL Add. MS 36707, fo. 82ᵛ). Richard Frewin, who held a Faculty Place in medicine from 1709 to 1714, also held the professorship of chemistry, though when Uffenbach visited Oxford in 1710 he complained that the laboratory in which Boyle had conducted his experiments lay neglected, the furnaces were uncared for, and 'not only are the finest instruments, crucibles and other things belonging to the place almost all of them lying in pieces, but everything is covered in filth' (W. H. and W. J. C. Quarrell (edd.), *Oxford in 1710, from the Travels of Zacharias Conrad von Uffenbach* (1928), 38). W. G. Hiscock has drawn attention to the syllabus of a course of lectures on chemistry delivered in about 1774 by John Parsons, who besides being a Faculty Student also held the Lee lectureship in anatomy. It is entitled *The plan of a Course of Lectures in Philosophical and Practical Chemistry* (W. G. Hiscock, *A Christ Church Miscellany* (1946), 210). The copy in Christ Church Library is in a bound volume of pamphlets referenced Z. 286/3, and is attributed to Parsons in a contemporary list of contents.

philosophy.[1] When this practice commenced is not known, for it was never the subject of a Chapter order, but it may have coincided with the arrival in Oxford of John Keill who entered Christ Church on 7 October 1702. Earlier than that, when the scientific works studied by undergraduates were based on Aristotle, practical demonstration was not involved, whereas the scientific discoveries of the latter part of the seventeenth century required the use of laboratories and apparatus, neither of which was at the disposal of the college tutor. Keill, a Newtonian, is remembered primarily as a mathematician, but after his incorporation from Edinburgh in 1694 he gave the first lectures at Oxford on natural philosophy. It may be that he was induced to come to Oxford by his friend David Gregory, who had held the chair of mathematics at Edinburgh before becoming Savilian Professor of Astronomy at Oxford in 1691. Shortly after his enrolment at Christ Church, Keill, describing himself as Deputy Professor of Natural Philosophy, gave notice in the *Oxford Almanac* for 1703 of a course of 'Mechanical and Experimental Philosophy'. The course consisted of three parts:

In the First are contain'd, 1. The *Principles* of the *Mechanicks, The Contrivance of Engines,* and the way of estimating their *Force.* 2. The *Laws* of *Nature,* and all the common *Appearances* which easily flow from them. 3. The *Centrifugal Force* of Bodies moving in a *Circle,* and several *properties* that arise from thence. 4. The particular *Laws* of *Motion,* the Rules of *Congress* of *Hard* and *Elastick* Bodies. 5. The *Acceleration* of heavy Bodies, the Reason, Rules, and Proportion of this *Acceleration,* their *Descent* upon inclin'd *Planes,* the *Motion* of *Pendulums, their* Equability, and their *Application* to Clocks for Measure of Time. All this shown and proved by *Experiments.*

The Second Part is upon the Nature of *Fluids,* which contains, 1. The *Principles* of Hydrostaticks, the *Pressure* of *Fluids* on *Fluids,* their *Respective* and *Absolute Gravitation* rationally and experimentally demonstrated, the various *Immersion of Solids* in *Fluids,* and the Method of examining their *Specifick Gravities* shown. 2. The *pressure* of the *Air,* and the *Effects* of it declared. 3. A Description of *Weather-Glasses,* viz. several sorts of *Barometers, Thermometers,* and *Hygrometers.* The Description and Con-

---

[1] *Report of the Oxford University Commission,* 1852, evidence, 188.

trivance of *Water-Engines*; and lastly a great variety of Experiments made by the *Air-pump*.

The Third Part is concerning *Opticks,* where the general Properties of *Light* are shown. 2. An Account of *Images* made by *Mirrours, Plane, Concave,* and *Convex,* and the several *Phenomena* that arise from their various *Combinations.* 3. The *Refraction* of *Light* entering different *Mediums,* and the various *Appearances* of *Objects* seen through such *Mediums* and *Multiplying-Glasses* are explain'd. 4. *Converse Glasses* are explain'd, and shown: as also an Account of their *Magnifying,* and *Force* of *Burning* when exposed to the Sun. 5. A Description of the *Eye,* the Use of it's Parts, and manner of *Vision,* the Faults of *Vision* in old, and purblind Men, and how they are to be rectify'd by *Convex* and *Concave Glasses,* or *Spectacles,* are demonstrated. 6. *Microscopes, single and double; Telescopes* of two or three or four *Glasses,* and other *Optical Machines,* as the *Magick Lanthorn,* the *Projection* of *Images* in a dark room, &c. are shown, and the reason of all those *Appearances* given.

Keill re-entered Christ Church as a Commoner Master on 4 July 1712 when he became Savilian Professor of Astronomy, a post he held until his death in 1721. His book *Introductio ad Veram Physicam,* published in 1702, was taken up to Collections in 1710–11, 1713–14, and 1716, and from 1763 to 1774 was a prescribed book, and his *Introductio ad Veram Astronomiam,* published in 1718, was also a prescribed book from 1768 to 1773. Keill's influence is perhaps found in other scientific works taken up to Collections in the early years of the eighteenth century. Amongst them were the following:

Willem Blaeu, *Institutio Astronomica de Usu Globorum* (1634); read in 1700
Pierre Gassendi, *Institutio Astronomica* (1647); read in 1706
Jean Le Clerc, *Physica* (1695); read in 1700, 1703–7, 1710
Jacques Rohault, *Traité de Physique* (1672); read in 1712–13
J. H. Suicerus, *Compendium Physicae Aristot.–Cartes. Methodo* (1685); read in 1707.

Keill was succeeded as Savilian Professor of Astronomy by James Bradley, who in 1749 became also Crewe Reader of Experimental Philosophy. He died in 1762. His notebooks record that fifty-seven members of Christ Church attended his lectures between 1747 and his death.[1] What appears to be the prospectus of a course of lectures by Bradley exists among the papers of William Perrin, who matriculated as a Gentleman Commoner at Christ Church on 7 November 1761. It is entitled *A Course of Mathematical Lectures and Experiments*.[2] Bradley purchased the scientific instruments, said to have been worth the enormous sum of £400, which had belonged to John Whiteside. In 1714 Whiteside became Keeper of the Ashmolean Museum, and was described by Hearne as 'an excellent Mathematician, and one of the best in England in Experimental Philosophy. He carried on a course of Experiments for many years at the Museum, to the great advantage of the youth of the University.'[3] It is not stretching the evidence unduly to suppose that the youth of the university described by Hearne included the undergraduates of Christ Church, for Whiteside was a chaplain at Christ Church when John Keill renewed his connection with the college, and on his death in 1729 was buried in the cathedral.

The topics treated in his lectures by Bradley were similar to those dealt with some fifty years later by S. P. Rigaud, who was Professor of Experimental Philosophy from 1810 to 1839. George Chinnery attended Rigaud's lectures in 1808 and has left a detailed account of them in his letters at Christ Church. Both lecturers discussed the theory and practical application of mechanics, optics, hydrostatics, and pneumatics, and Rigaud in addition lectured on electricity. The attendance registers kept by Rigaud show that many more undergraduates from Christ Church than from any other college attended his lectures. In Easter term 1833, for example, out of thirty-two present at the course twenty-nine were from Christ Church, and at the lectures in the following Michaelmas, the entire audience except for one person came from Christ Church.[4]

Owing to the munificent benefaction of Dr Matthew Lee, the undergraduates at Christ Church in the latter part of the eighteenth

---

[1] Bodl. MS Bradley 3.
[2] Ch. Ch. Archives, xlviii. b. 36, fos. 5–6.
[3] Hearne, *Collections*, x (1915), 191.
[4] Bodl. MS Savile e. 10.

century were able to study anatomy as well as experimental philosophy. Lee was elected to a Westminster Studentship in 1713
and proceeded MD in 1726. He was a contemporary at both Christ
Church and Westminster of David Gregory, son of the Savilian
Professor of Astronomy and a future Dean, whose enthusiasm for
scientific studies has already been noted. He was also a contemporary of John Keill, who re-entered Christ Church as a
Commoner Master in the year prior to Lee's matriculation, and
in his will Lee made a bequest to Keill's son James.[1] His filial
piety to Christ Church, nurtured by these early associations, was
further nourished when the Dean and Chapter leased to him the
valuable rectory of Chippenham in Wiltshire, the tithes of which
were worth about £260 a year. After practising in Oxford, he
became a prosperous and fashionable physician in London and
Bath, and in 1739 was appointed Physician to Frederick, Prince
of Wales. When he died in 1755 he bequeathed his estate to Christ
Church after the life interest of his wife, mainly for the foundation
of lectureships in anatomy and mathematics. Ten years later the
bequest was realized, and an estate at Butlers Marston and Hels-
thorpe in Warwickshire was purchased in 1768.[2]

By the terms of Lee's will, the Dean and Chapter were required
to elect an anatomical lecturer. He was to be a layman and a
Westminster Student, though a Canoneer Student or a Commoner
of Christ Church might be appointed in the absence of a suitably
qualified Westminster Student. The lecturer, who was to receive
a stipend of £100 a year, was to give instruction in anatomy,
physic, or botany, and was to deliver two courses of lectures a
year at each of which a human body was to be dissected. The sum
of £40 a year was allowed for anatomical preparations and for
procuring at least two adult human bodies. The Dean and Sub-
Dean were to nominate four Students and two Commoners to

---

[1] A James Keill was admitted to Westminster School in 1729, when he was
aged 10, and appears in the under-school list in 1731.

[2] The Lee benefaction was a favourite object of Cyril Jackson, himself a good
mathematician and a student of natural science. Towards the end of his life he
remarked that 'the only Xt.Ch. paper which has escaped the general burning is
a memorandum respecting my schemes about this very fund' (Ch. Ch. Archives,
Estates 90, fo. 300, Letter from Cyril Jackson, Felpham, 15 August 1818).

attend the lectures without payment, preference being given to those from Westminster. Lee did not specifically mention an anatomical theatre in his will, but his intentions could not be fulfilled without one, and the Anatomy School was erected to the designs of Henry Keene and was ready for occupation in the spring of 1768. It cost a total of £2,289, of which £1,209 was provided by the benefaction of Dr John Freind (d. 1728), and the rest by the Lee bequest.

John Parsons, a Westminster Student, was appointed anatomical lecturer, and on 22 January 1767 received £70 in payment for anatomical preparations obtained by him. He had studied medicine at Oxford, London, and Edinburgh, but at the date of his appointment had no degree in medicine. He had, however, been appointed to one of the Faculty Studentships in medicine on 10 June 1766, and became Bachelor of Medicine in 1769. In 1772 he became Doctor of Medicine and in the same year forfeited his Studentship, but not the anatomical lectureship, by marriage. When he died in 1785 at the early age of forty-three, he was succeeded by William Thomson, a Canoneer Student, who remarked that the value of the lectureship lay not in its modest emoluments but 'as an introduction to *practice*', and claimed that Parsons had made £1,400 a year from his practice besides £400 from his professorships.[1] Thomson took the degree of MB in 1785 and was made a Faculty Student. He immediately purchased the large house which Parsons had occupied, and filled half of it with the collection of fossils he had brought with him from Edinburgh. In a letter written soon after his appointment, he described the Anatomy School as he then found it:

As soon as ever my cabinets are ready, they will all be lodged in a room I am fitting up in the Anatomy School in Christ Church—a handsome stone building finely situated and secure from fire. It is endowed with a noble stock of anatomical preparations wet and dry, bones &c—a large apparatus and arched rooms for chemistry, and a few paintings from General Guise's collection ... these few were deemed too indecent to be shewn to company, and therefore were packed to the Anatomy

[1] National Library of Scotland, Adv. MS 29.5.8 (ii), fo. 35.

School and hung up in the lecture room, but there they shall appear no more—for obvious reasons. I am exceedingly busy in preparing to open my first campaign with credit in Lent. My predecessor left no catalogue of any thing, nor even a will behind him, so that I have laboured much in making out such a descriptive catalogue of the anatomical preparations as would be useful to my successor if I were to die tomorrow. In this I have been greatly assisted by Mr. Baillie from London, who was here lately. No one but an anatomist can form an adequate idea of the doubts and difficulties that occur in such an undertaking, where no notes are left nor the history of a single case among some hundreds.[1]

Thomson took no pupils, but his anatomical lectures were very well attended.[2] He was also an excellent mineralogist, and delivered what he claimed to be the first course of lectures on mineralogy at Oxford. It was estimated that the cost of cutting and polishing the specimens for one of these lectures was almost £60, and it is hardly surprising that the course seems not to have been repeated. In 1790 Thomson was suddenly deprived of his Studentship and expelled from the university for what as late as 1839 a correspondent of Philip Bliss described as 'a scandalous imputation' against him arising from his physiological experiments.[3] The nature of these imputations may be surmised from Thomson's own account in a letter to George Paton in 1790:

I am under great affliction, suffering a most scandalous imputation from an experiment performed on a man 4 years ago.

Tho I am personally safe, I shd hereafter feel unhappy in Oxford. My friends will be glad to hear that I have the fullest testimony of Mr. [John] Hunter and other experimentalists here, both as to the fairness of such a medical experiment and the reasonable manner in which I conducted it. Yet, not being guarded by any witness, the means I used to prevail upon the person to submit to the experiment (which I first explained to him) are now told against me. Mr. Hunter has published an account of some of his own trials, just as indecent, introducing thermometers into the penis and anus of men and beasts.[4]

---

[1] Ibid., fo. 35^{r,v}.
[2] Ibid., fos. 61^v, 71^v.
[3] BL Add. MS 34573, fo. 117.
[4] National Library of Scotland, Adv. MS 29.5.8 (ii), fo. 80.

Thomson retired to Italy where 'his medical attainments so far expiated his religious and other heresies' that he was appointed physician-in-ordinary to the Pope.[1] His departure from Christ Church seems to have taken place without acrimony, for in 1801 his father made discreet inquiries whether the Dean and Chapter would accept the bequest of Thomson's collection of minerals and fossils and allow him to found a professorship of mineralogy at Christ Church. It was said that he had 'a decided preference to Christ Church'.[2] He died at Palermo in 1807, and in his will offered his collection of fossils, minerals, and materia medica to Christ Church, and half his estate for the foundation of a lectureship of mineralogy. Apparently because of a problem concerning the endowment of the lectureship, the bequest was eventually declined and his collections were offered to the city of Edinburgh.[3]

Christopher Pegge, who succeeded Thomson, was neither a Westminster nor a Canoneer Student but a Commoner of Christ Church. After taking his BA degree he was elected to a Fellowship of Oriel, but within a few weeks of Thomson's deprivation he re-entered Christ Church, and on 8 December 1790 was appointed anatomical lecturer, an office which he held until 1816. Unlike his predecessors he was a Bachelor of Medicine at the time of his appointment. Although Pegge was knighted in 1799 and appointed Regius Professor of Medicine in 1801, he was never a Student, for Studentships were always awarded to undergraduates and Pegge ceased to be eligible for election in 1786 when he graduated.

From its foundation, the Anatomy School was less a place for the serious study of medicine than for what Acland called the 'recreation of amateurs'. Very few of those who attended lectures and dissections were intended for the medical profession,[4] and the lectures were not designed for the professional study of medicine. Of those given by John Parsons it was said that 'they were

---

[1] Holland, *Further Memoirs of the Whig Party,* 340–1.
[2] Ch. Ch. Archives, xi. a. 15, fol. 136.
[3] Ibid., fos. 142–5.
[4] There were of course exceptions, and the distinguished physician John Kidd may be accounted one of them.

calculated rather for the general philosopher than the medical practitioner'.[1] Christopher Pegge's lectures were no different. Lord Holland wrote of him that he 'could never render his anatomical school famous beyond the walls of the University or popular with the young men within them. There was a whisper among them that his science was superficial'.[2] Despite these limitations, the dissection of human bodies, which caused the Anatomy School to be known popularly as 'Skeleton Corner', continued with unabated enthusiasm into the nineteenth century, when Kidd, who succeeded Pegge in the lectureship, 'found unexpected difficulties in the way of providing subjects and procured permission to lecture from models and preparations'.[3] It was an eloquent tribute to the contribution made by jurisprudence to the study of anatomy that, no doubt with a view to ensuring a regular supply of cadavers, the accounts of the Anatomy School record from 1786 the payment of an annual subscription to the Association for Prosecuting Felons. In performing the dissections, the lecturer was assisted from 1768 to 1794 by John Grosvenor, and from 1795 to 1810 by William Stephens.

Gradually the Anatomy School acquired a large and varied collection of anatomical preparations. The sum of £40 a year which Lee had provided for their purchase and for the acquisition of human bodies proved insufficient, and until 1808 the lecturers made good the deficiency from their own pockets. As each of them gave up office, the Dean and Chapter purchased the preparations thus acquired. In 1785 they paid the sum of £45 for those of John Parsons, 'which', his biographer observed, 'for neatness and elegance have seldom been surpassed'.[4] In 1790, £240 was paid for William Thomson's preparations. At the annual visitations of the Anatomy School,[5] which began in 1796, the specimens and preparations acquired during the previous twelve months were noted. On shelves and in cupboards, bottled and dried, stuffed

[1] *A Short Account of the Late Dr. John Parsons* (1786), 5.
[2] Holland, *Further Memoirs of the Whig Party*, 340.
[3] *Report of the Oxford University Commission* (1852), evidence, 282.
[4] *A Short Account of the Late Dr. John Parsons*, 5.
[5] Ch. Ch. Archives, lii. b. 1.

and embalmed, was a microcosm of natural creation. Mammals, birds, and fish were plundered of organs demonstrating taste, smell, hearing, sight, digestion, respiration, and reproduction. Apart from domestic animals such as the horse, ass, and sheep, and a 'monstrous chicken with four legs', there were representative components of creatures from distant parts. In 1798 'two portions of armadillos' were acquired, and in 1800 the skull, stomach, and part of the intestines of a kangaroo. In subsequent years a secretary-bird, a Java pigeon, a tiger's head, and the foetus of a walrus were obtained, and in 1810 the jaw of a mammoth with two teeth well preserved, and the tooth of an elephant 'with the Asiatic character from America'. In 1823, two years before he became a Canon of Christ Church, William Buckland, who is remembered for munching his way through creation, and whose mouth must surely have watered at the contents of the Anatomy School, presented a cast of the fossilized head of a rhinoceros. *Homo sapiens* was not neglected, either in whole or in part. In 1799 the Anatomy School obtained the head of an old woman, the side view of the male pelvis 'dried and in oil of turpentine', an aorta, and a dried testicle. In 1804 a number of pathological specimens were obtained, among them a cancerous tibia, bones of the foot diseased from scrofula, a tumour from a woman's shoulder, and a couple of gallstones. The collections bore witness to the steady tramp of colonial expansion. In 1808 two skulls from New South Wales were acquired, and in 1810 the cranium of a young female native of Botany Bay. In the same year a naval surgeon presented the lower jaw of a New Caledonian citizen. A few years later the visitors recorded the woolly skull of a black male from Van Diemen's Land, a similar skull not woolly from New South Wales, and the head of a New Zealand native curiously tattooed.

The nature of the studies pursued in the Anatomy School is also reflected by the books acquired for the medical library which it contained. No details of them survive prior to 1796, but from that year until 1820 over eighty books and scientific journals are mentioned by name in the visitation reports, and to these other works not specifically mentioned may be added on the strength of payments to booksellers. The volumes noted individually in the reports tended to be expensive and often well-illustrated publications, but they give a general idea of the library's main areas of scientific interest. They show that, although the principal emphasis was placed on human anatomy, attention was increasingly paid to comparative anatomy, particularly after the purchase of George Shaw's *General Zoology* in 1807. The development of comparative anatomy accelerated the process which eventually caused the separation of the Lee Readership in Human Anatomy from the collections and specimens, which were later deposited in the University Museum. Even human anatomy covered areas which were not strictly medical, for it embraced phrenology, and, in such works as Charles Bell's *Essays on the Anatomy of Expression in Painting* and A. G. Camper's *Dissertation physique ... sur les différences réelles que présentent les traits du visage,* the study of art.[1]

No periodicals were taken until 1809, and it was not until Kidd succeeded Pegge in 1816 that the *Medical Transactions* of the College of Physicians, which began publication in 1768, and the *Edinburgh Medical and Surgical Journal,* which began publication in 1805, were acquired. Kidd had presented specimens to the Anatomy School as early as 1799, and it is likely that he was associated with it in other ways prior to 1816, particularly during the long period of Pegge's ill-health. In most cases the books were purchased near the time of publication from booksellers such as Remnant, Parker, Joshua Cooke, or, in the case of many of the French publications, from De Bosse. Some of the books, such as the *Anatome* of Thomas Bartholinus (1686), or *Observationum Anatomico-Chirurgicarum Centuria* (1689), of Fredrik Ruysch, where particular editions are mentioned, had long been out of print and were presumably obtained from antiquarian booksellers or by gift.

The books acquired for the library of the Anatomy School, as noted in the visitation reports from 1796 to 1820, were as follows.

---

[1] This is not the only evidence of a connection between the Anatomy School and the study of art. In 1819, for example, 'a model in wax of an adult female' was acquired, and Dr Alexander Hood presented the 'Anatomie du gladiateur combattant'. Had Ruskin studied anatomy at Christ Church, his private life, and perhaps even the history of art in the 19th cent., might have taken a different course.

1798[1] Albinus, Bern. Siegfried, *Tabulae Sceleti et Musculorum Corporis Humani* (1747).

1811 Baglivius, Georgius, *Opera Omnia* (1704).

1800 Baillie, Matthew, *Series of Engravings with Explanations which are Intended to Illustrate the Morbid Anatomy of . . . the Human Body* (1799–1803).

1799 Banister, John, *The Historie of Man* (1578).

1811 Bartholinus, Tho., *Anatome* (1686; this edn.).

1799 Bell, Charles, *System of Dissections, Explaining the Anatomy of the Human Body* (1798–1803).

1804 Bell, Charles, *Anatomy of the Brain, Explained in a Series of Engravings* (1802).

1807 Bell, Charles, *Engravings of the Arteries* (1801).

1807 Bell, Charles, *Essays on the Anatomy of Expression in Painting* (1806).

1804 Bell, John, 'Engravings of the Nerves', probably vol. iii of *Anatomy of the Human Body* (1802–4).

1805 Bell, John, *Anatomy of the Human Body* (1802–4).

1807 Bell, John, 'Engravings of the Bones', probably vol. i of *Anatomy of the Human Body* (1802–4).

1810 Bichat, Marie François Xavier, *Anatomie générale, appliquée à la physiologie et à la médecine* (1801). Another copy 1816.

1811 Bidloo, Govard, *Exercitationum Anatomico-chirurgicarum Decades Duae* (1704).

1801 Blasius, Gerardus, *Anatome Animalium* (1681).

1808 Blumenbach, Joh. Friedr., *Short System of Comparative Anatomy* (1807).

1811 Bonnet, Charles, *Contemplation de la nature* (1764; edn. of 1769).

1811 Borelli, Gio. Alfonso, *De Motu Animalium* (1680–1).

1813 Bosc, Louis Augustin Guillaume, *Histoire naturelle des vers,* (1802).

1799 Camper, Adriaan Gilles, *Dissertation physique . . . sur les différences réelles que présentent les traits du visage* (1791).

1810 Clark, Bracy, *Series of Original Experiments on the Foot of the Living Horse* (1809).

1798 Coleman, Edward, *Observations on the Structure, Oeconomy, and Diseases of the Foot of the Horse* (1798), 1802.

---

[1] The editions acquired are seldom known. However, in general the dates of the earliest editions in the British Library are noted here.

1810   Collins, Samuel, *Systeme of Anatomy* (1685).

1804   Cooper, Astley Paston, *Anatomy and Surgical Treatment of Inguinal and Congenital Hernia* (1804).

1814   Corvisart des Marest, Jean Nicolas, *Treatise on the Diseases and Organic Lesions of the Heart and Great Vessels* (1813).

1796   Cowper, William, *Myotomia Reformata, or an Anatomical Treatise on the Muscles of the Human Body* (1724).

1797   Cowper, William, *Anatomy of Humane Bodies, with Figures Drawn after the Life* (1698).

1809   Cuvier, Georges de, *Leçons d'anatomie comparée* (1800–5).

1808   Derham, William, *Physico-theology* (1713).

1813   Dumeril, André Marie Constant, *Zoologie analytique* (1806).

1804   Fox, Joseph, *Natural History of the Human Teeth* (1803).

1813   Fyfe, Andrew, *Outlines of Comparative Anatomy* (1813).

1801   Gautier d'Agoty, Jacques, *Exposition anatomique des organes des sens* (1775).

1811   Haller, Albrecht von, 'Disputationes Anatomicae', perhaps *Disputationes ad Morborum Historiam et Curationem Facientes* (1757–60).

1801   Haller, Albrecht von, *Icones Anatomicae* (1743–56).

1797   Harwood, Busick, *System of Comparative Anatomy and Physiology* (1796).

1811   La Ville sur Illon, Bernard Germain Étienne, Comte de Lacépède, *Histoire naturelle des quadrupèdes* (1787).

1811   Lawrence, Thomas, *De Natura Musculorum Praelectiones* (1759).

1813   Le Gallois, Julien Jean César, *Expériences sur le principe de la vie, notamment sur celui des mouvements du cœur* (1812).

1796   Lieberkühn, Johh. Nathanael, *Dissertationes Quatuor,* ed. John Sheldon (1782). Gift.

1798   Loder, Just Christian, *Tabulae Anatomicae* (n.d.).

1798   Ludwig, Christian Friedrich, *Icones Cavitatum Thoracis et Abdominis* (1789).

1819   Mascagni, Paolo, *Prodromo della grande anatomia* (1819).

1808   Mayow, John, *Tractatus Quinque Medico-Physici* (1674).

1813   Monet de Lamarck, Jean Baptiste Pierre Antoine de, *Système des animaux sans vertèbres* (1801).

1797   Monro, Alex., *Three Treatises. On the Brain, the Eye, and the Ear* (1797).

1810   Montfort, Denis de, *Histoire naturelle des mollusques* (1802).

1813   Nacquart, Jean Baptiste, *Traité sur la nouvelle physiologie du cerveau* (1808).

1808   Paley, William, *Natural Theology* (1802).

1810   Pennant, Thomas, *British Zoology* (1768–70).

1799   Pole, Thomas, *Anatomical Instructor* (1790).

1796   Pugh, John, *Treatise on the Science of Muscular Action* (1794). Given by the author.

1804   Rowley, William, *Schola Medicinae Universalis nova* (1794).

1811   Russell, Richard, *Oeconomy of Nature in Acute and Chronical Diseases of the Glands* (1755).

1811   Ruysch, Fredrik, *Observationum Anatomico-chirurgicarum Centuria* (1689; this edn.).

1807   Saunders, John Cunningham, *Anatomy of the Human Ear* (1806).

1796   Scarpa, Antonio, *Anatomicae Disquisitiones de Auditu et Olfactu* (1794).

1798   Scarpa, Antonio, *Tabulae Neurologicae* (1794).

1807   Shaw, George, *General Zoology* (1800–26).

1796   Sheldon, John, *Essay on the Fracture of the Patella* (1789). Gift.

1796   Sheldon, John, *History of the Absorbent System,* p. i (1784). Gift.

1802   Soemmerring, Sam. Tho. von, *Icones Embryonum Humanorum* (1799).

1807   Soemmerring, Sam. Tho. von, *Icones Oculi Humani* (1804).

1808   Soemmerring, Sam. Tho. von, *De Basi Encephali* (1791). Gift.

1815   Spurzheim, Joh. Gaspar, 'Craniology', perhaps *Anatomie et physiologie du système nerveux en général, et sur celui du cerveau en particulier* (1810).

         Stukeley, William, *Of the Spleen* (1723).

1816   Thompson, Thomas, *Annals of Philosophy* (1813–20).

1813   Turton, William, *Medical Glossary* (1797).

1808   Vaughan, Walter, *Exposition of the Principles of Anatomy* (1791). Gift.

1797   Vial de Saint Bel, Charles, *Anatomy of the Horse* (? 1795).

1796   Walter, Johann Gottlieb, *Tabulae Nervorum Thoracis et Abdominis* (1783). Another copy 1804.

1796   Weitbrecht, Josias, *Syndesmologia* (1742).

1808   White, Andrew, *Account of the Regular Gradation in Man* (1799). Gift.

1811   Zinn, Joh. Gottfried, *Descriptio Anatomica Oculi Humani* (1780; this edn.).

The periodicals acquired for the medical library were:

1810   *Annales du musée national d'histoire naturelle* (1802).
1816   *Edinburgh Medical and Surgical Journal* (1805).
1819   *Edinburgh Philosophical Journal* (1819).
1816   *London Medical ... Repository* (1814).
1816   *Medical Transactions* (College of Physicians in London, 1768).
1809   *Transactions Medico-chirurgicales* (1809).
1819   *Quarterly Journal of Science and the Arts* (Royal Institution of Great Britain, 1816).

At the time of Lee's benefaction, the study of medicine in Oxford was in decline. It had long been the practice for students of medicine to complete their studies overseas, usually at the universities of Leyden or Padua. The Sub-Dean's registers record the grant of leave of absence in the early eighteenth century to Noel Broxholme, John Wigan, Charles Kimberley, and Pierce Manaton for this purpose. In 1734 Erasmus Dryden and Anthony Parsons were given leave of absence 'they being ill and abroad under the care of Dr. Boerhave'. Neither of them took a medical degree, but in 1739 Parsons succeeded Wigan in his Faculty Studentship. George Dowdeswell, the stepson of Noel Broxholme, studied at Leyden in 1745, and William Oliver, having been expelled from Christ Church in 1751 for toasting the Young Pretender, studied at Leyden in 1753 and at Padua in 1755.[1] But it was not so much attendance at foreign universities which caused the decay of medical studies at Oxford as the rise of the new medical schools in Edinburgh and London. They were already much in evidence by the middle of the eighteenth century. The Sub-Dean's registers ceased to record the grant of leave of absence to Students after 1738, but when in 1760 the Chapter ordered that the regulations be more strictly observed it is apparent that many attended them. On 19 October 1763 Robert Cocks was permitted to attend physical lectures in Edinburgh, and on 30 November in the same year Lucas Pepys was allowed to attend anatomy lectures in London. On 24 July 1764 John Parsons was given a year's

[1] R. W. Innes Smith, *English-speaking Students of Medicine at the University of Leyden* (1932).

leave of absence, and on 8 July 1767 the same privilege was extended to another student of medicine, John Burges. In 1769 Thomas Russell attended physical lectures in Edinburgh. In all these cases leave of absence was given to Students who had taken at least their BA degree in Oxford. It was not, however, the invariable practice for a student of medicine to obtain an arts degree before commencing his medical studies. In the seventeenth century Nathan Lacy, who was elected Student in 1673, studied at Padua apparently without having previously taken a degree, and so successfully that he became physician to the Queen of Spain. Peter de Cardonnel, also a Student, entered at Leyden on 16 September 1681, but returned to Christ Church to take his degrees of BA and MA. In the latter part of the eighteenth century many who in past times might have come up to Oxford in order to take a BA or MA before entering on the study of medicine, began their medical studies without any such preliminaries.

Lee's foundation did little, if anything, to arrest the decline of medicine at Oxford, and perhaps was not intended to do so, for it is likely that his intention was not to restore it as a centre for medical studies but to provide a grounding in anatomy for undergraduates, and especially for Westminster Students, preparatory to the study of medicine in London or Edinburgh.[1] By the time his benefaction took effect, however, classical studies predominated at Westminster and Christ Church. Too late to encourage medicine at Westminster and excluded from the curriculum at Christ Church, anatomy was seldom a subject for serious study.

Human dissection [remarked Henry Acland, who was appointed to the Lee lectureship in 1845] is no fit recreation for amateurs, and ought not in my judgment to be brought forward in any lectures not intended exclusively for earnest students, and I question whether the receipt of a corpse in a box by coach and the consequent speculations and inquiries which undergraduates used to make at the Museum door, was not an evil which outweighed by many times any good that could be gotten by

---

[1] It is worth recalling that in Lee's youth Westminster School had produced some distinguished physicians, notably John Freind, Noel Broxholme, and John Wigan.

the Westminster Students from demonstrations upon it, lasting but three or four days.[1]

In conclusion, undergraduates at Christ Church appear to have studied science to a greater extent than has been supposed. But, although attendance at lectures in natural science was compulsory, the vacuum caused by the demise of Aristotelian science was filled by classical and not by scientific studies owing partly to the nature of the tutorial system but perhaps pre-eminently owing to the assumptions of liberal education, which were inimical to the practical application of science. As the boundaries of science expanded, the latent conflict was exposed between the need of the Industrial Revolution for a utilitarian education on the one hand, and the traditional concern to educate the clergy and gentry on the other. Stripped of its originally comprehensive character, liberal education became synonymous with classical education. Undergraduates indeed continued to study natural science, and at Christ Church it was enlivened by the creation of the Anatomy School, but they did not do so within the confines of the tutorial system, and scientific studies were not the avenue to tutorships or an object of ambition for Students.

[1] *Report of the Oxford University Commission* (1852), evidence, 283.

APPENDIX I

Specimens of Collections

PRIOR to 1768 the Collections Books do not specify the Collections submitted by undergraduates individually but record the reading prescribed for each *Classis*. The Collections of Noblemen and Gentlemen Commoners are not recorded until 1774.

MURRAY, WILLIAM. Westminster Student. BA. Lord Chief Justice and first Earl of Mansfield. (Tutor: Henry Sherman.)

1724   Hebraeum Psalterium; 4 first Articles of Bp. Pearson's Exposition; Ciceronis de Oratore Ll. 3; Homeri Iliad. Ll. 8 priores; Virg. Aeneid. Ll. 6 priores; Aldrichii Ars Logica.

1725   Liber Geneseos Hebraice; four middle Articles of Bp. Pearson's Exposition; Ciceronis de Claris Oratoribus et Orator; Hom. Illiad. Ll. 8 medii; Virg. Aeneid. Ll. 6 post.; Tullius de Officiis; Eustachii Ethica.

1726   Deuteronomium Hebraice; four last Articles of Bp. Pearson's Exposition; M. T. Ciceronis Quaestiones Tusculanae; Homeri Iliados Ll. 8 post.; Lucretius; Bartholini Physica.

1727   XXXIX Articulorum Expositio ab Ellisio; Burgersdicii Metaphysica.

(Ch. Ch. Archives, li.b. 1, fos. 44, 46^v, 49^v, 52.)

Identical Collections were submitted by Charles Wesley, Sir Francis Bernard, and William Markham amongst others.

ABBOT, CHARLES. Westminster Student. BA. Speaker of the House of Commons and first Baron Colchester. (Tutor: Thomas Pettingal.)

1775   Mich.   Soph. Oed. Tyr.; Tac. Vit. Agrica.; Hor. Ep. ad Aug.

1776   Hil.   Herodoti Ll. 4 post.; M. T. Cic. de claris Oratoribus.

        Pasch.   Thucyd. L. 1; Euclidis L. 1.

	Trin.	Thucyd. L. 2; Euclidis Ll. 2. 3. 4.
	Mich.	Thucyd. Ll. 6 post.; Euclidis Ll. 5. 6. 11.
1777	Hil.	Xenophontis *Ελληνικα*; Algebrae per Macl. pars 1.
	Pasch.	Xenophontis *Αναβασις*; Virgilii Georgica; Trigonometria Plana.
	Trin.	Xenophontis *Κυρου Παιδ.*; Trigonometria Sphaerica.
	Mich.	Aristotelis Organi quaedam; Aldrichii Log. L. 1; Xenophontis Memorabilia; Caesaris Commentarii.
1778	Hil.	Aldrichii Log. L. 2; Aristotelis Rhet. Ll. 2; Livii Ll. 10 priores; Grotius de Ver. Rel. Christianae.
	Pasch.	Polybii Ll. 5; Aristotelis Rhet. L. 3, ejusdem *περι ποιητ.* c. 6; Lockii de mente humana tractatus minor; Taciti dial. de causis Corrupt. eloquentiae.
	Trin.	[blank]
1779	Mich.	Juris studio nomen dedit.

(Ch. Ch. Archives, li.b. 2, p. 174.)

BISSET, GEORGE. Westminster Student. BA. Commended for excellent Collections (Chapter Act Book, 22 Dec. 1786). Clergyman. (Tutor: William Jackson.)

1783	Trin.	Oed. Tyr.; C. J. Caesaris B. Gal. Ll. 4.
	Mich.	Soph. Oed. Col., Antig.; Euripidis Iphig. in Aul. et Iphig. in Tauris; Euclidis Ll. 4 priores; C. J. Caesaris B. Gall. Ll. reliqui.
1784	Hil.	Euclidis Ll. 5, 6; *Ικετιδες, Επτ. επι Θηβ.*; Phoenissae, Medea; C. J. Caes. B. Civ.
	Pasch.	Algebrae per Maclaurin L. 1 pars 1; Herod. Ll. 1. 3. 4; Virgilii Georgica.
	Trin.	Herodoti Ll. 5. 6. 7. 8. 9; Trigonometria Plana.
	Mich.	[blank]
1785	Hil.	Thucyd. Ll. 3; Vitae Periclis, Themistoclis, Aristidis, Cimonis apud Plutarchum.
	Pasch.	Thucyd. Ll. 5 post.; vita Niciae apud Plutarchum.
	Trin.	Xenophontis *Ελληνικ. Κ Αναβ.*; Plut. vitae

	Pelopidas, Lysander, Agesilaus, Alcibiades.
Mich.	Diodori Siculi L. 11 et Ll. sequentes; Aristotelis Organ. quaedam; Aldrichii Logica.
1786 Hil.	Dionysii Halicarnass. Antiq. Romanae; Plutarchi Romulus, Numa, Publicola, Coriolanus; T. Livii Hist. Rom. Ll. 1. 2. 3; Aristotelis Rhetor. Ll. 1. 2.
Pasch.	Liv. Ll. 3–10; Plut. Camillus; Arist. Rhet. L. 3.
Trin.	Polybii Ll. 2 priores; Plutarchi Pyrrhus, Agis, Cleomenes, Aratus; Aristot. de Poet.
Mich.	Polyb. Ll. 3 et quae supersunt omnia; T. Livii 21–40; vitae Qu. Fabii et Marcell. apud Plutarchum.

Admissus ad gradum A.B.

(Ch. Ch. Archives, li.b. 2, p. 447.)

GLASSE, GEORGE HENRY. Canoneer Student. BA. Classical scholar. (Tutors: Joshua Berkeley and John Randolph.)

1775 Mich.	Xenoph. *Αναβ.*; Xenoph. *Κυρου παιδ.*; Liv. Ll. 10 priores; Eur. Med., Elect., Orest., Alc., Hipp.
1776 Hil.	Xenophontis *Απομνημουευματα*; Homeri Odyssea; M. T. Cic. de Oratore.
Pasch.	Herod. L. 5; Euclidis L. 1; Liv. Ll. 21–26; Demosthenis Philip. 1 et Olynth. 1; Cic. de claris Oratoribus et Orator.
Trin.	Homeri Ilias; Herod. L. 6; Virgil. Georgica; Liv. Ll. 26–35; Euclidis Ll. 2. 3. 4.
Mich.	Euclidis Ll. 5. 6 et 11 pars 1; Herod. Ll. 3 post.; Liv. Ll. 10 post.; Horatii Epistolae.
1777 Hil.	Maclaurin Algebrae pars 1; Caesaris Commentarii; Sallustii Opera.
Pasch.	Sophoclis Electra; M. T. Cic. de Natura Deorum; Demosthenis Olynth. 2. 3; Thucyd. L. 1; Trigonometria Plana.
Trin.	Thucydidis Ll. 2. 3. 4; M. T. Cic. Tusc. Quaest.; Trigonometria Sphaerica.
Mich.	Aristotelis Organi quaedam; Aldrichii Log. L. 1; Thucydidis Ll. 4 post.; M. T. Cic. De Finibus; quatuor Evangelia et Acta Apostolorum.

1778	Hil.	Xenophontis *Ελληνικα*; Taciti Annal.; D. Pauli et aliorum Epistolae; Aristotelis Rhet. Ll. 2 priores; Aldrichii Log. L. 2.
	Pasch.	Aristotelis Rhet. L. 3, ejusdem *περι ποιητ.* c. 6; Taciti Hist., Vit. Agric. etc.; Polybii Ll. 5; Grotius de Ver. R. Christianae; Horat. de Arte Poetica.
	Trin.	Aristotelis *περι ποιητ.* c. 20 post.; Sophoclis Oed. Tyr., Oed. Col., Antigone; Euripidis Phoenissae; Cellarii Geographia; Pearson in Symbolum.
	Mich.	Lucretius; Beveregii Instit. Chron.; Lockii de mente humana tractatus minor; Aristotelis Eth. Nicom.; Genesis et Psalmi Hebr.
1779	Hil.	[blank]
	Pasch.	Admissus ad gradum A.B.

(Ch. Ch. Archives, li.b. 2, p. 173.)

WOOD, WILLIAM. Canoneer Student. BA. Tutor and (1798) Senior Censor. (Tutor: Charles Sawkins.)

1786	Mich.	Euclidis Ll. 4; Homeri Ilias et Odyssea; C. J. Caes. B. Gallicum.
1787	Hil.	Eucl. 5. 6. 11; Herodoti Historia; C. J. C. B. C., Al., A., H.; Sophoclis Tragaed. septem; Euripidis Iphig. in Aul. et in Tauris.
	Pasch.	Thucyd. Ll. 3 priores; Plutarchi Theseus, Lycurg., Solon, Aristid., Themist., Cimon, Pericles; Alg. per Maclaurin capp. X.
	Trin.	Thucydidis Ll. rell.; Vitae Niciae et Alcibiadis apud Plutarchum; Algebrae per Maclaurin caput 13.
	Mich.	Xenophontis *Ελληνικα* et *Αυαβασις*; Diodori Sic. Ll. 11–20; vitae Artaxerxis, Alexandri, Lysandri, Pelopidae, Agesilai, Timoleontis, Eumenis, Demetrii et Demosthenis apud Plutarchum; Trigonometria Plana et Sphaerica.
1788	Hil.	Hamilton de Conicis Sectionibus Ll. omnes; Euripidis Tragaediae reliquae; Aldrichii Logica.
	Pasch.	Arist. Rhet. L. 1–10; Pindarus; Hesiodi quae

supersunt.

Trin.	Arist. Rhet. L. 1. capp. rell., L. 2; Demosthenis orationes ad rempublicam spectantes; Aeschinis Orationes 2.
Mich.	T. Livii 1–10; excerpta e Dionysio Halicarn.; Romuli, Numae, Publicolae, Coriolani, Camilli vitae apud Plutarchum; Arist. de Rhet. L. 3 et de Poet. capp. quaedam; Algebrae per Maclaurin partes 2 et 3.

1789	Hil.	Polybii Ll. 5. 6 quae supersunt; Livii Ll. 21. 22; Plutarchi Aratus, Pyrrhus, Fabius Maximus, Agis, Cleomenes; Arist. de Poet. capp. rell.; Longinus; Newtoni sectio de rationibus primis ultimisque.
	Pasch. et Trin.	Polyb. fragm.; T. Livii Ll. reliqui; Plutarchi Aemilius, Marcellus, Flamininus, Cato.
	Mich.	Platonis Dialogi.
	Hil.	Platonis de Republica Ll. 1–6, ejusdem Minos; T. Lucretii Ll. omnes.

Admissus ad gradum A.B.

(Ch. Ch. Archives, li.b. 2, pp. 262–3.)

CANNING, GEORGE. Canoneer Student. BA. Statesman. (Tutor: Phineas Pett.)

1787	Mich.	Sophocl. Oedip. Tyran. Hom. Il. Ll. 6 primi.
1788	Hil.	Euclid L. 1; Herodoti Historia.
	Pasch.	Euclid 2. 3; Thucyd. L. 1; Plutarchi Lycurgus, Solon, Themistocles, Aristides, Cimon, Theseus; Xen. Ath. et Lac. *Πολιτεια*.
	Trin.	Thucyd. Ll. reliqui; Plutarchi Pericles, Nicias, Alcibiades.
	Mich.	Xenophontis *Ελλην.* et *Αυαβ.*; Plutarchi Artaxerxes, Lysander, Agesilaus, Pelopidas; Iliados Ll. rell.; Algebrae per Maclaurin L. 1 capp. priora; Xenophontis *λογος εις Αγησιλαος*.
1789	Hil.	Diodori Siculi Ll. 11–20; Alexandri, Dionis, Eumenis, Demetrii, Phocionis et Timoleonis vitae apud Plutarchum.
	Pasch. et	Sophoclis Tragaediae reliquae; Aeneis; Aldrichii

	Trin.	Logica.
	Mich.	T. Livii Ll. 10; Polybii Ll. 2; Plutarchi Pyrrhus.
1790	Hil.	Polybii Ll. 3. 4. 5; T. Livii Ll. 21–30; Aristot. de Rhet. Ll. 2. 3; Vitae Marcelli et Fabii Maximi apud Plutarchum.
	Pasch. et	Polybii fragmenta; T. Livii Ll. rell.; Appianus;
	Trin.	Plutarchi vitae ad historiam Romanam spectantes 16; Sallustius; Aristot. de Rhet. L. 3, ejusdem L. de Poetica.
	Mich.	M. T. Ciceronis Orationes.
1791	Hil.	Demosthenes, Aeschines et Lysias.
	Trin.	Admissus ad gradum A.B.

(Ch. Ch. Archives, li.b. 2, p. 430.)

TRELAWNY, Sir HARRY. Nobleman. BA. Clergyman. (Tutor: Joshua Berkeley.)

	Trin.	
1774	Trin.	Demosthenis Orationes Selectae; Grotius de Veritate Rel. Christ.
	Mich.	Xen. Κυρου παιδειας Ll. 2 priores; Juvenalis Sat. 10.
1775	Hil.	Cellarii Geogr.; Log.
	Pasch.	[blank]
	Trin.	3 Epistol. Johan. Jud. 31 Gen. Heb.; Longinus.
	Mich.	Arist. Rhet. 3 lib.; Tull. de nat. deor.; Pauli Ep. Heb.; Locke on the cond. of ha. underst.
1776	Hil.	[blank]
	Pasch.	Admissus ad gradum A.B.

(Ch. Ch. Archives, li.b. 2, p. 145.)

BENTINCK, WILLIAM HENRY CAVENDISH. Nobleman. No degree. 4th Duke of Portland. (Tutor: Phineas Pett.)

1785	Hil.	Euclidis Ll. 6; Herod. Ll. 1. 3. 4. 5. 6. 7.
	Pasch.	Herodoti Ll. 8. 9; Thucyd. L. 1; Plutarchi Themistocles, Aristides, Cimon, Pericles; Algebrae per Maclaurin pars 1.
	Trin.	Thucyd. Ll. 2. 3. 4; de L. 11 Euclidis priori parte et de Trigon. Plana et Sphaer. Ulterius satisfaciendum.
	Mich.	Thucyd. Ll. 5–8; Aldrichii Logica.

1786	Hil.	Xenoph. *Ελληνικα* Ll. omnes; vitae Pelopidae, Lysandri, Agesilai apud Plutarchum.
	Pasch.	Diodori Siculi Ll. 15. 16. 17; Aristot. Rhet. L. 3.
	Trin.	Plutarchi vita Demosthenis; Demosthenis orationes 4; Arist. lib. de re poetica.

(Ch. Ch. Archives, li.b. 2, p. 460.)

KENYON, LLOYD. Nobleman. BA. Died 1801. (Tutor: George Illingworth.)

1794	Mich.	Herodoti Ll. 3 post.; Plutarchi vitae ad eam Historiam pertinentes; Euclidis Ll. 3 priores.
1795	Hil.	Thucydidis Ll. 2; Plutarchi Cimon, Themistocles, Aristides, Pericles; Euclidis Ll. 4. 5. 6.
	Pasch. et Trin.	Thucydidis Ll. reliqui; Algebra apud Maclaurin.
	Mich.	Xenophontis Hellenica, Cyri Exp.; Plutarchi Alcibiades, Lysander, Artaxerxes.
1796	Hil.	Diodori Siculi Ll. XVI–XX; Demosthenis Orationes 7.
	Pasch. et Trin.	Titi Livii Decas 1; Polybii Hist. Ll. 3 priores.
	Mich.	[blank]
1797	Hil.	T. Livii Ll. 21–40.
	Pasch. et Trin.	Admissus ad gradum A.B.

(Ch. Ch. Archives, li.b. 3, p. 171.)

PONSONBY, JOHN WILLIAM. Nobleman. Honorary MA. 4th Earl of Bessborough. (Tutor: Matthew Marsh.)

1799	Mich.	Herodoti Ll. 1. 3. 4. 5 et 6 pars 1.
1800	Hil.	Oedip. Tyrannus; Phoenissae; Georg. Virg.; Euclid. L. 3.
	Pasch. et Trin.	Xenop. Anab. L. 4; Juv. Satt.; Eucl. 4. 6.
	Mich.	Xenoph. Anab. Ll. rell.; Ciceronis orationes Catilinariae; Algebra pars 1.
1801	Hil.	Hom. Odyss. Ll. 1–10; Taciti de moribus Germ. lib.

	Pasch. et	
	Trin.	Tit. Liv. Decas 1; Odyss. Ll. rell.; Prael. Log.
	Mich.	Platonis Alcibiades uterque et Socratis apologia; T. Livii Decas 2.
1802	Hil.	T. Livii Ll. 30. 37; Eurip. Medea, Heraclidae, Iphig. in Aul.
	Trin.	Admissus ad gradum A.M. honoris causa.

(Ch. Ch. Archives, li.b. 3, p. 76.)

LEGGE, WILLIAM. Gentleman Commoner. BA. Died 1784. (Tutor: William Jackson.)

1774	Trin.	Herodotus; 10 Ll. Livii.
	Mich.	Thucydidis Ll. 2 priores; Liv. a L. 21 ad 27; Euclidis Ll. 2 priores.
1775	Hil.	Thucyd. 3. 4 lib.; Liv. Ll. post.; Ald. Log.
	Pasch.	Thucyd. L. 5; Sallustii op.; Eucl. Ll. 4. 5.
	Trin.	Thucyd. Ll. 6. 7. 8; Eucl. L. 6; Cic. Orats in Catilinam.
	Mich.	[blank]
1776	Hil.	[blank]
	Pasch.	Admissus ad gradum A.B.

(Ch. Ch. Archives, li.b. 2, p. 138.)

CONWAY, LORD WILLIAM SEYMOUR. Gentleman Commoner. BA. MP 1783–96. (Tutor unknown.)

1777	Mich.	Herodoti L. 6; Livii L. 1; Euclidis Ll. 3.
1778	Hil.	Herodoti Ll. 7. 8. 9; Livii Ll. 2–5.
	Pasch.	[blank]
	Trin.	Xenophontis Memorabilia; Livii Ll. 6–21.
	Mich.	Aldrichii Logica; Thucydidis Ll. 2 priores; Livii Ll. 22–24.
1779	Hil.	Thucydidis Ll. 3. 4; Aristotelis Rhet. Ll. 2; Livii Ll. 25–32.
	Pasch.	Thucydidis Ll. 5. 6; Aristotelis Rhet. L. 3; Livii Ll. 33–35.
	Trin.	Aristotelis περι ποιητικης; Thucydidis Ll. 2 post.; Livii Ll. 36–41.
	Mich.	Xenophontis Ελληνικ. Ll. 4 priores; Livii Ll. 4 post.

| 1780 | Hil. | Xenoph. Hellen. Ll. 5. 6. 7; Polyb. Ll. 1. 2. |
| | Trin. | Admissus ad gradum A.B. |

(Ch. Ch. Archives, li.b. 2, p. 226.)

FREEMAN, EDWARD DEANE. Gentleman Commoner. Honorary MA. High Sheriff of Cork. (Tutor: Joshua Berkeley.)

1778	Hil.	Homeri Il. Ll. 9–12; Demosth. Philip. 1; Livii L. 1; Virgilii Georgica.
	Pasch.	Homeri Il. Ll. 13–16; Demosthenis Olynth. 3; Livii Ll. 2. 3.
	Trin.	Sophoclis Oed. Tyrannus; Livii Ll. 4. 5.
	Mich.	Herodoti L. 6; Euclidis Ll. 3; Homeri Il. Ll. 17. 18.
1779	Hil.	Herodoti L. 7; Livii Ll. 21. 22; Euclidis Ll. 4. 5. 6 et 11 pars 1.
	Pasch.	Algebrae per Maclaurin pars 1; Herodoti Ll. 2 post.
	Trin.	Homeri Il. Ll. 6 post.; Trigonometria Plana et Sphaerica.
	Mich.	Thucydidis L. 1; Aldrichii Logica et Aristotelis Organi quaedam.
1780	Hil.	Thucydidis L. 2; Aristotelis Rhet. L. 1.
	Pasch.	Aristot. Rhet. Ll. 2 post.; M. T. Cic. de Oratore.
	Trin.	Aristotelis περὶ ποιητικῆς.
	Mich.	Thucydidis L. 3.
1781	Hil.	Admissus ad gradum A.M. honoris causa.

(Ch. Ch. Archives, li.b. 2, p. 229.)

RIDLEY, NICHOLAS. Gentleman Commoner. BA. 1st Baron Colborne. (Tutor: George Illingworth.)

1796	Mich.	Herodoti Ll. 3 post.; Virgilii Georgica Ll. 2 priores.
1797	Hil.	Thucydidis Ll. 3 priores.
	Pasch. et	
	Trin.	Thucydidis Ll. 4–7; Horatii Epistolae.
	Mich.	Xenophontis Hellenic. Ll. 2 priores et Cyri Expeditio; Juvenalis Sat. 1. 3. 8. 10; Euclidis Ll. 3–6.
1798	Hil.	T. Livii Decas prior; Juv. Sat. 4. 11. 13; Algebra.

	Pasch. et Trin.	T. Livii Decas 3; Euripidis Hippolytus; Trigonom.
	Mich.	T. Livii Ll. 31–40; Euripidis Andromache; Logices apud Aldrich. pars 1.
1799	Hil.	T. Livii Ll. reliq.; Appian. Mithrid. bellum; Persii Sat. 1. 2. 3; Arist. Rhet. quaedam.
	Pasch. et Trin.	Taciti Ann. Ll. 1–4; Pindari Olymp.; Arist. Rhet. quaedam; Persii Sat. Ll. 3 reliqui. Admissus ad gradum A.B.

(Ch. Ch. Archives, li.b. 3, p. 52.)

LEWIS, THOMAS FRANKLAND. Gentleman Commoner. No degree. MP 1812–55. (Tutor: Charles Thomas Barker.)

1798	Pasch. et Trin.	Homeri Il. Ll. 1–6; Horatii Sat. L. 1; Hist. Graec.
	Mich.	Homeri Il. Ll. 7–12; Horatii Serm. L. 2; Historiae Graec. quaedam; Euclidis El. Ll. 2 priores.
1799	Hil.	Homeri Il. Ll. reliqui; Euclidis El. Ll. 3. 4. 5. 6; Horat. Epist. L. 1.
	Pasch. et Trin.	Homeri Odysseis; Algebrae pars 1.
	Mich.	Livii. Ll. 1–5; Eurip. Medea; Trigonom. pl. et sp. el.
1800	Hil.	Livii Ll. 6. 10. 20. 25; Hecuba, Alcestis, Androm.; Prael. Log.
	Pasch. et Trin.	Livii Ll. 26. 36; Hippol., Heraclid. Euripidis; Aristotelis Rhet. quaed.
	Mich.	Livii Ll. rell.; Rhetorices Aristot. quaedam; Demosthenis Orat. quaedam; Euripidis Iphig. Taur. et Aulid.
	Hil.	Electra Eurip.; Elect. Soph; Aristotelis Rhet. Ll. rell.; Aristotelis Poet.; Virgilii Georgic.; Demosth. Orationes quaedam.

(Ch. Ch. Archives, li.b. 3, p. 220.)

STRACEY, EDWARD HARDINGE JOHN. Commoner. No degree. Barrister. (Tutor: Charles Henry Hall.)

1786	Mich.	Sophoclis Ajax, Electra, Trachiniae; Hom. Il. Ll. 8 priores; Euclidis Ll. 4.

1787	Hil.	Hom. Il. Ll. XVI reliqui, Odyssea; Euripidis Medea, Iphig. in Aul. et in Tauris, ejusdem *Ἱκετιδες*; Eucl. 5. 6. 11.
	Pasch.	Herodot. Ll. 7 priores; Maclaurin Algeb. pars 1.
	Trin.	Aeschyli Persae; Herodoti Ll. VIII. IX; Plutarchi Themistocles, Aristides, Cimon; M. T. Cic. de Officiis.
	Mich.	Thucydidis Ll. omnes; vitae Periclis, Niciae et Alcibiadis apud Plutarchum; Trigonometria Plana et Sphaerica.
1788	Hil.	Diodori Siculi Ll. XI–XIV; Xenophontis Hellenica ejusdem Anabasis; Plutarchi Agesilaus, Lysander, Pelopidas; Aldrichii Logica et Aristotelis Organi quaedam.
	Pasch.	Diodori Sic. Ll. XV–XVII; Pindari Olympica; Aristotelis Rhet. L. 1 capita 10.
	Trin.	Demosthenis Orationes publicae 10; Pindari Pythia; Diodori Sic. Ll. 18. 19. 20; Plutarchi Eumenes, Demetrius; Aristot. de Rhet. L. 1 capp. rell. L. 2.
	Mich.	Pindari Nemea et Isthmia; Demosthenis quae ad rempublicam spectant orationes reliquae, eadem Aeschinis; Aeschyli Tragediae *Επτα επι Θηβαις, Προμηθευς Δεσμωτης*; Arist. de Rhet. L. 3 et de Poetica capp. quaedam.

(Ch. Ch. Archives, li.b. 2, p. 126.)

ELMSLEY, PETER. Commoner. BA. Classical scholar. (Tutor: Charles Henry Hall.)

1791	Hil.	Euripidis fabulae omnes; Horatii Sermones.
	Pasch. et Trin.	Herodoti Ll. omnes; Solon et Lycurgus apud Plutarchum.
	Mich.	Thucydidis Ll. 1–5; Cimon, Pericles apud Plutarchum; Dionysius Halicarnass. de Thucydidis historia.
1792	Hil.	Thucydidis Ll. 5–8; Xenophontis *Ελληνικα*; Plutarchi Alcibiades, Nicias, Lysander, Agesilaus; Xenoph. *Αναβασις*; Aldrichii Logica.
	Pasch. et	Diodori Siculi 5 Ll. post.; Aeschylus; Hamilton

	Trin.	de sect. conicis Ll. 3 priores; Plutarchi vitae 7.
	Mich.	Demosthenis Orationes pub. argumenti.
1793	Hil.	Demosthenis et Aeschinis orationes περι Παραπρεσβειας; Demosthenis Midias, Leptines, Aristocrates, Timocrates; Aristotelis περι ποιητικης.
	Pasch. et Trin.	T. Livii Ll. 10; Dionysius praeter L. 1.
	Mich.	T. Livii Ll. 10–20; Polybii Ll. 5.
1794	Hil.	Pindarus.
	Pasch. et Trin.	[blank]
	Mich.	Admissus ad gradum A.B.

(Ch. Ch. Archives, li.b. 3, p. 76.)

HALLAM, HENRY. Commoner. BA. Historian. (Tutor: William Wood.)

1795	Pasch. et Trin.	Herodoti Ll. omnes; Plutarchi Lycurgus, Solon, Theseus; Maclaurin Algebra.
	Mich.	Thucydidis Ll. omnes; Plutarchi Themistocles, Cimon, Aristides; Trigonometria.
1796	Hil.	Xenophontis Hellenica; Plutarchi vitae quaedam ad historiam pertinentes; Aristophanis Plutus, Nubes et Ranae.
	Pasch. et Trin.	Demosthenis orat. 25; Aeschin. orat. 3; M. T. Cicero de oratore; Raleii quaedam.
	Mich.	T. Livii Decas 1; Polybii Ll. 2 priores; Plutarchi Romulus, Numa, Publicola; Aristophanis Εφηκες et Ορυιθες.
1797	Hil.	T. Livii Decas 2; Polybii Ll. 3–6; Arati, Agidos et Cleomenis vitae apud Plutarchum; Euripidis Alcestis.
	Pasch. et Trin.	T. Livii Ll. reliqui; Polybii fragmenta; vitae apud Plutarchum 4; Aristophanis fab. 4; Appiani Bell. Punic. et Hispan.
	Mich.	Appiani Bell. Civ.; Caesaris Bell. Civ.; Plutarchi vitae quaedam.
1798	Hil.	Aristotelis Rhetorices Ll. omnes; sect. con. per Hamilton Ll. 2 priores; M. T. Ciceronis

	orationes in Verrem.
Pasch. et	Arist. περι ποιητικης; Sect. Con. per Hamilton
Trin.	Ll. reliqui; Ciceronis orat. quaedam.
	Admissus ad gradum A.B.

(Ch. Ch. Archives, li.b..3, p. 49.)

ROBERTSON, ABRAHAM. Servitor. Savilian Professor of Geometry and Astronomy, Oxford. (Tutor: William Jackson.)

1775	Mich.	Ald. Log.; Macl. Alg. cap. 12 priora.
1776	Hil.	Trigonometria Plana et Sphaerica; Macl. Algeb. ptis. 1 cap. 13 et 14.
	Pasch.	Euclidis L. 1.
	Trin.	Euclidis Ll. 2. 3. 4.; Virgilii Georgica.
	Mich.	Matth. et Marci Evangelia; Hamiltoni de Sectionibus Conicis L. 1.
1777	Hil.	Hamiltoni de Sect. Cons. Ll. 2. 3; Xen. Αναβ. L. 1; Caesaris Bel. Gal. Ll. 6 priores.
	Pasch.	Xen. Αναβ. Ll. 2. 3; Caesaris Bel. Gal. Ll. 2 post.
	Trin.	Xen. Αναβ. Ll. 4. 5; Hamiltoni de Sect. Con. L. 4.
	Mich.	Xen. Αναβ. Ll. 2 post.; Homeri Il. Ll. 12 priores.
1778	Hil.	Aldrichii Log.; Aristot. Rhet. Ll. 2; Livii Ll. 2; Evangelia Luc. et John.
	Pasch.	Homeri Il. Ll. 13. 14; Arist. Rhet. L. 3; Livii Ll. 3. 4; Acta Apostolorum.
	Trin.	Admissus ad gradum A.B.

(Ch. Ch. Archives, li.b. 2, p. 170.)

BARNARD, JOHN. Servitor. BA. (Tutor: Charles Henry Hall.)

1786	Mich.	Xenophontis Απομνημονευμ. 2 priores; Euclidis Ll. 4 priores.
1787	Hil.	Iphigenia in Aulide; Xenophontis Απομνημονευμ. Ll. rell.; Euclidis Ll. 5. 6. 11.
	Pasch.	Homeri Il. Ll. 4 priores; Euripid. Iphig. in Taurid.; Maclaur. Alg. pars 1.
	Trin.	Homeri Il. Ll. 5–18; Maclaur. Alg. rel.
	Mich.	Herodoti Ll. 1. 3. 4.
1788	Hil.	Herodoti Ll. 5. 6; Xenophontis Oeconomica; Euclidis L. 1.

	Pasch.	Euclid. 2. 3; Herodotus 7–9.
	Trin.	Diodori Siculi Ll. 12. 13; Plutarchi Theseus, Solon, Lycurgus; Euclid. Ll. 4. 5. 6.
	Mich.	Diodori Siculi Ll. 14. 15. 16.
1789	Hil.	Diod. Sic. Ll. 17–20; Eucl. L. 11 pars 1; Trigonometria Plana et Sphaerica.
	Pasch. et Trin.	Plutarchi Aristides, Pericles, Eumenes, Phocion; T. Livii Ll. 2; Aldrichii Logica.
	Mich.	T. Livii Ll. 8 sequent.; Freinshemii 7; Aristot. quaedam.
1790	Hil.	Evangelia SS. Matthaei, Marci et Lucae; T. Livii Ll. 21–30; Arist. de Rhet. Ll. 2 priores. Admissus ad gradum A.B.

(Ch. Ch. Archives, li.b. 2, p. 242.)

PAYNE, EDWARD. Servitor. BA. (Tutor unknown.)

1793	Hil.	Evang. Matth. et Marc.; Grotii Ll. 2.
	Pasch. et Trin.	[blank].
	Mich.	Evang. sec. Lucam et Joannem; Grotii Ll. 3. 4.
1794	Hil.	Evang. sec. Lucam et Joannem iterum; Grotii Ll. 3. 4. 5. 6.
	Pasch. et Trin.	Evangelia omnia.
	Mich.	M. T. Ciceronis de Natura Deorum Ll. 2. 3; Apostolorum Acta.
1795	Hil.	D. Pauli Epp.; Sallustii B. B. Cat. et Jug.
	Pasch. et Trin.	Noelli Cat.; Grotii de ver. Xt. Rell.; D. Pauli Epist.
	Mich.	Juellii Apologia; Jenkin on Christianity; Pearson on the Creed. Admissus ad gradum A.B.

(Ch. Ch. Archives, li.b. 3, p. 21.)

APPENDIX II

Sources for the Identification of Tutors

PRIOR to the nineteenth century there are no lists of tutors in the records at Christ Church. Although tutors were appointed by the Dean, their relationship with their pupils was a private one, and they were paid for their services by the pupils themselves or their families. Because of the private nature of the arrangement, the college had no occasion to keep a record of it. Fortunately, however, the Treasurer kept financial records which, while not ostensibly concerned with the tutors, often enable them to be identified. For example, in entering the deposit and refunding of caution money, the payment of exhibitions, and the emoluments of Students, the Treasurer frequently recorded the identity not only of the undergraduate in whose name the transaction was made but also of the person who actually paid or received the sums concerned. Because from early times the tutor had a large measure of responsibility for the financial affairs of his pupils, these persons are often found to be tutors.

Of these records, the Caution Books, which survive from 1625, are amongst the most important.[1] Caution money was required from Noblemen, Gentlemen Commoners, and Commoners, but not from Students or Servitors.[2] The caution money paid by Commoners subsequently elected to Canoneer Studentships was refunded at the time of election. Caution money was paid to the Treasurer at or near the time of matriculation, and, unless extinguished by debts incurred in residence or contributed in the form of plate money to the college building fund, was repaid when the undergraduate concerned went down. Until the last quarter of the eighteenth century, caution money might be paid to the Treasurer either by the undergraduate himself, or by a relative, friend, or servant. Sometimes, however, it was paid by a Student. In due course it was repaid either to the person who had originally paid it, or sometimes

---

[1] The Receipt Books for 1612, 1613, and 1615 also contain accounts of caution money.

[2] But see p. 190.

to a Student even though that Student was not the original payer. Where a Student paid or was refunded the caution money of an undergraduate, he appears to have acted in the capacity of a tutor. In those cases where caution money was paid by and refunded to the same Student it may be concluded that the undergraduate in question had the same tutor throughout his residence. Where the Student who paid the caution was different from the Student to whom it was repaid, a change of tutor had probably occurred in the interval. In such cases it will often be found that the original tutor had given up his Studentship before the repayment of caution was due. From about 1774, caution money was almost always paid by Students and repaid to Students, and the records then become a more comprehensive source for the identification of tutors.

Since Students did not pay caution money, the Caution Books cannot be used to identify their tutors. These, however, may be ascertained from the Disbursement Books, which record the quarterly payment of Students' emoluments. The payments are often signed for by Students who were not the nominal recipients. That those who signed in such circumstances were tutors and not simply obliging friends may be established by the example of the Canoneer Students. It is then found that, when a Commoner was elected to a Canoneer Studentship and his caution money as a Commoner was repaid to a Student who had been his tutor, the same Student usually continued to sign for the emoluments of the newly appointed Canoneer Student. It may reasonably be concluded that the Canoneer Students thus had the same tutor before and after election. A similar cross-reference is not possible in the case of the Westminster Students, who were admitted as Students-elect, but it may be assumed that those who received emoluments on their behalf did so likewise in the capacity of tutors. On this assumption the receipt of payment for exhibitions awarded to Westminster Students were often made by the tutor. The Disbursement Books survive almost without interruption from 1577 to 1630, resume briefly from 1641 to 1644, and then continue without a break from 1658 to 1864. They provide the most comprehensive account of the tutors of any single group of undergraduates, and, because they record quarterly payments, enable changes to tutor to be dated with considerable accuracy. Neither the Caution nor the Disbursement Books enable the tutors of Servitors to be identified, but it is known from other sources that the Censors and college officers tutored them, and individual tutors may sometimes be traced through the ledgers of exhibitions for Servitors.

The hypothesis that certain categories of records at Christ Church are a source for the identification of tutors is confirmed by the internal evidence of the records themselves and by extraneous evidence from other quarters. The entries in the Caution Books, for example, are sometimes specific. Thus on 23 December 1671 it is noted that William Finmore's caution money was received 'of his Tutor Mr. Wheeler', and on 29 March 1672 William Baber's caution is described as received 'from his tutor Mr. George Walls'. In 1768 Joshua Berkeley paid the caution money of Charles Barton. When Barton was elected to a Canoneer Studentship in 1771 his caution was repaid to him and 'witnessed by his Tutor J. Berkeley'. The connection between tutor and caution money is clearly implied by the terms of the Chapter order on 10 December 1775 that 'in all future admissions of Noblemen or Gentlemen Commoners the Tutors be apprized that upon their leaving the College half of such persons caution money will be applied to the use of the college for plate money'.

Of evidence from other sources there is abundance. The evidence concerning John Locke is of particular interest. The recently published edition of Locke's *Correspondence* includes letters which establish that he was tutor to John Alford, Sir Charles Berkeley, Thomas Harborne, Corbet Owen, John Pickering, Henry Serle, Rowland Townshend, and Robert Williamson. Of these Corbet Owen was a Westminster Student and paid no caution, but the Disbursement Books show Locke in receipt of the emoluments of his Studentship. Locke paid the caution money of the remainder, except for two whose caution was paid by persons who were not members of the university. Locke's correspondence thus supports the evidence of the Caution and Disbursement Books, but these records in turn reveal the existence of other pupils not mentioned in the edition of the correspondence. The Disbursement Books show that Locke was also tutor to the following Students: William Duke, Morgan Godwyn, John Jones, William Lake, Edward Pocock, Aaron Rutland, Robert Stanton, and George Wall. The Caution Books show that, in addition to the pupils listed above, Locke was also tutor to Henry Clayton, Thomas Goode, John Pentlow, and John West. Thus between 1661 and 1664 he took at least twenty pupils. At Christmas 1663 Locke was appointed Senior Censor, and in this capacity was responsible for the performance of certain college exercises and was the recipient of addresses on various matters concerning college discipline. It is possible by means of the Caution and Disbursement Books to distinguish between those undergraduates who submitted exercises to Locke as Senior Censor and those to whom he was tutor. In the Bodleian Library is preserved

Locke's herbarium of dried and pressed plants which he mounted on the backs of the exercises he received as Senior Censor in 1664 and 1665.[1] To his account of these manuscripts in the *Bodleian Library Record*, Mr P. Long has added a list of the undergraduates whose exercises were used for this purpose.[2] It contains 123 names. Of these only fifteen were pupils to whom Locke is known to have been tutor. The remainder were undergraduates who submitted exercises to him in his capacity as Senior Censor.

Further evidence confirming the value of the Caution Books and other records at Christ Church for identifying tutors may be selected at random.

George Hooper, later Bishop of Bath and Wells, was lecturer in Greek in 1665 and 1666, and Senior Censor in 1667 and 1668. In her unpublished biography of him, his daughter Abigail Prowse wrote,

Whilst he continued at Oxford, which was near fourteen years, he had but five pupils, for he would not take the charge of more as he took a very particular care of them. It employ'd more of his time then one of his universal love of learning could spare. One of them Sr Thomas Bellot died young, the others were Mr Pelham, afterwards Lord Pelham, Sr Thomas Dyke, Sr Harry Gough, & Lord Lanesborough.[3]

Hooper paid the caution money of all of them. The Caution and Disbursement Books, however, suggest that he was also tutor to a further fifteen pupils including the Westminster Students elected in 1669.

The appointment of Maurice Wheeler as tutor to William Wake is well known from Wake's autobiography and Dr Norman Sykes' life of Archbishop Wake. On 28 February 1673 Wheeler paid Wake's caution.

Roger Altham was tutor to John Perceval in 1676[4]. He paid Perceval's caution on 18 May 1676.

Humphrey Prideaux was tutor to Charles Finch and John Dering in 1677.[5] Finch's caution was paid by Canon Woodroffe on 23 August 1676, but was repaid to Prideaux on 9 February 1680. Prideaux paid John Dering's caution on 23 May 1677, and it was paid back to him on 12 July when Dering became a Canoneer Student.

Richard Old was tutor to William Bromley.[6] On 8 April 1678 Old

---

[1] Bodl. MSS Locke c. 41 and b. 7.
[2] *Bodleian Library Record* (1964), vii, 185–93.
[3] Lambeth Palace Library, MS 3016, fo. 1^v.
[4] BL Add. MS 46953, fo. 72.
[5] BL Add. MS 46954A, fo. 172^v.
[6] Wood, *Athenae*, iv, 664.

paid Bromley's caution. Aldrich was tutor to Lord James Butler in 1679.[1]
He paid Butler's caution on 17 April 1679. Welbore Ellis was tutor to
Richard Steele in 1689.[2] Ellis paid Steele's caution on 23 December 1689.

Bentley at first believed that Aldrich was tutor to Charles Boyle, the
ostensible editor of the *Letters of Phalaris*. The claim was denied by
Atterbury,[3] and the belief grew that Atterbury himself and Robert Freind
were closely involved. This is in fact confirmed by the evidence of the
Caution Books, which show that Atterbury paid Boyle's caution on 25
June 1690, and that it was repaid to Robert Freind on 6 December 1695.

George Bull was tutor to Sir Bourchier Wrey in 1700.[4] Bull paid
Wrey's caution on 15 June 1700.

In 1721 Henry and Stephen Fox were sent to Christ Church, and
'recommend'd to Mr. George Wigan's care for a tutor, and that he be
desired to enter them in the college and provide chambers for them'.[5]
Wigan, who was described by Hearne as 'a great Tutor in Xt. Ch.',[6]
paid the caution of both on 3 March 1721. Hearne is also the source for
the tutor of John Potter, whose father the Bishop of Oxford made him
a Student in 1728. Hearne says that his tutor was Edmund Bateman,[7]
and the attribution is confirmed by the Disbursement Book for that year.
Boswell relates that when Johnson was seeking a tutor for his friend
John Taylor, 'He then made inquiry all round the University, and having
found that Mr. Bateman, of Christ-Church, was the tutor of highest
reputation, Taylor was entered of that College'.[8] Bateman paid Taylor's
caution on 25 February 1729.

Lord Shelburne remarked of his time at Christ Church, 'My tutor,
Mr. Hollwell, was a Commoner [Student], and was fool enough to set
himself up in a pointed opposition to the Westminsters'.[9] Holwell paid
Shelburne's caution on 17 March 1755.

William Jackson was tutor to Richard Colley Wellesley when the
latter was a Student.[10] Jackson's tutorship is confirmed by the Disbursement Book for 1779.

[1] HMC, *Egmont* (1909), ii, 79.
[2] Blanchard, *Correspondence of Richard Steele*, no. 3.
[3] Atterbury, *Short Review of the Controversy*, 40.
[4] HMC *11th Report*, app. vii (Bridgwater) (1888), 155.
[5] Earl of Ilchester, *Henry Fox, 1st Lord Holland* (1920), i, 22.
[6] Hearne, *Collections*, viii, 15.
[7] Ibid., x, 70.
[8] Boswell, *Life of Johnson*, i, 76.
[9] Fitzmaurice, *Life of Shelburne*, i, 13.
[10] *Wellesley Papers* (1914), i, 7.

Phineas Pett was tutor to George Canning in 1787. Josceline Bagot erroneously gives Pett's first name as Philip,[1] but the Pett–Canning correspondence in the possession of the Earl of Harewood removes all doubt that Phineas Pett was meant. Canning's caution was paid by Phineas Pett on 26 November 1787.

[1] J. Bagot, *George Canning and his Friends* (1909), i, 28.

APPENDIX III

The Vernon Studentship

IN 1601 Thomas Venables of Kinderton in Cheshire acquired by Act of Parliament[1] the right in perpetuity for himself and his heirs to nominate one of the hundred Students of Christ Church. The right was not acquired in recognition of a benefaction to the college, and Christ Church never laboured under the obligations of kin which afflicted All Souls. It was created in the unusual circumstances surrounding the settlement of a protracted and vexatious dispute between the college and successive generations of the Venables family concerning the ownership of the rectory of Rostherne in Cheshire. The rectory had been purchased from the Venables by Henry VII, who gave it to Launde priory in Leicestershire, but when the priory was dissolved in 1538 it was given by Henry VIII to his foundation at Oxford with a rent reserved to the Crown. Several unsuccessful attempts were made by the Venables family to recover it, their claim resting on an entail made in the reign of Edward IV, and in 1591 Thomas Venables sought to bring proceedings in Chester assizes by a writ of quare impedit. The Dean and Chapter, much alarmed because Venables was a man 'of great and strong alliance' in the county, petitioned for the case to be heard in the Privy Council, and an injunction was granted staying further proceedings while the Lord Treasurer and Sir John Fortescue made a report. Venables refused the compromise proposed in this report and threatened further legal action, whereupon the Dean and Chapter petitioned the Queen, who ordered the proceedings to be suspended. Undaunted by the prospect of the royal displeasure, Venables continued to press his case at law, and, when reminded of the penalty for contempt, 'Mr. Venables hath sayd it was but to ly by it, meaninge belike that it was but a matter of imprisonment for a time'. Finally, in 1599, an award was made by Archbishop Whitgift, Sir Thomas Egerton, Lord Buckhurst, and Sir John Fortescue, and was duly enacted in Parliament. In return for surrendering his right to the rectory of Rostherne to Christ Church, Venables received the sum of

[1] 43 Eliz. I, c. 8.

1,000 marks and the advowson.[1] The patronage of a Studentship was probably included in order to secure the presentation of a Student to the living, but if such was the intention it proved remarkably unsuccessful. When Sir Peter Venables died in 1679, the right to nominate a Student was inherited by his daughter Anne, who in 1687 married Montagu Bertie, Lord Norreys of Rycote, later (1699) 2nd Earl of Abingdon. On her death it passed to Ann, niece of Peter Venables and wife of Henry Vernon, whose son George Venables Vernon was created Lord Vernon, Baron of Kinderton, in 1762.

Except in the manner of their nomination, no distinction was observed between the Vernon and other Studentships. The college kept no roll of them and did not systematically enter appointments in the Chapter Act Books until 1730. The identification of Students before this date often depends on chronology and circumstantial evidence. In the following list conjectural appointments are indicated in brackets.

(Richard Fowler, 1664–8[2]).
Venables Keeling, 1669–76.
Ralph Walley, 1676–81.
Shirley Okeover, 1685–8.[3]
D'Oyley Norton, 1688–95.[4]
(Charles Bertie, 1695–1703[5]).
Richard Jenkinson, 1704–14.
(Edward Bertie, 1714–27[6]).
(Thomas Hill, 1727–30).
John Repington, 1730–9.
Gilbert Repington, 1739–44.
John Chawner, 1744–74.
Edward Venables Vernon, 1774–8.

[1] Papers concerning the suit are Ch. Ch. Archives, Estates 16, fols. 74–131.

[2] Richard Fowler was the son of Richard Fowler of Harnage Grange, Salop. Anne Venables (d. 1677) was the daughter of Peter Venables (d. 1669) and married Francis Fowler of Harnage Grange.

[3] Okeover was nominated on 19 Mar. 1681 but did not matriculate until 5 Jan. 1685.

[4] Norton was nominated by Lord Norreys 'in the right of my wife the now Baroness of Kinderton' (Chapter Act Book, 28 Sept. 1688).

[5] Charles Bertie was brother of Montagu Bertie, 2nd Earl of Abingdon.

[6] Edward Bertie was nephew of the 2nd Earl of Abingdon.

Joshua Powell, 1778–91.
Henry Anson, 1791–8.
Frederick Anson, 1798–1800.[1]

[1] On 12 Dec. 1800 the Chapter ordered that Gaisford be placed on the roll immediately after the Sub-Dean's nomination 'in consideration of his great diligence and proficiency in learning and of the uniform regularity of his behaviour'. They also resolved that Gaisford's nomination be exchanged with Lord Vernon for his turn of nomination then vacant. Gaisford was duly elected on 23 December 1800 (Chapter Act Book).

APPENDIX IV

The Faculty Students 1660–1800

IN the seventeenth century the appointment of Faculty Students took place at the annual elections of officers in December and is seldom specifically recorded in the Chapter Act Books. From 1708 the appointments were made at varying times during the year and are always noted in the Chapter Act Books.

MEDICAL 1

Nathaniel Hodges, 1660
Samuel Jackson, 1661
John Locke, 1675
William Breach, 1684
John Freind, 19 April 1708
Richard Frewin, 24 December 1709
John Wheeler, 24 March 1715
James Impey, 13 November 1749; died 1756
Robert Cocks, 11 July 1764
John Parsons, 10 June 1766
Lucas Pepys, 1 August 1772
Sir John Russell, 18 December 1772
William Eden, 16 December 1774
Archibald Macdonald, 7 December 1776
David Murray, 26 February 1778
Charles Abbot, 20 October 1783
Osborn Markham, 2 February 1797–25 June 1806

MEDICAL 2

Isaiah Ward, 1660
Henry Croone, 1662
John Luke, 1667
John Richards, 1677
Edmund Norden, 24 December 1688

Matthew Lee, 18 November 1720
Peirce Manaton, 20 January 1730
Henry Willis, 18 March 1743
William Lewis, 7 June 1746; resigned 8 April 1751
William Russell, 9 November 1758
John Heath, 2 November 1764
Sir Scrope Bernard, 12 July 1781
William Thomson, 1 August 1785
Thomas Carter, 10 November 1790
John King, 24 December 1791
John Erskine, 12 June 1792 – 13 November 1802

LAW 1

Thomas Bedingfield, 1660
Ralph Tounson, 1663
Henry Croone, 1679
John Ellis, 1681
William Wall, 11 July 1738
Robert Greenhill, 24 December 1791–24 December 1836

LAW 2

Edward Fettiplace, 1660
Thomas Armstead, 24 December 1687
Edward Hannes, 23 December 1693
John Urry, 16 March 1699
Richard Ince, 12 November 1715
Thomas Carter, 9 November 1758
William Spry, 25 August 1759
Earl of Cork, 10 December 1762
John Monck, 28 March 1764
Robert Freind, 28 March 1767
Francis Burton, 22 June 1776
William Robert Hay, 18 January 1788
Henry Legge, 12 February 1793–21 December 1829

HUMANITIES (THURSTON)

Thomas Ireland, 1665
William Allestree, 1675
William King, 23 December 1693

Henry Watkins, 18 July 1713
John Wigan, 25 May 1727
Anthony Parsons, 25 April 1739
William Lewis, 18 April 1740
John Bettesworth, 7 June 1746
Charles Gould, 1 February 1753
John Skynner, 22 December 1757
John Thomas Batt, 22 June 1776
William Garthshore, 6 February 1794
Nicholas Vansittart, 2 February 1797–28 July 1806

INDEX

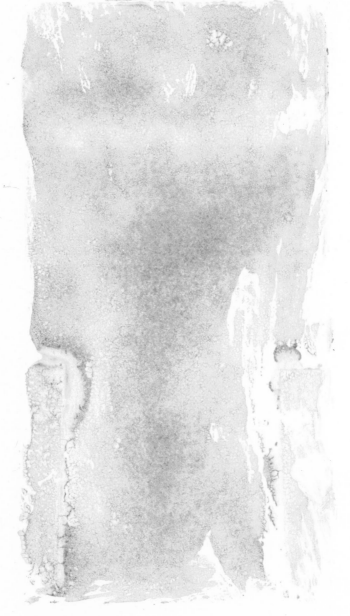